MILESTONES
Turning Points in
New Zealand History
Second Edition

6/10/2001

Dear Judy,

After we were shepherded around Dunedin by Tom Brooking, I thought you might enjoy reading his witty and engaging history of ....

Enjoy!

Love,
Louis

MILESTONES
Turning Points in New Zealand History

Second Edition

**Tom Brooking
and Paul Enright**

Picture research Harry Mills

Second edition 1999
Dunmore Press Ltd
Palmerston North
New Zealand

ISBN 0-86469-309-5

Front Cover Picture:
Encampment of General Chute's forces near
Te Putahi Pa on the Whenuakura River, 7 January 1866.
A pen and watercolour by Gustavus Ferdinand von Tempsky.
Alexander Turnbull Library.

First edition 1988
Mills Publications Ltd
Lower Hutt
New Zealand

ISBN 0-908722-30-3

Edited by Anna Rogers
Typeset by Linotype Service (1987) Ltd, Palmerston North
Design and production by Lindsay Cuthbertson
Maps by Jo Mayo
Printed in Hong Kong through Bookprint Consultants, Wellington

Contents

Contents continued

Acknowledgements

In writing this book I have incurred as many debts as the New Zealand economy. The list which follows is, of necessity, very abbreviated.

I would like to thank the staff of the following overworked and underfunded institutions: Hocken Library, Dunedin, Early Settlers' Museum, Dunedin, Dunedin Public Library, University of Otago Central Library, National Museum, Wellington, Alexander Turnbull Library, Wellington, National Archives, Wellington, General Assembly Library, Wellington.

Some individuals also made special contributions. Many provided information, ideas, inspiration, especially Claudia Orange, Gordon Parsonson, Fergus Sinclair, Erik Olssen, Roberto Rabel, Dorothy Page, Barbara Brookes, Charlotte MacDonald, Terry Hearn, Lawrence Jones, Hardwicke Knight, Claire Matthewson, Jeff Sissons, Helen Leach, Atholl Anderson, George Griffiths, Roger Collins, Tim Garrity, Annette Facer, Harry Morton, Bill Oliver, Michael King, James Belich and Peter Gibbons. I also owe a considerable debt to ten years of students. Thank you one and all.

Much gratitude goes to the long-suffering typists who converted my appalling scrawl into typescript. Thank you Trish Brooking, Flora Kirby, Liz Malthus and Jan Stoddart.

Special thanks goes to Paul Enright for researching and writing the two First World War milestones, and to Mary Boyd for checking the manuscript and for her many helpful suggestions. Finally, thanks to Harry Mills for the fine production of this book and to Trish, Rachel and Peter Brooking and Peg Cadigan for support.

Tom Brooking

The selection and quality of the illustrations owes much to the skill and dedication of the staff of the over 30 libraries, museums, art galleries, government departments, newspapers and private companies who contributed illustrations. Each illustration used in the book is individually acknowledged at the end of its particular caption. My warmest thanks for the special efforts made by Janet Davidson, Marian Minson, Herb Kawainui Kane, Geoffrey Rice, Mary Boyd, Bill Cooper, Sidney Moko Mead, Peter Webster, Tim Ryan, William Main, George Kaye, Eugenie Sage, Gary Couchman, Noel Hilliard, Peter McIntyre, Barry Thomson, Ian Burnett and Kevin Wells.

Harry Mills

Preface

This book is intended to be an introduction to New Zealand history, a kind of aperitif to whet the appetite for further reading and inquiry. It is expressly aimed at high school and lower level university students, tourists, and the large number of New Zealanders who were turned off the subject at school but who now want to learn more about the fascinating history of this small country. The book makes no claims to be comprehensive, but rather tries to direct all those interested in learning more to fuller and more complex accounts listed under the 'Further Reading' section.

The book is shaped around the idea that history is circular rather than linear, so it begins with the arrival of Maori and ends with the Maori resurgence of recent times. The significance of each of the key events chosen as milestones could be disputed, but they are intended as a means of providing a focus for the reader. Timelines at the back provide a narrative framework in which to set the incidents highlighted by the text. Particularly exciting episodes have also been chosen to make clear the richness of our history and to demonstrate that the great themes of world history have been played out here in most intriguing ways.

Periodisation of any country's history keeps shifting. Writing New Zealand history from the supposed heights of welfarism achieved around the late 1930s makes little sense from the perspective of 1999. The enormous changes that have occurred since 1984 have made the New Zealand of the first edition almost unrecognisable, so we have added a chapter on these momentous economic, political and ideological shifts and we have updated major developments in the Maori world.

Historical scholarship itself has also advanced since the first edition, so we have directed attention to the key publications released since 1987 in the reading list and attempted to incorporate new findings where appropriate. Many areas, nevertheless, remain seriously under-researched, so we hope that this introductory history will stimulate students of whatever age to dispute and challenge our interpretations. It would be even better if some readers were provoked into carrying out their own investigations into our past, thereby providing the basis for more comprehensive general histories in the future.

Tom Brooking and Paul Enright
July 1999

Introduction and Overview

Milestones looks at 22 events that have dramatically shaped New Zealand's past. These events are labelled turning points because they have altered the course of life in this country.

Common threads emerge from the list of milestones: issues involving race relations, war, the quest for economic security and the search for social justice dominate.

The first Polynesians landed in New Zealand about 800 AD. From this landfall an indigenous and distinctive Maori culture evolved. This carefully researched painting by Hawaiian Herb Kawainui Kane is of an East Polynesian double canoe on a settlement voyage. It is carrying pigs, dogs and poultry to use as food sources in the new lands. *Courtesy Herb Kawainui Kane and Island Heritage Ltd, Hawaii.* **(See Milestone 1.)**

EASTERN HEMISPHERE.

North Pole

South Pole

Engraved by Samuel John Neele, N.º 352 Strand.

Master mariner and explorer James Cook established, by circumnavigating it, that New Zealand was not part of a mythical southern continent but two large islands. Cook's accounts gave Europeans their first insights into Maori society and encouraged further exploration, economic exploitation and settlement.

WESTERN HEMISPHERE.

North Pole

South Pole

Engraved by Samuel John Neele N.º 352 Strand

Cook discovered and charted much of the Pacific we know today. These maps of the Eastern and Western Hemispheres are from Sydney Parkinson's *A Journal of a Voyage to the South Seas, 1784.* **(See Milestone 3.)**

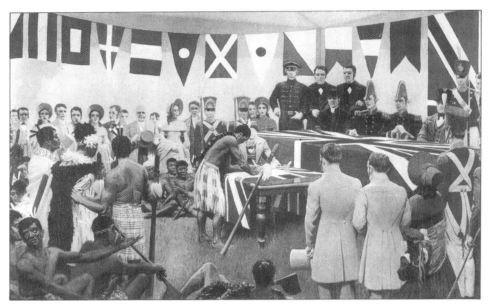

In 1839 the British government despatched Captain Hobson to New Zealand to persuade the Maori chiefs to recognise Queen Victoria's authority so that New Zealand could become a British colony. The British offer, set out in the Treaty of Waitangi, guaranteed the Maori the possession of their land and property and bestowed the rights and privileges of British subjects. To the Maori the treaty was a 'sacred pact'; to the Pakeha it was a 'scrap of paper' to be conveniently ignored. Debate over what was promised has continued ever since.

This reconstruction of the signing of the Treaty of Waitangi on 6 February 1840, is by Marcus King. Hobson is incorrectly portrayed wearing a full dress uniform. Compare this with the more accurate reconstruction on p.51. The Ngapuhi chief Tamati Waka Nene, pictured signing the treaty, was a supporter of British protection. Nevertheless even he warned Hobson: 'You must not allow us to become slaves. You must preserve our customs, and never permit our lands to be wrested from us.' *Alexander Turnbull Library.* (See Milestone 5.)

Disagreements over what the Treaty of Waitangi meant in practice quickly emerged.

Hone Heke showed his disillusionment with the treaty by chopping down the flagstaff bearing the British flag — the symbol of British rule — at Kororareka in 1844. The protest, which turned into open rebellion, became the first of a series of campaigns, called the New Zealand Wars of 1845-72, to resist European expansion. In the painting by Major Cyprian Bridge, HMS *North Star* is destroying Pomare's pa at Otiuhu in the Bay of Islands, 1845. *Alexander Turnbull Library.* (See Milestone 7.)

By 1840 2000 Europeans lived in New Zealand. Reports of good farming land and 'co-operative natives' attracted increasing numbers of settlers. A number came under colonisation schemes planned by Edward Gibbon Wakefield and the New Zealand Company. Wakefield's scheme was based on buying land at bargain prices from the Maori and selling it on to speculators and farmers at a much higher price. The first Wakefield settlement was established at Wellington. Charles Heaphy painted this view of Wellington — looking towards the south-east — in 1841. *Alexander Turnbull Library*. **(See Milestone 6.)**

Although sealing, whaling and gold served as economic stimulants, New Zealand's prosperity depended on farming. Exports, however, were restricted to non-perishable commodities such as wool and wheat. The breakthrough came when the Albion Line's sailing ship *Dunedin* successfully took a pioneer shipment of frozen meat to Britain. Refrigeration also meant a dairy industry could develop based on the export of butter and cheese. The painting is by H. L. Mallitte. *Alexander Turnbull Library.* (See Milestone 10.)

Most of New Zealand's European immigrants came from Britain. Some came to make a quick fortune and return home. Others wanted to escape the social evils of the old world and build a more just and equitable society.

Increased immigration placed more pressure on the Maori to sell their lands. In 1860 the Pakeha population surpassed the declining Maori population.

This lithograph by E. Noyce shows English families waiting to depart for the colonies. *Alexander Turnbull Library.*

Taking Leave of Old England

14

Pioneering life in New Zealand called for different skills and attitudes. Out on the farms women were much more than house-keepers; they shared in virtually all the farm work. In a small community like New Zealand, activists for women's franchise such as Kate Sheppard could more easily mobilise public opinion. So in 1893 New Zealand became the first country to give women the vote. The *Auckland Weekly News* photograph shows women voters going to the polling booth on election day in Auckland, 15 December 1899. *Auckland Institute and Museum.* (See Milestone 12.)

New Zealand did not always escape the social evils of industrial Britain. A sweat-ing scandal, for example, broke out in 1889. Open class conflict erupted from time to time, in particular in 1913 and 1951. In the picture of the 1913 Waterfront Strike, striking watersiders scatter before oncom-ing mounted 'specials' wielding long batons. *Alexander Turnbull Library.* (See Milestone 13.)

By the turn of the twentieth century a distinctive New Zealand national identity was beginning to emerge. The Boer War (1899-1902) gave the young nation its first chance to prove its manhood on foreign battlefields. But it was at Gallipoli in 1915 that New Zealand had its national 'baptism in blood'. Of the 8556 New Zealanders who served there, 2721 died and 4752 were wounded. This portrait of Simpson and his donkey rescuing the wounded at Gallipoli was painted by Horace Moore-Jones, who served with the 1st Company of New Zealand Engineers. *Aigantighe Art Gallery, Timaru* (See Milestone 14.)

The search for a distinctive national identity quickened after 1915, but progress was erratic. Significant advances were made in the 1930s and as a result of the Second World War, but the momentum was lost in the 1950s and 1960s. Then, when Britain's entry into the EEC coincided with a decline in immigration and an increase in the number of young New Zealanders travelling overseas, a stronger sense of nationhood began to develop. This has also been expressed through a more independent foreign policy and the move to create a bicultural society. Since 1973 an artistic flowering has emphasised the uniqueness of New Zealand culture. Denys Watkins' 1985 painting *Bi-lingual* is representative of this new attitude. *National Art Gallery, New Zealand Collection.*

NOTICE

—TO—

EPICENE WOMEN.

ELECTIONEERING WOMEN

ARE REQUESTED NOT TO CALL HERE.

They are recommended to go home, to look after their children, cook their husband's dinners, empty the slops, and generally attend to the domestic affairs for which Nature designed them.

By taking this advice they will gain the respect of all right=minded people—an end not to be attained by unsexing themselves and meddling in masculine concerns of which they are profoundly ignorant.

HENRY WRIGHT.

103, Mein Street, Wellington.

Perhaps the most important milestones are those which irrevocably change attitudes. This poster prepared by Henry Wright in 1895 in reaction to women winning the vote in 1895 reminds us how far we have come in our short history. *Alexander Turnbull Library.*

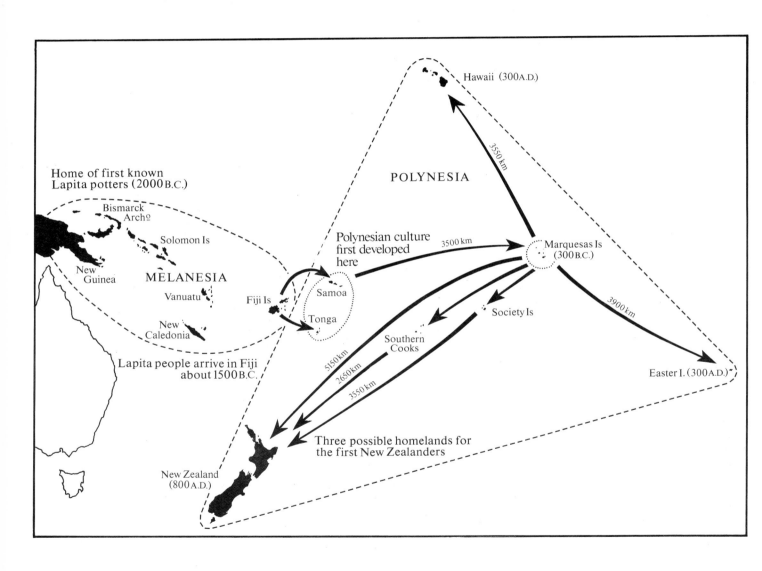

Home of first known
Lapita potters (2000 B.C.)

Bismarck
Archⁿ

Solomon Is

New
Guinea

MELANESIA

Vanuatu

New
Caledonia

Fiji Is

Lapita people arrive in Fiji
about 1500 B.C.

POLYNESIA

Hawaii (300 A.D.)

3550 km

Polynesian culture
first developed
here

3500 km

Marquesas Is
(300 B.C.)

Samoa

Tonga

Society Is

Southern
Cooks

3900 km

5150 km

2650 km

3550 km

Easter I. (300 A.D.)

Three possible homelands for
the first New Zealanders

New Zealand
(800 A.D.)

1. 1000 AD Vikings of the Sunrise:

East Polynesian Voyagers Discover Aotearoa

DAWN broke over a large land mass. Clouds were clustered around distant mountains rising beyond lines of green hills. This new land looked like a giant fish whose back had been flayed by angry fishermen. It was unlike any other island in Polynesia.

The unknown Polynesian adventurers who found Aotearoa around 1100 AD must have been filled with awe as well as the relief that the sight of land always brings to sailors after a long and arduous voyage. Te Ika a Maui (the North Island), Te Wahi Pounamu (the South Island) and Rakiura (Stewart Island) were huge by Polynesian standards; the land area of Aotearoa was several times greater than all the others islands of Polynesia put together.

This new country was isolated from animals and humans. The only mammal native to the islands was a fruit-eating bat. Only birds could conquer the barrier of distance and they ruled supreme for countless millennia. Because there were virtually no predators, the curious flightless parrots and swamp hens which evolved walked the floor of the verdant rain forests untroubled by enemies. Some of these biological oddities grew to exceptional size, the most famous being the giant moa, which stood over 3 metres tall. Nearly everywhere else in the world the earlier appearance of people and animals had eliminated such obvious and defenceless targets; the reign of birds and forest was now clearly threatened.

The climate was as different as the flora and fauna. It was much cooler and more changeable than balmy, tropical Polynesia. Coconuts, bananas and breadfruit would not grow so far south and even the hardier kumara needed special care to survive. Daylight was also much longer in the summer. Some historians believe that the name Aotearoa actually refers to 'land of the long daylight' rather than 'land of the long white cloud' because tradition has it that the discoverers of Aotearoa arrived at the time when the pohutukawa was in bloom. A cooler climate and a harsher environment added up to a need for change and adaptation.

The navigators who found Aotearoa came from East Polynesia. The tools and ornaments they brought with them point to the Cook Islands or the Marquesas and Society Islands as their immediate homelands. The discoverers sailed in double-hulled canoes 20 to 25 metres long which they paddled and sailed southwards for several weeks. Careful observation of sea currents, wind patterns, bird flight and the stars enabled the Polynesians to voyage considerable distances in quite deliberate fashion. Aotearoa was relatively easy to find because it was a big target compared with most Pacific islands.

Sailing back from Aotearoa to those small islands was another matter, but by no means an impossibility. Latter-day voyages by historian sailor David

Polynesian voyagers used a variety of clues and signs to help them navigate.

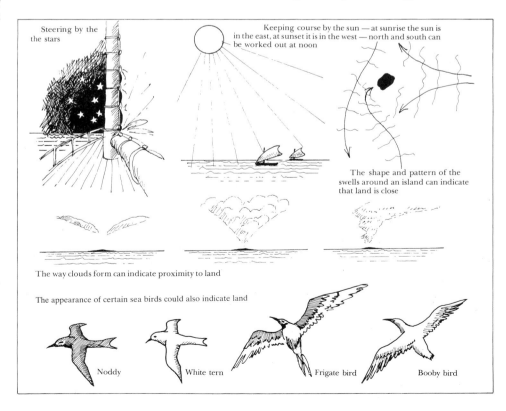

Steering by the the stars

Keeping course by the sun — at sunrise the sun is in the east, at sunset it is in the west — north and south can be worked out at noon

The shape and pattern of the swells around an island can indicate that land is close

The way clouds form can indicate proximity to land

The appearance of certain sea birds could also indicate land

Noddy   White tern   Frigate bird   Booby bird

Changes in Maori food sources 800-1800 AD. *Auckland Institute and Museum Educational Service.*

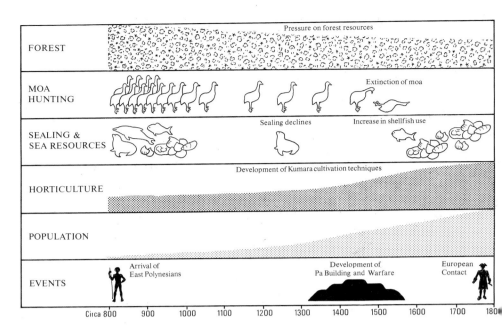

Lewis have demonstrated the extraordinary skills of Polynesian navigators and sailors. By using traditional methods Lewis sailed 1800 kilometres the 'wrong way' across the Pacific against the currents and winds and landed within a couple of kilometres of his intended destination. Modern research has, therefore, supported Te Rangi Hiroa's (Sir Peter Buck) claim that Polynesians were the greatest of all pre-scientific navigators.

Accidental voyaging did occur when fishing parties were blown off course, but it seems unlikely that Aotearoa was found by a fishing party, for two main reasons. First, they would not have had enough food on board to survive the lengthy journey, and second, there must have been women on board for the Maori voyagers to have multiplied in Aotearoa. Given that Polynesian women were not taken on deep sea fishing expeditions, it seems probable that the East Polynesians who discovered Aotearoa were deliberately searching for a new home after being driven from their native land by war, famine or oppression. Archaeological evidence indicates that they settled in New Zealand between 800 and 1200 AD; after the 14th century contact with Polynesia ceased.

The first arrivals from East Polynesia quickly learned to exploit Aotearoa's natural resources. The forests were abundant with berries and birds, while the surrounding seas were full of shellfish, fish, seals and dolphins. In the South Island forests in particular there were large numbers of the huge, meaty flightless moa. This key food source led some anthropologists to call these Archaic Maori the Moa Hunters. The Archaic Eastern Polynesian culture was based primarily on hunting and gathering. Food was plentiful. These were peaceful times; no weapons have been found and there is no evidence of cannibalism.

After the settlement period 800-1200, there was rapid change and expansion down to 1500. Forests on the eastern side of the South Island and parts of the North Island were fired to encourage the growth of fern. Large areas were also burnt accidentally and became grasslands. The 20 species of moa as well as other birds were exterminated not only by fire but by human hunters, dogs and rats. A cooler climate and erosion made some land more difficult to cultivate. Some kinds of shellfish disappeared while gardening of crops such as kumara increased. New types of tools, ornaments and weapons were developed.

The northern part of the North Island with its warmer climate, fertile soils and rich fisheries, prospered. Population expanded; by the 15th century some three-quarters of all Maori were living in that region. There was greater competition for food and land and fighting escalated. The losers were forced to migrate southwards and resettle.

Hunting and gathering remained more important than anywhere else in

---

The Great New Zealand Myth

For generations New Zealand schoolchildren were taught this version of Maori discovery and settlement.

925 AD Kupe chased a giant squid from his homeland Hawaiki all the way to New Zealand. On his return home he left instructions on how to find the large islands which he had discovered.

Some time later another group of mixed Melanesian/Polynesian heritage settled New Zealand. These people were called the Tangata Whenua or Moriori.

1125 AD A sailor, Toi, set out from Central Polynesia to find his grandson, Whatonga, who had disappeared in an interisland canoe race. Eventually Toi landed and settled at Whakatane.

He was later joined by Whatonga. Together they conquered and intermarried with the local Moriori.

1350 AD A great fleet of seven canoes journeyed from Hawaiki. They landed in various parts of the country and all tribes trace their ancestry back to these canoes.

The 'fleet' Maori in turn conquered the Moriori and Toi's descendants and established a vigorous martial culture.

This version has an English parallel: the Maori have their own Norman conquest, with 1350 AD the equivalent of 1066. It is,

however, myth not history.

● Carbon dating has shown that the Maori arrived well before 925 AD.

● The man responsible for much of the myth, the 19th-century Surveyor-General, Stephenson Percy Smith, based his 925 AD date on unreliable whakapapa or tribal tradition. Kupe, Toi and Whatonga are 14th-century characters who appear in a number of tribal traditions.

● It is unlikely that there was a Great Fleet at all; canoes may have come at various times. Archaeologists now think that the Great Fleet in Maori tradition refers to a migration within Aotearoa. Northland, with its warm climate and better soils, underwent a population explosion between 1400 and 1500 AD. As competition for scarce agricultural land increased, so did warfare. The losers were forced to move from Northland (their Hawaiki) and settle further south.

● New Zealand was not settled by the Moriori. There is no evidence of any people other than the Maori settling pre-Pakeha Aotearoa. The Moriori were simply Maori who journeyed to the Chatham Islands from New Zealand. After a long period of isolation they developed their own distinctive culture.

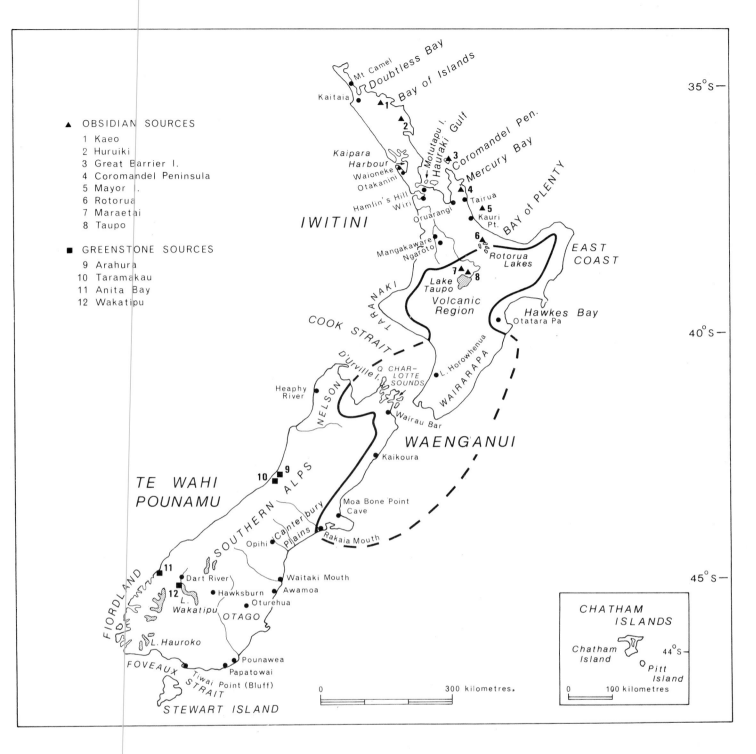

OBSIDIAN SOURCES
1 Kaeo
2 Huruiki
3 Great Barrier I.
4 Coromandel Peninsula
5 Mayor I.
6 Rotorua
7 Maraetai
8 Taupo

GREENSTONE SOURCES
9 Arahura
10 Taramakau
11 Anita Bay
12 Wakatipu

Archaeological map of New Zealand. Wherever Maori settled they had to adapt to the local area's climate, soil and food resources. *Courtesy Peter Bellwood.*

Polynesia. Fern root was supplemented by seal meat, shellfish, birds and berries. Life was physically tough, the diet often monotonous. A staple food, fern root wore away the teeth. For those who had to eat such a spartan diet life expectancy was not much more than 30 years; kaumatua (elders) were probably only about 35 years old.

Maori infant mortality was probably much lower than that in pre-industrial Europe. There was also enough food on Aotearoa to support a population of 100,000 or more.

Warfare played an important part in Classic Maori culture and tribal traditions abound with tales of constant skirmishing. Toa (warriors) attained higher status than in other Polynesian societies and the art and weapons of war were developed to a more sophisticated level. Large-scale warfare, however, was comparatively rare.

The concept of tapu controlled Maori attitudes and beliefs. Roughly translated, it means sacred or holy. Both animate and inanimate could be declared tapu. If an object was tapu it had to be approached or handled according to a strict set of rituals. A high chief was so sacred when communicating with the gods that he had to be fed by another person with a stick. Food sources such as eel weirs and shellfish beds were protected by declaring them tapu for certain periods

of the year. In this way tapu was used to conserve resources and deter outsiders.

The principle of utu (recompense, reciprocation or revenge) meant that an insult or an attack from a neighbouring tribe had to be repaid in kind. A careful count was kept of breaches of family and tribal honour. Utu could be effected in several ways. Minor breaches of etiquette and unintentional insults were usually avenged by muru or formal plundering raids. The experience of bad luck, for example the loss of a canoe, could also be satisfied by the exercise of muru. More serious offences such as contravention of tapu, sexual philandering or accidental death or serious illness, were avenged by murder. A small taua (war party) would be formed by the offended individual or hapu (clan) and swift reprisal taken. Very occasionally a large taua would be created over a long period of time, forging alliances with other hapu and iwi (tribes). Sometimes a major campaign would be launched many years after the incident which caused the initial grievance had taken place though this was very unusual before the coming of the European. Generally utu kept a check on excessive fighting because everyone knew the lore and accepted it.

Maori society was clannish. It was structured around the whanau (extended family), hapu (clan) and iwi (tribe), but the hapu — a tightly knit group of extended families — was always most important in terms of identification and loyalty. Each member of a hapu could trace their descent to a common ancestor. In this way Maori also differed from the Aborigines of Australia who moved around in small family groups of 20 to 30. Maori preferred to live in relatively large fortified villages which could house up to 2000 people. More important, the centrality of the hapu ruled out the development of a system of kingship. No one chief or tribe ever became sufficiently dominant to be considered leader of all the tribes of Maoridom.

Maori society was hierarchical in structure. The paramount chief of the iwi was the ariki, the chief of the hapu the rangatira. Chiefly rank was ascribed by birth and seniority of descent, usually through the male line. Nevertheless, a relatively minor or low born chief like Te Rauparaha could win mana (prestige) through military conquest. On the other hand that same ambitious chief once spared the life of his arch enemy, Te Wherowhero, because the latter was the eldest son of a first wife and could trace his whakapapa (genealogy) back to the tribal ancestor through the tuakana (senior descent line). Despite the hierarchy chiefs were expected to work and fight along with everyone else. Below the

rangatira were tutua (commoners) who came from the junior descent line (teina). Taurekareka (slaves), usually war captives, were not numerous before the coming of the musket and the intensification of tribal warfare. They were generally well treated and were never a hereditary caste; their children were automatically born free. Their punishment took the form of loss of mana or spiritual power.

Leadership in Maori society was usually exercised by men although women of character and ability were often a powerful influence behind the scenes. Whereas all men except slaves were tapu, women were noa, the opposite of tapu, except during menstruation and childbirth. Women were also confined to strictly prescribed roles. Men felled the trees and loosened the soil for planting; women sowed and cared for the crops. Open sea fishing was men's work. Cooking was left to the slaves and women. Women were encouraged to act as cheerleaders in battle but rarely took part in the fighting. Despite their obviously inferior status, Maori legend and tribal tradition suggest that some Maori women of high birth did hold considerable power and authority.

The Maori never built elaborate temples or tombs. Their sacred objects were nearly always works of nature: mountains, lakes, giant trees, outcrops of rock, clusters of stone. Although tohunga were important and powerful, they never developed into a theocracy like that of Tahiti or Easter Island. The word tohunga means specialist rather than priest and these men were treasured more as keepers of whakapapa, guardians of tribal tradition, storytellers and poets than as priests. Some tohunga were actually carvers or canoe builders. Only a minority were considered capable of makutu (sorcery) and were consulted as seers, but even so they had an incredible psychological hold over their hapu. Despite the psychic power of some tohunga most Maori carried their religion within them rather than expressing it in elaborate outward forms. They believed that everything, living or inert, creature, tree, or stone, had its own life force or mauri. The bush was literally alive with the ghosts of departed ancestors, good and evil spirits. Rivers had their taniwha (evil spirits) as well as their magical guardians. Land, water and bush filled Maori with awe. People, land, rivers, sea, trees, fish and birds were united in a strange, mystic union.

Debate continues as to whether a higher school of tohunga believed in a supreme being known as Io. It seems likely that most Maori were more concerned with explaining and describing natural phenomena in human terms than with ascribing the creation of life to any one God.

In the Maori view the natural and supernatural were so inextricably linked that separation of one from the other was unnecessary. The great divide in the Maori universe was not between God and man but between earth (papa — the mother of creation) and sky (rangi — the father of creation).

Early European explorers, settlers and missionaries had great difficulty in coming to terms with the world view of the Maori. Christianity saw life in simple moral terms of right and wrong, good and evil, whereas the Maori view was much more subtle and complex.

Specifically Maori forms of clothing, architecture and art had emerged by the 15th century. Captain Cook noticed that Maori wore more clothes than other Polynesians and were altogether more utilitarian and less flamboyant in their dress. Their housing was warmer and more functional. Open structures were quite impractical in chilly Aotearoa and innovation was apparent in the carefully constructed houses built to store food. Maori art and artefacts were also unique and extremely sophisticated. Carving was more highly developed than elsewhere in Polynesia with quite distinctive motifs decorating meeting houses and canoes. Given the limits of their stone tools, Maori work with greenstone was quite extraordinary. Weaving was also developed to a remarkably high degree; the intricate patterns (taniko) deeply impressed early Europeans.

By the time Europeans came to New Zealand, Maori society seems to have reached about as high a level of development as was possible for a stone age technology. Its people lived in relative harmony with the environment and with one another. The Maori were relatively healthy and were free of infectious diseases such as yaws which caused so much harm elsewhere in the Pacific. Captain Cook reported that they were about 5 feet 7 inches (170 centimetres) in height when the

A reconstruction of Maori war parties meeting at sea, by Hawaiian artist Herb Kawainui Kane. This work is based on the Toki, a Taupiri war canoe in the Auckland Museum. *Courtesy Herb Kawainui Kane and Island Heritage Ltd, Hawaii.*

This composite picture is taken from *The New Zealanders Illustrated* (1847) by G. F. Angas:

1. Mode of fishing with nets on Lake Taupo.
2. A fishing weir, or eel trap, on the River Mokau.
3. Wooden fish-hook.
4. Fish-hook generally in use.
5. Eel trap, formed of twigs.
6. A wooden digging stick.
7. A pounder for beating flax.
8. Wooden flute.
9. Bark bucket.
10. Flax basket.
11. Ancient wooden bowl for kumara.
12. Flax sandals.
13. Flax sandals.
14. An aged slave woman.

height of the average Englishman was about 5 feet 3 inches (160 centimetres). He described them as well made but lean and generally free of serious physical defects.

This reasonably happy condition had been reached because of Maori capacity to adapt to a new environment in a relatively short time. They seem to have built into their social structure and world view an ability to accommodate change and new challenges. This was in marked contrast to the Australian Aborigines who had settled their country up to 80,000 years before. The Aborigines lived in such perfect harmony with their environment that change seemed unnecessary and even unthinkable; the status quo became absolute. The past was always important to the Maori but they never lost their perception of the future and always realised that change was part of the human condition. Both this capacity to cope with change and their considerable military skill explains why the Maori of Aotearoa were so much better equipped to adjust to the European intrusion than the Aborigines of Australia.

2. 1642 In Search of the Southern Continent:
Tasman Discovers New Zealand

LITTLE is known about the first European to discover New Zealand. Abel Janszoon Tasman was born in the Dutch village of Lutjegast in 1603 and the next record we have of his life is the December 1631 proclamation of his marriage in Amsterdam to Jannetje Tjaers, which took place in January of 1631. In this document the 28-year-old widower is described as a sailor.

In 1633 Tasman sailed to Batavia on a three-year contract with the Dutch East India Company and within a year rose to become mate. Three months later he became master of the *Mocha*, joining other ships to investigate a new route between the spice islands of Amboina and Banda. He was promoted to commodeur (commodore) in 1636. His chief vice seems to have been a taste for rum and he was once disciplined for disobedience. Tasman sailed to Holland in 1636, returning to Batavia with his wife in 1638 to take up a 10-year contract.

Anthony Van Diemen, the Governor General of the Dutch East Indies from 1636 to 1645, had dreams of building a vast trading empire stretching from mainland Asia in the north to the as yet undiscovered South-land in the southern oceans. In the pursuit of trade, profits and knowledge, he sent an expedition in 1636 to explore the north-west coast of New Holland (Australia). Three years later Tasman went as second in command on an expedition to search for the islands of 'gold and silver' in the seas east of Japan. In 1640 Tasman led his own four-ship expedition to Japan, and further trading voyages to Cambodia and Formosa followed.

By now Van Diemen was confident enough of Tasman's abilities to con-

Abel Tasman, a sketch by James McDonald. *National Museum.*

tract him in 1642 to lead an exploratory expedition to the southern latitudes in search of the supposedly fabulously wealthy South-land. Tasman was put in command of two small ships, the *Heemskerck* and the *Zeehaen*. Franchoys Jacobszoon Visscher, the chief pilot, was instructed to draw up a plan to reach the southern continent and open up access to Chile. Visscher set daunting objectives, ones that could not possibly be accomplished by one man or one expedition.

The final instructions of 13 August 1642 suggest that the Dutch East India Company's directors had even grander dreams than Visscher. The Hon. Justus Schouten penned commands which pointed out the enormous gains that resulted from the discoveries of Vasco da Gama and Christopher Columbus in the Northern Hemisphere. He further argued with a confidence born of ignorance that:

> there must be similar fertile and rich regions situated south of the equator, of which matter we have conspicuous examples and clear proofs in the gold — and silver — bearing provinces of Peru, Chili, Monomatapa or Sofala so that it may confidently be expected that the expense and trouble that may be bestowed in the eventual discovery of so large a portion of the world, will be rewarded with certain fruit of material profit and immortal fame.

The message was clear — the expedition must cover costs and win material gain. Schouten then instructed Tasman to sail to Mauritius to refit and take on supplies. Thereafter he was to follow Visscher's plans and also search for a passage between New Guinea and Eendrachtsland (Western Australia). The coast of any land found by Tasman was to be followed and mapped and trade opportunities exploited. The directors doubted that Tasman would find any civilised people but he was to find out what commodities were produced by countries occupied by 'savages' and ascertain whether these people prized silver and gold. If any people were unaware of the value of gold and silver Tasman should give the impression that the Dutch prized copper and lead. Finally, he was ordered to be careful as well as deceitful. Small craft were not to be landed among warlike savages and the bloodshed which marred the discovery of North America was to be avoided. Violence would reduce trade and cost money as well as lives. The Dutch continued to think and act as traders and investors rather than as conquerors and empire builders.

Tasman's two ships, although relatively new, were quite unsuited to the demands of such an expedition. They were small, capable only of a maximum of 5 knots and quite unmanoeuvrable. The flagship, the *Heemskerck*, was little more than a 60-tonne yacht. Short and squat, it sat high out of the water and 60 men were squeezed into its cramped quarters. The supporting ship, the *Zeehaen*, was longer, sleeker and faster, and had a draught suited to sailing in shallow waters. The 100-tonne flute carried 50 men and conditions on board were less restricted. Unfortunately, however, its

Tasman's ships the *Zeehaen* and *Heemskerck*. Taken from Tasman's diaries. *National Museum.*

upper half was rotten and it required extensive repairs. Even more serious, neither ship could tack against the wind and both were forced to run before the breeze. Compared with contemporary English craft this was a serious handicap. Because the ships came from the merchant navy rather than from the armed forces, an unusual command structure operated for the voyage. Tasman was not given total command but acted as president of a council made up of all senior officers, making decisive action difficult.

Tasman was sailing into the unknown. Dutch maps of the area consisted of little more than disconnected lines. He possessed neither sextant nor chronometer so he could not calculate longitude accurately. He had on board an astrolabe, a cross staff and an hourglass but probably relied more on 'dead reckoning'. Tasman, it must be remembered, sailed at the start of the Scientific Revolution, which meant that he was hampered by more than inadequate navigational technology. His mind was also full of the myths and monsters of the Middle Ages. Like his crew he still believed in giants and sea monsters. The burdens of superstition and a very real fear of the unknown made his difficult voyage even more courageous.

Tasman sailed in his inadequate and overcrowded vessels on 14 August 1642, arriving at Mauritius in early September. So appalled was the commander of Mauritius at the condition of the ships that he held them over for a month for refitting, so that Tasman finally sailed on the main part of the adventure on 8 October. Heavy mists surrounded the tiny ships and no land was sighted. Storms and big seas were encountered on 6 November and the weather became so cold that Visscher agreed to break with his plan and they turned east at latitude 49° 4'. Temperatures did not rise and Tasman sailed back up to 44° before resuming the easterly course. At last on 24 November land was sighted about 65 kilometres away. Tasman named the hilly new country Van Diemen's Land in honour of the Governor General.

The clumsy ships were becalmed the following day until a storm blew up and got them under way again on 26 November. They beat their way around the southern tip of Van Diemen's Land (later called Tasmania to honour its discoverer) and sailed up the east coast to Storm Bay. On 1 December Tasman dropped anchor at Green Island and sent men ashore to collect fresh vegetables and water. Smoke was seen rising in the distance but his men did not encounter any human beings. They noted with some alarm, however, that there were foot notches on the trees spaced some 1.5 metres apart. Tasman immediately suspected that giants lived in the vicinity and when no drinkable water was found he gladly sailed away on 4 December. The expedition tried to sail north to discover the relationship between Van Diemen's Land and New Holland. Unfortunately they were beaten off by a head wind and turned east on 5 December. Bass Strait had to wait another 150 years for its European discoverer.

Tasman continued for a few days, then, just before noon on 13 Decem-

calm of what is now called Golden Bay. Smoke was rising from a low coast covered in sand dunes. It was time to seek a safe harbour so on 18 December the cockboat and pinnace were sent out to scout around. In the late afternoon the storm-beaten ships dropped anchor in Wharawananga Bay.

Lights shone on shore and an hour or so later two double-hulled canoes were spotted paddling out to the ships. As the men in the canoe came near

seemed to be made out of a cotton-like material. The canoe travelled fairly fast and was propelled by long, narrow pointed paddles. When a loud yell from the visitors interrupted Tasman's thoughts, he held up white linen and knives, gesturing to the Maori to come on board. They declined but seemed so friendly that Tasman decided to move closer in.

Before he could weigh anchor seven more canoes began paddling towards the ships. The *Zeehaen* sent its quar-

ber, he recorded in his journal: 'saw a large land, uplifted high [groot hooch ver heven landt] south east of us for about fifteen miles.' It was the Southern Alps of New Zealand. The coastline was covered in clouds and he could not see the mountain tops. Huge breakers crashed into the shore and the country looked inhospitable. Tasman compared what he saw with Formosa and named it Statenlandt, assuming that it was a continuation of the coastline given the same name by Jacob le Maire when he rounded the Horn of Tierra del Fuego in 1610.

Landing on such a dangerous coast was quite impossible and Tasman ran out to sea to escape the heavy swell. Then he turned north and followed the distant coastline until it fell away around Cape Farewell on 17 December. The squall disappeared as he sailed around Farewell Spit into the

they shouted out in 'a rough, loud voice'. None of the Dutch sailors could understand a word; the language was quite different from that of either the Solomon Islands or New Guinea. Then the natives blew a horn which Tasman thought sounded like a Moorish trumpet. (It was probably a conch shell.) Tasman responded by ordering his men to play a tune on a trumpet and other instruments. The impromptu concert continued until darkness forced the canoes to retreat.

The next morning after daybreak another canoe paddled out towards the ships. Tasman noted that the men in the canoe were brown to yellow in colour, of ordinary height and strong boned. They had thick black hair tied in tufts rather like the Japanese and a white feather crowned each head. Naked from the waist up, they wore on their lower bodies woven mats which

A Maori canoe, 1642. Derived from a drawing from Abel Tasman's journal entitled 'A View of Moordaerers' Bay, as you are at anchor there at 15 fathoms, 1642.' The original was the first image of a Maori by a European artist. Instead of drawing the Maori accurately the artist depicted them in the way most 17th-century artists painted naked bodies. *Alexander Turnbull Library.*

termaster and six sailors in the cockboat to warn the *Heemskerck* not to take too many natives on board. On its return to the *Zeehaen* the boat was rammed by the biggest canoe. Three sailors were clubbed to death and a fourth was fatally wounded. The quartermaster and the remaining two sailors managed to swim back to the safety of the *Heemskerck*. In the meantime the Maori collected one body and set the cockboat adrift. Tasman picked up one body and the

seriously wounded man and fired over the heads of the Maori. He weighed anchor as quickly as possible and sailed out into the safety of Cook Strait.

Tasman's mind was made up: 'no friendship could be made with these people', the inhabitants of this country were 'enemies'. He named the place Murderers' Bay. After this tragic beginning to New Zealand's Pakeha history Tasman was reluctant to land anywhere else near Statenlandt and so opportunities to learn more about the geography, resources and people of this new land were lost. This unfortunate incident also denied ethnographers and anthropologists an insight into 17th-century Maori life.

Tasman had clashed with an obscure tribe known as the Ngati Matakokiri, who were themselves destroyed by other tribes in the 18th century. They probably attacked because Tasman arrived in summer, the season when taua (war parties) were likely to strike without warning. Unlike later explorers, Tasman carried little that would attract the Maori. On a positive note, the very brief contact left the Maori unaffected by European disease. The impact of Tasman's visit was slight and localised. The incident with the Dutch sailors receives scant mention in tribal traditions and the Maori did not tell Cook about Tasman.

Although Tasman described the area around Cook Strait as 'a beautiful, fine land', he was not prepared to risk another landing and instead sailed east to Chile but was driven back by strong easterly winds. For reasons that are still unclear, Tasman guessed that he was in a giant bay and drew a line suggesting that the coastline ran beyond him in the east. Once the wind switched to the south he sailed northwards, charting the west coast. He failed to see Taranaki because of cloud but he did spot Mount Karioi behind Raglan Harbour. He noted little else of interest.

On 4 January Tasman reached a cape which he named Maria van Diemen after the Governor General's wife. After sailing around the cape he turned north to the Three Kings Islands, so named because he found them on Twelfth Night. At long last it seemed he had found a safe landing which provided fresh water and veget-

ables. Unfortunately the following morning he saw 30 to 35 men of huge stature, who called once again in rough voices and waved lethal-looking clubs. A fearful Tasman was convinced that he had seen giants who 'took enormously large steps and strides'. The apparition and an awkward heavy surf proved too much; he departed from New Zealand shores on 6 January 1643.

Tasman sailed back to Batavia via the Friendly Isles (Tonga) and on through Fiji, the Solomon Islands and New Ireland. He failed to find any passage leading from northern New Guinea to Western Australia and arrived back home on schedule on 14 June 1643. He had lost only 14 men, a virtual record for such a long voyage. To have travelled 8000 kilometres in slow and poorly designed boats was a remarkable feat of courage and skill.

Unfortunately, Van Diemen and the Dutch East India Company were not impressed. Tasman and the officers were paid a token bonus of two months' extra salary while the men received one month's extra pay. The Governor General complained that Tasman had left 'the main part of his task to be executed by some more inquisitive successor' and lamented the lack of treasure and trade deals. Furthermore, Tasman had failed to establish the Chile route and had added only a little to the geographical knowledge of the Dutch. What little Tasman had found was brought into question later in 1643 when Hendrik Brouwer discovered that Statenlandt was nothing more than a small island off the coast of Tierra del Fuego.

Despite his disappointment, however, Van Diemen still had sufficient faith in Tasman and Visscher to send

them off on another expedition in 1644. This time they were instructed to find a strait which led directly from Northern New Guinea to the Southland. Tasman traced the outlines of the Gulf of Carpenteria instead and only found a poor and primitive people. The Governor General and the company directors in Amsterdam were unimpressed. These businessmen, uninterested in geographical discovery, complained the voyages were too costly and, worse, there were no immediate profits. They condemned Van Diemen's vision as too grand; future expeditions should concentrate exclusively on India, Taiwan and Japan. Geographic inquiry could be left to larger, richer nations.

When Van Diemen died in April 1645, his grand design of a Dutch empire encompassing most of the Pacific died with him. The Dutch continued to believe in the great South-land until the 18th century but introduced the name of Nieuw Zeeland once Brouwer knew that Statenlandt was no more than an island. After 1645 the Dutch concentrated their trade activities in South Asia and remained content with a map which was full of gaps and showed only three sides of Australia.

Tasman returned to normal duties. He fell from favour for a time because of a vicious drunken assault upon two crewmen, but he soon won back his captain's title and in 1656 set up his own shipping business. By the time of his death in 1659 he was one of Batavia's largest landowners. Tasman's contribution was not recognised until many years after his death. At first only Dutch map makers acknowledged the importance of his discoveries and it took Sir Joseph Banks and

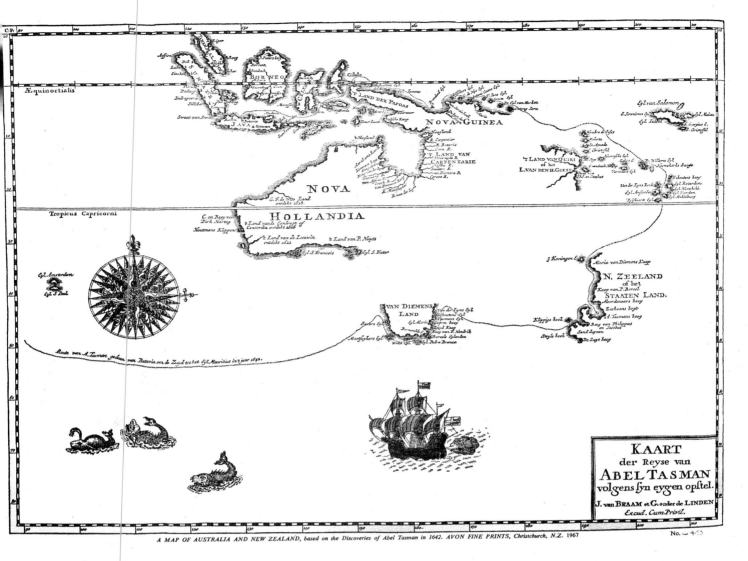

A MAP OF AUSTRALIA AND NEW ZEALAND, based on the Discoveries of Abel Tasman in 1642. AVON FINE PRINTS, Christchurch, N.Z. 1967

the English historian of exploration, James Burney, to bring Tasman's extraordinary feat to the attention of the world. Banks called Tasman a 'great man' and ever since he has occupied a prominent place in the Pacific hall of fame.

Banks' glowing judgement must be qualified. While undoubtedly a brave and skilful sailor Tasman was neither great nor clever. He was a professional doing a job designed by a superior mind. He never appreciated the geographical importance of his discoveries and showed minimal intellectual curiosity about the flora, fauna and people he encountered. Although Tasman made an important beginning, it

Tasman's map of Australia and New Zealand. *National Museum.*

was left to his successor to rise above the category of sailor and move beyond the instructions of his superiors to become discoverer, geographer, scientist and ethnographer. James Cook was that successor.

29

3. 1769 Master Mariner:

Cook Circumnavigates New Zealand

THE transit of Venus was due on 3 June 1769. Observations of the previous transit in 1761 had been ruined by heavy cloud and this time British and European scientists were determined to get things right. In England, the Royal Society calculated that its chances of success would be much improved if the path followed by Venus across the face of the sun could be viewed from a high point in an area of clear skies. They needed a ship and an able commander to accomplish such a mission so they turned to the Admiralty for help.

Alexander Dalrymple, an eminent Scottish hydrographer, was first approached to lead the expedition, in 1767, but he resigned when the Navy refused to allow him to appoint his own crew. The Navy then turned to one of its own officers, a master who had done excellent work as hydrographer, chart maker and surveyor in the St Lawrence River area and Newfoundland. Why the Navy chose James Cook rather than a score of other competent candidates remains a mystery, but their selection of a professional rather than a nobleman of good family would be vindicated many times over.

James Cook was born on 27 October 1728 at Marton-in-Cleveland in Yorkshire where his father, James Cook Senior, was the manager of a local farm, a position which allowed James, an intelligent lad, to receive a reasonable education. At 17 he took up an apprenticeship with William Sanderson, grocer and haberdasher of Staithes, but the life proved dull and

Captain Cook. A 19th-century engraving after a portrait by Nathaniel Dance painted in 1776. *National Museum.*

Engraving of the bark the *Endeavour*, Cook's ship on his 1769-70 voyage to New Zealand. *National Museum.*

after 18 months James moved to an apprenticeship with John Walker, a Whitby coal shipper.

James quickly learned the skills of seamanship on coal ships plying from Whitby to London. It was a tough job, with only half a day off per week, but the experience gained on the strong, ungainly 500-tonne vessels was invaluable. By 1752 Cook had risen to the rank of mate and showed promise as a navigator.

Now 26 years old, James seemed to want greater challenge in his life and on 17 June 1755 he volunteered for the Navy at Wapping, then joining a 60-gun warship, the *Eagle*, at Portsmouth. Within a month he became mate and two years later had passed his exams and went on to be master of a 24-gun frigate, the *Solebay*. A master was the chief professional on board a naval ship responsible for navigation, pilotage, soundings, charts and keeping the log; as such, he was a combination of captain, mate, lieutenant and midshipman. Nevertheless in the 18th century masters ranked below fighting men and few ever received a commission.

Cook was first sent to flush out French smugglers around the Scottish coast. Then, in October 1757, he was transferred to the *Pembroke*, a big, new, 64-gun, 1650-tonne ship. Early the next year he was ordered to Halifax, Nova Scotia, to take part in actions against the French. It was during General Wolfe's Quebec campaign that Cook chartered the St Lawrence and impressed as a sailor and chart maker.

In 1762 Cook returned to Britain where he married Elizabeth Batts of Barking in Essex. Elizabeth, who came from a respectable family of artisans and small businessmen, was a devoted, supportive wife who bore six children, none of whom lived past 30.

Cook returned to Newfoundland in 1763 where he spent four years surveying and mapping the southern and western coastlines. Then, late in 1767, the Admiralty asked him to lead the expedition to observe the transit of Venus; Cook agreed.

The Navy decided on a collier for the voyage because its strength, stability and shallow draught would make it ideal for exploration and surveying, and the four-year-old *Earl of Pembroke*, built at Whitby, was chosen.

Some 30 metres long and 9 metres wide, it weighed 368 tonnes. Extensive refitting was required and the name was changed to the more appropriate *Endeavour*.

While the *Endeavour* was being overhauled, Captain Samuel Wallis returned from a long Pacific voyage to report the discovery of Tahiti. The high mountains, fine climate and friendly inhabitants of this island made it an ideal site from which to observe the transit. Cook, now a first lieutenant, was instructed to sail to Tahiti with a crew of 85 and 12 marines. He was also to be accompanied by several scientists. Mr Green was instructed to take charge of the astronomical observations and two botanists were appointed: Joseph Banks, a young Englishman of a landed and wealthy family, and Dr Daniel Solander, a favourite pupil of the great Swedish botanist Linnaeus. Banks also took along for company two secretaries and four servants, two of them black. The expeditionary party was completed by two artists, Sydney Parkinson, an expert at drawing flowers, and the epileptic landscape painter Alexander Buchan.

Cook was very much better equipped for accurate navigation than Tasman; dead reckoning would be a thing of the past. The *Endeavour* was much more manoeuvrable than the Dutch ships, and could tack against the wind. Even more important, Cook sailed with a mind free of giants and monsters, and he was driven by an insatiable curiosity rather than by a fear of the unknown.

Cook's instructions were first to sail to Tahiti for the transit, via Plymouth, Madeira and Cape Horn. Second, he was to sail south to latitude 40° in search of the southern continent and then sail west to New Zealand.

The expedition departed on 25 August 1768 and reached Tahiti on 13 April, seven weeks before the transit. Despite being only the second English commander to sail to Tahiti, Cook encountered no special navigational problems and his crew remained remarkably well, none dying of sickness. The transit, observed in perfect weather, was later judged a success. On 9 August Cook left the Society Islands with a native interpreter, Tupaia, on board and headed south-west. The goal now was to find either the southern continent or the east coast of New Zealand.

Eventually, almost two months after the *Endeavour* had left Tahiti, the young servant boy Nicholas Young spotted land at 2 p.m. on Saturday 7 October; Cook recorded: 'saw land from the mast head bearing WBN'. Banks thought that the southern continent had been discovered but the more sceptical Cook suspected that he had found Tasman's Nieuw Zeeland. Next day Cook wrote:

> The land on the sea coast is high with white steep cliffs and back inland are high mountains, the face of the Country is of a hilly surface and appears to be clothed with wood and verdure.

Sighting canoes and houses on shore, Cook decided to land and investigate the 'Indians', whom he described as being 'strong raw boned, well-made active people rather above the common size, of a very dark brown colour with black hair'. Their speech was close enough to Tahitian for Tupaia to talk to them but communication did not lead to a warm welcome; the locals did not want strangers landing on their territory. Cook ordered a shot fired to deter an attack and one native was killed. As Cook's boat was rowed back to the *Endeavour*, it was attacked by a canoe and three more Maori were killed.

Cook and Banks were upset; their beginning had been as bad as Tasman's. Unlike Tasman, however, Cook persisted and three young Maori men were taken on board to parley. As individuals they seemed friendly enough but when the *Endeavour* moved nearer the shore a 200-strong war party could be seen performing a frenzied war dance. Cook finally gave up and sailed away, having named the area Poverty Bay 'because it afforded us no one thing we wanted'.

Sailing south, Cook called the south-west point of Poverty Bay Young Nick's Head and the servant boy also won a gallon of rum for first sighting New Zealand. Near present day Napier, several canoes approached the *Endeavour* and a number of Maori tried to drag young Taiata, Tupaia's servant, aboard their canoe; two Maori were killed in the rescue. Cook named the point where the incident occurred Cape Kidnappers and the wide, open, shallow bay

he christened Hawke Bay, after the First Lord of the Admiralty.

Continuing south, Cook reached Cape Turnagain on 17 October and reversed his course. The journey north brought a change in fortunes. Friendly Ngati Porou greeted Cook at Uawa Bay (which Cook thought was Tolaga Bay) and on 19 October he traded nails, beads and tapa cloth for kumara and fresh fish. Cook's persistence was paying off and he stayed 10 days in the bay taking on fresh water and provisions.

On 29 October he resumed his northern journey, rounded East Cape on 30 October and named Hicks Bay after his second lieutenant Zachary Hicks. The following day he scared off war canoes at Cape Runaway and sailed on to discover the 'well inhabited' and heavily cultivated Bay of

Plenty. The local Whaka-tohea and Ngati Awa, although hostile at first, warmed after warning shots were fired. Cook sailed into Mercury Bay on 4 November and while anchored there observed the transit of Mercury. During his 10-day stay he made good friends, explored the area and was shown over a large and impressive fighting pa.

Eighty years later the old chief Te Horeta Taniwha told European settlers of his childhood memories of Cook's visit to Mercury Bay. The boat seemed supernatural and he wondered if the sailors had eyes in the backs of their heads because they rowed with their backs to the shore. The thunder and lightning sticks frightened the

Cook's chart of New Zealand, a masterpiece of cartography. *National Museum.*

A tattooed Maori face by Sydney Parkinson, 1770. *British Museum.*

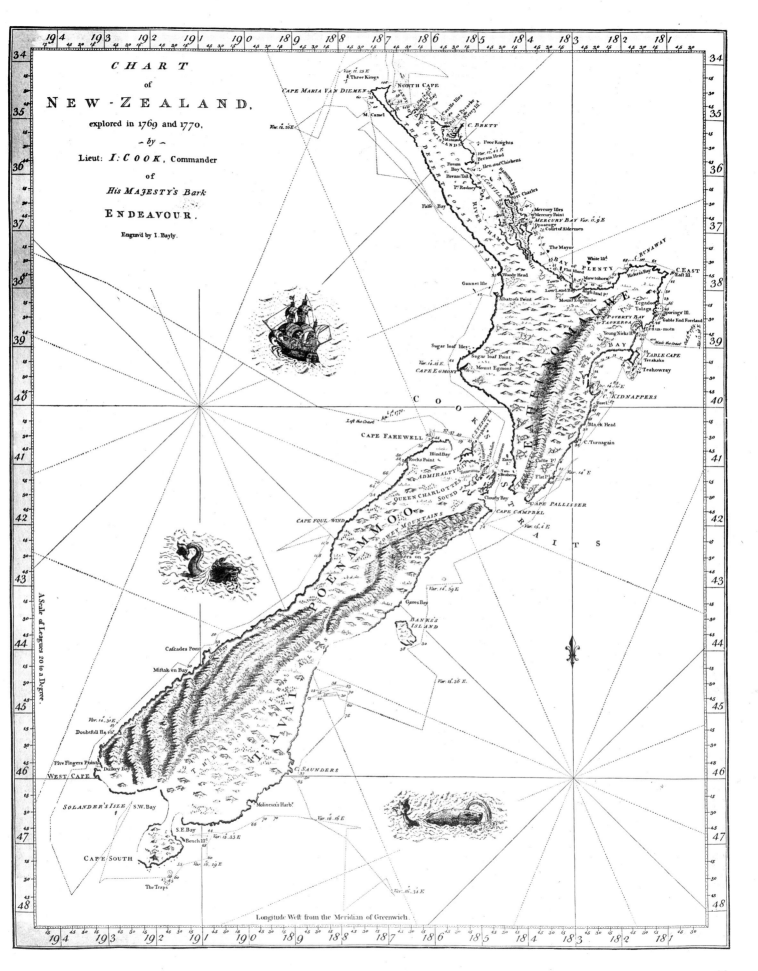

women and children away (one Ngati Maru was shot during the visit) and yet the tupua (goblins or demons) seemed kind. They gave food (potatoes) and goods in exchange for fish and cloaks. Te Horeta remembered going on board and having his head patted by a tall man who gave him a nail. This man said little but was obviously the rangatira. Te Horeta may have engaged in some poetic licence in front of his credulous audience but he certainly sensed Cook's mana. As he said, 'e kore te tingo tangata e ngaro i roto i te tokomako' (a veritable man is not hid among many).

At Mercury Bay Cook claimed the area for George III without, naturally, bothering to consult the Maori living there; it was an ominous event for the future of Maoridom. He sailed out of the bay on 15 November and rounded Cape Colville, which he named after his naval commander. The area on the leeside of the Coromandel Peninsula he called the Firth of Thames: the estuary reminded him of London's famous river. The site seemed ideal for future European settlement.

At the Bay of Islands, where Cook landed on 29 November, the Ngapuhi threatened to attack but became friendly once cannon was fired over their heads. The surrounding country was fertile, with numerous kumara patches supporting a large population. Cook's intention to treat Maori and Briton alike was demonstrated when he had one of his men flogged for raiding a kumara patch.

Once Cook left the Bay of Islands

Joseph Banks, the botanist who travelled with Cook on his 1769-70 South Pacific exploration. Banks' observations are one of New Zealand's most important early historical records. *National Museum.*

on 5 December the weather worsened and for nearly two months extremely difficult, squally and unseasonable conditions hampered charting. The *Endeavour* did not reach the Three Kings Islands until Christmas Eve and only with some difficulty rounded Cape Maria van Diemen. Cook then worked his way down the inhospitable west coast to reach the Kaipara Harbour on 4 January 1770. Conditions

proved too treacherous for landing so the whole west coast of the North Island was charted from the sea. Cook named the high Taranaki Mount Egmont after John Perceval, second Earl of Egmont, a former Lord of the Admiralty. Eventually on 14 January Cook sailed into a big strait and the following day found Ship Cove in Queen Charlotte Sound, where he decided to reprovision.

Ship Cove delighted Cook and it became a favourite spot to which he returned on later voyages. Banks was especially impressed by the 'melodious wild musick' of the birds. While at Ship Cove, Cook heard of the misfortune of the French explorer Jean François Marie de Surville, who had sailed past the Hokianga at the same time as Cook was battling the wild winds north of the Bay of Islands in December. De Surville, who had landed with 60 men dead from scurvy, upset the local Maori and was expelled by force. Cook took heed of this tale and was careful thereafter in dealing with the warlike natives of New Zealand.

Interestingly, during extensive study of the people of the sounds area Cook never heard mention of Tasman's visit. The natives were cannibals who defended the practice stoutly against the criticisms of Tupaia. Cook also heard about the South Island which he called 'Tovy-poenammu' and proved that the

A reconstruction of Cook's landing at the mouth of the Turanginui River by F. F. C. Huddleston. *Gisborne Museum Collection.*

water running between the islands was a strait rather than a bay, by climbing the tall hill of Kaitapeha which provided views over the whole sounds area. Cook took possession of the area around Queen Charlotte Sound, again without consultation. The Ngati Kuia were glad to see him go on 5 February since the visit had seriously depleted their food sources.

Later that day Banks persuaded his modest commander to name the strait after its discoverer. Cook then sailed north to convince his officers that the North Island was in fact an island, before turning south to circumnavigate the South Island. He sailed past the Kaikoura Mountains on 14 February. Cloud covered Banks Peninsula so that Cook mistook it for an island. Ten wild days off the South Canterbury and Otago coast followed. Cook saw Cape Saunders on the tip of the Otago peninsula but did not enter Otago Harbour. Passing Stewart Island on its southern side, Cook thought that it was joined to the mainland by a peninsula, but he drew it in on the map with dotted lines just in case. On 14 March he reached

Dusky Bay in Fiordland, an area that so impressed him with its spectacular beauty that he determined to return.

The voyage up the West Coast was as rough as Tasman's had been. A fierce nor'-wester off Westport led Cook to name the coastal promontory Cape Foulwind. He did not reach Cape Farewell until 23 March and failed to see Golden Bay as it was obscured by cloud; he called the place Blind Bay instead. The circumnaviga-

tion was completed by four days spent replenishing supplies at Admiralty Bay outside Queen Charlotte Sound.

Even in the rough weather he encountered, Cook produced a chart showing some 3840 kilometres of coastline. His only serious mistakes concerned Banks Peninsula and Stewart Island and even then he was

Queen Charlotte Sound, a painting by J. Webber. *Alexander Turnbull Library.*

Reproduced from Rex and Thea Rients,
The Voyages of Captain Cook, Hamlyn.

prepared to admit that he could have drawn these portions incorrectly. The South Island and North Island were also located a little too far east. Despite these failings Cook's chart of New Zealand was, in the words of his biographer J. C. Beaglehole, 'one of the very remarkable things in the history of cartography'.

The chart was only one of several achievements. Banks and Solander had collected over 400 varieties of new plants, and Cook's careful observations of Maori society have proved invaluable to scholars ever since. On Saturday 31 March 1770 as he sailed out of New Zealand waters Cook noted with almost prophetic perception:

> So far as I have been able to judge the genius of these people it doth not appear to me att-all difficult to strangers to form a Settlement in this Country. They seem too divided among themselves to unite in opposing by which kind means and gentle useage the Colonists would be able to form strong parties among them.

Cook also wrote that the 'natives' (the word Maori had not yet come into common usage) were 'a strong raw bred well made Active people rather above rather than under the common size' who enjoyed 'a good state of hilth and many of them live to a good old age'. He commented on tattoos, clothing, food, houses, pa, canoes, tools, musical instruments and cannibalism. He remarked on the similarity between the myths, legends and language of the New Zealanders and of the other Polynesian peoples. Although he could find no easy explanation for them, the similarities fascinated him for the rest of his life.

Cook's voyage back to Britain was as remarkable as his circumnavigation of New Zealand. He discovered the east coast of Australia, navigated the Great Barrier Reef at considerable risk, sailed through the treacherous

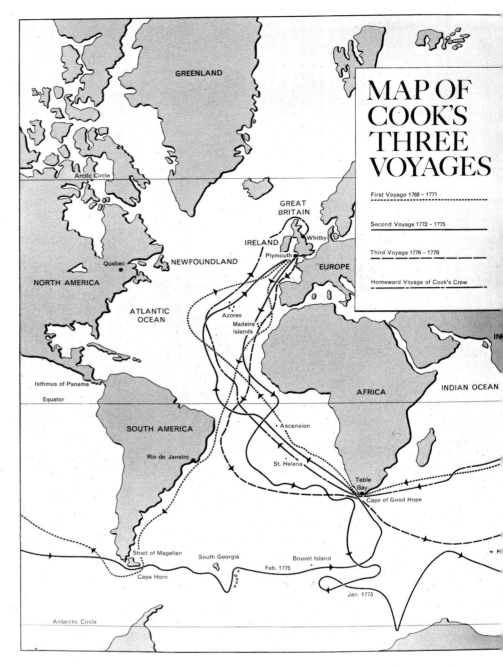

MAP OF COOK'S THREE VOYAGES

First Voyage 1768 – 1771

Second Voyage 1772 – 1775

Third Voyage 1776 – 1779

Homeward Voyage of Cook's Crew

Torres Strait. In Indonesia he lost 29 men from scurvy. He arrived in England on 13 July 1771 to a sensational reception. Banks was awarded an honorary Doctorate of Law from Oxford; Cook was promoted to captain.

Cook remained unsatisfied and wanted to learn much more, so two

more voyages followed — in the years 1772-75 and 1776-79. The second voyage, primarily concerned with proving once and for all that there was no great southern continent, involved long periods sailing Antarctica's icy perimeter. On this voyage Cook learned to use citrus to ward off the

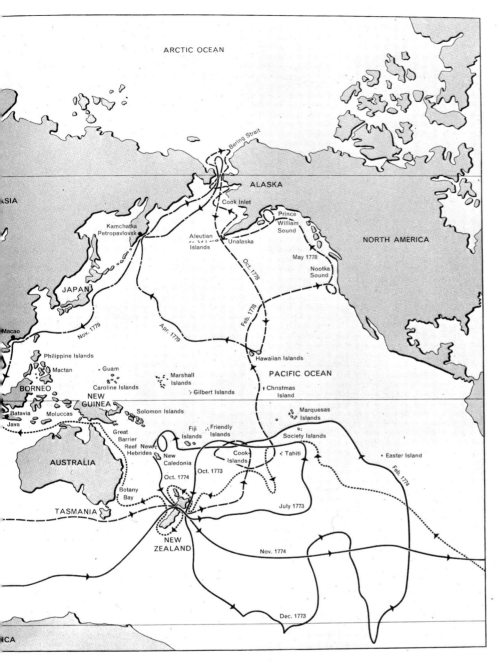

Pacific Oceans. He failed to find the passage but learnt much more about the geography of the Pacific. Cook's desire to learn eventually led to his death on 14 February 1779 when he was killed by a religious cult in Hawaii for ritualistic reasons. Cook's usual caution and good sense deserted him and he lingered too long. Beaglehole has put this fatal error of judgement down to fatigue but Gordon Parsonson's explanation that the intrepid social scientist refused the chance of a rare observation in the field is more compelling.

Cook's achievements as sailor, commander, discoverer, geographer, scientist and ethnographer were extraordinary, yet this self-effacing sailor should not be portrayed as a superman. His achievements were, after all, dependent upon the talented scientists and artists who accompanied him and the efforts of his anonymous group of disciplined seamen must not be forgotten either. Cook had his faults. He was often testy, he remained aloof and he shared the arrogance of his superiors in claiming territory by right of discovery.

Captain Cook superman has become part of the New Zealand mystique. Early settlers were especially pleased that their colony had been rediscovered by one of the greatest explorers and pioneers seemed to follow his advice in subduing the Maori by taking advantage of internal divisions. The interwar generation of schoolchildren were taught that Cook was an explorer without peer. In more recent years, however, the Cook mythology has faded, despite the 1969 bicentenary celebrations and the large corpus of Beaglehole's writing. The modest Yorkshireman would have been amused by Prince Charles' recent discovery that the statue of Cook in Gisborne had on the wrong uniform and was wearing its hat back to front. It seems the sculptor had used the Dominion Breweries emblem as a model. Thus are the truly great men of history reduced to the ranks of ordinary mortals.

ravages of scurvy during long periods at sea. He also proved that the natives of New Zealand practised cannibalism, noted the potential for sealing and whaling in southern waters and discovered the Marquesas, New Hebrides, Lord Howe Island and New Caledonia.

During the voyage of 1113 days and 112,000 kilometres Cook lost four men, three in accidents and one from sickness. Not one died of scurvy.

Driven on by insatiable curiosity, Cook set out again in 1776 to search for the north-west passage which supposedly connected the Atlantic and

Link: From Cook to Hongi

Cook's rediscovery did not radically alter life within New Zealand. The outside world became more aware of the island group but the enthusiasm of Banks and Cook failed to persuade any European power to colonise the country. Some of the explorers who continued to visit after Cook lacked the diplomatic skills of the inquisitive Yorkshireman and prompted Maori aggression. Marion du Fresne, for example, was killed along with 26 of his crew in 1772. These later voyages filled in gaps in Cook's knowledge but their combined influence was slight and Maori life continued much as before.

Pigs and potatoes enabled Maori to provision European shipping. Fences were erected to keep pigs out of potato and kumara patches and gardening flourished. Yet despite the beginnings of a mini agricultural revolution within Maoridom the old balance between agriculturist and hunter gatherer underwent only minor changes. Iron tools and nails aided the construction of pa and canoes and made possible more elaborate carving. Muskets only became significant from about 1818. The Maori took two generations to learn how to use these weapons effectively.

European diseases caused a noticeable increase in mortality but their influence has been exaggerated by overgenerous estimates of pre-European population levels. Cook's figure of 100,000 was probably too low but 120,000 seems more reasonable than the 200,000 suggested by some scholars. Gonorrhoea certainly reduced fertility, while measles, tuberculosis and influenza caused severe losses in local areas. On the other hand, many of the diseases which devastated indigenous populations in other parts of the world colonised by Europeans — particularly typhus and cholera — were absent in New Zealand. The Indian population of Central America, for example, fell by over 90 per cent as a result of the Spanish conquest and the ravages of smallpox, while Aboriginal numbers in Australia fell to over 85 per cent below pre-European figures after colonisation began. The Maori population was also reduced dramatically by some 60 per cent at its lowest point of 42,113 in 1896. But Maori society was not sent tumbling into rapid and terminal decline by its brief encounter with Cook, as has been suggested by Harrison Wright and other proponents of the fatal impact theory of colonisation.

After the explorers Europeans on sealing ships from Sydney, Hobart, North America and Britain began harvesting the large seal populations of southern New Zealand from 1792 onwards. Contact between these wild,

The Assassination of Marion du Fresne, Bay of Islands, New Zealand, 1772. Painted in 1848 by Charles Meryon, it could hardly have portrayed the event more inaccurately. Look at the way the Maori are drawn. Greek style pillars support the entrance to the village. French explorer Marion du Fresne visited the Bay of Islands in 1772 and was killed with 26 of his men for seemingly breaching local custom. In revenge the French levelled the guilty village and massacred 250 Maori. Alexander Turnbull Library.

rough men, many of them ex-convicts, and the Maori was brief, infrequent and often violent. We know from John Boultbee's reminiscences that sealing was an extremely brutal industry which tainted all those associated with it. Seals were slaughtered indiscriminately; one vessel berthed at Sydney in 1806 with 60,000 sealskins aboard. By 1810 sealing was no longer profitable, although there was a brief revival in the 1820s and 1830s.

Whaling lasted much longer than sealing and left a much deeper mark on Maori society. The first whaling ship called at Dusky Sound in 1792 but regular visits were not made until the new century. Most of the early visitors were deep sea factory ships which anchored in northern harbours, especially the Bay of Islands, to take on fresh water and provisions and seek out female company. More permanent

Maori involvement in whaling, including lifelong liaisons between whalers and Maori women, resulted from the development of shore or bay whaling along the east coast south of Mahia peninsula and around Cook Strait from the late 1820s.

Quite large numbers of Maori crewed on whaling ships; several Ngapuhi chiefs sailed to Sydney and Hobart. Most decided that trade and contact with Europeans would bring more benefits than problems, provided that they dictated the terms of trade and controlled the level of contact. Some Maori even hoped that the wealth generated by whaling would enable them to build cities like Sydney which would combine the best of European and Maori worlds. Such cities would enhance their mana in Maoridom, while attracting more trade and muskets to secure their domination.

Deep sea whaling opened up the Bay of Islands to regular contact with European sailors, trade and technology. The production of pork and potatoes was encouraged and later wheat and maize growing. A timber trade developed in the Hokianga and flax was grown by tribes in the southern North Island. Prostitution, previously unknown in Maori society, flourished when the whale fleet was in port.

Sealing, whaling and the flax and timber trades introduced the Maori to a limited range of goods. In combination tools, weapons, plants and animals caused some social, economic and political changes in Maori communities, especially in coastal areas. Yet these changes should not be exaggerated.

Missionary influence in New Zealand began with the enthusiasm of Yorkshireman Samuel Marsden, who arrived in New South Wales in 1794, as chaplain to the penal colony. During his time in Australia, Marsden met and was impressed by Maori who had crossed the Tasman at various times on trading or whaling vessels. Among these men was Ruatara, an influential Ngapuhi chief from the Bay of Islands and nephew to the famous Hongi

Samuel Marsden was the driving force behind the setting up of missions in the Bay of Islands. He is often credited with conducting the first church service in New Zealand on Christmas Day 1814 at Rangihoua, Northland. While this is true for Maori, almost certainly earlier European voyagers to New Zealand held services for their men. *National Museum.*

Hika. These contacts fuelled Marsden's interest in setting up a mission in New Zealand and he travelled back to England to convince the Church Missionary Society of his plan.

With their backing and taking with him his chosen missionaries John King, William Hall and Thomas Kendall, he then returned to Sydney. From there the brig *Active*, with Hall and Kendall aboard, sailed to Rangihoua in the Bay of Islands in March 1814. This preliminary trip, during which the Englishmen developed contacts with the chiefs of the area, including Hongi, lasted until August. Later that year the full missionary complement, headed by Marsden, arrived in the Bay of Islands to establish the mission and at Oihi Marsden preached New Zealand's first Christmas sermon to Maori.

Before Marsden returned to Sydney in 1815 (he visited New Zealand several times before his death in 1838), his friend Ruatara fell ill and died. Patronage of the mission then passed to his uncle, Hongi (or Shunghee, as Marsden called him). The chief totally dominated the missionaries, who were largely dependent upon him for their economic survival and for military protection.

The first Anglican mission at Rangihoua by an unknown painter. *Rex Nan Kivell Collection, National Library of Australia.*

4. 1821   Utu:

Hongi Hika Launches the Musket Wars

IN 1807 a tired 500-strong Ngapuhi taua (raiding party) rested at Moremunui (also spelt Moremonui) just north of modern day Dargaville. They felt safe with their two muskets. Suddenly a Ngati Whatua war party led by Murupaenga, which had been lying in wait in the toetoe and flax bushes, ambushed them. After fierce fighting the Ngati Whatua triumphed in a battle which became known as Te Kai-a-te-Karore, the seagulls' feast, and which left some 150 Ngapuhi dead; prisoners were taken.

Among the defeated Ngapuhi was a minor chief, Hongi Hika from Kerikeri. Two of his brothers were among the corpses littering the battleground. Hongi Hika was born about 1788. Little is known about his early life except that he came from a senior line of rangatira. His father was an ariki and the death of Hongi's two older brothers enabled him to assume the senior position. Hongi never forgot the humiliation at Moremunui and he also seems to have resented deeply the several punishing defeats inflicted by the Ngati Maru of Coromandel and Ngati Paoa of Tamaki.

Hongi impressed most Europeans he encountered. CMS missionary Thomas Kendall considered him 'a man of mild disposition' and 'great ingenuity', like most Europeans finding it hard to imagine that the amiable Hongi could be responsible for the slaughter of so many of his own people. Europeans regarded Hongi, too, as an innovator who grew wheat, drank tea and used such new tools as hoes, spades and axes. Thomas Kendall taught him to write.

An engraving of Hongi by James Barry.
Alexander Turnbull Library.

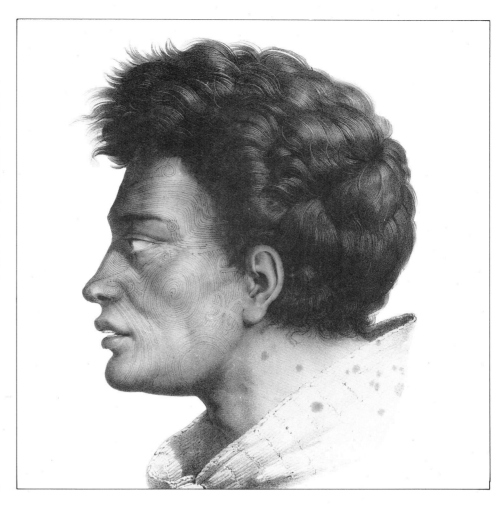

Natai, a chief of Bream Bay. A lithograph taken from Jules d'Urville's Pacific exploration of 1826-28. *National Museum.*

Hongi's reputation as a warrior increased considerably when in 1818 he led a war party of 800 down the east coast to Tolaga Bay. On the 11-month expedition Hongi, with about 50 muskets, swept all before him. Most of the tribes he fought had no experience of guns and fled at the first volley of shots. Reputedly, some 500 villages were burned, several chiefs were killed and some 2000 prisoners were taken. Such a large number of captives was new in Maori history; Hongi needed extra slaves to raise wheat and flax which he could sell for even more muskets.

Although his campaign had been highly successful, Hongi wanted still more firepower; trained warriors equipped with patu and taiaha (short and long clubs) were still hard to beat. Muskets were cumbersome, slow to reload, unreliable under pressure and inaccurate over more than 50 metres; they were a guarantee of success only when used on a massive scale. Hongi

Slaves preparing food at Kororareka, painted by Augustus Earle. *Rex Nan Kivell Collection, National Library of Australia.*

Even though the death of their great chief was a bad omen, the Ngati Paoa fought on. Hongi built a high wooden tower from which his men picked off the pa's defenders. Eventually sheer firepower enabled Hongi to take the pa and kill nearly everyone in it. This victory so decimated the ranks of Ngati Paoa that it virtually cleared the Auckland isthmus of Maori settlement.

Undaunted, Hongi paddled and marched on to the even more formidable Ngati Maru pa of Te Totara on the Waihou river near modern day

also needed more spectacular victories to head off the challenge of his chief Ngapuhi rival, Te Morenga. To add to Hongi's problems his key strategist and chief wife, Tarikatuhu, had gone blind. He was, therefore, delighted when his brother-in-law Titere, recently returned from a trip to London with 'Tommy' Tuai, told him that there were a 'thousand thousand guns at the Tower'. Hongi easily persuaded the missionary Thomas Kendall to travel to England with himself and the young chief Waikato and the unlikely trio left in March 1820 to arrive in England in August.

No first-hand written description of this visit has survived but later oral accounts suggest that Hongi resented CMS patronage and went his own way. Meeting George IV, Hongi is supposed to have said, 'How do you do, Mr King George?' to which the monarch is said to have replied, 'How do you do, Mr King Shunghee?' The King presented Hongi with two muskets and a suit of armour and helmet. Kendall became alarmed when he learnt that what most fascinated Hongi was his visit to the Woolwich arsenal. The only other events to arouse his interest were a visit to Cambridge and the sight of an elephant in a zoo.

Hongi failed to purchase enough muskets in England but was laden with gifts which could be bartered for guns in Sydney, where Hongi, Kendall and Waikato arrived in May 1821. Hongi sold all his presents other than the suit of armour, the helmet and an officer's regimental jacket. He struck a

good bargain and returned to the Bay of Islands in July 1821 with 300 muskets. At last he had sufficient firepower to avenge past humiliations.

Hongi returned from Sydney with Te Hinaki, ariki of Ngati Paoa, and Te Horeta, rangatira of Ngati Maru. Soon after arriving home he insulted both chiefs by brazenly displaying his muskets and requesting his guests to drink milk. Both men were unable to drink the unfamiliar liquid and Hongi rubbed it in by downing the entire bucket. Hongi then swore vengeance for the lost battles of the past.

Preparations complete, in October 1821 Hongi led a war party of 2000 men south; at least half the warriors were armed with muskets. Hongi's first target, the great Ngati Paoa pa at Mokoia (Panmure), proved much harder to take than he ever imagined. Stakes driven into the seabed made landing by canoe difficult and heavy earthworks nullified musket fire. After four days of heavy and largely futile fighting, Hongi and Te Hinaki resorted to traditional combat.

The duel was a remarkable sight. Hongi was dressed in his suit of armour, helmet and regimental coat. Te Hinaki was equally resplendent in a full officer's uniform given to him by Governor Macquarie. Both men were armed with muskets rather than taiaha. Hongi fired first over Te Hinaki's head. Te Hinaki returned the fire, knocking Hongi to the ground. At this, two Ngapuhi warriors rushed forward and killed Te Hinaki. Hongi had been saved by his armour.

Thames. After two days' heavy fighting Hongi could gain no advantage so he resorted to tika (or trickery for the advantage of the tribe). He made a false peace and then attacked at night when Ngati Maru were sleeping. About 1000 were killed and nearly 2000 taken as slaves. The musket had not won the siege but it had made possible a level of killing unprecedented in Maori history.

Hongi returned in triumph to Kororipo pa in Kerikeri with more than 2000 captives. Local missionaries were horrified by the feasting which followed; past humiliations inflicted by Ngati Paoa and Ngati Maru were being repaid many times over. Yet Hongi was still not completely satisfied. His son-in-law, Tete, had been killed in

the campaign and his death had to be avenged. So with 3000 warriors Hongi set out again in February 1822 to hunt down the remnants of Ngati Paoa and Ngati Maru who had fled into the Waikato for protection.

The slaughter continued. The Waikato warriors who were protecting the Ngati Paoa and Ngati Muru survivors had never experienced musket fire and fled at the first volley. During the Waikato campaign, Hongi's men had also killed an Arawa chief. Arawa took utu by ambushing and killing 15 Ngapuhi warriors. A furious Hongi retaliated later that year by joining forces with Te Morenga on an expedition which travelled down the coast to Tauranga, dragged and paddled its canoes across country to Lake Rotor-

ua and then took the island fortress of Mokoia in the middle of the lake. Heavy losses were again inflicted and 500 Arawa were taken prisoner.

Such demanding expeditions took their toll on the Ngapuhi confederation. Maori society had never been geared to long campaigns and even large numbers of slaves could not compensate for neglect of crops and gardens. The confederation was also a shaky affair constantly threatened by the old rivalry between the Hokianga and Bay of Islands hapu and ambitious younger chiefs like Pomare seeking to

New Zealand warriors presenting trophies of conquest to the Queen Turero. A painting by Augustus Earle. *Rex Nan Kivell Collection, National Library of Australia.*

Meeting of the Artist and Hongi at the Bay of Islands, November 1827. **A painting by Augustus Earle.** *Alexander Turnbull Library.*

topple Hongi's supremacy. There had also been serious disagreement over some of Hongi's tactics, especially at Mokoia. What Hongi now needed was one more spectacular act of utu to heal the rifts and head off challenges to his leadership. Moremunui remained the most obvious score to be settled and in February 1825 Hongi set off to avenge the massacre.

Waning enthusiasm for another bloody campaign reduced the war party to only 350 men. The Ngati Whatua proved tough opponents and it took all Ngapuhi's firepower to win a narrow victory. Unfortunately for the Ngati Whatua they had killed Hongi's favourite son Hare and an enraged Hongi killed all his prisoners rather than saluting a gallant enemy for their bravery. Moreover he now had reason to seek further utu and rampaged through the Kaipara district killing every member of Ngati Whatua he could find. Butcherings were followed

by vindictive raids into the Waikato which culminated in the taking of Te Rauroha's pa at Noho Awatea where further remnants of Ngati Whatua, Ngati Paoa and Ngati Maru were disposed of while their Ngati Haua hosts withdrew to safety.

This was Hongi's last major southern expedition; all his tribe's main grievances had been avenged. The upheaval caused by the large-scale killing was compounded by the large number of slaves taken. The musket gave Hongi a practical military advantage but it proved more effective as a mechanism for executing utu than for winning battles.

By 1825 the brief Ngapuhi dominance was ending. Other tribes were buying muskets, and were learning how to make their pa 'musketproof'. Earthen embankments, heavy palisades and trenches were commonplace by 1830. Pa were moved from hill top sites onto flat areas, giving defenders a wider field of fire. In addition to the re-establishment of a balance of power Ngapuhi themselves seemed unable and unwilling to sustain such a large military effort.

An ageing and tired Hongi spent his last two years in the Bay of Islands embroiled in interhapu strife. In 1826 he suffered several pieces of bad luck: he was pinned under a tree, his daughter died from tuberculosis and his second wife, Taniwhare, committed suicide. News of the death of Pomare in battle further lowered Hongi's spirit. The despondent chief began to believe that he had breached tapu and incurred a hara or spiritual penalty from his tupuna (ancestors).

For reasons which are quite obscure, the irascible chief decided to move from Kerikeri to Whangaroa in December 1826. He stripped the Methodist mission on 10 January and a few days later, in a fit of pique, murdered a large group of his kinsmen at Kaitangata. The infuriated Ngati Uru hapu retaliated and in a skirmish on 19 January 1827 Hongi was shot through the lung and seriously wounded. He lived on for 13 months despite paralysis down his right side and an injury that made his breathing sound like a whistling steam train. Inevitable decline of mana followed and both missionaries and Bay of

Islands Maori lived in dread of an attack by the Mahurehure confederation of Hokianga led by Tamati Waka Nene. The war lord finally died on 6 March 1828. He is reputed to have left instructions to his people to be brave and to allow the missionaries to stay.

Hongi's dying words summed up the dilemma facing the fiercely competitive Maori society: how to extract the benefits of European trade and technology without submitting to European domination. Trade had become a permanent part of New Zealand life because a tribe without muskets would be dominated by other tribes with muskets. Once Maori entered the world of the European there could be no return to the pre-European past. Even though Maori could reject European religion and law and continue to behave in distinctively Maori ways they had been trapped by their own confident belief that they could control the extent of European intrusion.

Hongi left few tangible gains. He did not win any new territory for his tribe and he did not establish a dynasty. He even failed to mould Ngapuhi into a single unit and left unhealed a serious rift between the Hokianga and Bay of Islands hapu which would play a critical role in the history of northern New Zealand over the next two decades. Hongi's bloody campaigns had won nothing more than mana and satisfaction. Despite his skill in using European technology he was, as historian Gordon Parsonson argues, a man of the past who conformed strictly with the dictates imposed by the classic Maori institutions of tapu, utu and muru. He acted for peculiarly Maori reasons and was unconcerned with personal or tribal aggrandisement. His battles were not about land but retribution.

Two other major conclusions can be drawn from Hongi's story. First, Maori history had its own separate existence and its own special dynamic. Hongi acted from essentially Maori motives and made a Maori history that was quite distinct from European history in New Zealand or the history of relations between the races in this country. But when motivations from the pre-European past combined with destructive European technology the results could be catastrophic. The musket enabled Hongi to execute utu on an unprecedented scale and to almost annihilate three tribes.

Second, despite the disruption wrought by the musket, Maori society adapted to the new military technology remarkably quickly. Within a few years after Hongi's death large-scale battles gave way to ineffectual long-range skirmishing. At Tauranga in 1837, for example, the danger element in a battle between Ngapuhi and Ngai te Rangi was so low that women and children were sent out to pick up spent bullets during exchange of fire. In the same year Bay of Islands trader Sam Polack reported that 20,000 rounds were fired in a battle between Ngapuhi chiefs Pomare and Titore without causing a single casualty. The same pattern unfolded in other areas like the Waikato where the musket's initial deadly impact was soon nullified by changes in pa construction and fighting tactics.

The old balance of power was restored by the late 1830s. Missionaries claimed credit for the return of peace but they acted as arbitrators on relatively few occasions. Cessation of large-scale tribal warfare had much more to do with equalisation in the arms race and successful adaptation to military change.

Hongi caused so much mayhem because his campaigns coincided with the most disruptive phase of the adjustment of a competitive society to the challenge issued by a new and much deadlier military technology.

Te Rauparaha's fleet approaching 'Kaiapohia', north of Christchurch, on a raid. While Hongi was waging war in the north, Ngati Toa chief Te Rauparaha came to dominate much of the south-west North Island and the north of the South Island. *Alexander Turnbull Library.*

Link: From Hongi to the Treaty

'Kororadika Beach', Augustus Earle, 1838. Earle visited Kororareka in 1827. *Rex Nan Kivell Collection, National Library of Australia.*

After Hongi's death whaling, trading and missionary activity expanded rapidly and this growth had attracted some 2000 British subjects by the time New Zealand was annexed in 1840.

About 80 shore-based whaling stations operated between 1829 and the early 1840s. Most were on the East Coast but some were scattered around the bottom end of the South Island and there was one on Te Rauparaha's Kapiti Island fortress. Shore whaling brought Maori from coastal areas into contact with Europeans, providing a useful apprenticeship in race relations. Intermarriage between the races was not uncommon. Increased contact also, however, meant a multiplication of the epidemics caused by the introduction of European diseases.

During the 1820s and 1830s American ships, along with Canadian, French, Norwegian, Danish, German and Portuguese vessels, visited New Zealand waters, making fleeting contact with Maori. These visits generated rumours that the United States and France wanted to colonise New Zealand, even though their interest was purely commercial.

Shore and deep sea whaling gave New Zealand its first staple industry. Edward Jerningham Wakefield estimated in 1844 that 68 whalers employing 650 men were operating. Whaling was, however, also a depletable industry, which declined rapidly after 1847.

Contact with an international industry stimulated activities such as timber felling, flax growing and farming, and drew attention to New Zealand's economic potential. Increasing numbers of traders came to cash in on the servicing of the whaling industry. The influx of whalers, traders, land speculators and other opportunists caused the European crime rate to soar, and this, along with interhapu skirmishing, led to calls for Britain to annex New Zealand. James Busby was appointed British Resident in 1833 but the problems continued. In 1838 the settlers at Kororareka (now Russell) in the Bay of Islands formed a vigilante association.

The fortunes of the Anglican missionaries began to improve with the arrival of Henry Williams in 1823. Williams built a ship, the *Herald*, to trade with tribes other than the Ngapuhi and he founded a mission station at Paihia. Maori welcomed the trade but few converted to Christianity. The first conversion did not take place until 1825 when a dying chief requested baptism from Henry Williams. After the arrival of the printer and Maori scholar William Colenso in 1834, prayer books and scriptural passages translated into Maori became available. Maori enthusiasm for literacy ensured a rapid spreading of the missionary message, as did the release and escape of ex-slaves to areas like the East Coast.

Missionaries found that Maori already knew the gospel message well. By 1840 the Anglicans had 19 mission stations throughout the North Island and it seemed that a genuine Maori conversion was under way. A typical

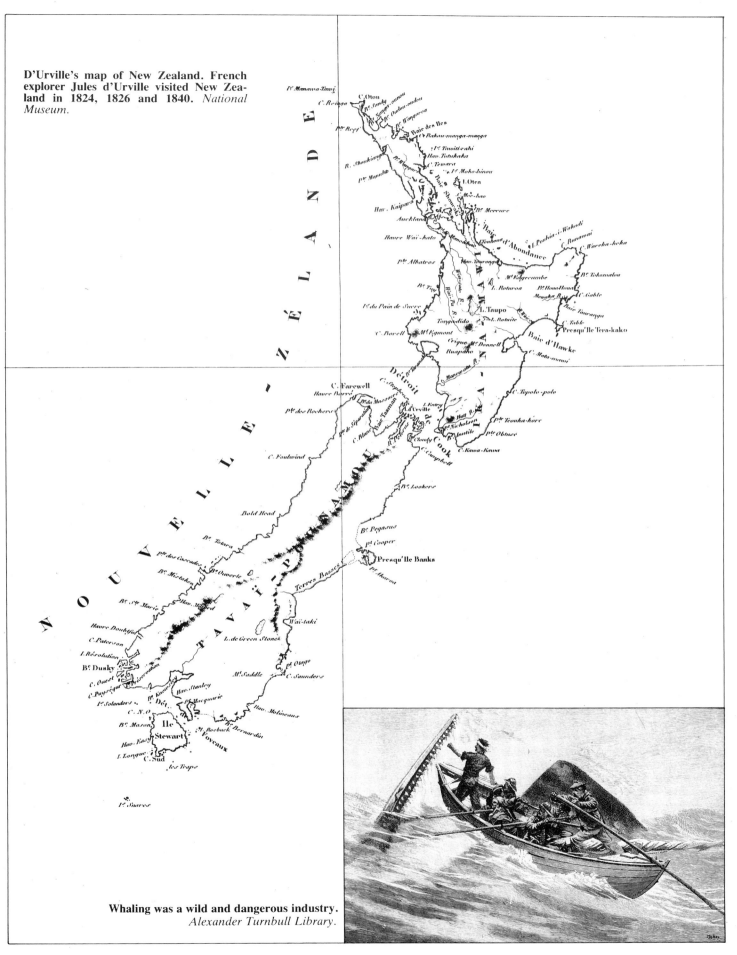

D'Urville's map of New Zealand. French explorer Jules d'Urville visited New Zealand in 1824, 1826 and 1840. *National Museum.*

NOUVELLE - ZÉLANDE

IKA - NA - MAOUI

TAVAI - POENAMOU

Détroit de Cook

Terres Basses

Whaling was a wild and dangerous industry.
Alexander Turnbull Library.

Baptism of the Maori chief Te Puni in Otaki Church, 1853, painted by Charles Barraud. The painting depicts the baptism as taking place in the elaborately designed Rangiatea church at Otaki. The baptism actually took place in a much plainer undecorated chapel at Petone. *Rex Nan Kivell Collection, National Library of Australia.*

mission station consisted of a missionary's house, a chapel and a school. The schoolroom had accommodation for children and Maori trainee teachers. A farm and orchard usually completed the settlement. From such a base the missionary would spread the gospel to surrounding villages. The Anglicans claimed in 1840 that 30,000 Maori were attending church, nearly 5000 of whom were interested in joining the faith. Some 284 were communicant members.

A Wesleyan mission established in 1822 set up bases at Whangaroa and Hokianga. The Wesleyans claimed over 1500 'members' by 1840. A French Catholic mission arrived in 1838 and, despite language difficulties, claimed 1000 converts after two years.

Missionary claims of 'conversion' should be treated sceptically; missionaries exaggerated their success to justify their efforts both to their backers in Britain and to themselves. Maori did not so much surrender to a 'superior' religion as take what they wanted to fit their own ends and reject the rest. They learnt from the missionaries skills such as reading and writing because the written word held the key to knowledge, the source of European power. They took from the Bible story the elements closest to Maori experience. The Old Testament proved much more popular than the New because Maori identified strongly with the Jews as a chosen people. Missionary Christianity soon gave way to distinctively Maori versions.

Often, hapu were more interested in the material and technological benefits brought by the missionaries than in their message. We should not forget, either, that some tribes, such as Ngati Maniapoto and Tuwharetoa, had no contact with missionaries and were completely unaffected by Christianity.

The missionaries' motives were not always the purest. CMS missionaries acquired some 160,000 acres (65,000 hectares) of land. (Wesleyan missionaries were not allowed to own land.) Henry Williams, who argued that each child needed 1000 acres (405 hectares) for their support, came to own 11,000 acres (4500 hectares). More than greed was involved, however. The missionaries showed genuine concern over Maori welfare and tried

hard to protect Maori from the worst effects of European settlement.

It is easy to exaggerate the impact European imports such as muskets, iron tools, blankets and clothes had on Maori life in the 1830s. Outside the mission settlements Maori society changed very little, and what major disruptions there were were caused by Maori politics which had little to do with European influence. The most important instance was Te Rauparaha's decision to migrate south with his Ngati Toa tribe from Kawhia down the west coast of the North Island to Kapiti Island. Driven out by Ngati Maniapoto and Waikato war parties, Te Rauparaha in turn conquered, displaced or made alliances with Ngati Raukawa, Ati Awa and Taranaki.

Armed with muskets, Te Rauparaha and his Taranaki allies moved into the South Island, overcoming local Maori as far south as Kaikoura. In 1830 Te Rauparaha and his warriors sailed south to Akaroa on the brig *Elizabeth*, and on landing the Ngati Toa destroyed three enemy pa. These raids opened the way for European settlement of Canterbury. The disruptions caused by Te Rauparaha's resettlement also played a significant part in the land disputes that contributed to the Wairau incident of 1843 and in the outbreak of hostilities in Taranaki in 1859. In short, between 1820 and 1840 both Maori and Pakeha were altering the face of New Zealand settlement.

While Te Rauparaha was conquering the south an important agreement was reached in the north. In 1835 British resident James Busby persuaded 35 Ngapuhi chiefs to sign a Declaration of Independence, creating a body known as the Confederation of the United Chiefs and Tribes of New Zealand. The chiefs adopted and swore allegiance to a flag which they had chosen in 1834. The Confederation has been dismissed as a device to head off the threat posed by the plans of the eccentric Baron Charles de

Thierry to found a feudal utopia in Hokianga, but closer examination reveals direct links to the Treaty of Waitangi. Both the Colonial Office and Ngapuhi treated the Confederation very seriously. The chiefs regarded it as a guarantee of their independence and 13 extra signatures were added by 1839. The Colonial Office accepted the Confederation as bestowing 'indisputable' Maori 'title to the soil and to the sovereignty of New Zealand'. British recognition of 'Sovereign independence' meant that a formal negotiated treaty with the Maori would be needed if the British were ever to govern New Zealand.

The rights of indigenous peoples were already under review in Britain. Lord Glenelg, Secretary of State for the Colonies and a noted humanitarian, was becoming increasingly sympathetic to the idea of a British protectorate, in part to insulate the Maori from the abuses associated with colonisation.

Moves by Edward Gibbon Wakefield to found the New Zealand Association in 1837 pushed the idea of

a protectorate further forward. Wakefield's colonisation plans were ominous for the Maori. The Colonial Office, suspicious of the association, imposed strict conditions upon it which Wakefield and his colleagues refused to meet. The association then reformed in 1839 as a joint stock company — the New Zealand Company — and plans were made to despatch the *Tory* on a land-buying expedition.

There seemed little choice for the Colonial Office but to annex New Zealand; Crown intervention and formal government appeared to be the only alternative to bloodshed and chaos. The missionaries lacked power to restrain Wakefield or land speculators from Sydney. Only Her Majesty's Government could protect British citizens and Maori alike. Accordingly, on 14 August 1839, Captain William Hobson RN was sent to New Zealand to reach an agreement with the Maori about the establishment of a British colony.

5. 1840 Scrap of Paper or Sacred Pact? :
The Treaty of Waitangi

ARRIVING in New Zealand on 29 January 1840, Captain Hobson faced a daunting task: he had to convince the Maori people to place their land under British control. His instructions offered little help, being strong on principle but weak on practical detail; Hobson was expected to improvise. Nowhere was there mention of a treaty as such — Hobson was 'to treat with' (negotiate) so as to win 'the free and intelligent consent of the natives'. For a man who had joined the Navy at the age of 10 and who lacked both legal and diplomatic training, the creation of an agreement for the establishment of a new colony represented a formidable challenge.

International recognition did not of course greatly worry the most powerful nation on earth. The British were more interested in passing on the benefits of the best system of law and government in the world. British institutions would protect the Maori against European criminals and stop the 'process of war and spoilation' that usually accompanied European colonisation. It was Hobson's job to persuade Maori of the advantages of British rule and to stress that no humiliation was involved. The Colonial Office conceded that Maori would at first be suspicious and fear loss of

One of G. F. Angas' paintings of life in a Maori pa in the 1840s. He described it as 'Tu Kaitote, the Pa of Te Wherowhero on the Waikato, Taupiri Mountain in the distance.' *Alexander Turnbull Library.*

A reconstruction of the signing of the Treaty of Waitangi. At the rear table Hone Heke — reputedly the first chief to sign the treaty — shakes hands with Governor Hobson. *Treaty House, Waitangi.*

A Comparison of the English and Maori Versions of the Treaty of Waitangi

Official English Text of the Treaty of Waitangi

First Article of the Treaty

The Chiefs of the Confederation of the United Tribes of New Zealand, and the separate and Independent Chiefs who have not become members of the Confederation, cede to her Majesty the Queen of England, absolutely and without reservation, all the rights and powers of Sovereignty which the said Confederation or individual Chiefs respectively exercise or possess, or may be supposed to exercise or to possess, over their respective Territories as the sole Sovereigns thereof.

Second Article of the Treaty

Her Majesty the Queen of England confirms and guarantees to the Chiefs and Tribes of New Zealand, and to the respective families and individuals thereof, the full, exclusive and undisturbed possession of their Lands and Estates, Forests, Fisheries, and other properties which they may collectively or individually possess, so long as it is their wish and desire to retain the same in their possession; but the Chiefs of the United Tribes and the Individual Chiefs yield to Her Majesty the exclusive right of Pre-emption over such pieces of land as the proprietors thereof may be agreed upon between the respective Proprietors and persons appointed by Her Majesty to treat with them in that behalf.

Third Article of the Treaty

In consideration thereof, Her Majesty the Queen of England extends to the Natives of New Zealand Her Royal Protection, and imparts to them all the Rights and Privileges of British subjects.

Comments

First Article

There is no exact Maori translation for the English word 'sovereignty'. Kawanatanga, meaning governorship, was used in the Maori text but Maori acquaintance with the word was limited.

The meaning was therefore ambiguous. Critics of the treaty argue that if the much stronger word 'mana' had been used, the chiefs would never have signed. (The word mana was used in the 1835 Declaration of Independence.)

Second Article

The English version promised 'the full, exclusive, and undisturbed possession of their Lands and Estates, Forests, Fisheries and other properties'; the Maori wording was much less specific.

The English version granted the Crown the exclusive right of pre-emption (strictly the right of first refusal). The Maori translation was confusing. Did the Maori agree they could only sell to the Crown or did it mean that the Crown merely had the right of first offer?

Third Article

This granted Maori full British citizenship — yet Crown pre-emption in the previous article had taken away one of their rights as British subjects to sell their land to anyone.

The Maori Version: Te Tiriti o Waitangi

Literal translation of the Maori text

The Chiefs of the Confederation and all those chiefs who have not joined in that Confederation giving up to the Queen of England for ever all the Governorship (Kawanatanga) of their lands.

Literal translation of the Maori text

The Queen of England agrees and consents [to give] to the Chiefs, the Hapus, and all the people of New Zealand the full chieftainship (Rangatiratanga) [of?] their lands, their villages and all their possessions but the Chiefs of the Confederation and all other Chiefs give to the Queen the purchasing of those pieces of land which the owner is willing to sell, subject to the arranging of payment which will be agreed to by them and the purchaser who will be appointed by the Queen for the purpose of buying for her.

Literal translation of the Maori text

This is the arrangement or the consent to the governorship of the Queen.

The Queen will protect all the Maori people of New Zealand and give them all the same rights as those of the people of England.

Overall Impression

'It appears that Maori were left with the impression that there would be a sharing of power between Maori and European, an arrangement that would leave a substantial degree of authority in Maori hands.' Historian, Dr Claudia Orange

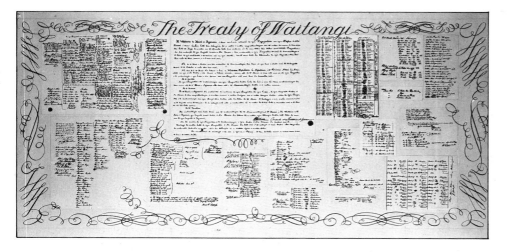

A montage of the Treaty of Waitangi showing the signatures. *National Archives.*

independence, but Hobson was to 'gradually overcome' such fears by 'mildness, justice and perfect sincerity'. He was also to use missionaries and respectable settlers to win over the Maori. More than benign paternalism was involved in these lofty instructions; the Colonial Office was also under pressure from British taxpayers to avoid another expensive frontier war like that in Cape Colony.

Another important feature of Hobson's instructions was the belief that there were ample 'waste' or unused 'wild' lands available in New Zealand for European settlements. No one appreciated that the Maori 'owned' the whole of New Zealand and needed far more land than they occupied simply to subsist. This mistaken belief led Europeans to assume that they could settle designated areas without disruption to Maori society. The Colonial Office also insisted on the Crown controlling all future land purchases. Existing claims would be carefully investigated and declared null if found improper. Land taken from Maori would be returned to its rightful owners after compensation had been paid. The Crown would then negotiate any new sales at a fair price.

Hobson's instructions were clearly an awkward mixture of humanitarian and paternalistic concern to protect the Maori and British subjects and a desire to avoid a costly war. Realising these intentions would have been daunting even for a highly experienced statesman. Hobson proceeded with great speed. As soon as the *Herald*

anchored in the Bay of Islands in January 1840 he declared himself Lieutenant Governor, changing his uniform accordingly. This action contradicted his orders which suggested that he remain a consul until an agreement had been reached. Hobson was Governor of a British colony which did not yet exist.

On 30 January invitations were sent out to the chiefs who had signed the 1835 Declaration of Independence and then the drafting of an agreement began. Hobson called on his secretary, J. S. Freeman, and on British Resident James Busby for help. There is debate as to who did most of the drafting; Busby later claimed that the treaty was essentially his but Hobson, although sick at the time, certainly had an input.

Undue haste and Hobson's ill health help to explain the ambiguity in the treaty's wording and the drawing up of five different English versions, three of which contain significant variations. These problems were compounded when Henry Williams was given a draft at 4 p.m. on 4 February to translate into Protestant missionary Maori by the next day. Henry was not a very able linguist but his linguistically talented brother William was away so Henry and his son Edward did the best they could in the short time available.

Misunderstanding was inevitable when a literate culture sat down to negotiate with an oral culture. Few chiefs could read the Maori version of the treaty, and practically none could read the English text since the mis-

sionaries had only ever taught the Maori to read in Maori. Accurate translation and explanation was vital if the treaty was to hold much meaning for either party: unfortunately both translation and explanation were vague and misleading. To make matters worse, Henry Williams apparently rewrote the treaty to make it more palatable to the chiefs because his translation diverged from the English version at key points (see p.52).

Williams has been criticised for translating the treaty into missionary Maori. This is quite unfair. Missionary Maori was the only written Maori and many Maori, especially Ngapuhi, were familiar with its lofty metaphorical tone. But did Williams perpetrate deliberate deceit? Tony Simpson argues that Williams engaged in subterfuge to protect his 11,000 acres (4500 hectares) of land. Yet British rule was more likely to undermine Williams' claim than support it. It is more probable that Williams saw the treaty as the only available means of controlling colonisation and of retaining missionary influence within New Zealand. The treaty's bicultural tone and emphasis on co-operation reflected missionary views rather than those of land speculators, rapacious settlers or the New Zealand Company. If Williams was engaged in perpetrating a fraud it was a pious fraud which he genuinely believed was best for all parties. His actions remain questionable nevertheless.

A hastily drafted, ambiguous, inconsistent and contradictory document was presented to the assembled chiefs on 5 February at Waitangi — the waters of lamentation. Hobson arrived at 9 a.m. on a sunny morning to address the gathering. He began his speech around 11 a.m. once the official party had taken their seats. Henry Williams translated the dull and uninspired statement which soon palled beside the fine oratory of many of the chiefs.

Hobson stressed that the Queen wished only good for both the New Zealanders and her subjects living among them. The benefits of British law could not be extended, however, unless the chiefs gave their assent. Once the treaty was signed the Queen would be able both to protect and restrain her subjects. Hobson concluded by emphasising that he had asked for the agreement in public rather than from individuals, in the open rather than in secret. It was best for the Maori chiefs that they sign such an honest and honourable document. Hobson then read out the treaty without further explanation. Williams translated again.

Every Bay of Islands chief rose and spoke against any agreement. Te Kemara would not be 'low, small, a worm, a crawler, he down, the Governor up'. He complained that all his land had been taken by Williams and Busby (who had purchased 11,000 acres (4500 hectares) and 45,000 acres (18,000 hectares) respectively). Rewa of the Ngai Tawaka hapu asked the missionaries Richard Davis and George Clarke to return his lands and the Governor to go back. Moka of the Patuheka hapu extended the criticism of excessive land purchases to Europeans other than missionaries, including the American consul James Clendon. Tareha then engaged in a dramatic parody by standing up in a filthy piece of matting and waving a fern root to suggest that the Pakeha was of no use to the Maori. His point was well received by an appreciative audience. Soon after, Busby and Williams found themselves defending their land purchases against a tirade of criticism.

Even Hone Heke expressed doubts about such a treaty, but later in the afternoon he began to change his mind and suggested that since it was now too late to reject Europeans it was better

A painting by George F. Angas depicting the tomb of Huriwenua, a late chief of the Ngati Toa tribe 1847. *Alexander Turnbull Library*.

to accept them on the best possible terms. Tamati Waka Nene and his older brother Patuone of the Mahurehure Confederation in the Hokianga developed Heke's argument. They pointed out that the land had already gone and the Pakeha was here to stay. If they had been asked to speak on this matter in older times when there were few Pakeha they would have asked the Governor to go back, but now it was too late and he must stay. Bay of Island chiefs could not bear the thought of the Hokianga hapu cashing in on European trade at their expense and Waka Nene won the day.

Te Kemara protested but even he ended up shaking hands with Hobson saying, 'How d'ye do eh Mister Governor.' The gathering was then dispersed and asked to meet again two days later on Friday 7 February for further debate. The chiefs, however, returned the following morning to debate the document further. Food was running short because Waitangi was a barren place and Busby and Williams advised Hobson to get the issue settled quickly before there was time for doubts to develop.

The chiefs gathered again at 4.30 a.m. on 6 February huddling together in small groups to discuss the treaty. A flustered Hobson arrived around midday in plain clothes and dress hat and announced brusquely that there was to be no further discussion. William Colenso protested — the chiefs did not understand the treaty and required further explanation. Henry Williams brushed aside the protest, assuring the chiefs that the treaty was a sacred contract binding on all parties. This speech helps to explain why the treaty

soon came to mean more to the Maori than the Pakeha. Heke rushed to the defence of the senior missionary and argued that because the Maori were children in such matters they should follow the advice of their missionaries; the signing went ahead. Most chiefs seemed to share the view expressed later by Nopera Panakareao of Rarawa, from the Kaitaia area, that the shadow of the land would pass to the Queen while the substance would remain with the Maori.

Tradition has it that Heke was the first to sign but there is no concrete proof of this. Eventually all 52 chiefs came forward and added their marks or signatures. It is very hard to know what they understood by the treaty. Certainly they were not as naive as some radicals suggest, but on the other hand there was no way in which they could have realised just how many settlers would come to their shores. Nor did they understand the idea of freehold, that is alienating land for good rather than lending it out for a lifetime. Consequently, interhapu rivalry more than anti-British sentiment shaped their thinking. They were also probably lulled into a false sense of security by Williams' soothing words and by the Governor's bicultural pronouncement, 'He iwi tahi tatou' (We are now one people), made to each chief as he added his signature to the document.

As far as Hobson was concerned the 52 Ngapuhi signatures were quite suf-

54

A feast at Mata-ta. A painting by G. F. Angas, 1847. *Alexander Turnbull Library.*

ficient for the purposes of securing the treaty but he sent officials and missionaries out to collect 'testimonials of adherence' to the original document. In all 512 signatures were collected. Explanations of the treaty differed markedly from collector to collector, and many chiefs were cajoled with gifts of blankets. Seventy-two chiefs wrote their own names.

The chiefs south of the Bay of Islands were misled into thinking that the treaty had been signed in the north after the customary period of long debate. Such verbal consensus made the treaty far more binding within Maoridom than any written document. It assumed the status of wairua or sacred compact in the Maori rather than the missionary sense. Anyone who breached such an agreement would face very serious consequences.

Significantly, older ariki like Te Wherowhero of Waikato and Te Heuheu of Tuwharetoa refused to sign, dismissing the treaty as nothing more than an agreement with the untrustworthy Ngapuhi. Ngati Maniapoto and Arawa tribes shared this suspicion and refused to sign. Although the Arawa later fought with the British, none of these dissenting tribes initially regarded the treaty as wairua.

In May 1840 Hobson proclaimed all New Zealand from latitude 34° 30′ north (a mistake) to 47° 10′ south and from longitude 166° 5′ to 179° east a British possession. He took this action to head off the establishment of a republican municipality at Port Nicholson. The North Island was claimed by cession and the South Island by right of Captain Cook's discovery.

Humanitarians in Britain, the missionaries and other philo-Maori like William Swainson, New Zealand's first Attorney-General, were delighted with the treaty. Governor Robert Fitz-Roy, who arrived in 1843 to replace Hobson after his premature death in 1842, enthusiastically referred to the treaty as New Zealand's 'Magna Carta'. Although FitzRoy almost immediately breached this new treaty when he abolished Crown pre-emption in 1844, his analogy has proved popular with optimistic Pakeha ever since. Few of FitzRoy's contemporaries, however, European or Maori, agreed with his glowing judgement.

Meanwhile the Colonial Office was surprised by Hobson's interpretation of the clauses relating to land. They thought that there was plenty of waste land for purchase but had to accept Hobson's establishment of a Crown monopoly over the whole country. The New Zealand Company, which had its 20 million-acre (8 million-hectare) claim reduced to 282,000 acres (113,000 hectares) was even less impressed. Company spokesmen in England labelled the treaty 'a device to amuse and pacify naked savages'. The House of Commons Committee to whom the company made submissions in 1844 agreed that the treaty was 'contradictory' and 'ambiguous' and constituted a serious block to the progress of the new colony. Soon after the committee's report Earl Grey, Secretary of State, instructed the new Governor, Captain George Grey, to move away from the bicultural intention expressed in Hobson's statement 'He iwi tahi tatou — we are now one people'. Assimilation emerged as the preferred policy even though Grey kept control of native affairs out of the settlers' hands. Most settlers applauded the change of policy but continued to condemn it as favouring the Maori.

The treaty meant different things to Maori and Pakeha in 1840 and has continued to do so ever since. To the Maori it was a sacred compact which suggested the possibility of equal partnership. To most Europeans it was little more than a scrap of paper which made possible a convenient co-existence.

Link: From Waitangi to Colonisation

Britain in the 1830s witnessed the emergence of a group of intellectuals, propagandists and politicians who saw overseas settlements as a means of solving discontent at home. At that time Britain was not unlike many developing countries of today, its sprawling, unsanitary and over-crowded cities beset by ill health and high crime rates.

The most colourful and persuasive of the colonial reformers was Edward Gibbon Wakefield. Born in 1796, the eldest of a large family, Edward was a difficult child. After a year at Westminster School he refused to return and lasted just two years at his next school in Edinburgh.

His first wife died young, leaving him with two children. In 1826 he ran away with Ellen Turner, a schoolgirl heiress, carrying her off to Scotland to marry her. Ellen's family prevented the marriage and Wakefield was arrested and imprisoned for three years, along with his brother and accomplice. It was in prison that he formulated his theories of 'systematic colonisation'. One of the two books he wrote in prison, *A Letter From Sydney* (1829), outlined some of his ideas and attracted the attention of some prominent citizens. Wakefield elaborated further on his views in *England and America*, published in 1833.

Wakefield argued that colonisation had failed in the past because it was unplanned and lacked a guiding theory. His new theory would provide an organisational framework and systemise the whole process. A proper balance would be achieved between the three cornerstones of any economy: capital, land and labour — through the device of the 'sufficient price'. If the price of land was set high enough labouring men would not be able to buy land immediately and the chronic labour shortages which had plagued both Australia and North America would thereby be avoided. Capitalists would also be attracted by such a lucrative investment and the prospect of increased value brought about by the labour of immigrants. Undercapitalisation, the bane of all new colonies, would also be overcome by the sufficient price. Furthermore, a relatively high land price would enable a portion of money from land sales to be set aside to fund further migration and public works. On the other hand, the price should be low enough to enable labouring men to purchase land after four or five years' work for an employing landowner. This would lure the respectable lower middle and working classes and deter loafers and petty criminals.

Wakefield wanted more than economic experimentation. He wished to turn back the clock and establish a hierarchical social order that he imagined had existed in rural England before the Industrial Revolution. He believed in the 'Aristocratic Ideal', that all healthy societies should be led by a natural and morally responsible aristocracy. Such leadership would ensure that everyone knew and accepted their place in society. Stability would thereby be encouraged and the excessive social mobility and disorderly behaviour of North America avoided.

The 'Aristocratic Ideal' had a strong following in the 1820s. Wakefield claimed he could realise the ideal by transplanting carefully selected slices of British society to Australasia. Gentlemen capitalists, farmers, the 'uneasy class' of small businessmen and white collar workers and the skilled and respectable working class would be encouraged to migrate. Manufacturers, the industrial working class and the lumpen proletariat would be left behind.

The rough, uncivilised and democratic tone of North America and Australia would be tempered by basing colonies on grain farming and concentrating settlement around market towns like those of south-eastern England. Concentration would make social control easier and encourage the development of civilised communities. Married couples with few or no children would be given priority to avoid the drunken excess of single men and the drain on resources of large numbers of dependent children. Women were seen as agents of civilisation and Wakefield aimed for a rough balance between the sexes. Immigration agents were to be paid 40 shillings for married couples as against 10 shillings for single persons to ensure the right social mix. Instant civilisation was his objective.

The theory looked good on paper. Even the critical Karl Marx rated Wakefield as 'the most notable political economist' of his time.

The major problem with his fine sounding theory was that Wakefield's lack of fieldwork made him unaware that Australia and New Zealand were not well suited to the transplanting of the farming patterns of south-east England. Wakefield had also not given enough thought to the role to be played by Aborigines and Maori. He imagined that Aborigines would be shunted off to reservations while Maori chiefs would be gradually converted into a cigar-smoking, claret-sipping native aristocracy who would personally own much smaller areas of land than the tribe. The possibility of armed resistance was ruled out because such an intelligent people as the Maori would soon see British civilisation offered a superior way of life.

The theory was also made unworkable in practice by Wakefield's deliberate encouragement of speculative investment. Absenteeism was promoted as beneficial rather than harmful and property was to be sold unseen via a lottery system. Investors had no idea of the quality of the land they were buying and took pot luck.

An able promoter, Wakefield was what his contemporaries called an expert 'puffer'. With enthusiastic support from powerful and wealthy backers, he first tried out his ideas in South Australia in 1836. They failed, but Wakefield explained away the failure by claiming that the 12 shillings per acre price of land set by the British government was too low.

This explanation was accepted and even more MPs, churchmen and entrepreneurs supported his establishment of the New Zealand Association in December 1837. Joseph Somes, England's leading shipping magnate, added his support when the association became the New Zealand Company in May 1839. The City also showed much interest and the company boasted a capital of £100,000 when Edward's brother, Colonel William Wakefield, and Edward's only son Edward Jerningham Wakefield, departed on a land-buying adventure in May 1839.

An engraving by George Cruikshank. 'She died for love and he for glory'. This tells the story in picture and verse of a pickpocket who is hanged and his wife who is transported. This was the very sort of 'settler' Wakefield tried to keep out of his settlements. *Alexander Turnbull Library.*

She DIED for LOVE and He for GLORY.

A filching lass a footpad lov'd!
For daring deeds renown'd in story!
Her passion was by him approv'd!
And love and pillage all their Glory!

Soon after she became a bride,
And in the Hue and Cry reported!
For Glory He at Tyburn died!
And She for Love was quite transported!

G L.

Pub.ᵈ March 15, 1815 by Wᵐ Holland Nᵒ 11 Cockspur Street.

6. 1840 Frontier Towns: Europeans Establish Settlements at Wellington and Auckland

WELLINGTON was to be Wakefield's first 'planned' settlement in New Zealand. Yet its foundation was notable for its totally inadequate preparation and lack of planning.

The first five ships which left England in September and October 1839 were superior to many North American migrant ships but were still over-crowded and uncomfortable. The food was adequate but monotonous and no one had allowed for the extremely lengthy voyage. One hundred and fifty-seven cabin passengers as against 647 in steerage seemed reasonable enough but only a handful of the cabin group brought much money with them. Nearly all the biggest investors stayed in London to watch the experiment from the comfort of their clubs.

When the *Aurora* finally reached Wellington on 23 January the high hopes of its 146 passengers were quickly dashed. Wellington was anything but an 'earthly paradise' set in the

Thorndon Flat and part of the city of Wellington. A painting by Charles Heaphy, 1841. *Alexander Turnbull Library.*

midst of smiling farmland. The disappointed migrants found instead a harbour with virtually no foreshore locked in by 'steep, abrupt and rugged slopes' covered with 'dense forests'. The surrounding mountains were larger and higher than anything in England and rose 'in the blue distance, ridge above ridge in continued succession'.

Even worse shocks were to follow. The unfortunate migrants, dumped on the beach at Petone, found that no preparations had been made for their arrival. Surveying had not progressed very far and efforts had been abandoned to establish a grid pattern over the ridges and gullies of Te Aro on Lambton Harbour, the chosen site. Chosen instead was the area around the mouth of the Hutt River. This river valley was blocked by heavy bush a mere 5 kilometres from the coast, but at least it was flat and the Maori were friendlier than those around Lambton Harbour. The marking out of boulevards for the new town had begun just a few days before the immigrants arrived.

The 800 odd migrants who arrived by early March were kept alive by the Ngati Toa and Ati Awa who had made the Hutt their home during Te Rauparaha's resettlement of the southern North Island. Although grateful for this vital assistance, the arrivals resented being dependent on the local Maori and floods which drove them out of their tents in the Hutt convinced them that Lambton Harbour had better prospects.

The Lambton area, however, with its potato patches and gardens, was much prized by the Maori. The New Zealand Company offered 100 acres (40 hectares), much of it unfarmable, in exchange — hardly a fair swap for 600 acres (240 hectares) of cultivated land. Not surprisingly, the Maori refused to move or to sell. So Edmund Halswell, appointed by the company to ensure fair dealings with the Maori, took advantage of the settlers' superior numbers and in May 1840 drove the Maori from the area. George Clarke (junior), Sub-Protector of Aborigines, protested but Halswell dared not upset the disillusioned and angry settlers.

Te Rangihaeata, Te Rauparaha's nephew, who was living in the fertile area around Porirua posed a much more serious threat to settlement. He refused to allow any European settlement and invited Ngati Rangitahi of Wanganui to join him. This resistance

held back Pakeha development of the area until Governor Grey forced him to negotiate in 1848. Ngati Rangatahi also joined Ngati Toa in 1841 at Heretaunga in the northern part of the Hutt Valley, thereby pinning the Wellington settlement to the harbour area. To make matters worse, most of Colonel Wakefield's land deals were investigated and cleared by Commissioner Spain and by 1843 development had virtually ground to a halt.

A dispute between Te Rauparaha and the New Zealand Company over an attempted survey of land in the Wairau Valley led to the 'Wairau Affray' on 17 June 1843. Twenty-two Pakeha and six Maori were killed. This setback in race relations caused problems for the other Wakefield settlements — Nelson (founded in 1842), Wanganui (founded in 1840) and New Plymouth (founded in 1841) — and hurt Wellington's development as a port and entrepreneurial centre servicing the newer settlements. Race relation difficulties and the unfavourable publicity which they inspired were compounded by chronic absenteeism, the slow speed of surveying and the high cost of clearing bush country.

Nearly 60 per cent of the sections in early Wellington were owned by absentee speculators. If local landowners were lucky enough to have picked

Regulations of New Zealand Company's Emigrant Ships. Extracts from a New Zealand Company poster of 1842. *Hocken Library.*

a farmable property rather than a sheer cliff face they were still faced with the refusal of absentee neighbours to fence and drain their properties or to clear them of bush and weeds. Large blocks of absentee land also put big distances between the urban and rural sections of local landowners, causing considerable inconvenience and raised costs.

Grain was difficult to grow on the windswept, hilly country. Even if they succeeded in producing wheat against considerable environmental odds, there was no market for the product. Land could also cost up to £60 per acre to clear, a cost for which no allowance was made. Little wonder that farmers concentrated on subsisting or abandoned their 100-acre (40-hectare) properties for small businesses in town. The 1843 burgess roll revealed few big farmers; only two are recorded along with six agriculturalists. Visitors to early Wellington remarked on the large numbers of small businesses and shops and the lack of farms. This impression is confirmed by the 1848 census which shows that only 11 per cent of the population were agricultur-

Colonel Wakefield's Wellington residence on the present site of the Beehive. From a painting by Samuel Brees, 1847. *Alexander Turnbull Library.*

alists whereas 38 per cent were mechanics and artisans; 33 per cent were labourers. Only 1700 acres of land had been cultivated.

The failure of agriculture led to economic decline. Immigration virtually ceased after 1842 and by 1846 Auckland's 4655 citizens outstripped Wellington's 3977. As late as 1845 only 7000 acres (2800 hectares) out of a total of 110,000 (44,000 hectares) had been surveyed. By 1848 only 85 of the original 436 settlers remained; the rest had sailed back to Britain or moved to more prosperous Auckland.

Wellington's 'selected' migrants were not as superior as Wakefield had hoped. The sexes balanced up reasonably well, with 80 women for every 100 men, but the fact that 43 per cent of the population was under 14 years old placed a considerable strain on the slender resources of the settlement. Labour was in short supply and the influence of Chartism was obvious in the efforts of working men to form unions; somehow the lumpen proletariat had slipped through. By 1843 Wellington could boast 20 hotels and grog

shops to quench the thirst of 2000 adults. Brawling was a popular pastime and thieving and prostitution had found their way into utopia. Church attendance was low and children roamed the settlement like Huckleberry Finns.

Wakefield blamed such problems on whalers who visited the town, but whalers alone could hardly be held accountable for the corruption which accompanied municipal elections in 1843. Bribery and treating were blatant and newspapers were full of personal invective. Apart from a small elite who organised balls and concerts, most early Wellingtonians' behaviour was anything but genteel. On the other hand, the lifestyle of these migrants was not as bad as credulous missionaries pictured it. Compared with many other settler societies, early Wellington was relatively law abiding and orderly, simply a mixture of good, bad and indifferent characters rather than the 'most splendid settlers' of the British Empire as several generations of schoolchildren were taught.

Wellington's main problem was lack of capital. Few capitalists came and most of those who did soon left. What saved Wellington was the very antithesis of what Wakefield wanted: pastoralism. Younger sons of lesser gentry

like Frederick Weld and his cousin Charles Clifford put their capital to work by opening up the Wairarapa and Hawke's Bay for sheep farming from 1845 onwards. They responded to a growing demand among Australian squatters to find more reliable rainfall areas in which to depasture their sheep. Profits were generous and quickly realised if a man was blessed with enough money. The rapid return on investment was reflected by the fact that there were some 60,000 sheep in the province by 1851.

Pastoralism encouraged a very different social order — dispersed, transient and male dominated. It provided the engine of development which Wakefield had failed to find. His theory had proven to be more of a hindrance than a help to development. Once the sufficient price of £1 an acre and the notion of concentration were dropped, Wellington raced ahead. The most Wakefield could claim was a tempering of the worst excesses of the Australian pastoral industry.

The weaknesses of Wakefield's grand theory were further emphasised by the fact that Auckland, an unplanned settlement much despised by all the Wakefield settlers, fared far better in its early years than Wellington. Even though Auckland was supposed-

Kaiwarrawarra Sawmill, on the outskirts of Wellington. A painting by Samuel Brees, 1847. *Alexander Turnbull Library.*

ly settled by the 'dregs and sweepings of Sydney', it had become New Zealand's premier town by 1845, a position it held until the discovery of gold in Otago in 1861.

Auckland was established as New Zealand's second capital — Okiato in the Bay of Islands was the first — by Governor Hobson in September 1840. Hobson wanted a capital sited outside the territory of the domineering Ngapuhi and closer to the rest of the colony. Auckland's excellent harbour, ready access to the west coast via the Manukau and absence of a large Maori settlement proved ideal. Officers settled in Official Bay and the artisans lived in Mechanics Bay. Hobson himself did not take up residence in the new Government House until 14 March 1841, in time to declare New Zealand separate from New South Wales on 3 May 1841.

The New Zealand Company settlers in Wellington protested strenuously against Hobson's decision to site the capital in Auckland and so the intense and bitter rivalry between the two towns began. Hobson was unimpressed but his new capital struggled nearly as much as Wellington in its first two years of existence. The economy of the entire new colony was hit hard by depression in Australia. Even successful early established merchants like William Brown and John Logan Campbell could not lift the struggling settlement out of the doldrums. Hobson's premature death on 10 September 1842 added to the gloom.

In 1843 there was still no wharf and no formed roads. Raupo huts and tents were common and the small houses of rough-hewn weatherboard which replaced them had little aesthetic appeal. More serious was the lack of drains and sewers. Constant outbreaks of diarrhoea in the summer quickly earned the town an unhealthy reputation.

These problems were aggravated by the arrival of two large groups of immigrants in 1842. On 9 October some 500 artisans and their families from Paisley, Scotland reached Auckland harbour on the *Jane Gifford* and *Duchess of Argyle*. The second group comprised 92 inmates of Parkhurst reformatory aged between 12 and 20 years. There was little work for either group and most went on to government-subsidised public works.

Weavers and other artisans who came from an industrial and urban environment were not ideal colonists. They were reluctant to learn new skills and their old skills were of little use in a farming-based colony. Nevertheless the incentive of a high daily wage of 8 shillings and the availability of relatively cheap land encouraged hard work and lured labour away from Wellington. The drift north began early in New Zealand's history.

The Parkhurst group did not fit in so well and Auckland became notorious for its high crime rate; visitors commented that every third building seemed to be a grog shop. Statistics bear out this impression. In 1847 one in eight of the population had been arrested for drunkenness. The town reportedly housed 28 brothels for a population of 5167. Figures such as this earned Auckland a reputation as an 'Australian' colony with an inferior tone to the Wakefield settlements.

Early Auckland's basic problem was the same as Wellington's — undercapitalisation. Land sales started slowly partly because unchecked speculation forced prices to absurd levels. In 1841 some city land was valued at £550 per acre and country land was set at £1 per acre. Speculation encouraged excessive subdivision and the central area became a jumble of narrow streets. Surveyor Felton Mathew's more spacious design was thereby ruined. Once land prices fell to more realistic levels the province made more rapid progress, but that did not happen until 1845 when Grey ended the war in the north.

Auckland's saviour was increased government spending, the garrisoning of troops and the growth of Maori agriculture and trade.

Once Grey had suppressed the northern rebellion he stepped up public works and Auckland flourished, much to the annoyance of Wakefield settlers. The arrival in 1847 of 500 pensioner soldiers, known as the Royal New Zealand Fencibles, to protect Auckland against possible Maori attack, added a further fillip to development. In this happier economic climate the entrepreneurial skills of merchants like Brown and Campbell flourished. Maori agriculture also came into its own and a lucrative export trade to Australia was established for Maori grain growers. Sydney-based entrepreneurs responded by pumping more money into Auckland, and a kind of economic take-off was achieved. By 1851 Auckland was well placed to take advantage of the Victoria goldrushes.

Even though Auckland was not a Wakefield settlement a reasonable age-sex balance was achieved. There were 78 women for every 100 men in 1843 and children made up only 36 per cent of the total population. Yet, like Wellington and most settler societies in the early phase of development, it was a very young society devoid of grandparents.

The religious mix was much the same as Wellington's. Anglicans predominated (65 per cent as against Wellington's 55 per cent), the Church of Scotland was in second place (21 per cent as against 22 per cent) while

Auckland from Smales' Point, drawn by Patrick Hogan, 1852. *Alexander Turnbull Library.*

Auckland looking from the new wharf, showing Queen Street, the foot of Shortland Street, the Market House, the Wesleyan Chapel and College. *Alexander Turnbull Library.*

Roman Catholics made up 12 per cent of the population as against 5 per cent in Wellington. Methodists, however, made up a mere 1 per cent in Auckland as against 15 per cent in Wellington. Auckland's reputation as the most Irish of New Zealand cities came later with the arrival of Imperial soldiers, goldminers and Australian-Irish labourers.

Remarkably, even though Auckland did not exercise a selective immigration policy it reproduced the class structures of Britain more exactly than Wellington. A census taken in 1843 revealed that 13 per cent were landed proprietors, merchants and professionals; 11 per cent were shopkeepers and retailers; 27 per cent were mechanics and artisans; 16 per cent were gardeners, stockmen and agriculturalists and 22 per cent were dependants. As early as 1843 clear-cut residential zones had also emerged. Official Bay was characterised by spacious grounds, elegant buildings and open parkland whereas Mechanics Bay was notorious for poor housing, overcrowding and a complete absence of parkland or basic urban facilities. From the very beginning there were two Aucklands. Unbridled capitalism created a class-based society more rapidly and effectively than Wakefield's deliberate attempt to remake old England at the bottom of the world.

Auckland grew at the expense of the Bay of Islands. Depression set in soon after Hobson moved south and the downturn worsened with the decline in Australian demand for New Zealand timber and a sharp fall in the number of whaling ships calling at Kororareka (renamed Russell in 1840). Areas nearer to Auckland also proved more suitable to European style farming and the southern tribes benefited most from the growth of Maori agriculture.

Hone Heke became alarmed about the economic decline of the far north and soon realised that the Treaty of

Auckland from Britomart Barrack, showing Commercial Bay with Queen Street. Drawn by Patrick Hogan, 1852. *Alexander Turnbull Library.*

Auckland from Hobson Street South, drawn by Patrick Hogan, 1852. *Alexander Turnbull Library.*

Waitangi had not brought the advantages he anticipated. Nothing seemed to offset the loss of chiefly mana. He determined to protest against this unsatisfactory state of affairs in as striking a manner as possible.

7. 1844 Rebellion in the North:
Hone Heke Chops Down the Kororareka Flagstaff

AT dawn on Monday 8 July 1844 Hone Heke, Ngapuhi chief, chopped down a flagstaff at Russell. Although he had signed the Treaty of Waitangi he had become disillusioned with the way it was operating. Maori custom, for example, was under threat. A minor Ngapuhi chief, Maketu, had been executed under British law in 1842 and the police magistrate at Kororareka (Russell) was imposing British law wherever he could. In short, Heke's mana and chiefly authority were being undermined. And the fact that the capital had moved to Auckland exacerbated the situation. Customs duties and restrictions on felling certain types of timber were imposed.

Heke's protest was carefully calculated. He did not want to frighten the European settlers who contributed so much to his hapu's prosperity, so he attacked the symbol of British authority — the Union Jack. To underline his demands for a fair share of power Heke flew two flags above Kororareka — the Union Jack and the ensign of the Confederation of the United Chiefs of New Zealand.

Governor FitzRoy and Bishop Selwyn were reluctant to acknowledge Heke's calls for dual authority. Several meetings were called to appease the chief; customs duties were cut. When this failed to satisfy Heke, FitzRoy blamed the influence of 'bad men', mainly Americans, French and rogue Englishmen living in the bay. Bishop Selwyn pointed to Heke's rebellious youth, arrogance and unpredictable behaviour.

FitzRoy now contemptuously re-erected the flagpole. Heke chopped it down again on 10 January 1845. This time FitzRoy put up a third flagpole

Hone Heke. Engraving by J. R. Ashton. *T. Ryan Collection.*

clad in iron and guarded by a blockhouse. Heke's actions were assuming the proportions of a Boston Tea Party and war became imminent as tensions increased and attitudes hardened. Heke's action threatened the very basis of FitzRoy's authority and settlers urged him to take a firmer stand with the Maori. Heke had to be taught a lesson — there was one government in New Zealand, and it was British.

Heke allied himself with the formidable warrior and Kawakawa chief Kawiti, who had been the strongest opponent of land sales in the north. As well as FitzRoy, Heke faced opposition from Tamati Waka Nene and a number of other chiefs who saw war as a chance to right some old grievances.

Kawiti planned to attack Kororareka to divert the troops while Heke took the flagstaff on Maiki Hill. One week in advance the citizens of Kororareka were warned, to avoid civilian casualties; Kawiti's and Heke's war was with the British government, not with British settlers. Heke also offered Thomas Beckham, the magistrate, the withdrawal of the invading forces on Monday 10 March, if the flag was taken down. Beckham refused. The attack began at dawn the next day.

Heke and Kawiti attacked at 4 a.m. They broke into two groups, Kawiti leading 300 men against the one gun battery and the lower blockhouse to lure soldiers out of the town. This enabled Heke and 150 men to steal up and quickly capture the blockhouse guarding the flagstaff. Soon after the flagstaff fell for the last time.

Meanwhile Kawiti met unexpected opposition at the battery outside Kororareka, where Commander Robertson and 45 sailors and marines from HMS *Hazard* were improving entrenchments. It took heavy fighting to force the marines to withdraw. Early in the afternoon Sam Polack's magazine was blown up. Rapid evacuation of the town followed. No civilians were harmed but rum proved tempting for the warriors and they sacked the town, killing three drunks as utu.

At the end of the fighting some 13 Maori lay dead and 28 were wounded. The British had lost 20 men and had 23 wounded. British reports immediately inflated Maori casualties to 34 killed and 68 wounded. Estimates of the number of Maori warriors multiplied to well over 1000. Then the British command was blamed for gross incompetence.

The point of this excuse making was to deny the military capability of the Maori. According to the prevailing British view, native peoples were incapable of thinking strategically. Kawiti's and Heke's carefully planned victory was dismissed and blamed on overwhelming Maori numbers and the unprofessional conduct of the British commander. Meantime, Auckland citizens shivered in their beds while FitzRoy awaited reinforcements from Sydney.

Tamati Waka Nene had other ideas; he confronted Heke. Fighting was conducted in a very traditional and chivalrous fashion, and was confined to daylight. At the end of the day all prisoners were returned and combatants rubbed noses before exchanging news of casualties and sharing the latest family gossip. Although all rather ritualistic, it was enough to seriously delay Heke's building a new fighting pa at Puketutu.

Meanwhile 215 troops arrived in Auckland and a British force led by Lieutenant Colonel William Hulme, an able and experienced soldier, sailed north on 26 April. Soon after reaching the Bay of Islands, they took the neutral chief Pomare II hostage and to punish him for supplying Heke with food and materials destroyed his evacuated coastal pa.

Hone Heke was far from ready when Hulme, his 300 troops and 500 Maori allies under Nene appeared. Kawiti and his 140 men had only just arrived and furious last minute alterations had to be made to strengthen the Puketutu pa. Heke's men covered the palisades with layers of woven flax to absorb musket and cannon fire. Kawiti then camped out in the bush, leaving Heke inside the fortified pa with about 800 warriors. Overall Heke held a

Hone Heke fells the flagstaff at Kororareka. A modern reconstruction. *Alexander Turnbull Library.*

small numerical advantage.

Fighting began on 8 May. The British stormed the weak back section of the pa and almost gained the upper hand, but Kawiti attacked from the bush and a party led by Heke emerged from the pa to secure the victory. The costs for both sides were high, each suffering about 52 casualties. Maori deaths outnumbered British by 28 to 13. The British predictably downplayed the loss by exaggerating Maori casualties to 200 killed. FitzRoy even claimed victory because Hulme had taken the pa when Heke and Kawiti deserted it a few days after the military action.

While the Governor contemplated future action, Heke suffered a serious reversal at the hands of Tamati Waka

Nene at Te Ahuahu. Heke eventually escaped to Ohaeawai pa to join Kawiti.

Colonel Henry Despard, the new commander of the British forces, decided to strike while Heke was still licking his wounds. He prepared to attack Ohaeawai pa on 24 June with 615 men and four cannon. Had he known of the extraordinary modifications Kawiti had made to the pa, Despard would have been less confident.

The most striking feature of the new pa was the firing and communication trenches which gave Kawiti's men

Hone Heke and his wife Harriet and four attendants. Painted by Joseph Merrett c. 1846. *Alexander Turnbull Library.*

maximum protection while allowing rapid movement within the pa. Kawiti was one of the first military engineers to build anti-artillery bunkers set into the ground under cover of logs, stones and matted flax. Inside these rua warriors were safe from bombardment. The palisades were also more strongly built than in earlier pa and an inner fence of heavy puriri logs provided an effective second line of defence. Kawiti's engineering efforts, well in advance of their time, were not duplicated in European warfare until the Boer War.

For six days Despard shelled the pa with 6- and 12-pound cannon. Much to his surprise this produced little effect and so on 1 July he brought up a 32-pounder, by far the biggest gun ever used in New Zealand. Kawiti hit back with a provocative sally. Despard countered by sending 250 hand-picked men in a direct assault on the pa. He assumed that the constant shelling had

caused massive damage and undermined morale. Instead his soldiers were mown down in a hail of deadly crossfire. A mere 100 Maori warriors repulsed the attack, leaving 39 soldiers dead and 70 wounded. Only one Maori was killed in the desperate assault. This ignominious defeat was immediately blamed on the obvious scapegoat, Despard.

After the British defeat Heke and Kawiti surprised their opponents by abandoning the pa on 11 July. Once again they made clear that their protest was against their loss of sovereignty, was not anti-Pakeha and involved no desire for territorial gain. Kawiti reinforced this point by returning to his home territory and Heke took care to leave mission buildings, farms and bridges unharmed. Despard took the empty pa and made a futile claim of victory.

FitzRoy seemed to be making progress towards peace when he was dismissed in late September. The Colonial Office believed that his soft bicultural approach had failed; his successor was instructed to assimilate

the Maori rather than to allow the evolution of a dual system of authority.

FitzRoy's replacement, Captain George Grey, who arrived to take up his position on 14 November 1845, became one of the most striking and enigmatic figures involved in the colonisation of New Zealand. He was able, energetic and achieved much in a relatively short time. He was also nakedly ambitious, self-serving, autocratic and deceitful. Like Wakefield he was an artful 'puffer' who greatly exaggerated his achievements in his despatches home.

On the other hand, the debunking of Grey has gone too far. His darker side should not be allowed to obscure the fact that he genuinely believed that modernisation, progress and civilisation were inherently good while the primitive and savage state was inherently bad. Maori should be transformed into brown-skinned Europeans as quickly as possible, for their own sake. Legends and traditions should be preserved only as a means of demonstrating Maori advance from their primitive background. In Grey's eyes Maori were children who needed to be taught a severe lesson before they could grow into true adulthood. He was a visionary but his vision was flawed by cultural arrogance and notions of racial superiority.

Unlike FitzRoy, Grey had the troops and firepower to teach the 'rebels' a lesson. He had 800 regulars, 400 naval men, 80 sailors, 60 volunteers from Auckland and artillerymen from the East India Company's forces. About 400 Maori also offered their services. For the first time Heke and Kawiti were heavily outnumbered. Grey was also supported by five war ships and had 13 cannon including three 32-pounders.

A detachment of Maori allies under Makoare Te Taonui was sent to prevent Heke, who was still at Hikurangi, from joining forces with Kawiti at his formidable fighting pa, Ruapekapeka or the Bat's Nest. He succeeded. When the government troops arrived at Ruapekapeka with their 30 tonnes of artillery dragged over rugged bush country, they outnumbered Kawiti's warriors four to one.

Heavy bombardment started soon after Christmas. At first shelling had little effect because Ruapekapeka was as well constructed as Ohaeawai. It incorporated the latter's innovations and added stone walls and World War One style dugouts, each a miniature

The bombardment at Ruapekapeka Pa, January 1846. A painting attributed to Major Cyprian Bridge. *Alexander Turnbull Library.*

Maori war dance c. 1845. Painted by Joseph Merrett. *Rex Nan Kivell Collection, National Library of Australia.*

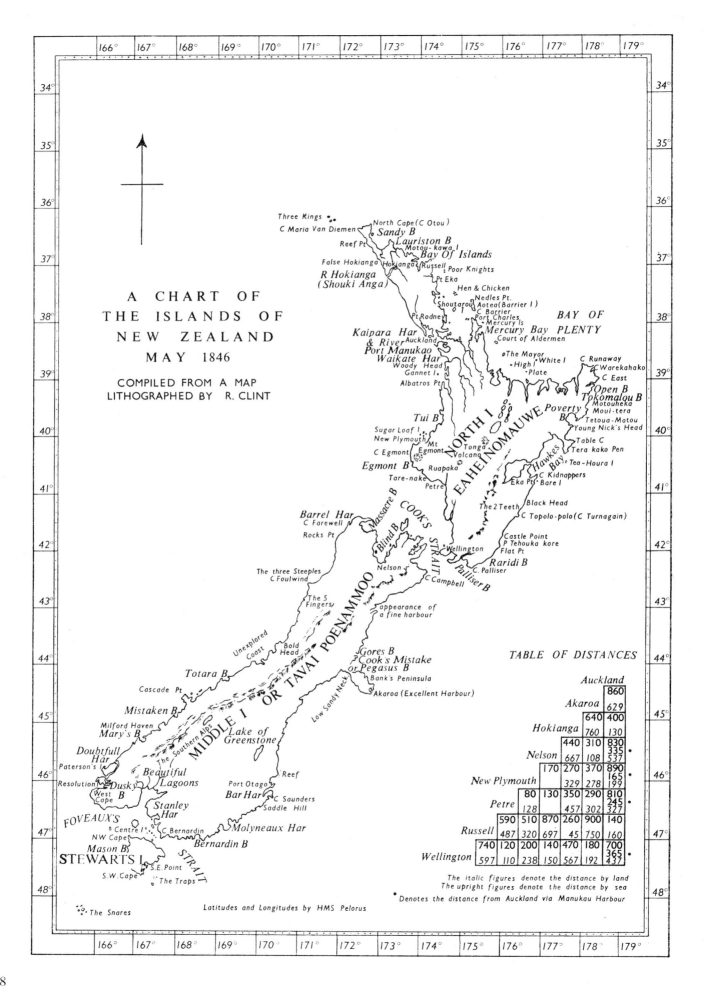

fortress in itself. Shelling continued throughout the season of peace and began to take its toll by the time Heke arrived with 60 warriors on 10 January.

On Sunday 11 January 1846, the pa appeared to be abandoned. Attackers discovered Kawiti and a dozen warriors inside, who fled and linked up with other Maori sheltering in the bush. Heavy fighting followed. Three hours later the Maori retreated with some 30 casualties, leaving the British tending 45 casualties.

Despard claimed victory. The Maori rather saw such desecration of the Sabbath as yet another example of Pakeha hypocrisy. Historians have followed this contemporary Maori and missionary interpretation by arguing that nearly all of the Maori garrison had left the pa to attend divine service. Yet, as James Belich has recently pointed out, fighting continued at Ohaeawai on Sunday and there was nothing naive about either Kawiti or Heke. More likely, the Maori forces deliberately abandoned the pa. Once in the bush they held a considerable advantage over the British soldiers and defences erected outside the pa suggest that they were trying to spring a trap. What saved the British from heavier losses was the rumour that Kawiti had been captured or killed. This news persuaded some warriors to return to the pa on a mission of rescue or utu.

On balance Ruapekapeka was a draw rather than a British victory, but it did push Heke and Kawiti into negotiating for peace through the neutral chief Pomare II. Grey reacted magnanimously by pardoning the 're-

Tamati Waka Nene. Engraving by J. R. Ashton. *T. Ryan Collection.*

bels' and sensibly did not erect another flagpole. He also cleverly promoted peace as a huge success.

The Colonial Office, most contemporaries and subsequent generations of New Zealanders were impressed. As *Our Nation's Story*, the textbook for two generations of schoolchildren puts it, 'wise and clever' Grey beat the rebels and 'won the respect of Maori and settler alike'. So the legend of 'Good Governor Grey' first created by W. P. Reeves was popularised.

More recent historians have been less impressed. Both Ian Wards and Alan Ward stress the enormous military advantages Grey held over Fitz-Roy. Along with Belich they also note the manner in which Grey exaggerated his success in subjugating the Ngapuhi. Kawiti, admittedly, lived out the remainder of his life in poverty and converted to Christianity before his death in 1854, but neither Ngapuhi nor Heke suffered great losses from the war. At most 60 men had been killed and 80 wounded even though Grey boasted 500 Maori casualties. Economic strains were apparent but the tribe was still socially intact. Grey's decision to keep extra troops in New Zealand proved that he continued to view Heke and elements of Ngapuhi as dangerous.

Heke himself does not seem to have lost much mana. F. E. Maning and Henry Williams, admittedly both opponents of Grey, considered Heke the real power in the north until his death from tuberculosis in 1850. Heke continued to administer native law and was well regarded by all Bay of Islands hapu. Belich concludes Grey won the propaganda war even though the real victors on the battlefield were Kawiti and Heke.

Such revisionism has gone too far, however. Grey's decisive military action had a greater impact on a warlike people than vacillation followed by an ill-considered campaign. Grey also revealed diplomatic skill as well as conceding military weakness in not re-erecting the flagstaff. Even though the peace he secured was anything but lasting he at least pacified the powerful Ngapuhi tribe. Their neutrality during the wars of the 1860s would be of considerable advantage to the British.

The Governor ignored the essential point of Heke's and Kawiti's protest — that they wanted partnership in government and control of their land — and, along with his contemporaries, he was equally incapable of conceding the military achievement of the Maori.

A painting attributed to Major Cyprian Bridge. View of Maori pa with potato plantings around. There are loopholes for musket fire at the foot of the palisade. Intertribal wars were limited by the need to return home to gather food and harvest crops. *Alexander Turnbull Library.*

Link: From Heke to Gold

After pacifying the north Grey turned his attention to the southern North Island. Troops cleared the Hutt Valley of Maori 'rebels' and Te Rauparaha was placed under house arrest in 1846. Even his uncompromising nephew Te Rangihaeata retreated to the south of the Manawatu River; forced to give up his raiding, he lived in peace. A minor rebellion at Wanganui was stamped out in 1848. Within two years of arriving in New Zealand Grey had secured peace.

The Governor now concentrated on 'civilising' the Maori and amalgamating the races. George Clarke, Chief Protector of Aborigines, was dismissed and his department dismantled. Resident European magistrates and Maori assessors were appointed to some Maori districts. A tiny sum of money was set aside for building Maori schools and hospitals. Cheap loans were also made available to chiefs interested in developing European style farms. Wheat growing flourished in the Waikato and mills sprang up to supply Auckland, Melbourne and Sydney with grain.

Sales of Maori land continued. During Grey's stay almost the entire South Island was purchased for a mere £50,000. The buying of land opened the way for the settlement of Otago and Canterbury and the development of New Zealand's only viable industry — pastoralism.

In 1848 278 Scottish settlers led by Captain William Cargill arrived in Dunedin to establish an Otago settlement. Organised as an improved version of the Wakefield settlements, the group's Free Church Presbyterianism would provide the social cement lacking in the other communities.

The problems the settlers encountered on their arrival must have made them think they had sailed back in time to the 17th century. Preparations were inadequate. There was no wharf, no immigration barracks and only half-formed tracks. Surveying was incomplete. Like their Wellington counterparts the Otago pioneers had to start from scratch. More serious, the venture attracted even fewer capitalists than its northern counterparts and land sales languished.

The only people with any capital also happened to be English and Anglican and a serious rift soon developed between the majority Scots and the 'little enemy'. Grain farming also proved difficult. The whole 'godly experiment' might well have foundered but for the tenacious leadership of Cargill, the grim determination of Thomas Burns, the minister to the first congregation in 'New Edinburgh', and the desire of most settlers to achieve a 'modest self-sufficiency'.

Otago's future, like Wellington's, lay with pastoralism, yet Cargill clung to the sufficient price of £2 per acre until 1856. Once he cut the price to 10 shillings the fortunes of the struggling settlement improved markedly. Immigration resumed in 1858 and population rose from 3796 in 1856 to reach 12,691 by 1860. Sheep numbers increased even more spectacularly.

Canterbury, settled in 1850, realised the Wakefield ideal more completely than any of the other special settlements. It was more successful because it was adequately capitalised. Bishops and wealthy clergy of the Church of England gave generous financial support, as did respectable Anglican gentlemen and entrepreneurs. Substantial early investment made Canterbury the best prepared of all the Wakefield settlements. The first settlers, or 'pilgrims' as they called themselves, found that surveying had been completed. They were able to live in proper immigration barracks rather than tents until they set up their own homes. Wharves and roads were progressing.

Canterbury was also successful because significant numbers of investors came to seek their fortune. Their money was put to work quickly because Canterbury was far more suited to grain growing than any other area of New Zealand. The region was free of heavy bush and there was no Maori resistance to delay the making of 'newest England'.

Canterbury was lucky, too, to have a younger, better educated and more flexible leadership than Otago. John Robert Godley and James Edward FitzGerald were sons of the Anglo-Irish gentry who had been educated at Oxford and Cambridge respectively. Quickly realising that Canterbury's future lay with pastoralism, they abolished the sufficient price of £3 per acre on second and third class land even before they received permission from the New Zealand Company and, unlike in Otago, no attempt was made to limit the area of runs.

The bait worked and several squatters from New South Wales arrived to burn off the prickly matagouri and take full advantage of some of the best sheep farming country in the world. The demise of the New Zealand Company at the end of 1850 gave the leadership an even freer hand and they opened up the area to all comers. Recently arrived British migrants soon joined the Australians and prospered. One such was the young novelist, Samuel Butler, who doubled his father's £4,000 advance in four years and returned to Britain to live out his leisurely literary life in comfort.

There were failures, of course, especially among those with little money. Rapidly rising prices of stock brought from Sydney and driven overland from Marlborough hit the undercapitalised hard. Droughts, flash floods and the dreaded Australian stock disease scab also caused problems and occasional bankruptcy. Even so, Canterbury flourished. By 1861 the province

William Cargill, Resident Agent for the New Zealand Company and later Otago's first Superintendent. *Hocken Library.*

boasted 16,000 people whose prosperity rested on 877,000 sheep.

Even though Canterbury's population contained many more younger sons of the British gentry than anywhere else in New Zealand (some 17 per cent of Canterbury's provincial councillors were connected with gentry families) it was still not as genteel as Wakefield would have liked. Over 60 per cent of the first group of migrants were labourers or domestic servants, and worse, some undesirables and Irish slipped through the screening process. Early Canterbury was just as liquor-filled as the rest of colonial New Zealand. By 1858 it boasted six breweries and consumption of spirits was six times higher than it would be a century later. Canterbury, too, was never exclusively Anglican, crime and prostitution were present and its migrants were not as literate as the Scots to the south. Even so, much of the atmosphere and appearance of rural south-eastern England was transplanted in Canterbury. Christchurch's classic grid pattern, its gracious parks, square and cathedral still impart an English air.

The immigrants who settled Otago and Canterbury were as enthusiastic about self-government as the settlers in Nelson and Wellington. Governor Grey managed to delay the introduction of a constitution in 1846 but was forced to relent by introducing a new constitution in 1852.

The 1852 Constitution Act provided the settlers with representative gov-

ernment but left foreign affairs under control of the British Foreign Office. A bicameral legislature was established, made up of a nominated Legislative Council of not less than 10 members and an elected House of Representatives of between 27 and 42 members. Thirty-seven members sat in the lower house during the first Parliament of 1854. The provincial councils soon assumed more power than the authors of the 1852 Act had intended, including control over the sale of waste lands (that is land purchased by the Crown from the Maori for settlement) in 1855. The politicians themselves were generally well educated men of capital who could afford time away from business or farm. No clear parties formed and debate was notable for its pragmatic content rather than for ideological division. Cliques formed around personalities and a rough division gradually emerged between 'centralists', who wanted greater government control, and 'provincialists', who wanted greater local automony. Only the more leisured citizens took much notice of politics and apathy was widespread.

The franchise was relatively wide. Freeholders who owned property worth £50 annually and leaseholders who paid an annual rental of £10 were entitled to vote. Holders of tenements in town areas worth £10 a year were also enfranchised. This meant that one in five of the population, or about two-thirds of adult males, could vote, as against one in 30 in Britain.

Yet the New Zealand franchise was not as democratic as the universal franchise introduced in South Australia and Victoria in 1856. There was also no secret ballot in New Zealand and the potentially corrupt practice of plural voting was allowed. Inevitably women were excluded. The majority of settlers were cynical about the system, even after the introduction of responsible government in 1856. Elections generated excitement, but only a minority of settlers bothered to exercise their democratic rights. Turnout at elections was notoriously low. Nearly all Maori were excluded because of their communal system of landownership.

By the late 1840s Maori began to resist ever growing land sales. An anti-land selling movement expressed dissatisfaction in Taranaki and grew into the King Movement between 1854 and 1858. The idea was that the land should be placed under the mana of a Maori King. Support came mainly

Port Lyttelton, Canterbury, 1851. From here settlers had to climb the Port Hills before reaching Christchurch. By William Fox. *Alexander Turnbull Library.*

from Taranaki and the major central North Island tribes — Tuwharetoa, Ngati Maniapoto and Waikato. Northern tribes and the wealthy and powerful Ngati Porou of the East Coast remained neutral. Despite failure to win the support of all tribes the King Movement reflected a growing Maori nationalism, and its mere existence made clear a Maori desire for local self-government.

The Waikato ariki Te Wherowhero was crowned as Potatau I in 1858 and the movement had its own flag, parliament and newspaper. It made and administered its own laws and was strenuously opposed to further land sales. The symbols and mechanisms of government which it borrowed from the British were derivative but the desire for a higher and more united Maori political identity was obvious. They did not want war; they wanted a partnership with the Pakeha.

This direct challenge to the British policy of political amalgamation troubled Grey's successor, Governor Thomas Gore Browne, and the settlers saw the King Movement as an attempt to block their acquisition of more land. Yet hostilities did not begin with the Waikato-based Kingites. Fighting broke out in Taranaki when a minor chief, Teira, sold some land at Waitara to which he was not entitled. When surveyors were sent in, the owners of the land pulled out their pegs. Gore Browne treated the protest as an act of rebellion and declared martial law.

The growing racial tension coincided with declining wool prices. By 1860 New Zealand had become the ugly duckling of the Australasian colonies and now its progress seemed to be blocked by the racial crisis and an uncertain economic future.

8. 1861 Eureka:
Gabriel Read Finds Gold

DUNEDIN in 1861 was a sleepy village of 2000 people. The stern Calvinist leadership — nicknamed 'the old identity' by goldfields balladeer Charles Thatcher — knew that gold existed in Otago but they feared that a rush would destroy their religious experiment. The establishment did not want thousands of rough Victorian miners descending on the province, lowering the religious tone and making a mockery of the social hierarchy. They therefore turned a deaf ear to Hindu prospector Black Peter's claim that he had found large gold deposits.

But when respectable Tasmanian geologist and gold hound Gabriel Read wrote in early June 1861 that he had found, in Central Otago's Tuapeka River, gold shining 'like the stars in Orion on a cold frosty night', even Richardson, the new provincial superintendent, took notice. He passed Read's letter on to the *Otago Witness*, who published it with great fanfare.

Hydraulic mining at Gabriel's Gully, 1884. Twenty years earlier individual miners had dominated the gully. Now mining was run by companies who could afford equipment for 'hydraulicing' or sluicing. *R. P. Hargreaves, T. J. Hearn, New Zealand in the mid Victorian Era,* **John McIndoe.**

There was no sudden stampede, however. Apathy and a long record of false alarms, including a shortlived rush to the Lindis area earlier that year, had made the populace sceptical.

This scepticism broke down in late June when respected settlers like James MacIndoe and T. B. Gillies confirmed the accessibility and size of the field. Goldfields regulations were passed on 28 June to give the superintendent special powers to control proceedings. The rush had begun.

Tents sprang up along the side of Gabriel's Gully. By mid-July 500 were camped out; by early August there were 2000. 'Gold, Gold, Gold, is the universal subject of conversation,' proclaimed the *Witness*. As Vincent Pyke, the soon to be appointed goldfields warden, put it, local society was 'temporarily unhinged'. Thomas Burns wrote to his brother in Scotland: 'Every blacksmith's forge is blown out, the carpenters have bolted, the sawmill is silent'. Read was rewarded with a payment of £500 in November, later increased to £1,000, but Black Peter's claim to be the original discoverer was ignored.

From August a ragged army of Victorian miners began flooding into the area. Accessible alluvial gold had been well worked out in Victoria and these men jumped at the chance of joining a new rush. By the end of the year over 17,000 had arrived, swelling Otago's population to 30,000. Some 14,000 miners were working the Tuapeka field by the end of 1861. New Zealand's most backward province suddenly held a third of the colony's population.

Dunedin boomed. Its population trebled and its prim three hotels became 30 by early 1862. The number of ships visiting the port exploded from 68 in 1860 to 256 in 1861. Manufacturing, financial development and retailing were also stimulated. But such an influx of population brought problems as well as gains. Dunedin soon became a disorderly collection of shanties and tents jammed into gullies and scattered along ridges. Open drains and sewers failed to cope and the arrival of summer saw the rapid spread of infectious disease. A commission reported in 1864 that rates of diphtheria and dysentery were higher than in contem-

porary London. The orderly Wakefieldian village had become a wild, frontier town.

Despite the upheaval in Dunedin the Tuapeka fields were remarkably orderly. Otago's leaders learned from the mistakes made in Victoria. A modest miner's right was introduced from the outset rather than the high licence fees which had been bitterly resented and had led to open rebellion at the Eureka Stockade in Australia. Vincent Pyke, brought in from Victoria as warden of the goldfields, won the support of miners and the confidence of the older Otago establishment with his efficient and fair administration. Claim jumping was much less of a problem because Gabriel Read's 24-square foot (2.2-square metre) claims worked better than the 8-square foot (0.75-square metre) claims of Victoria. Police were handpicked, highly disciplined and were generally confined to escort duties. The mounted gold escort functioned so well that it was never attacked. Settlement of disputes was left to wardens and the police corruption and brutality which had characterised the Victorian rushes were almost

entirely absent in Otago.

As a result there was little violence and bushranging was rare. Even the best known bushranger, Henry Garrett, who worked the Maungatuas, treated his victims well. The pipes of the miners he held up were filled and lit and brandy was distributed to keep out the cold until help arrived. Garrett's chivalrous criminal activity was not tolerated as in Victoria and he was soon captured and imprisoned.

One reason for the miners' near universal condemnation of anti-social behaviour was the fact that many were highly trained artisans. As in Victoria they raised the education and literacy levels of the population. Athenaeums and Mechanics Institutes were well supported in both Lawrence and Waitahuna. Although the miners drank hard and scorned the pretensions of the 'old identity', they were also concerned with respectability and self-improvement. Many stayed on as farmers, storekeepers and publicans after the easily mineable gold ran out.

The Tuapeka rush was followed by bigger, more spectacular rushes to the Dunstan area around Cromwell in August 1862, and the Arrowtown and Queenstown district in November and December of the same year. The land and the climate were much harsher in these areas and conditions were markedly rougher than at Tuapeka. Mining the beaches along the edges of the swiftly flowing Clutha was dangerous and demanding. Snowstorms and flash floods claimed many lives. Pyke's effective administration retained a semblance of order but claim jumping and brawling rose dramatically, along with the level of violence. Armed conflict broke out on occasion. Even so, when the Otago rush began to fall off late in 1864 it remained the most orderly goldrush in history.

News of the West Coast rushes reached Otago in early 1865 and some miners left to join others coming from Sydney and Melbourne. The Coast produced about the same amount of gold as in Otago and involved similar numbers of miners, but its impact was much greater because it made something out of nothing. Gold brought life to the West Coast and left a lasting stamp on the character of the region. The difficulty of crossing the Southern Alps meant these rushes benefited Sydney and Melbourne more than Canterbury.

By 1867 most of the easily mined gold on the West Coast had been extracted. A smaller and less important rush to the Thames/Coromandel area followed, but this region yielded little easily mineable gold and panning and digging was soon replaced by company-operated quartz mining.

A similar pattern unfolded in both Otago and the West Coast after the easily mineable gold had been extracted. First, co-operatives were formed to carry out elaborate sluicing operations. Cornishmen were particularly prominent in this phase and their ingenious engineering has left obvious scars on the landscape in places like the Blue Lake at St Bathans.

Second, companies were formed in Dunedin and Auckland to bring in expensive machinery and employ larger numbers of miners to work deeper seams. Company mining created a

Panorama of Jones Flat and the upper township of the goldtown Ross, Westland, 1868. *Canterbury Public Library.*

A Chinese goldminer, Central Otago. Chinese did not arrive in significant numbers on the goldfields until 1866. They were encouraged to come by the Dunedin Chamber of Commerce who were concerned that Europeans were deserting Otago for the new West Coast fields. *Presbyterian Church Archives.*

quite different social order from alluvial mining and established a clear-cut division between management and men. This type of mining was most important around Thames and was more important on the West Coast than in Otago. The biggest company operations, especially at Thames, also attracted British and Australian capital.

Third, some 5000 Chinese miners came from Victoria to rework older fields. Their acceptance of appalling working conditions and low living standards unleashed bitter resentment from European miners and in response the government passed discriminatory legislation against Chinese migrants. Yet even though miner dislike of the Chinese resulted as much from racism as from fear of unfair competition, physical violence against the Chinese in New Zealand was never as bad as in Victoria and California.

Fourth, a brief dredging boom revived the goldmining industry in the 1890s. Largely financed by Dunedin's commercial elite, it established a heavy industrial base in the city. The bubble soon burst in Otago but West Coast dredging operations continued for much longer.

The goldrushes were not as important to New Zealand as they were to either Victoria or California. All three New Zealand rushes combined pro-

duced about 17 million ounces over a 50-year period (West Coast: 6.55 million, Otago: 6.52 million, Thames: 3.7 million). In comparison Victoria produced 28 million ounces over a 10-year period. New Zealand exports contributed a mere 4 per cent of the world's gold in the second half of the 19th century as against Australia's 27 per cent and North America's 36 per cent. The Klondike, Kalgoorlie and South African rushes were also much larger than New Zealand's.

The problem with these broad comparisons is that they conceal the impact of what were relatively small rushes by international standards on a tiny colony of 100,000 people. New Zealand's smallness, newness and failure to find export staples other than wool meant that the goldrushes had a bigger influence on the nation than their relatively small size and short duration would suggest.

The goldrushes gave a badly needed shot in the arm to a stagnant economy. Gold became a second export staple for a decade during which time it contributed more than half of the colony's export earnings. Without gold New Zealand would have declined and become little more than a giant sheep run. Most important, gold lured people to the bottom of the world. By the end of the golden decade the colony's population had increased two and a half times to a quarter of a million. Such a rapid influx of people brought about an economic take-off by creating an internal market. Manufacturing was made viable for the first time. Such miscellaneous Dunedin industries as brick making and soap manufacture trace their beginnings to the goldrushes. Breweries multiplied to quench the miners' big thirst and the printing industry expanded to meet a greatly increased demand for newspapers. Engineering and clothing manufacture started and flour and sawmilling became profitable.

Farmers did even better. Although initially hostile to the miners, runholders soon realised that miner hunger could be turned into profit. Sheep numbers increased several fold in Otago from 600,000 in 1860 to reach 2.4 million by 1867. Grain farmers benefited from the demand for flour.

Urban merchants and financiers gained most from the boom. Importing and exporting were suddenly lucrative. Banks were established. The Auckland-based Bank of New Zealand, founded in 1861, and its main rival, the Bank of New South Wales, rofited most. Dunedin financiers were too slow; the Bank of Otago did not begin operations until 1863 and always struggled, winding up in 1874.

That peculiar New Zealand combination of mortgage company, export agency and supplier of seeds and materials known as the stock and station agency also gained a foothold in the 1860s. Beginning as local operations like Donald Reid and Wright, Robertson and Stephenson, such agencies later attracted the competition of larger Australian and London-based operations such as Dalgetys (1861) and the National Mortgage Agency (1873). Insurance companies like Auckland's New Zealand Insurance Company (1859) also prospered. A definite financial infrastructure was created during the 1860s which benefited Auckland, Wellington, Christchurch and many small towns as well as Dunedin.

Storekeepers, transport operators and publicans also did well. Few miners, however, scratched out more than a bare living. Estimates for Victoria that eight out of 10 made little money or worsened their position are probably also true for Otago. Big strikes worth £2,000, like that of Hartley and Reilly, were rare indeed.

The demographic impact of the rushes was considerable. Most miners were young single males without children; two-thirds of them were between 21 and 39 years old. This influx undermined Wakefield's familial ideal. Before the rushes there were 83 women for every 100 men in Otago; by the end of 1862 there were 66 women per 100 men, about the same ratio as for the rest of the colony. On the Otago goldfields themselves the average was 32 women for every 100 males and in some cases there were no women at all. The sexual imbalance was even more marked on the previously completely unsettled West Coast.

Such a situation encouraged heavy drinking and prostitution, the very things which Wakefield detested about uncontrolled colonisation. Quiet Dunedin supported 80 hotels and four breweries by 1865. The New Geneva had its own notorious red light district — the 'Devil's half-acre' — where tiny hovels, some of them one-woman brothels, were jammed together around a stinking open sewer. The arrival of the Chinese, who played fan-tan and pakapoo in the smallest and most rundown of the cottages, added to the area's notoriety. Hokitika was even wilder; its population of 5000 supported 102 hotels.

New ethnic elements were introduced to Otago by the rushes. The Southern Irish, a mere 4 per cent of the population before the golden decade, rose to 10 per cent by 1867. The proportion of Roman Catholics rose from a miniscule 1 per cent to 10 per cent. The Scottish sector declined dramatically from 66 to 32 per cent. The Irish presence in Otago was quite small compared with the West Coast where one in three miners claimed Irish parentage, a figure well above the 15 per cent for New Zealand as a whole.

By 1870 the struggling village of Dunedin had been transformed into a prosperous town of 14,000 people — 2000 more than Auckland. Its status as the premier town of the colony was confirmed by substantial banks and office blocks in the business area and fine homes in the new suburbs. The

Women faced additional difficulties on the heavily male dominated West Coast goldfields. This is probably a digger's wife and child at Donaghues, Ross, 1868. *Canterbury Museum.*

A wagon train arrives at Waikino from Paeroa about 1904 with coal for the Waihi Mine's Victoria Battery, mining equipment stores, and some barrels of beer. *Waihi Art Centre and Museum, Waihi.*

establishment of a boys high school in 1864, a university in 1869 and a girls high school in 1871 made Dunedin New Zealand's undisputed educational leader.

Province benefited as well as town and by 1871 some 70,000 people were living in Otago. The goldrushes had shifted the economic focus from north to south. Economic and political leadership became firmly rooted in Otago and Canterbury until the 1890s. The ongoing development of pastoralism and grain farming pushed the South Island further ahead.

Contrary to popular myth, miners were opponents rather than supporters of closer settlement; they wanted to exploit the land rather than nurture it. They disputed access to valuable water resources with farmers who did not want their stock drinking polluted water. Miners called on the central government to arbitrate such disputes because they felt that provincial government, dominated by big pastoralists and farmers, was unsympathetic to their needs. The state responded by altering individual property rights in ways which would have been considered quite unacceptable in Britain. This early instance of state intervention to foster economic development helps to explain why later governments, especially Seddon's, had little hesitation in using the state to solve the country's problems.

Once goldmining declined, however, the goldfields area was substantially reduced and the government responded to the demands of the more numerous small farmers by experimenting with various forms of leasehold to promote intensive farming. Mining was restricted to high yield areas, special mining tenures were introduced and the advantages given miners in the 1860s were withdrawn.

Despite the impact of the goldrushes, farming always held more sentimental appeal as the economic saviour of the nation. It was the burning desire to own and farm land, not to mine gold, which drove the majority of rural migrants who came to New Zealand and exacerbated the growing racial tension in the North Island where goldmining did not offer a major alternative to farming.

The goldrushes accelerated the development of Otago, created an inhabited West Coast out of the bush and boosted a depressed economy. Wakefield's ideals were undermined more completely by gold than by pastoralism, and the state became involved in colonial development earlier than would otherwise have been the case. But farming continued as the mainstream of New Zealand's development; goldmining was never more than an important and relatively shortlived tributary.

'Wild Missouri' on the Thames goldfield with its wooden water-wheel, flumes, races, trestles and railway. Mines such as these needed larger sums of capital than individual miners could attract so company mining developed. *Auckland Public Library.*

Link: From Goldrush to War

Hostilities broke out in Taranaki on 17 March 1860 when Colonel C. E. Gold attacked Wiremu Kingi's pa at Waitara. Initially local Maori warriors, bolstered after May by 500 Kingite allies from the Ngati Maniapoto and Waikato tribes, used their local knowledge to great advantage. In June they scored a major victory over Gold and Major Thomas Nelson at Puketakauere.

Gold was replaced by Major General T. S. Pratt on 3 August. Pratt countered the Maori use of fighting pa by digging zigzag 'saps' or trenches up to the palisades. On 6 November he inflicted heavy losses on a party of Ngati Haua warriors he caught in the open at Mahoetahi. Something of a stalemate eventuated as 3500 Imperial troops faced 3000 Maori warriors (1500 Kingite warriors came from the Waikato during the fighting). So when Wiremu Tamihana of Ngati Haua secured a truce with Governor Gore Browne on 8 April 1861 both sides seemed relieved. The opening campaign had been fierce; the British lost 238 killed and wounded, and the Maori suffered 200 casualties, many of whom were killed.

Sir George Grey was recalled from South Africa to resolve a difficult situation. The Colonial Office instructed him to make the ministers assume responsibility for native affairs. Local politicians hoped, however, that the Colonial Office would continue to pay for military operations. Sir George responded to the challenge by acting as an autocrat who knew what was best for Maori and settler alike. He returned in September 1861 to a hero's welcome and spoke of peace while preparing for war.

He promised to investigate the Waitara purchase and dismissed as outrageous Gore Browne's idea of invading the Waikato. He also pledged to increase Maori participation in government. He and William Fox introduced runanga (councils) to encourage Maori involvement in local government. At the same time, Grey built a 'defensive' road south towards the Waikato and kept all 3500 Imperial troops in New Zealand under the pretext that the situation was precarious. By 1863 Grey had even increased troop numbers to 4000, nearly 8 per cent of the total of 41,000 troops stationed throughout the Empire.

As well as building military roads and undermining the King Movement, Grey refused to negotiate with moderate leaders like Wiremu Tamihana. He rejected, for example, Tamihana's offer to negotiate with Taranaki Maori who had taken the Tataraimaka block as compensation for Waitara, and by constant talk of digging around the King he further hardened Kingite resolve.

THE FIRST TARANAKI WAR.

PROCLAMATION.

The inhabitants will in future be required to have a candle or lamp at their front windows at night ready to light in case of alarm, and are desired to secure their doors and lower windows. The Police to see to this.

C. E. GOLD,

Colonel Commanding the Forces

New Zealand.

New Plymouth, 20th April, 1860.

A warning to European settlers in New Plymouth, April 1860. Hostilities had broken out in March. *Alexander Turnbull Library.*

Then Grey waited for his ministers to agree to the recommendation of the official committee of inquiry that Wiremu Kingi's land be returned. The ministers did not act on this matter until 11 May, and Sir George Grey reoccupied the Tataraimaka block on 4 April 1863 before making the announcement that the official committee of inquiry had reported in favour of Kingi's claims to ownership of the Waitara. The ministers further delayed action on this decision until 11 May.

Rewi Maniapoto meantime assumed Grey's action signalled a resumption of hostilities and ordered the ambushing of the blockade at Tataraimaka on 4 May. Nine soldiers were killed in the raid, adding fuel to Grey's concerted propaganda campaign against the Kingites. Grey had been talking of a

possible attack on Auckland since 1862. All Kingites were 'extremist' and the warlike Rewi Maniapoto was portrayed as their undisputed leader whereas the moderates Tamihana and King Tawhiao were still very much in control. Grey then wrung every emotive advantage from the unpunished rape of a British settler within Kingite territory. As elsewhere in the Empire, the rape of a white woman by a coloured man unleashed a flood of racist condemnation from the settler press and politicians. Here was proof that the Maori were incapable of ruling themselves.

By May 1863 Grey had made up his mind to invade the Waikato. Rumours of an impending attack on Auckland and Rewi's hot-headed action provided very convenient excuses. Offensive action could now be portrayed as defensive. Hostile Maori rhetoric was interpreted as a declaration of war and in June Grey produced letters from Kingite leaders which supposedly talked of an attack upon Auckland. The correspondence was in fact fraudulent and only three of the 18 letters cited by Grey were written before 24 June, after official approval had been given for the invasion.

Grey's actions received little censure because many settlers were enthusiastic about invading the Waikato. Would-be small farmers wanted to convert that lush green country into farmland, while big Auckland financiers such as Frederick Whitaker, J. C. Firth and Thomas Russell saw a major speculative opportunity; they would benefit more than anyone from the military defeat of the Maori.

Most missionaries also changed sides during 1863. Bishop Selwyn and the CMS had supported Kingi's Waitara claim and had opposed the Taranaki war. But Selwyn signalled a change of heart by offering his services as army chaplain once the invasion was agreed upon in June. He believed the Maori would only be brought to their senses if they were given a sound thrashing. Nearly all the CMS missionaries followed his example and supported the war; only Octavius Hadfield stood firm in his opposition. The Wesleyans stayed silent and the Roman Catholics remained neutral. All missions had failed to make much progress after 1845 and most Protestants had come to believe that the use of force was the only way in which the Maori could be directed back onto the

path of civilisation.

There were also sound military reasons for attacking the Waikato rather than other areas. It was flatter and more open than most Maori strongholds and would enable the British commanders to employ their traditional strength of massed formations. The Waikato River would also allow gunboats to provide additional artillery and auxiliary support. The only settler opposition to the invasion came from some South Island politicians. They did not question such action on moral or military grounds but were concerned that the use of many troops would cost them dearly in taxes.

Governor Grey retook Tataraimaka in early June, killing 24 Maori warriors. An ebullient Premier Alfred Domett then gave the invasion his official blessing on 24 June. A fortnight later, on 9 July, Grey declared that all Maori would have to swear the oath of allegiance or be expelled into Kingite territory. Then two days later he announced that he intended to build military posts on the Kingite side of the Mangatawhiri Stream; any Maori who resisted the construction of these forts would be arrested and have his land confiscated. The Kingite leaders did not receive this advice until 17 July, five days after the invasion had

The 57th Regiment taking a Maori redoubt on the Katikara River in the Taranaki, 1863-64. *Alexander Turnbull Library.*

begun.

Alan Ward has labelled this action 'the climactic event in New Zealand race relations' because it marked the end of all efforts at moral persuasion. The Maori were to be amalgamated whether they liked it or not and the British system of law and government was to be forced upon them. Kingites were supposedly in breach of the Treaty of Waitangi but to many Maori it seemed to be the other way around.

9. 1863   Crushing the Kingites:

Governor Grey Orders the Invasion of the Waikato

GENERAL CAMERON invaded the Waikato by crossing the Mangatawhiri Stream with 3000 troops on 17 July 1863. At first things went well. Cameron's superior firepower won an easy victory at Meremere on 31 October. Kingite resistance at Rangiriri on 21 November was fiercer but Cameron killed 36 Maori warriors and took 183 prisoners. Ngaruawahia, the Kingite capital, was taken on 8 December without a fight. Thereafter Maori resistance stiffened as Cameron moved cautiously down the Waikato River and cleverly constructed fighting pa continued to cause problems for the experienced General.

On 21 February 1864 Cameron took and fired the supply village of Rangiaowhia. Two victims of this harsh act of war were the daughters of the chief Kereopa, a name which would later strike fear into European hearts. This action also seemed to harden Maori resolve so that Rewi Maniapoto and his Ngati Maniapoto warriors provided the most determined opposition of the campaign at the nearby pa of Orakau between 30 March and 2 April 1864.

Cameron's use of saps forced Rewi into an impossible situation but the redoubtable chief refused to give in. Reduced to using wooden bullets, he lost 80 warriors but when asked to surrender by Cameron replied, 'E hoa, ka whaiwhai tonu ahau kiakoe ake ake.' (My friend, we will fight you forever, forever.) These words later inspired the Maori Battalion in a very different kind of campaign. British troops were so impressed by Rewi's gallantry that they erected a memorial to him and his men at nearby Te Awamutu. This was only one of two instances where this happened; the other was at Rorke's Drift in South

The 14th Foot attacking Waikato Pa, 1863. A painting by Orlando Norie. *Alexander Turnbull Library.*

Africa after the British had defeated the Zulu. Orakau was nearly as significant to Maori as Culloden to Scottish Highlanders, although Rewi's command was superior to that of Bonnie Prince Charlie.

Orakau was the last major setpiece of the wars and after it fighting became much less chivalrous. Ngai te Rangi and remnants of the Kingites nevertheless managed to win a dazzling victory at Gate Pa near Tauranga some three weeks later. On 24 April 1864 overconfident British troops charged Maori fortifications after they had been subjected to a level of shelling which James Belich estimates was equivalent to that of the Somme. They did not realise that the Maori had developed an elaborate trench and bunker system which enabled them to survive the bombardment and move their warriors well forward of the palisades. The hidden warriors caught the British completely by surprise and killed 111 troops. Such sophisticated earthworks were not used again until the Western Front.

The reverse of Gate Pa was avenged at Te Ranga, also near Tauranga, on 21 June 1864. On this occasion the better armed British forces overwhelmed local Maori resistance and killed 120 warriors in the bloodiest action of the wars. British troops were slowly withdrawn after this battle and colonial militia and Maori auxiliaries came to play a more important role. Both militia and Maori allies (kupa-

pa), however, were less well disciplined than the Imperial troops and the fighting became noticeably dirtier, with atrocities against civilians increasing on both sides as skirmishing continued down to 1872.

During the later part of the wars the colonial forces were led a merry dance by Te Kooti in the central North Island and Hawke's Bay areas and the Ngati Ruanui leader Titokowaru in South Taranaki. Both leaders combined classic guerilla tactics with the use of fighting pa; Titokowaru constructed a diamond-shaped pa which was virtually impregnable. Both men deserve to be called generals because they knew their enemy better than themselves and followed carefully devised military strategies. Titokowaru's support collapsed in 1869 and he eventually became a follower of the pacifist prophet Te Whiti. Te Kooti escaped into the King Country and set about finding a peaceful new religion — Ringatu.

The extraordinary resistance put up by the Kingites and their allies constituted the fiercest and most effective opposition made by an indigenous people against the relentless march of British Imperialism. Waikato, Ngati Maniapoto, Tuwharetoa and allies from other tribes fought so hard because they were defending their land and their way of life.

The British never won an absolute military victory but pacification of the Maori was made virtually inevitable by their huge superiority in troop numbers and firepower. Nearly 12,000 Imperial troops were used in the Waikato campaigns, approximately the total number of adult Maori males for the whole of Aotearoa. The well-drilled and experienced professional soldiers were joined by up to 4000 colonial militia and several hundred kupapa or 'loyalist' Maori (mainly Arawa). Belich estimates that 50 million troops would have had to serve in India to secure equivalent numerical domination.

Despite the efforts of contemporaries to blame setbacks on an incompetent command, the British were well led. The much maligned Cameron was, in fact, highly regarded, while his successor, Major General W. C. T. Chute, was a tough, ruthless soldier who practised the scorched earth policy with the enthusiasm of a Sherman or a Von Kleist. The film *Utu* made a serious mistake in portraying the British commander as a bungling upper-crust nincompoop.

The Maori also suffered from other disadvantages. Most important, the Maori were divided between Kingites, loyalists and neutrals. Also, they could

'A Fortified Pa' believed to be Paparatu Pa in the Waikato painted by Major Gustavus von Tempsky. *Auckland Institute and Museum.*

not sustain long campaigns since despite the successful development of Maori farming in the Waikato, they still relied upon food gathering for survival. In addition they had little artillery, limited ammunition and could not match the British bayonet in hand to hand combat. The only area in which they were roughly equal was in firearms; their shotguns were a match for the relatively old-fashioned rifles used by the British.

The Maori put up a heroic fight against overwhelming odds and even won several stunning victories because of their skill as strategists and military engineers, not because of British incompetence. Several astute Maori military thinkers emerged during the campaigns, though prevailing British attitudes denied the possibility of strategists among the 'natives'. Prejudice also blinded British observers to the fact that the Maori were able engineers as well as guerilla fighters.

Some 2000 Maori supporters of the King were killed in the New Zealand wars as against 560 British troops and 250 kupapa. This bitter and bloody struggle was much more than a minor war. About 4 per cent of the Maori population were killed as compared with under 2 per cent of New Zealand's population killed during the First World War. Such losses were appalling. An element of horror was added when the pressures of war converted Pai Marire (good and peaceful religion) from a pacifist adjustment cult into fanaticism. The term 'hauhau' (the battle cry of followers of the cult) sent a chill through the nation.

Kereopa was the most notorious member of the cult. He is remembered, wrongly, as the man who beheaded the Anglican missionary Carl Sylvius Volkner in his church at Opotiki. This

This imaginative picture of an assault on a Hauhau stronghold in the Taranaki shows how little credit was given to the Maori's sophisticated skills in the art of fortification. *Alexander Turnbull Library.*

action, along with Te Kooti's 'massacre' of 37 innocent Maori and 33 Europeans at Matawhero near Gisborne, have become imbedded in national mythology as examples of Maori excess. Yet these folk memories do not tell us that Kereopa had two daughters killed when the British burned Rangiaowhia on 21 February 1864.

Te Kooti's pursuers also committed atrocities. The Matawhero 'massacre'

was avenged a few days later in grim fashion at Ngatapa Hill near Gisborne when 120 of his followers were summarily executed. General Chute burned villages, destroyed crops, looted and shot prisoners during his pursuit of Titokowaru. Ropata Wahawaha (Major Kemp), the most famous of the 'loyalist' kupapa, did not take prisoners. A quick strike action into the Waikato became a damaging and vicious nine-year war.

The New Zealand wars produced three major results. First, they accelerated the alienation of Maori land. Second, Maori were confined to a smaller area and although the racial frontier was expanded the two races came to live in largely separate worlds. Third, they added complexity to the unusual pattern of race relations which unfolded in the colony because the Maori's heroic resistance had won a begrudging respect.

In 1864 Governor Grey gave in to pressure from ministers who were determined to punish 'rebels' and pay for the war by confiscating land. Soldier settlements were also promoted on the edge of Maori territory to cement British military domination. Some 3¼ million acres (1,300,000 hectares) in the Waikato, Bay of Plenty and Taranaki were confiscated from 'rebels', neutral and loyalist Maori alike but the Ngati Maniapoto lands

This engraving of Rangiriri reproduced in *Cassell's Picturesque Australasia* gave readers a totally misleading picture of Maori fortifications in the New Zealand wars. Rangiriri was not a fort at all, but a defensive line of earthworks. See below. *Alexander Turnbull Library.*

remained untouched and provided a base for the continuation of the King Movement. Eventually about a half of this land was returned and some compensation was paid in response to ongoing Maori protest. The unfortunate exercise did not pay for an expensive war. All it did was make Maori even more wary of Pakeha duplicity.

The Native Land Court established in 1865 promoted the amalgamation of Maori titles and accelerated land sales. By the time the Liberals came to power in 1891 the Maori had sold off 5 million acres (2 million hectares) of prime North Island Maori land to add to the 7 million acres (2,800,000 hectares) which had been sold before the wars. The Maori were left with about 11½ million acres (4,600,000 hectares), much of it marginal, less than half of the North Island's useable land.

Maori forced into more isolated districts in the central North Island, the East Coast, the area in the back of Wanganui and North Auckland responded to the advancing European frontier in different ways. Some tribes tried to cut themselves off from contact while others co-operated with government. Maori participation in seasonal agricultural tasks such as shearing and fencing increased but afterwards Maori labourers usually retreated to their pa. Some tribes coped better than others with adjusting to the loss of land and participating in the market economy. Outside racial frontier zones racial interaction decreased. Intermarriage continued but slowed.

As the physical separation of the races continued, the myth of the noble Maori, the most superior of all native peoples, took hold of the national psyche. What had formerly been viewed as arrogance was reinterpreted as courage. Maori were placed on a pedestal with such other martial peoples as the Sikhs, Pathans and Zulu. Elaborate racial hierarchies were devised under the influence of social

Rangiriri was a sophisticated, elaborately engineered defensive line of earthworks. It stretched for 300 metres. The defence consisted of a parapet of banked-up earth and a double ditch. The parapet was 4 to 7 metres high from the bottom of the ditch. *Alexander Turnbull Library.*

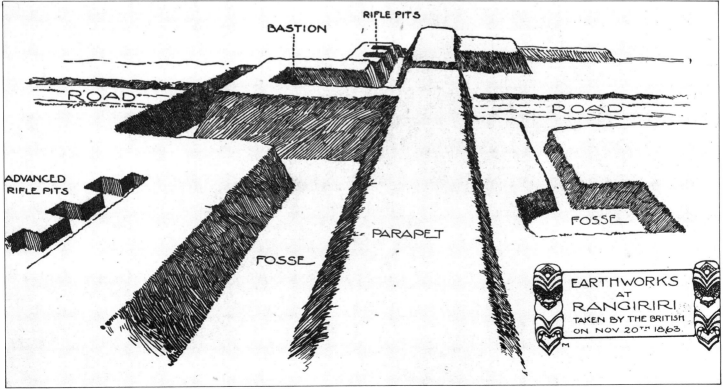

RIFLE PITS

BASTION

ROAD

ROAD

ADVANCED
RIFLE PITS

FOSSE

PARAPET

FOSSE

EARTHWORKS
AT
RANGIRIRI
TAKEN BY THE BRITISH
ON NOV 20TH 1863.

Darwinism. Some of these schemes were drawn up as the tree of man, in which the Maori were always placed at the top of the coloured races, immediately below such inferior caucasians as Slavs and Latins. In contrast, Australian Aborigines and Kalihari bushmen were placed at the base of the trunk. Chinese and pacifist Hindus were placed in the middle, just above black people, but well below the Maori.

Maori were still inferior second class citizens, but they were the best of all second class citizens and had the intellect and physical ability to elevate themselves into brown-skinned Britons. This belief was the greatest compliment which ethnocentric 19th-century Englishmen could pay any native people. Furthermore, the noble deeds of the Maori were to be celebrated and preserved in national history rather than obliterated from the national memory.

This view of the Maori was, of course, comfortable because it was generally believed that they would die out like all inferior peoples who came into conflict with superior Europeans. The Pakeha's task was to make the inevitable passing of a noble people as dignified as possible. To be fair to the European settlers, at least, there never was any attempt at genocide as happened in Tasmania or Argentina and no one ever tried to poison off whole tribes as happened in Australia.

Fortunately for Aotearoa, the Maori soon began to devise alternative forms of resistance to warfare. One truly extraordinary conciliatory gesture of the British settlers — establishing four Maori seats in the House of Representatives in 1867 — was taken up by the Maori while they set about developing more traditional structures to cope with limited military defeat and the loss of their land.

The surrender of the Ngai te Rangi tribe at Te Papa, Tauranga, 1864. Unlike some other artists of his time, Lieutenant Robley tried to picture battle scenes as realistically as possible. *National Museum.*

Captain Porter in the centre of the photograph poses with his Ngatai Maori auxiliaries outside a Gisborne stockade and blockhouse c. 1870. The wool shawl dress proved practical in the bush. *National Museum.*

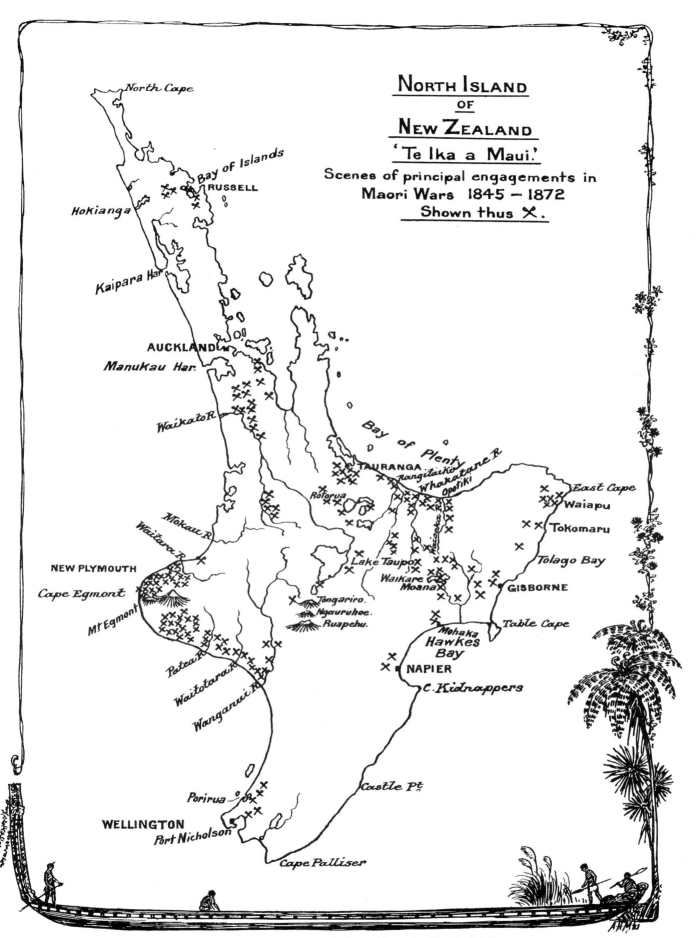

NORTH ISLAND
OF
NEW ZEALAND
'Te Ika a Maui.'
Scenes of principal engagements in
Maori Wars 1845 – 1872
Shown thus ✕.

North Cape
Bay of Islands
RUSSELL
HoKianga
Kaipara Har.
AUCKLAND
Manukau Har.
Waikato R.
Bay of Plenty
TAURANGA
Rangitaiki R.
Whakatane R.
Opotiki
Rotorua
East Cape
Waiapu
Tokomaru
Mokau R.
Tolago Bay
Waitara R.
Lake Taupo
Waikare
Moana
GISBORNE
NEW PLYMOUTH
Tongariro.
Cape Egmont
Ngauruhoe.
Ruapehu.
Table Cape
Mt Egmont
Mohaka
Hawkes
Bay
Patea R.
NAPIER
Waitotara R.
C. Kidnappers
Wanganui R.
Castle Pt
Porirua
WELLINGTON
Port Nicholson
Cape Palliser

James Cowan, *The New Zealand Wars*. *Alexander Turnbull Library*.

Link: From War to Refrigeration

The gold began to run out before military hostilities ceased. After depression set in during 1869, there was a desperate search for economic solutions. The new Colonial Treasurer, Julius Vogel, came up with a drastic proposal in his public works budget of 28 June 1870: borrowing on an unprecedented scale. He wanted to borrow £10 million over the next decade to fund a massive programme of public works and immigration.

Most New Zealanders responded enthusiastically to Vogel's plan. The impetus for development had to come from overseas and a large loan would obviously help New Zealand to shake off its image as the ugly duckling of the Australasian colonies. A few cautious politicians expressed concern over the size of the loan but no one questioned the concept. There was nothing unusual about borrowing by new colonies. Capital was critical to their development and all were forced to borrow to promote economic growth.

What was new was the scale of the loan which eventually doubled to £20 million. By 1880 New Zealand's per capita debt was higher than that of any other Australasian colony and several times higher than Canada's.

Vogel's bold plan was cited by contemporaries as a cause of the severe depression of the 1880s. Such an interpretation is, however, unfair because, even without the loan, New Zealand would have been affected by the major downturn in international economic activity. Rather, the loan exacerbated short-term economic problems while bringing mid- and long-term advantages. Later development would have been considerably hampered without the 1100 miles (1760 kilometres) of railway, 2500 miles (4000 kilometres) of road and numerous bridges built during the 1870s. Some 4000 miles (6500 kilometres) of telegraph poles and a link-up with the international telegraph cable in 1876 also assisted development.

Equally important, nearly 200,000 immigrants helped double New Zealand's population. Financial institutions flourished during the artificially induced boom and New Zealand won a reputation as a 'working man's paradise'. The cumbersome provincial system was done away with in 1876 in an endeavour to secure more favourable terms on the London loan market. Vogel's imagination and faith in the future development of the colony helped hasten economic recovery once the international economy picked up in the mid-1890s.

Unfortunately, provincial jealousies undermined Vogel's concept of a national estate. The interest bill became a serious burden and there was no attempt at any kind of cost benefit analysis. Roads, bridges and railways were built in the wrong places. Branch lines, for example, tended to run onto the properties of wealthy landowning politicians rather than systematically linking the economic hinterland to the ports. Generally the wealthier Otago and Canterbury provinces gained more than the less developed North

Island with the notable exception of Hawke's Bay. Easy credit also encouraged speculation and land values soared to unrealistic levels. The personal indebtedness of both large and small landowners increased dramatically along with the national debt.

Many of these problems were offset by the composition of the immigrants who arrived in such large numbers. About 115,000 came from Britain, Scandinavia and Germany under the government's assisted immigration scheme. A further 60,000 found their own way to win the high wage of £2 a week for unskilled labourers. (Such a wage was nearly double that paid in Britain.) Most of the 'unassisted' group came from Australia.

Initially assisted migrants received a very bad press. Older settlers labelled them 'certificated scum' and everything from an increase in drunkenness to the economic depression was blamed on their arrival. Such condemnation was quite unjustified. The migrants of the 1870s were generally hardworking, law abiding and highly literate, despite the fact that most belonged to such 'low status' occupations as agricultural and general labourers, domestic servants and 'navvies' (road and railway builders). The major difference from earlier waves of migration was the absence of members of the lesser gentry and the professional classes. The 1870s also saw the first major influx of single women. Otherwise they were very similar to earlier groups: about 60 per cent of them were male and young.

The 4500 Scandinavians (mainly Danes), 2000 Germans, 34,000 Irish and 22,000 Scots who came as assisted migrants were also hardworking and generally successful settlers. Some from cities such as Dublin, Glasgow and London found the rigour and isolation of pioneering in rural New Zealand too demanding and retreated to the main towns, but most thrived on their new found independence. There were few criminals and the large numbers of single women boosted the marriage rate and hastened the development of family life. The rate of drunkenness and violent crime fell dramatically as a result.

Most migrants were keen to establish a more equitable social and economic order and they soon found plenty to protest about as large areas of prime farming land were converted into huge freehold estates during the 1870s. Even though there was also considerable subdivision during the same decade, the trend towards monopoly dominated. By 1890 some 584 individuals and companies owned 56 per cent of New Zealand's freehold land.

Huge profits were made on downland country by combining wool growing with grain farming, some estates making up to £30,000 in good years. By contrast woolgrowing in high country areas was more marginal and failure more common. In the east coast lowland areas grand houses were built and exclusive schools established. Some big landowners of Canterbury and Hawke's Bay in particular aped the lifestyle of the English gentry and carefully controlled the marriages of their children. As a group they held considerable but never total political power. The emergence of this wealthy and conspicuous elite was deeply resented by the new arrivals. They had migrated to escape the evils of a class-dominated society and were determined to prevent their reduplication in the 'Britain of the South'.

The other key development of the 1870s was the introduction of a national system of free, secular and compulsory primary schooling in 1877. This innovation had a revolutionary impact on everyday life by removing a major source of free labour, although the effect was not felt immediately because truancy levels remained high until the 1890s and it took time to build schools and train teachers. Nevertheless, the already high literacy levels rose rapidly from around 70 per cent to over 90 per cent by 1890. As a result newspaper circulation grew twice as fast as the population between 1870 and 1890. Support for elementary schooling was widespread, since parents saw its introduction as improving the prospects of their children. There was little interest in higher education but it was widely hoped that compulsory education would make New Zealanders more efficient farmers, businessmen, artisans and workers.

The Maori population was just be-

Rivers, particularly when in flood, caused considerable headaches to settlers. This panorama was shot south of Greytown by Bragge after a flood in December 1875. *Wellington Harbour Board.*

Life on board an emigrant ship, 1875. In the 1870s 180,000 new settlers emigrated to New Zealand. The three-month journey called for patience and some fortitude. *Alexander Turnbull Library.*

Part of Taranaki chief and prophet Te Whiti's community at Parihaka photographed by Dunedin's Burton brothers in 1885. A street lamp can be seen to the left just above the roofs. *National Museum.*

ginning to adjust to the painful reality of European domination. In Taranaki Te Whiti o Rongomai led the first post-war non-military resistance movement. The Lutheran-educated chief practised a form of non-violent non-co-operation similar to the Indian pacifist Mahatma Gandhi. Like Gandhi, he was also deeply concerned with improving the health of his people and established an efficient sanitation system in his model pa at Parihaka. He obstructed the survey and roading of confiscated land for settlement and provoked the fury of the government. In one of the tawdriest instances of Pakeha mistreatment of the Maori, Te Whiti and his leading followers were arrested and imprisoned by Native Minister John Bryce and his 'brave twelve hundred' soldiers.

Te Whiti's example suggested that the old capacity to adjust and survive was very much alive. Hope was restored in several communities and the Maori birth rate began to recover in the 1880s.

10. 1882 Colonial Entrepreneurs: The First Successful Shipment of Refrigerated Meat

ON 24 May 1882 the 1320-tonne sailing ship SS *Dunedin* arrived in London with the first cargo of frozen meat despatched from New Zealand. The specially constructed freezing chamber held 22 pig carcasses, 3347 carcasses of mutton and 491 of lamb. A few frozen hams, rabbits and turkeys were also on board along with 2256 sheep tongues and 246 kegs of butter. The mutton and lamb arrived in especially good condition despite the long 98-day voyage and a difficult time in the tropics.

London salesmen were pleased with the quality of the produce and *The Times* remarked that the voyage was 'prodigious'. The lamb sold for 7½ pence a pound and the mutton averaged 6¾ pence, more than twice the price they fetched in New Zealand. John Swan and Company, major buyers in the Smithfield market, told the press that there was 'a bright future' for New Zealand as a producer of quality lamb and beef. English farmers were so worried by the glowing reports that a request was made in the House of Lords that meat from the colony should be labelled 'New Zealand' to prevent its sale as an English product.

Much hard work lay behind this epoch-making voyage. William Soltau Davidson, the astute and farsighted manager of the Glasgow-based New Zealand and Australian Land Company had begun negotiations in March 1880 with the Albion Shipping Company and the American refrigeration manufacturers Bell Coleman and Company. The absence of a refrigerated works in New Zealand posed real problems as did the unavailability of a steamship. Davidson solved these difficulties by deciding to fit a Bell and Coleman freezing unit on a sailing ship.

The freezing chamber was installed in the SS *Dunedin* in Glasgow between May and August 1881 and the New Zealand and Australian Land Company agreed to supply 7500 sheep from the crossbred Lincoln and Leicester flocks of the Totara estate. The sheep would be slaughtered on the estate and chilled before being sent on the five-hour train journey to Port Chalmers. Five butchers were employed to process 500 carcasses a day. Loading would take several weeks and the whole unwieldy operation was very risky.

The SS *Dunedin* arrived on 28 November 1881 and killing began immediately. Disaster struck on 12 December when a crank shaft in the freezing chamber broke and 1000 carcasses had to be sold off locally. It took some time for a replacement to be shipped in and operations did not recommence until 14 January 1882. Such a lengthy delay caused the venture to lose money and it only continued because of the ample capital resources of the New Zealand and Australian Land Company and Davidson's determination to see the experiment through.

Loading was eventually completed

The refrigerated vessel *Dunedin* leaving Port Chalmers for London in February 1882 carrying the first cargo in what would become a huge frozen meat export industry. *Alexander Turnbull Library.*

A Manawatu settler's first home. Such dwellings were often makeshift affairs. *Palmerston North Public Library.*

on 14 February and the ship sailed the following day. Captain Whitson and chief engineer, Alex MacAllister, experienced serious technical problems. Sparks generated by the freezer constantly threatened the sails which caught fire on one occasion; freezing chambers were more suited to steamships. The heat and still air of the tropics made it difficult to maintain air circulation and the freezer was only kept going by MacAllister's and Whitson's constant vigilance. The captain well deserved the £20 bonus paid by the Albion Shipping Company and the £100 paid by the New Zealand and Australian Land Company when he delivered his cargo in good condition.

Another Scot, Thomas Brydone, who managed the Totara estate, also played a vital role in ensuring that the loading was completed successfully. New Zealand's Agent-General, Sir Francis Dillon Bell, helped by ensuring that the venture was well publicised in London and alerted major meat-buying companies to the experiment. But more than anything else, it

is Davidson's vision of New Zealand as a country of family farms specialising in intensive stock raising and his extraordinary organisational ability which explains why the New Zealand and Australian Land Company stole a march on its Dunedin-based rival, the New Zealand Refrigerating Company. Ironically, it is Brydone's contribution which has been commemorated by a large and conspicuous monument outside Oamaru, while recognition of Davidson's input has been confined to a thesis and a scholarly article.

In this instance it was a large privately owned company which was responsible for converting New Zealand from a one- to a three-staple export economy. The state allowed the biggest private landowner in New Zealand to take the risk before offering much assistance. A Stock Branch was created in 1881 under the auspices of the Colonial Secretary to improve control of sheep scab and a dairy expert was appointed in 1883, but the fully fledged Department of Agriculture was not established until 1892 when the infant frozen meat and dairy industries had proven their worth. During the 1880s these new industries were left to fend for themselves.

The immediate impact of refrigeration was not great. Only big estate owners could afford to hire ships to transport frozen cargo and there was no appreciable upturn of prices until 1896. As late as 1891 only 200,000 tonnes of frozen meat and 20,000 tonnes of dairy produce were exported and there were 21 freezing works, 1581 freezing workers and 491 specialist dairy farmers. Yet within a decade meat exports would double in quantity and value while butter exports grew five times in quantity and six times in value. Butter factory numbers exploded from 74 in 1891 to 247 by 1901. Wool still earned 45 per cent of export revenue in 1891 as against the combined 10 per cent of frozen meat and dairy products. Within the following decade wool's share had fallen to a third of export receipts while frozen meat and dairy products earned nearly a quarter of export income.

It took time for New Zealand lamb and butter to prove their worth. The take-off of the new industries also depended upon the recovery of the troubled British economy. Once that recovery occurred a much bigger market opened up as the standard of living of the British working class rose from the mid-1890s. For the first time this large group of consumers could regularly afford meat, butter and cheese.

The cheapest meat available was jerked and frozen beef from Uruguay and Argentina and frozen lamb from New Zealand. It soon became clear that the New Zealand product was of superior quality and it won a larger share of this fast growing market. New Zealand butter and cheese were also markedly cheaper than Danish products and won a reputation for reliable quality. Strict quality control measures introduced by the Liberal government and executed by the new Department of Agriculture brought marked improvements in standards. Regulation from cowshed through creamery and dairy factory to port of export meant that New Zealand butter and cheese were entrenched sellers on the London market by 1900.

Many historians have exaggerated the influence of refrigeration on the pattern of land settlement. A technological innovation alone did not enable small and medium-sized farms to replace the big estates as the key unit of production. Much more than the magic of applied science was involved in this vital transformation. Subdivision was underway before refrigeration and both smaller farmers and big estate owners benefited from the increased sale of oats and wheat to Victoria. These more modest operators achieved a limited viability during the 1870s and always heavily outnumbered the big property owners.

New Zealand farmers had played an active role in local government from the beginnings of settlement. The new system of county administration introduced in 1877 was generally controlled by farmers operating units of several hundred acres rather than by big estate owners. After 1890 New Zealand farmers also became very active at the parliamentary level.

Many rural labourers aspired to become farmers at some future date and supported the call for closer settlement. Small town businessmen wanted to benefit from subdivision of land and added their voice to the call to 'burst up' the big estates.

The Liberal government was a government of small farmers and small townspeople and of urban working men and women. Such a government naturally reacted favourably to the demands of rural voters and undertook a whole range of actions (see Chapter 11) to promote closer settlement. The effects of the Liberals' land reform programme should not be exaggerated but there can be little doubt that positive action accelerated the move to more intensive forms of land usage. Such a change would probably have happened without the land reform programme, given the structure of rural society, the aspirations of the majority of settlers and the expanding market, but strong state action ensured that the change occurred and that it happened sooner rather than later.

Refrigeration had another major consequence: it locked New Zealand into producing three export staples for a single market — London. Strong economic ties with Australia and the west coast of the United States of America were largely dismantled by 1900. In 1886 about 20 per cent of New Zealand's exports went to Australia but that figure had fallen to about 8 per cent by 1901. Both the Australian and American markets only became important again after Britain entered the EEC in 1973.

Tariffs erected by Victoria and the United States from 1890 stifled New Zealand's growing textile industry and the country became almost totally reliant upon exports of wool, meat, butter and cheese for its economic survival. Alternative primary industries such as fishing, horticulture and viticulture were largely ignored as export earners once a new prosperity was achieved on narrow and insecure economic foundations. New Zealand became more colonial in the economic sense after the turn of the century and it was to remain little more than Britain's outlying farm until 1973.

There were not many economic alternatives. An absence of iron ore ruled out heavy industrialisation, while protectionism instituted by such newly emerging industrial powers as the United States and Germany severely reduced the potential for lighter industries. The internal market was also too small to sustain anything more than the production of such necessities as soap and building materials and luxuries like boots and beer. High wages and the extreme distance from overseas markets made it easier to import most manufactured goods. English manufacturers also saw to it that New Zealand entry to the British market was conditional upon buying British goods and maintaining colonial tariffs at relatively low levels.

W. B. Sutch's lamentation that New Zealand lost an opportunity to achieve economic take-off in the 1890s by concentrating exclusively on the development of its pastoral industries for export pays little heed to the prevailing economic reality. Refrigeration offered a new economic opportunity and New Zealanders seized it with both hands. They became world leaders in industries where the rivalry was not as intense as in viticulture and horticulture. On the other hand Sutch is correct in pointing out that other potentially rich resources were largely ignored. New Zealanders virtually

Clydesdales with a load of woolbales, Kurow, North Otago. *Alexander Turnbull Library.*

A town milk supply farm at Temuka in the late 1890s. *Alexander Turnbull Library.*

turned their back on the sea which produced food that most people wanted. Serious anomalies were built into the fishing industry which we are still struggling to untangle. Forestry was ignored as a replaceable resource until the 1920s. By then most of the easily millable timber had been ripped out. The amazing capacity of the country to grow a vast range of top quality fruit and vegetables was only realised in a few areas.

Specialisation brought spectacular short-term rewards but created long-term environmental and aesthetic problems as well as placing the new prosperity on too narrow a base. At one extreme, marginal country best suited to growing timber was stripped of forest and the systematic destruction of unique rain forest was begun in earnest. At the other end of the spectrum prime country best suited to specialised crops was covered in lush green grass. Smoke from huge fires lit to burn off the bush cleared to reveal a monotonous landscape of endless pad-

docks covered in charred tree stumps.

Such a dramatic transformation warmed the hearts of most contemporaries who wanted the bush replaced by the world's most productive farmland. They were unaware of future problems of secondary growth and erosion. Prosperity was welcome after 15 years of depression and they pursued that prosperity with enthusiasm and energy. At last it seemed that a majority of settlers would realise their vision of becoming independent landowners in country, small town or suburb.

Dependency also brought more intangible losses. The healthy, vigorous nationalism which emerged during the 1880s and 1890s soon gave way to a slavish adherence to British models. Politicians, bureaucrats and intellectuals during the 1890s had looked all over the world for solutions to problems. Danes were consulted when the dairy industry was founded and an Italian-Yugoslav with Victorian experience (Romeo Bragato) was brought in to expand the wine industry. North American, German, Swiss and Argentinian models were also given careful consideration.

Such borrowing was more than im-

itation because overseas precedents were considerably adapted to meet the peculiarities of the New Zealand situation. John McKenzie's Department of Agriculture, for example, incorporated aspects of its British, North American and Australian counterparts as well as developing distinctive New Zealand approaches of its own. George Hogben searched all around the world in his efforts at overhauling the education system early in the new century. William Pember Reeves and his undersecretary Edward Tregear corresponded regularly with British, French and American intelligentsia when introducing a wide-ranging series of labour reforms.

But all this changed in the new century as New Zealand moved economically closer to London than to Sydney or Los Angeles.

Guessing what would have happened without refrigeration and the open British market is of course fraught with difficulties, but one thing is quite certain — the success of the *Dunedin's* experimental voyage changed the pattern of the colony's economic development irrevocably.

A portable steam engine driving a threshing mill c. 1899. *Palmerston North Public Library.*

Mutton slaughtermen at the Belfast Freezing Works. *Alexander Turnbull Library.*

11. 1889 Sweating: Work or Slavery?
Reverend Waddell Preaches on the 'Sin of Cheapness'

O N 30 September 1888 the Reverend Rutherford Waddell delivered a sermon to the St Andrew's congregation of central Dunedin on the 'sin of cheapness'. It was to prove the most influential sermon in New Zealand history.

The small Ulsterman of Scots-Irish parentage was well known as a Christian socialist and an advocate of the social gospel. He had already established a Friendly Society to help his poorer parishioners cope with problems caused by the depression of the 1880s. Always a fierce social critic, he urged his congregation not to commit the 'sin of cheapness'. Constant seeking of bargains only forced down wages, causing misery to working people. Dunedin was fast becoming like London where middlemen 'sweated' labour to enhance their profits. Women were the most common victims of this iniquitous practice; Waddell cited the case of a widow who was paid 2 pennies for finishing a pair of trousers.

These disclosures shocked his listeners, some of whom wrote to the *Otago Daily Times*. Their letters caught the attention of the paper's managing director, George Fenwick, who sent reporters out to investigate the operation of the factory system in Dunedin. This inquiry revealed many abuses and a full-scale scandal broke in the early part of 1889.

Journalists discovered that the worst abuses were being perpetrated on women working in the textile industry and boys involved in shoe making and printing. During the 1880s big pastoralists and urban merchants switched their capital from farming into textile manufacture to offset falling wool prices. Several large mills employing

Reverend Rutherford Waddell (1849-1932), the Presbyterian minister and social reformer, whose sermon on the 'sin of cheapness' sparked off a sweating scandal. *St Andrew's Church, Dunedin.*

up to 600 people sprang up around Dunedin. High levels of male unemployment forced more women out to work; by 1890 3000 women were employed in Dunedin.

Because women earned much less than men, they helped employers reduce costs. Most worked long hours for low rates of pay in dirty, noisy and sometimes dangerous conditions. A 72-hour week made up of six 13-hour days was common and the standard rate for such long hours was a meagre 9 shillings a week. Factory workers, however, were better off than those who took work home on a piece rate basis.

Outworkers were very poorly paid.

One bag maker was paid 2 shillings for stitching a gross (144) of 25-pound bags. She in turn employed girls whom she paid 7½ pence per gross of 25-pound bags. After paying all her expenses the woman's income had been reduced from £1 2s 6d to 18 shillings a week while her girls were paid the merest pittance.

These revelations won woman textile workers wide support and led to the establishment of the Tailoresses' Union in July 1889. Backed by Waddell and the Seamen's Union, the tailoresses immediately succeeded in raising wages and improving conditions. The take home system of piece work was virtually brought to an end. Foundation secretary Harriet Morison's sterling work soon won her a reputation as a hard negotiator and determined champion of women workers. Public support for the new union was widespread. In Dunedin, newspaper editorials and local notables compared their brave tailoresses with the courageous London match girls who also established a union in 1889.

Boys were increasingly being employed to replace men especially in printing and shoe making. Working conditions were cramped, poorly lit and often smelly, and apprenticeship contracts were blatantly broken. In some printing businesses one man worked with a dozen or more boys who were hired and fired at will. Twelve- and 13-year-old boys worked more than 12 hours a day, six days a week, for wages of 8 shillings. In one workshop boys were allowed to use the toilet only once a day, at 10 a.m. Orthodox unions had no jurisdiction over such practices; a comprehensive new labour code was needed to control the abuse of boy labour.

The Royal Commission promised by the 'conservative' Atkinson government in June 1889 was finally appointed on 28 January 1890 and reported on 5 May. The majority report, while denying the existence of 'sweating', conceded that many abuses were evident, especially in Dunedin, and called for a comprehensive new Factory Act to end the exploitation of female and boy labour. The introduction of boards of conciliation and arbitration was also recommended, along with the establishment of Bureaux of Statistics to collect reliable data on New Zealand industry. A system of indenturing employers to apprentices was proposed to solve the problem of apprenticeship breaking.

Rutherford Waddell, D. P. Fisher and Colin Allan added a minority report which claimed there was ample evidence that 'sweating' as defined by Beatrice Potter existed in New Zealand. There were: '(1) overcrowded or insanitary workshops or living rooms, (2) long and irregular hours, (3) constantly falling prices and low wages.' And unless 'prompt legislative action' was taken these 'evils' would strike deep roots in the new colony.

Working men shared the concerns of the writers of the minority report. Formerly high wages had fallen to British levels and seemed liable to fall further. The once proud boast that New Zealand working men were blessed by 'eight hours' work, eight hours' sleep, eight hours' play and eight bob [shillings] a day' sounded hollow. Increasingly it became replaced by a lament that the lot of manual workers in New Zealand was little different from that of the hard pressed London dockers.

There was less public sympathy for the problems of working men than for women and boys. Only the *Otago Workman*, edited by rumbustious republican, Sam Lister, expressed much support for the struggles of unskilled working men. The Seamen's Union founded in 1880 battled on alone while apathy led to the rapid demise of the Otago Trades and Labour Council set up in 1885. The seamen won a victory in 1888 when they ran their own ship in competition with the Northern Shipping Company.

This success inspired the unskilled to set up the first large union of the unskilled on 28 October 1889. The

Roslyn Woollen Mills, Dunedin. *Alexander Turnbull Library.*

Maritime Council, a federation of seamen, wharf labourers, lumpers, railwaymen, storemen and coalminers, was deliberately modelled on the 'new' unskilled unions being formed in Britain.

A dispute across the Tasman pulled the Maritime Council into industrial strife in August 1890. Even before the struggle between Australian seamen and the shipping companies broke into open conflict, strikes were called by coalminers at Shag Point in May and printers in Christchurch soon after. Railway workers went out in June. The miners won but the printers and railwaymen were beaten before the Maritime Council struck in August. Although the Council had grown to a membership of over 20,000 it was not big enough to take on the combined strength of the shipping companies and the government. By 10 November the strikers were forced to capitulate and the union movement was smashed.

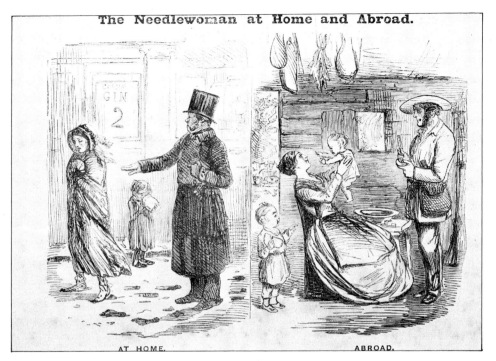

The Needlewoman at Home and Abroad.

AT HOME. ABROAD.

This *Punch* cartoon of 1850 hints at why sweating in New Zealand, especially among women and children, became such an issue in the 1890s. Immigrants came to New Zealand to escape the evils of the old world. *Alexander Turnbull Library.*

St George (with the face of Harriet Morison) slays the sweating monster. *New Zealand Observer, 25 June 1892*

The public and some politicians were very critical of the strikers — industrial militancy was regarded as an old world evil on a par with sweating. There was no place in New Zealand for either exploitation of labour or class conflict. Support for the strikers was confined to skilled working men and urban radicals so that despite the ultimate defeat, important political links were forged between the unskilled, the so-called 'labour aristocracy' and some politicians. In Dunedin and Christchurch a small Labour Party was established which ran ordinary working men as parliamentary candidates for the first time. Five of these men won seats in the December election. They were a boot maker, a boot operative, a brass finisher, a carpenter and a tailor. An informal alliance was also made between working men and the 'Liberal' group of candidates led by the radical journalist John Ballance.

The election of 1890 was a watershed in New Zealand history although it took until 1891 for a governing party to emerge when the five Labour members threw in their lot with the 33 Liberals and seven independent small farmer MPs. So was formed New Zealand's first modern political party, the Liberal Party.

It always was an unlikely alliance of left and right of centre, of city, small town and country, and of working men, lesser professionals and small town businessmen. Tensions between the frequently opposing interests of these groups eventually tore it apart but initially it was united by opposition to the old oligarchy of big estate owners and wealthy merchants. Ballance also won over working men by his sympathetic attitude. His decision to give his Minister of Labour, the very able William Pember Reeves, ample scope for experimentation and innovation further increased the Liberals' popularity with working men.

The sweating scandals of the 1880s had a significant impact on the Liberals' policies, with Reeves passing a mass of laws between 1891 and 1894 to improve the lot of labouring people. Hours were shortened and a half-day holiday made compulsory. Conditions of work were strictly monitored by an army of inspectors employed by a new Department of Labour. Truck Acts ensured that workers were paid in cash rather than kind and Labour Bureaux were set up to help the unemployed. After Reeves left to become Agent-General in London in 1896 his energetic undersecretary, Edward Tregear, continually improved the administration of Reeves' protective legislation.

The centrepiece of Reeves' industrial reforms was the introduction in 1894 of a compulsory system of Arbitration and Conciliation which remained the basis of New Zealand

industrial relations down to 1986. This system of taking industrial disputes to an independent court worked well at first and gave New Zealand 12 years of industrial peace. The success prompted Californian Henry Demarest Lloyd to write a book about New Zealand entitled *A Country without Strikes.*

Reeves' new system revitalised the shattered union movement. He actively encouraged the formation of new unions to avoid the trauma of 1890. Like other Fabian Socialists he wished to do away with class conflict altogether and hoped to make New Zealand a harmonious, one-class, roughly equal society. Most workers were happy with the new arrangement at first because limited security and protection was preferable to the open, uncontrolled class battles of the late 1880s.

The question remains: why did the problem of sweating, which was largely confined to one city, have such a widespread impact? The answer seems to be that the prevailing climate of opinion was receptive to the call for reform of working conditions. The severe depression of the late 1880s created a climate in which moral panics and crusades flourished. Constant reference was made in newspapers and at public meetings to such related problems as drunkenness, larrikinism (juvenile delinquency), smoking and prostitution, as well as to the abuse of female and child labour. New Zealanders were also growing alarmed at the incidence of disease and insanity in their new Eden.

Organisations that attempted to address these problems proliferated in the late 1880s. The Women's Christian Temperance Union, the Anti-Smoking League and the Society for the Protection of Women and Children (the Auckland branch added 'Animals') were established to halt the breakdown of the family and the spread of old evils. In Dunedin the Amenities Society was confronted the problem of urban degeneration. Free kindergartens were established in 1889 to provide childcare for working mothers.

Heading for the first issue of *Labour*. Although planned it was never published. The small illustrations represent the unions behind the magazine. *Alexander Turnbull Library.*

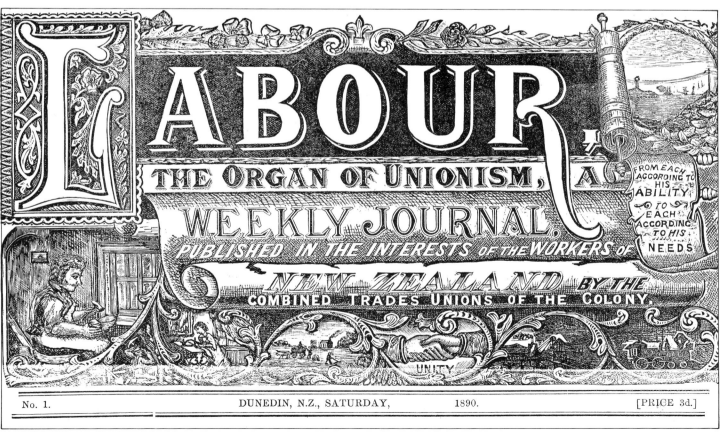

No. 1.   DUNEDIN, N.Z., SATURDAY,   1890.   [PRICE 3d.]

Significantly this service was started in St Andrew's Hall. The Shetland-born free-thinking radical Sir Robert Stout tried to drag boys off the streets by arranging night classes in which they would be introduced to Shakespeare and the world of the intellect. Much to his chagrin but to no one else's surprise, the boys stayed on the streets. Despite such instances of naïveté, New Zealanders seemed to experience at this time what W.H. Oliver has called 'a loss of colonial innocence'.

The climate of opinion that generated the sweating scandals and labour reforms also made way for significant changes to land reform. The shift from large estates to smaller accelerated. More intensive farming was already under way when the Liberals took office and among the other goals proposed in their 1890 election campaign they had promised to 'burst up the big estates' and 'put the small man on the land'. As Minister of Lands and Agriculture it was John McKenzie's task to put these

Two formidable Liberal politicians Prime Minister Richard John Seddon (left) and his Minister of Lands John McKenzie are drawn quarrelling over a minor issue. *National Archives.*

A pensioner couple outside their home. Seddon's pension provided £18 a year, less than a quarter of the annual earnings of a male factory worker. *Alexander Turnbull Library.*

promises into practice. The more extreme land reformers, influenced by American Henry George and English Liberal John Stuart Mill, called for a single land tax on land or land nationalisation.

His Land and Income Tax Act of 1891 taxed large landholdings but was so modest as to be ineffective. In 1892 he introduced the lease in perpetuity scheme which gave Crown leasees a 999-year lease on a low fixed rent. This offered farmers lacking capital all the advantages of freehold at a bargain price. McKenzie went further than any Australian state government in obtaining power to compel owners of large estates to sell their land for subdivision, but compulsory repurchase was invoked only 13 times between 1894 and 1912. The Lands for Settlement Act of 1894 enabled the purchase of large underused estates for subdivision and between 1893 and 1912 the government bought 200 estates covering 1,300,000 acres (525,200 hectares). An Advances to Settlers Act provided cheap credit to buy stock, seed and machinery and to erect buildings and fences.

There was a widespread desire to achieve a balance between the right to own property and the need for a reasonable degree of social justice and equality. In this sense, McKenzie's land resettlement programme and Reeves' legislation complemented each other.

The Liberal vision of a nation run for hardworking, self-made, ordinary people rather than for well-educated large landowners brought about a dramatic change in the style of New Zealand politics. Richard John Seddon, who took over as leader in 1893 after Ballance died, turned ordinariness into a political asset. Loud, rough and with only an elementary education, Seddon sold himself as an ordinary bloke who understood the needs of ordinary people.

Seddon's humanitarianism resulted in a number of welfare measures to improve the lot of the hardworking and deserving poor. Wages and conditions for labourers and miners were regulated and the Old Age Pensions Act of 1898 provided a modest pension of 7s 6d a week for a small group of elderly poor who had lived in New Zealand for 25 years. Registration of nurses in 1901 and midwives in 1904 led to improvements in childcare as did the establishment of St Helen's Hospitals in which working class mothers could have their babies.

The Liberals' actions earned New Zealand a reputation as the world's 'social laboratory'. Several overseas intellectuals visited New Zealand to view the programme at first hand.

Working conditions in an engineering workshop c.1900. *Trevor Plaisted Collection.*

From France came Albert Métin and André Siegfried, along with the American progressives H. D. Lloyd and Professor Frank Parsons and the English Fabian Socialists Beatrice and Sidney Webb. They concluded that a democratic rather than a socialist order had been established and that the government programme of reform was 'sans doctrine'. Pragmatism was the keynote of the new administration. The vision shaping their actions was modest and limited and likely to produce conservative rather than radical results. Siegfried predicted that a respectable and prosperous peasantry would inhabit the countryside and prevent any revolutionary developments in the towns. Capitalism was controlled and tempered by the Liberals' reforms but it was not challenged.

All agreed that the radical moment of 1890-93 soon faded. After 1894 most energy seemed to go into consolidating the gains made in those years and very little new happened once Reeves left for London. One radical action which had particularly caught the attention of all these observers was the granting of the women's franchise in 1893.

12. 1893 New Zealand First: Women Win the Vote

I N *State Experiments in Australia and New Zealand* published in 1902 the former Liberal cabinet minister turned historian William Pember Reeves wrote: 'So, one fine morning of September 1893, the women of New Zealand woke up and found themselves enfranchised.' Ever since New Zealanders have congratulated themselves on being the first nation to grant women the vote. (Australia was the second nation to enfranchise women, in 1901.)

Reeves argues that women's franchise was a fortuitous by-product of the temperance movement to ban the sale of alcohol. This interpretation held sway among most male historians down to the 1950s. Before then the most serious challenge came from Lady Anna Stout in a lecture celebrating the 25th anniversary of the reform. Lady Stout declared that 30,000 women had signed a petition in support of the vote for women, not for prohibition. She further argued that both women and male politicians played a vital role in bringing about this important reform.

A more detailed study published by Patricia Grimshaw in 1972 conceded that the franchise movement used the Women's Christian Temperance Union as an organisational springboard and that the two movements were linked, but also demonstrated conclusively that the franchise movement had a separate life of its own.

Women's franchise in New Zealand was a cause with a long history. It went back to Mary Ann Muller in Nelson in the 1850s, became a major issue during the 1870s and easily pre-dated the establishment of the Women's Christian Temperance Union in 1885. Male politicians became interested in 1877

Kate Sheppard (1848-1934) played a crucial part in the success of the suffrage campaign. She was described as 'the woman whose life and person made the deepest mark upon New Zealand's history.' *Auckland Public Library.*

when Sir George Grey's government of 1877-79 advocated the introduction of a full women's franchise. Women ratepayers had already been granted the vote in local body elections in 1875 and were entitled to vote for and sit on school committees with the introduction of compulsory education in 1877. Universities had always been open to women; Kate Edger was the first woman to graduate in 1877. Granting the full vote seemed a logical progression.

Grey, Stout and Sir William Fox were all convinced Liberals who had read J. S. Mill's *Subjection of Women* published in 1869. Their views were well in advance of many of their

colleagues yet they won a surprising amount of support from many conservatives such as John Hall, a self-made large runholder from Canterbury. All these men believed that women were morally and spiritually superior to men. Participation by women in politics would, therefore, raise the tone in Parliament and on the hustings. Nineteenth-century electioneering was often accompanied by riotous and drunken behaviour which would supposedly be inhibited by the presence of women. These conservatives also thought that women, being more civilised than men, would instinctively support cautious conservative government rather than radical and disruptive change.

Hall led a ministry between 1879 and 1882. He introduced a women's franchise bill in 1879 but it was defeated, like that of Grey and Stout in 1878, by social conservatives from both sides of the House. Little happened between 1882 and 1887 apart from the introduction of the important Married Women's Property Act in 1884, which enabled married women to own property in their own right; previously all of a woman's property passed to her husband upon marriage. Women also won the right to vote for licensing committees in 1882 and for Hospital and Charitable Aids Boards in 1885. Then, in 1887, the generally ineffectual government led by Vogel and Stout introduced a women's suffrage bill which nearly passed the House.

Vogel himself was an enthusiastic supporter of the women's franchise. Initially his bill was well received and a clear majority in the House of Representatives was in favour. Seddon, the most determined and consistent oppo-

New Zealand women voting for the first time. *Alexander Turnbull Library.*

nent of women gaining the vote, was alarmed and tampered with the bill in its committee stage. He inserted a clause that the vote should be limited to women property owners knowing full well that such a restriction was unacceptable to both Liberal MPs and the women's movement. The bill was defeated by 22 votes to 19.

The matter was raised again in 1890. Now some MPs were afraid that women would vote against them for opposing universal franchise in the past. Also attempts to limit the franchise to married women or those who had matriculated were unacceptable to the more committed Liberal members. Divisions within government ranks brought about a predictable defeat.

While the male politicians talked the Women's Christian Temperance Union (WCTU) organised a campaign. The WCTU was founded in 1884 in Invercargill. Then after a visit from the United States of Mary Clement Leavitt in 1885 branches quickly sprang up throughout the country. Although it was established as a temperance movement, the vote for women soon became one of the WCTU's chief goals. In part it was influenced by the ideas of the American feminist Mary Colclough who, writing under the pseudonym Polly Plum, had caused quite a stir in Auck-

land during the 1870s.

As New Zealand's first nationally organised women's society, the WCTU battled for a wide range of women's issues. The union promoted improved women's health through dress reform and better nutrition for wives and mothers. It campaigned for equality in marriage and for more support and protection for mothers and children. Some of its causes were anything but genteel. Members called for the age of consent to be raised from 12 to 16 to prevent sexual abuse of children and sought an end to prostitution. They wanted the blatantly discriminatory Contagious Diseases Act, which applied only to women as suspected carriers of venereal disease, repealed. Collectively, the WCTU's protests were an attack on the Victorian double standard.

Early leaders of the WCTU tended to be unmarried women or older married women with grown children. Most, like the temperance movement in general, had connections with the non-conformist denominations. This very visible leadership and the advanced and sometimes daring nature of the organisation's views soon earned it a reputation for 'eccentricity'. Yet, despite constant abuse from some male politicians and journalists, the strength and determination of these

women won much support from the public and the majority of male politicians alike. Harriet Morison of the Tailoresses' Union, Learmonth Dalrymple, the staunch Dunedin-based advocate of secondary education for girls, and Kate Edger, by now a headmistress of a Nelson girls' school, were already well known. Katherine Wilson (Kate) Sheppard, who became undisputed leader of the WCTU by the late 1880s, was even more formidable.

The Scots born 39-year-old was appointed foundation Franchise Superintendent in 1887. She was already notorious as a proponent of equal status in marriage, an advocate of children's rights and one of the first woman cyclists. She soon saw that every WCTU branch appointed one person to concentrate exclusively on suffrage agitation. An expert propagandist, she tirelessly wrote articles, distributed pamphlets and delivered lectures all over the country. Her forceful personality persuaded several reluctant newspaper editors to print her articles and won her the support of several prominent politicians, including Sir John Hall. Charges that the WCTU was full of eccentric old ladies fell flat when the public saw the dynamic and striking-looking Mrs Sheppard in action.

After the new Liberal government became established in 1891, Kate Sheppard turned the WCTU into a very effective single-issue pressure group. For the first time the call for women's suffrage was directed beyond the better educated middle class to all women. Harriet Morison, secretary of the Tailoresses' Union, enlisted the help of the Dunedin suffrage superintendent, Helen Nicol, to convert all members of her union into suffragists. Well-educated women were drawn into the campaign even if they did not support temperance objectives. Ordinary women in domestic situations, especially those on farms, were harder to reach, but a petition provided a solution to the problem of including this large group.

In 1891 Kate Sheppard set about organising an ambitious nationwide signature-gathering campaign, which women supported enthusiastically, few refusing to sign. Dunedin produced the most signatures because of the help of the Tailoresses' Union but 10,000 signatures were collected from all over New Zealand. A better organised effort the following year collected 20,000 signatures, by far the biggest petition ever presented to a New Zealand Parliament.

This success led to the formation of a suffrage organisation separate from the WCTU in 1892. The Women's Franchise League (WFL) set up branches in the main centres and leagues also sprang up in smaller towns such as Gore and Feilding. In Christchurch a more ardently feminist and self-consciously intellectual Women's Institute was formed by women and men associated with the university.

Public meetings were held more frequently and on a larger scale than ever before. Kate Sheppard rented a page in the *Prohibitionist* which had a circulation of over 20,000 and newspaper reports were full of women's franchise news. The *Auckland Evening Star, New Zealand Herald, Evening Post* and *Dunedin Evening Star* strongly supported the cause.

The most vigorous opponents of women's franchise were brewers and the liquor trade who feared that women would vote for prohibition. The Catholic and Anglican churches were also unsympathetic. Individual politicians were extremely sexist. Henry Fish, the most notorious, said that if women were given the vote it would be

'. . . analogous to taking the bloom off the luscious peach — you destroy its principal beauty'.

In opposition to Fish many Labour and more radically inclined backbench Liberal MPs spoke in favour of women's suffrage, and they worked with conservative members to bring the matter before the House in 1891. Once again the Lower House favoured the bill but Seddon shrewdly added a clause allowing women to stand for Parliament. This addition proved too much for the conservatives in the Legislative Council and the bill was once again rejected. Things looked brighter in 1892 until Seddon again intervened and added electoral rights or postal voting to the bill. Most Liberals were ardently committed to the secret ballot and could not accept such a breach of a basic tenet of the Liberal faith.

In 1893 the WFL made greater

Ethel Haggit and Gertie Tewsby c. 1896, smoking pipes to signal their emancipation from oppressive restrictions on women's behaviour. *Alexander Turnbull Library.*

efforts, by organising an even bigger petition; over 30,000 signatures were collected, a quarter of the adult women of New Zealand. No government could ignore such a significant statement, but what actually won women the vote in 1893 was not the petition but the caprice of male politicians.

Seddon opposed women's franchise for a complex of reasons. He feared that women would vote for the conservative politicians who had supported women's franchise in the past and that temperance would inevitably follow women's participation at the polls. He had already been forced to introduce the compromise of the local option to defuse the temperance agitation. Under this system a 60 per cent vote in any electorate could force an area to go dry. If the whole country went dry the brewers, private allies of Seddon, would be deeply angered, as would working men who were Seddon's most loyal supporters. So once again, Seddon moved to delay the introduction of women's franchise until the 1896 election by adding electoral rights to the bill.

What upset Seddon's plan was the decision of two of his most bitter opponents in the Legislative Council, W. H. Reynolds and E. C. J. Stevens, to spite the Premier by voting for the women's franchise without electoral rights. Previously they had always insisted on electoral rights but this time they changed tack to call Seddon's bluff. Their ploy worked and women got the vote. The long campaign of women was brought to triumph by male perversity.

This ironical end to the story does not adequately explain why New Zealand women were the first to get the vote. More deep-seated causes were involved. Grimshaw isolates as critical the newness of New Zealand and the absence of conservative inertia, the favourable climate of opinion, the underdeveloped nature of party politics, the highly developed organisation of the WCTU and the WFL and the drive, energy and ability of Kate Sheppard. Most remarkable, women could have got the vote even earlier but for Seddon and the liquor lobby.

Grimshaw's analysis does not go far enough, however. We need to understand the role played by women in colonial New Zealand society, and male attitudes towards women. Late 19th-century New Zealand women led a rather different kind of life from their British contemporaries. In a raw colonial society there was little place for ornamental females and New Zealand women were useful in ways that their British middle class counterparts were not. Women in New Zealand were more like partners in founding farms or businesses, as well as being mothers to their husbands' children. In a country short of labour women were essential to the success of a farm or a business.

The *New Zealand Farmer* was quick to respond to women's demands by publishing a women's section made up of recipes, home hints and short stories. The editor made it clear that married men were more successful

A cartoon by Ashley Hunter, *NZ Graphic*, 18 November 1893. Some people thought that if women won the vote they would clean politics up and raise its tone. *Auckland Institute and Museum.*

farmers because in their youth wives could carry out a multitude of chores, thus freeing their young husbands for heavier physical tasks. Then, as farms developed, the tireless homemakers would supply free labour in the form of large families. A rural woman was expected to be a combination of labourer, domestic and child-producing machine.

Ideal and reality did not always match so neatly, however. Childbirth away from midwives and other women could be harrowing and dangerous, and raising large families without the help of grandmothers and aunts was daunting. Nevertheless, the majority of women seemed to relish being in demand and took advantage of the shortage of their sex to secure advantageous marriages; few women migrants of the 1870s stayed single for long. The shortage of domestic servants was also a continuing problem as young women left paid service to marry. Once married, New Zealand women had one of the highest per capita incomes anywhere in the world at their disposal in the 1870s. Most considered themselves much better off than their British sisters.

Nineteenth-century rural women were expected to perform a wide range of jobs as this anonymous ditty, published in the *New Zealand Farmer* in 1885, shows.

The Farmer's Wife

By the kitchen fire stood his patient wife,
Light of his home and joy of his life,
With face all aglow and busy hand,
Preparing the meal for her husband's band;
    For she must boil
    And she must toil,
    And she must broil,
    All for the sake of the home.

How briskly the wife steps about within —
The dishes to wash and the milk to skim
The fire goes out and the flies buzz about —
For the dear ones at home her heart is kept stout;
    There are pies to make,
    There is bread to bake
    And steps to take,
    All for the sake of the home.

But the faithful wife from sun to sun,
Takes the burden up that's never done;
There is no rest, there is no pay,
For the household good she must work away;
    For to mend the frock,
    And to knit the sock,
    And the cradle to rock,
    All for the good of the home.

This drawing from a Victorian medical book used in New Zealand homes was captioned 'Family Life *versus* Single-Blessedness'. Women were expected to be homemakers and find complete happiness within family life.

Property ownership was a more complex indicator of the position of women in colonial New Zealand. About a quarter of adult women owned property in 1882. Although over half of adult males owned property, the proportion of women property owners was very high by world standards. After the passing of the 1884 Married Women's Property Act women in urban areas started making wills along with their husbands. Usually property was left to the spouse and surviving children and there was no attempt, as in Britain, to keep property in the male line.

New Zealand women got the vote before their Australian sisters because New Zealand was a single entity rather than a series of competing states; Australian women got the vote immediately the new Federal Commonwealth was established in 1901. There was also no convict background in New Zealand with its negative stereotypes of women as 'damned whores'. A separate chauvinistic male

culture did develop but not to the same extent as across the Tasman.

The other obvious reason for the speed with which New Zealand women won the vote was the country's smallness. In New Zealand access to politicians was easily gained and it was simpler in a small population to collect the signatures of a quarter of the adult female population.

Did winning the vote bring about much change for women in New Zealand? The short answer is no. Reeves delighted in reporting that women generally voted the same way as their husbands or fathers and that little was different in terms of relations between the sexes. Like other women across the world New Zealand women found that winning the vote did not raise their status very much. Other battles had to be won.

Winning the vote seemed to take the momentum out of the New Zealand feminist movement. In contrast, the long, hard struggle of British and American women sustained the movement through the difficult interwar years. In 1894 the suffrage journal *Daybreak*, which had predicted a bold new future for New Zealand women, was forced to add a page of recipes and fashion notes. Pipe smoking and trous-

er wearing did not remain fashionable for long. The WFL, no longer necessary once its ultimate goal had been achieved, was replaced by the National Council of Women in 1896.

The council, which concentrated its energies on improving the lot of the family and children, did its work so effectively that it wound down temporarily in 1914. Yet women were not entitled to stand for Parliament until 1919. The first woman MP, Elizabeth McCombs, was elected in 1933 after the sudden death of her parliamentarian husband, James. Women moved into a much wider range of occupations in the new century, especially in office work. But women dominated only the worst paid of the professions — teaching and nursing and domestic service remained by far the largest employment category. There were relatively few married women in the workforce until the Second World War when a feminist movement intent upon achieving equal wages and occupational equality for women got under way.

It has been suggested that male politicians bought women off by granting the vote. The trade-off was an unwritten agreement that women would remain in the traditional 'sepa-

A woman with dairy equipment, pails, cheese dishes and a butter churn. Women were much more than housekeepers on most farms. *Canterbury Museum.*

rate sphere' of the home. Certainly there was little apparent opposition (Emily Siedeberg, New Zealand's first woman doctor, and Lady Stout excepted) to the views advocated by male social engineers like Dr Frederic Truby King that women were more suited to nurturing activities than to participation in the rough world of paid employment. The secondary school curriculum pushed many girls into areas separate from boys and the University of Otago Home Science School (1909) tried to divert women away from entering professions.

The problem with such an argument is that it attributes the aspirations of modern feminism to late 19th-century women. In fact the feminists of the 1890s were much more concerned with improving the lot of women and children within the family context than in the workforce. After all, the everyday experience of the majority of women was much more immediately affected by what happened in the domestic sphere than in the workplace. Single working women probably missed out on the gains made by the women's movement.

Nevertheless in terms of their limited objectives, the National Council of Women made very real gains, including raising the age of consent, abolishing the Contagious Diseases Act and improving divorce law. The 1898 Divorce Law made it easier for women to divorce violent or wayward husbands and the Testators Family Maintenance Act of 1900 forced husbands to pay some maintenance towards the upkeep of wives and children. These laws may have helped to reduce the high level of wife desertion. Registration of nurses and midwives made birth a less risky business for both mother and baby and the inci-

dence of prostitution fell rapidly in the new century.

In total these reforms made women's lot more comfortable and there is no doubt that the women activists of the 1890s and early 20th century were able to pass on many positive achievements to their daughters and granddaughters. Frenchman André Siegfried summed up the situation neatly when he wrote:

That which in 1893 was regarded as slightly ridiculous is now treated as a very natural state of things, and no one is surprised to find women voting, making speeches, in a word, taking their part as citizens in public affairs. It can therefore be said that the feminist movement has left the heroic age and is now in the era of slow and practical realities.

Link: From the Old Century to the New

'On 28 September 1899, a fortnight before Britain declared war on the Boers, Premier Richard Seddon proposed to the House of Representatives that New Zealand should send a contingent of mounted rifles to South Africa. Seddon had always been an enthusiastic Imperialist and he had no doubt that New Zealand was bound by 'duty' and 'blood' to support the mother country. The protests of the Christchurch socialist Tommy Taylor that such a war would be costly and unjust were swamped in a surge of jingoistic fervour. Parliament agreed by 54 votes to five and the public supported the decision with considerable enthusiasm. Large fund-raising concerts were organised and the streets were filled with endless parades.

Eventually 6495 men with 8000 horses served in South Africa, the largest proportion of representation from any British colony. In South Africa the New Zealanders earned a reputation for strength, speed and stamina. The expert horsemanship of the New Zealanders, Australians and Canadians made them into the most effective of the British troops in a war where mobility was all important. By the end of the conflict the New Zealand soldiers also believed they were more resourceful than their professional British equivalents. The press at home proclaimed them 'natural soldiers'.

The Boer War was a chivalrous affair at first and the New Zealanders developed a real respect for the tenacity and courage of the Boers, but as the fighting dragged on the war became dirtier. The British eventually established concentration camps and engaged in a scorched earth policy, finally forcing the Boers to surrender in May 1902.

New Zealand casualties were low, with 70 killed in action and 158 dying of wounds; a further 166 were wounded but survived the journey home. These losses were slight compared with those suffered by the British troops and both soldiers and public were delighted by the young colony's

'Roughriders' in their distinctive New Zealand uniforms in South Africa c.1900. *Alexander Turnbull Library.*

first performance in a 'real' war.

Historian Sir Keith Sinclair has suggested recently, however, that the Boer War represented an important moment in the development of New Zealand nationalism. Certainly, the soldiers were forced to think of themselves as New Zealanders rather than Aucklanders or Cantabrians. The impact of the Boer War was not, however, as great in New Zealand as in Australia. There was no literary school like that of the *Bulletin* in Sydney to turn incidents such as the execution of Breaker Morant into key moments in the development of a national identity. Australia was also an older, bigger and more urbanised society further along the path to national development. The Boer War shows how Imperialist and nationalist sentiment were tied together in New Zealand but its importance should not be exaggerated.

Meanwhile within New Zealand, a

108

new kind of Maori leadership emerged during the 1890s based around a group of highly talented men who had attended Te Aute College. Although known as the Young Maori Party, the group was never a party as such but simply a loose association of like-minded individuals. During their time in this Church of England school, these men came under the influence of the charismatic headmaster, John Thornton, an advocate of piety, diligence, sobriety, thrift and industry. Thornton also taught that if a weaker race came into contact with a stronger, it would die out unless it adopted the ways of the stronger.

The Te Aute Old Boys Students' Association established in 1897 met on a regular basis until 1910 and pursued four major objectives: to improve Maori health and education, to promote Maori farming on a communal basis, to stop land sales and to preserve chiefly mana. Te Aute old boys were avowed modernisers who saw the European parliament as holding the key to removing Maori grievances.

The three giants of the group were Apirana Ngata, Te Rangi Hiroa (Peter Buck) and Maui Pomare, all three much influenced by the half-caste politician and adviser to Seddon on Native Affairs, James Carroll. Ngata was the most important of the three because he retained stronger links with the Maori world and served nearly 40 years in Parliament.

Ngata, who was born into a high-ranking Ngati Porou family in 1874, graduated with an MA Honours and an LLB from Canterbury University College. Between 1900 and 1905 he helped Seddon and Carroll form Maori councils to slow land sales and improve Maori health. Elected MP for Eastern Maori in 1905, Ngata stayed loyal to the Liberals all his life. He was Native Minister in the United and Coalition governments between 1928 and 1934. During this time Ngata won Maori farmers greater access to credit and developed co-operative farming ventures in the East Coast area. Unfortunately, he resigned from Cabinet office in 1934 after the Native Affairs Commission reported that there were irregularities in the administration of land development schemes. He continued as MP for Eastern Maori until 1943 when he was defeated by the Ratana-Labour alliance. Ngata's strong Ngati Porou associations limited his influence within Maoridom but he held many hui to promote feelings of unity and promoted a reviv-

3575- TAUMARANUI - KING COUNTRY -

This King Country scene was photographed c.1885. The woman standing is weaving a flax cloak. The house has a bark roof. Ponga logs form the walls. *National Museum.*

al of Maori arts, crafts, songs and oral traditions. He died in 1950, a worthy champion of his people.

Born, it is believed, in 1877, Te Rangi Hiroa (Peter Buck) graduated in medicine from the University of Otago in 1904. The following year he became Medical Officer for Maori Health under Maui Pomare, another member of the Young Maori Party, and the two men established health councils and village committees to improve standards of sanitation. In 1909 Te Rangi Hiroa became MP for Northern Maori but he never liked politics and was somewhat relieved to be beaten (in a European seat) in the 1914 election.

He joined the Army instead and fought in Egypt and at Gallipoli. After the war he resumed his position as Medical Officer, and from 1919 until 1927, when he left New Zealand, he

was Director of the Health Department's Division of Maori Hygiene. Te Rangi Hiroa's anthropological work, pursued and developed since the war, led to his becoming Director of the Bishop Museum in Hawaii in 1927 and later Professor of Anthropology at Yale. He became the world authority on Polynesian exploration of the Pacific and had a number of books to his credit. He died in 1951.

Maui Pomare's grandfather was a European and his grandmother one of the few Maori women to sign the Treaty of Waitangi. He put his medical degree, won from the Seventh Day Adventist College in Michigan in 1897,

3515 - VILLAGE SCENE - KORONITI - (CORINTH) WANGANUI RIVER.

A Maori village at Koroniti on the Wanganui photographed by the Burton brothers in 1885. The wearing of blankets and European clothing was common at that time in this part of the country. *National Museum.*

to good use. As a health officer between 1901 and 1905 he burned 1256 unhygienic whare and built 2103 new houses and over 1000 latrines. He urged Maori to adopt Western practices, institutions and technology; to Pomare, tribal customs such as tohungaism, the tangi and hui were outmoded.

He was elected to Parliament in 1911. Once he switched from the Liberals to join Massey's Coalition, he urged Maori to sell their land and become European style farmers. As Minister of Health in 1923 he tried to overhaul New Zealand's backward mental hospitals. Before he died in 1930, Pomare managed to win some compensation for Maori whose land had been confiscated.

The importance of the Young Maori Party's influence should not be exaggerated. Maori mistrust of the European system worked against men who were prepared to fight for reforms through participating in that system. Overall, these Te Aute graduates were more important as individuals than as a group. More traditional leaders such as Eru Ihaka in the far north, King Mahuta, Princess Te Puea and the king maker, Tupu Taingakawa in the Waikato, were much more powerful figures within Maoridom. Both the King (essentially supported by the Waikato and Ngati Maniapoto tribes) and the Kotahitanga (essentially an alliance of Ngapuhi, Arawa and Ngati Kahungunu) Movements were more popular than the Young Maori Party in the tribal areas they represented. Prophets such as Te Whiti, Te Kooti and Rua had far greater mana amongst their own people. European historians have sometimes exaggerated the influence of the Young Maori Party because its members succeeded in the Pakeha world and were well known to Europeans.

13. 1913   Cossacks on the Streets:
The Waterfront Strike

ON 22 October 1913, the Wellington Watersiders' Union held a stopwork meeting. Two hours later they returned to find their places had been taken by 'free' labour brought in by the shipowners. The wharfies deemed this action a lockout and called another meeting. About 1500 gathered and demanded that their places be returned. Their employers refused. Two years of constant industrial strife now exploded into the great Waterfront Strike of 1913.

The watersiders were confident of victory even though other unions were less enthusiastic about a strike. Coalminers were reluctant now that winter had passed, while seamen, a generally older group with strong memories of the defeat in 1890, were even more hesitant. The leadership of the United Federation of Labour (UFL) or Red Feds, normally renowned for their fierce pronouncements, also hoped that a strike could be averted. Such reticence failed to deter the ebullient Wellington militants.

Further meetings between the watersiders and their employers failed to produce a settlement. On 26 October over 1000 strikers prevented any work from being done on the Wellington wharves and a large boisterous meeting followed at the Basin Reserve. Such bold action and the fiery speeches of the militants frightened the new government of William Ferguson Massey which had only come to power in July 1913. A call went out for volunteers to enlist as special constables.

While a 'Farmers' Army' assembled Prime Minister Massey presided over a special conference between employers and unionists on 28 October. The shipping companies requested that the

Ships wait out in Wellington Harbour during the Waterfront Strike. *Wellington Public Library.*

watersiders come to arbitration even though their union was not registered under the Arbitration Court. The union refused and then rejected the alternative of a good behaviour bond of £500. Bill (W. T.) Young and Pat Hickey, the acting executive of the UFL, were now called in to see if they could settle the dispute. The government hoped that these two notorious hotheads might be able to restrain their fellow Red Feds.

Tension increased as mounted specials flocked in from country districts. Farmers, determined that the export of perishable goods would not be halted, also wanted to teach the more militant unions a lesson and jumped at the opportunity to take a break from the tedium of farm work. Their commanding officer, Colonel Newall, claimed that the farmer specials were 'born soldiers'. Massey reinforced these enthusiastic volunteers by putting the Navy on full alert. The aptly named HMS *Psyche* was ordered to stay in Wellington Harbour and HMS

Pyranus returned to Auckland on 29 October.

Natural soldiers or not, the mounted specials behaved in ill-disciplined fashion on 30 November when they batoned a crowd of women and children at Post Office Square in Wellington. This brutal display earned the specials the title of 'Massey's Cossacks' and hardened union opposition to the government. Labour MP Paddy Webb called for a full commission of inquiry and civil war threatened.

Massey responded by suggesting that the captain of the *Psyche* land officers and men to maintain order. Luckily wiser counsel prevailed and the Prime Minister was persuaded to ask instead for ratings to parade on the wharves. More specials were also recruited as outbreaks of fighting continued in the streets.

The UFL responded to Massey's

provocative actions by ordering out the watersiders in Lyttelton and Dunedin. In Auckland an uneasy peace prevailed as the police superintendent persuaded 'free' labour to go home. Wellington remained troubled as regular soldiers paraded with a machine gun and bayonets uncovered. Work was confined to King's Wharf because it was served by a railway.

In a last desperate attempt to restore industrial peace a large delegation of unionists, Labour Party representatives and the retired Liberal leader Sir Joseph Ward urged Massey to call another conference with the shipping companies. Massey was also asked not to employ any more 'free' labour. Unfortunately the Citizens' Defence Committee made up of the Employers' Federation, Farmers' Union and Sheepowners' Federation had other ideas. They were frightened by the wild talk of Bill Young at public meetings in which he boasted that 10-15,000 armed men would march on Wellington if 'free' labour was used. The determination of the Citizens' Defence Committee to keep the ports open saw the conference with Massey collapse on 3 November.

The UFL still hoped for a settlement but they could not stop the strike spreading. Wharfies closed down the ports in Dunedin and Christchurch and riots continued out of the wharf area in Wellington. In Auckland Mayor C. J. Parr exchanged conciliation for provocation and seized the wharves. By 8 November about 1700 farmers occupied the Auckland wharves under cover of machine guns. 'Free' labour soon loaded the waiting ships in both Auckland and Wellington.

Employers decided to outmanoeuvre the watersiders by forming a separate new union under the Arbitration Act to replace the older Watersiders' Union which operated outside the ambit of the arbitration system. The Red Feds responded to this initiative and the heavy-handed tactics of Massey and Parr by calling a general strike of the 24 non-registered unions representing 11,000 workers. Eighteen registered unions representing 5000 workers joined the UFL action. The strikers comprised 5000 watersiders, 4000 miners, 2000 seamen and 5000 from assorted smaller unions.

Even more significant was the fact that 55,000 members of registered unions did not join the strike. Two unions in particular reduced the chances of success by failing to give

their support. Shearers, who could have drawn the specials back into the countryside, remained aloof as did railwaymen, who had been requested to block the supply of exports to the ports. In some smaller centres such as Wanganui and Gisborne employers and employees mixed happily at dances when the strike was at its height. Disunity within the union movement and a lack of enthusiastic support outside Wellington and Auckland crippled the strike. Massey was presented with a chance of smashing the notorious Red Federation once and for all.

The Prime Minister seized this opportunity with both hands. On 11

The 1913 Waterfront Strike was preceded by a period of increasing industrial militancy as unions lost faith in the arbitration system. Here Peter Fraser (a future Labour Party Prime Minister) addresses a meeting during the 1911 labourers' strike. Michael Savage (New Zealand's first Labour Prime Minister) is kneeling on the right. *Auckland Institute and Museum.*

November he imprisoned several of the UFL leaders, including Bob Semple, organiser of the UFL, Peter Fraser, secretary of the Social Democrat Party, Harry Holland, editor of the vociferous *Maoriland Worker*, and G. Bailey, chairman of the Wellington strike meetings. Three of these wild young men later became cabinet

ministers. Bill Young, president of the UFL, was gaoled on 12 November. A rather dubious collusion between employers and government was suggested by the fact that the jury which tried Holland and Young was made up entirely of businessmen and professionals. Older union suspicions about the judiciary were confirmed when the Chief Justice starved the strikers of funds by ruling that it was illegal for trade unions registered under the Industrial Conciliation and Arbitration (IC and A) Act to contribute funds to unions which were out on strike.

The combined power of employers and the state proved too much for a divided union movement. As early as 24 November the general strike had collapsed. On the following day decisive action taken by specials under the direction of the Union Steamship Company opened Lyttelton up for business. Port Chalmers in Dunedin returned to work on 28 November when the Dunedin strike committee was arrested. Despite the watersiders' rapid defeat the seamen and miners stood firm. A month later the seamen capitulated, leaving the miners alone. Hickey begged the miners to return to work but they held out until 13 January 1914 when they were forced to form a new union registered under the IC and A Act.

Pressures induced by the strike exacerbated the chronic factionalism which had beset the labour movement for some time. Relative moderates who favoured political rather than industrial action could not agree with

the militants who pinned their hopes on strikes. Even syndicalists who wanted 'One Big Union' and believed that one big strike by all workers would bring down the capitalist system could not agree among themselves. Some were heavily under the influence of the 'wobblies' (the Chicago-based IWW or Industrial Workers of the World, who became increasingly anarchic from around 1908). Others preferred the teachings of Professor de Leon of Detroit who broke from the 'wobblies' to found a party which would operate as a revolutionary vanguard. The more reformist American socialist Eugene Debs also had his supporters and Arthur McCarthy of Dunedin was a recent convert to British Guild socialism. More orthodox Marxists felt that industrial action alone was insufficient to bring about real change. Doctrine had become important to even the most moderate and pragmatic socialists by 1913, despite the virtual absence of such influences at the turn of the century.

The failure of the 1913 strike taught all factions of the labour movement some painful lessons. First, unity was critical if they were to have any hope of bringing about change. Doctrinal purity was a luxury they could ill afford. A heady and exciting moment had passed and labour leaders now had to forget their differences and undertake less spectacular but more solid organisational and educative work. Second, the political option seemed to be the only realistic alternative in a country where employers and

Twenty people were injured when special police charged this crowd of demonstrators in Wellington. *Auckland Institute and Museum.*

farmers held control of the government and the mechanisms of the state could be used to crush direct action. The electorate appeared to be very intolerant of any extreme action and had to be educated if attitudes were to be changed. Many of the syndicalists were reluctant to undertake such a dramatic change of course but they had little choice. On the more positive side unity was now much easier to achieve because there was a clearly identifiable enemy to unite against — Massey and his farmer government.

How had the situation arisen in which doctrinaire socialism exerted such an influence in a country well known for the pragmatic nature of its politics? Why had 'A Country Without Strikes' been subjected to two years of serious industrial disruption? Most explanations have focused on the conjunction between growing dissatisfaction with the arbitration system within New Zealand and the rapid spread of industrial militancy and internationalist socialism throughout the Western world in the period between 1906 and the First World War.

West Coast miners discovered at Blackball in 1908 that they could win more gains by operating outside rather than within the arbitration system. A strike to extend the lunch break from a miserly 15 minutes to half an hour produced almost instant success. The

113

speed and ease of the victory persuaded local miners to form a Federation of Miners, and the following year miners extended their organisation into a national federation championing the interests of several unions.

The Federation of Labour, known colloquially as the Red Feds, linked several watersiders' unions, shearers, flaxmillers, Auckland tramway employees and general labourers' unions from various parts of the country. The Red Fed and socialist leadership was dominated by men born outside New Zealand. All of them were fiery orators whose exotic ideas and distinctive accents made it easy for conservative politicians and press to dismiss them as 'foreign agitators'.

Despite such claims the 'bacillus socialismus', as one labour paper put it, spread like a contagion after 1911, especially in Auckland and Wellington. Working people seemed to gain enormously in confidence throughout 1911 and 1912 and political parties like the New Zealand Labour Party, founded in 1910, appeared to be unnecessary as the militants marched to victory through direct industrial action. Industrial disputes escalated throughout 1911.

Things first became serious at Waihi between May and November 1912. There a long strike by miners employed by goldmining companies turned sour when Massey's new government tried to force the miners back to arbitration. Imprisonment of several of the miners' leaders and provocative police action eventually led to an outbreak of violence on 12 November in which a shot was fired at a policeman and a striker was clubbed to death. Fighting continued for a few more days but the strike was broken.

The labour movement responded to this setback by calling two large unity conferences in January and July 1913. Unity was not achieved. The United Federation of Labour was formed to undertake further industrial action with support from a minority of unions. A new party, known as the Social Democrat Party, was also established but its avowedly socialist objectives of nationalising the 'means of production, distribution and exchange' frightened off the more moderate wing of the labour movement. Real unity was not achieved until the failure of the 1913 'general' strike closed off the industrial option.

The outbreak of industrial militancy from 1908 onwards had much to do with the declining popularity of the

Soldiers with drawn bayonets in Buckle Street, Wellington during the 1913 strike. *Alexander Turnbull Library.*

Special constables armed with long batons on their way to confront the striking watersiders. *Alexander Turnbull Library.*

Liberal Party among working people. Once the charismatic Seddon died in 1906 the dandyish merchant Joe Ward proved a much less attractive leader. The right increasingly joined Massey's small conservative party of self-made men, which called itself Reform from 1909. Massey adopted the populist style of Seddon and kept many of the Liberals' innovations in order to broaden his support base. The party lacked a guiding doctrine but basically it opposed socialism and the growing menace of Labour. It also promised to reform the corrupt and expensive Liberal bureaucracy.

The Reform Party attracted support from the North Island's growing bloc of prosperous farmers located in particular around Auckland. And these rural men found ready allies in the increasing number of respectable businessmen who lived in the main centres and the larger towns. By 1911 the North Island had edged ahead of the South with 56 per cent of the population and Auckland city passed the 100,000 mark. The Liberal Party, meanwhile, remained essentially a South Island party, its power base of small towns in relative decline.

These key demographic and economic changes were reflected in the 1908 election results when, for the first time, a large group of small farmer MPs representing North Island constituencies entered the House of Representatives. Their arrival heralded the golden age of farmer influence in Parliament; farmers remained the single biggest occupational group in the House until 1935.

A decade of prosperity increased the chances of Reform's success. In the 1911 elections Reform won 36 seats to the Liberals' 30; there were six independents, four Labour-Socialists and four Maori MPs. Joseph Ward resigned as Prime Minister and Liberal leader in March 1912 in the hope that a new leader might be able to hold the Liberal-Labour majority together. A new leader, Thomas Mackenzie, was elected but lasted just three months. Several Liberals crossed the floor to join Massey in July 1912, so ending 21 years of Liberal rule. Massey became Prime Minister at the head of a Reform ministry and remained in office until his death 13 years later.

Now even the militant unionists were caught up in the rush to be comfortable. The 1912 Cost of Living Commission revealed that working people had much higher expectations than in 1890. Red Feds and other radical critics believed that they were not winning their fair share of the new prosperity. They held that their real incomes had fallen behind rises in prices and profits.

Unions who worked outside the arbitration system and used direct action to further their ends made a

number of tangible gains between 1908 and 1913. (Several more militant unions believed that the Arbitration Court was simply a tool of the employers and the government to keep workers subjugated.) But limited success was followed by extravagant action which pushed the new conservative classes past their limits. The newly propertied perceived militant unionists as threatening their hard won prosperity. When this perception is set alongside the belief of working people that

Special constables approaching Queen's Wharf, Wellington during the 1913 strike. *Alexander Turnbull Library.*

their share of the national wealth is declining, industrial warfare becomes understandable. The combination of small property, big business and the state welded together by the threat of revolution from below proved too much for the labour movement when open conflict broke out in October 1913.

Link: From Wharves to War

On 4 August 1914 Germany declared war on Belgium, immediately crossing the Belgian frontier. New Zealand responded enthusiastically to Britain's declaration of war on Germany on 4 August 1914. There was no constitutional need for a separate declaration of war and no need for any political discussion. It was New Zealand's duty to do all it could to meet this challenge to the freedom of the world, and on 7 August New Zealand's cabled offer of the services of an Expeditionary Force was quickly accepted. The enthusiasm was not restricted to politicians. New Zealanders had been educated extensively in the glories of the British Empire and its civilising role. This was a conflict between Freedom and Justice, and Autocracy and Greed; it was clear where New Zealand must stand.

The New Zealand Defence Act of 1909 had made provision for a conscripted citizen army of 30,000 designed to complement the Imperial Army in time of need, and by 1914 there was a considerable reservoir of New Zealanders with some military experience. During his visit in that year General Sir Ian Hamilton, then Inspector-General of the Overseas Forces, reported he had inspected 18,807 territorial and permanent troops and 17,868 cadets, a total of 36,675 or 70 per cent of the Defence Forces. The following year Major General Sir Alexander Godley, commandant of the New Zealand forces, estimated that 89,000 partially trained men were available to the New Zealand forces.

As a result the New Zealand government was able to respond swiftly to a request from the British Secretary of War on 6 August 1914 to take the German wireless station at Samoa. A volunteer force of 1413 men drawn from territorial units in Auckland and Wellington sailed from Wellington on 15 August. The convoy arrived in Apia, Samoa without incident and occupied the German possession without firing a shot on 29 August.

In the meantime preparations for the Expeditionary Force proceeded. Each of the four military districts mobilised to provide their contribution and the process of equipping and training proceeded apace. The force was well equipped with modern artillery pieces and machine guns and the hardy and reliable .303. In June Sir Ian Hamilton concluded his report to Sir

G. R.

MILITARY TRAINING.

DOMINION OF NEW ZEALAND.

NOTICE AS TO MILITARY TRAINING.

NOTICE IS HEREBY GIVEN that every male inhabitant of New Zealand who, on the 1st day of March, 1911, had attained the age of fourteen years or upwards, but had not attained the age of twenty-one years, and who is a British subject and has resided in New Zealand for at least six months, IS HEREBY REQUIRED before 7 p.m. on the 2nd day of June, 1911, to fill in a prescribed form of registration in respect of military training under the Defence Acts, and to post or deliver the same to the Area Sergeant-Major of the territorial area in which the applicant for registration resides.

Forms of registration may be obtained at any Post Office or Police Station. No postage is required where the form is posted as aforesaid.

Any person to whom this notice applies who fails to take any step necessary to secure his registration as aforesaid is liable to a fine of FIVE POUNDS, and shall not be eligible for employment in any branch of the Government Service.

Dated at Wellington, this 10th day of April, 1911.

GEO. FOWLDS,
Acting Minister of Defence.

All males between 14 and 21 were required to register for military training after 1911. *Alexander Turnbull Library.*

James Allen, New Zealand's Minister of Defence, with these words: 'The army of today puts its best into its work; it is well equipped; well armed; the human material is second to none in the world; and it suffers as a fighting machine only from want of field work and want of an ingrained habit of discipline.' His words were soon to be tested in Egypt and at Gallipoli.

The Expeditionary Force sailed from Wellington on 16 October, the 8574 men and 3818 horses crammed onto 10 transports. After rendezvousing at Albany, Western Australia, with the ships carrying the 1st Australian Division, the 'armada' headed for the Suez Canal. Most expected they would go on to England for further training but as the convoy entered the Red Sea, word came that they were to

disembark in Egypt for training and to reinforce the troops defending Egypt and the Canal Zone against the attack which was expected following Turkey's entry into the war on the side of the Central Powers on 31 October.

After disembarking at Alexandria the New Zealanders moved to Zeitoun on the outskirts of Cairo where a dusty stretch of desert was soon transformed into a military camp. The training began immediately, with drill, route marching and musketry the order of the day. Cecil Malthus, a private in the 1st Canterbury Infantry Battalion, later recalled the 'normal programme' as 'a long march out into the sand dunes, a scorching sun, dry bread and biscuit for lunch . . . and hours spent in digging useless trenches or elaborately attacking an imaginary enemy. Then a weary struggle home to a comfortless camp, a ravenous meal of stew, and so to bed.'

While most Europeans supported fighting in a European war there were a number of conscientious objectors. Conscription was introduced in 1916 and the speaker Bob Semple was gaoled for advocating its repeal. Semple later became Minister of Public Works when the Labour Party first won office in 1935. *Alexander Turnbull Library.*

Lantern Lecture
Entitled
"THE GHASTLY HORRORS OF WAR"

Will be delivered by

MR. ROBERT SEMPLE

at ___MUNICIPAL___ ___CONCERT___ ___HALL___

CHRISTCHURCH

on ___SUNDAY, MAY 13,___ 7.30 p.m.

Another World's War will, according to eminent authorities, end our civilization. The People only can prevent it.

COME IN YOUR THOUSANDS

The Wellington Battalion departs for overseas. *New Zealand Herald.*

14. 1915   Trial by Ordeal: Gallipoli

The writing and research for Milestones 14 and 16 was carried out by Paul Enright.

AT 9.30 on the morning of Sunday 25 April 1915 the first members of the New Zealand Expeditionary Force — 1725 men — waded ashore onto a beach on the Dardanelles Peninsula. It had no name then but it would soon be known as Anzac Cove. This was what the New Zealanders had trained for; they were the equal of any soldiers, volunteer or regular. The hardships, triumphs and defeats they would share would set them apart forever. Their achievements would allow New Zealanders back home to stand tall.

The Gallipoli campaign was conceived as a 'promising sideshow' by the

Anzac Cove, 1915. The beach, 600 metres long, was little more than a dent in the shoreline. It had no name when the Anzacs went ashore on 25 April — some 2 kilometres north of their intended landing place. *Noel Hilliard.*

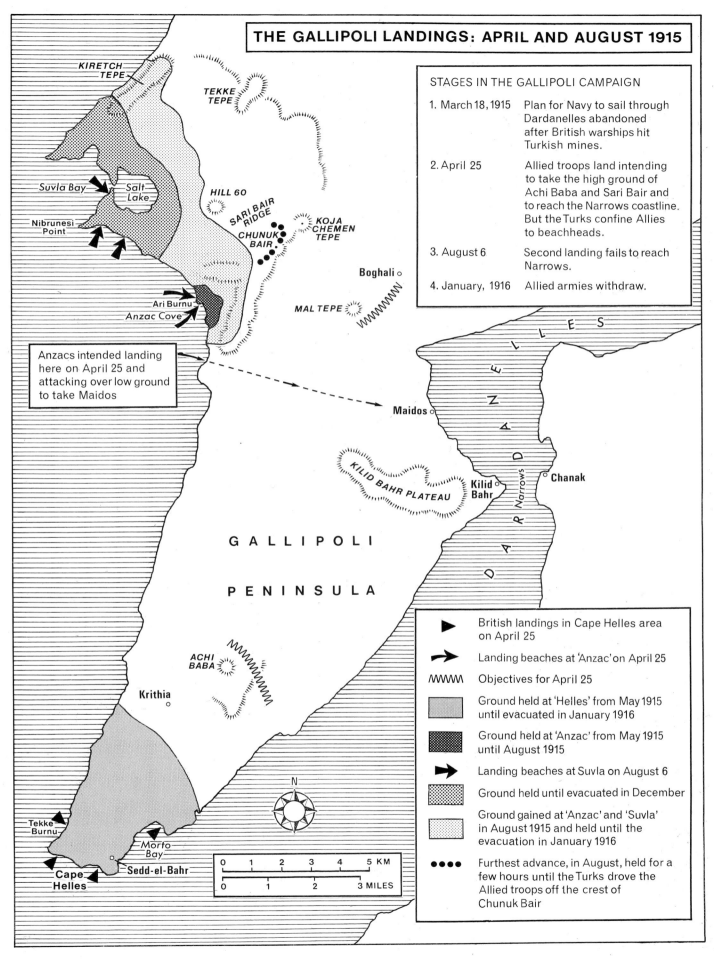

THE GALLIPOLI LANDINGS: APRIL AND AUGUST 1915

KIRETCH TEPE

TEKKE TEPE

Suvla Bay

Salt Lake

HILL 60

Nibrunesi Point

SARI BAIR RIDGE

CHUNUK BAIR

KOJA CHEMEN TEPE

Boghali o

Ari Burnu

Anzac Cove

MAL TEPE

STAGES IN THE GALLIPOLI CAMPAIGN

1. March 18, 1915   Plan for Navy to sail through Dardanelles abandoned after British warships hit Turkish mines.

2. April 25   Allied troops land intending to take the high ground of Achi Baba and Sari Bair and to reach the Narrows coastline. But the Turks confine Allies to beachheads.

3. August 6   Second landing fails to reach Narrows.

4. January, 1916   Allied armies withdraw.

Anzacs intended landing here on April 25 and attacking over low ground to take Maidos

Maidos o

DARDANELLES

KILID BAHR PLATEAU

Kilid Bahr

Narrows

Chanak o

GALLIPOLI

PENINSULA

ACHI BABA

Krithia o

N

Tekke Burnu

Morto Bay

Cape Helles

Sedd-el-Bahr

| 0 | 1 | 2 | 3 | 4 | 5 KM |
| 0 | 1 | | 2 | | 3 MILES |

British landings in Cape Helles area on April 25

Landing beaches at 'Anzac' on April 25

Objectives for April 25

Ground held at 'Helles' from May 1915 until evacuated in January 1916

Ground held at 'Anzac' from May 1915 until August 1915

Landing beaches at Suvla on August 6

Ground held until evacuated in December

Ground gained at 'Anzac' and 'Suvla' in August 1915 and held until the evacuation in January 1916

•••• Furthest advance, in August, held for a few hours until the Turks drove the Allied troops off the crest of Chunuk Bair

First Lord of the Admiralty, Winston Churchill. The Western Front had settled into the stagnant battle of attrition and in the east Russia was being hard pressed by the Germans. Churchill convinced the British cabinet that seizure of the Dardanelles Straits, that narrow strip of water connecting the Black Sea and the Mediterranean, could lead to an early Allied victory. Control of the straits would allow the Royal Navy to threaten Constantinople, the Turkish capital, and could force Turkey out of the war and relieve Russia. Initially the campaign was planned as a naval operation but when the fleet proved unable to force the passage, soldiers were committed and a Mediterranean Expeditionary Force, made up of some 70,000 British regulars and

Anzac wounded being evacuated off the Gallipoli peninsula to hospital ships which then transported them to hospitals in Egypt. *New Zealand Herald.*

French Colonial troops, was placed under the command of Sir Ian Hamilton. The Anzacs were included after Lord Kitchener had assured Asquith that they were 'good enough'.

On that first Anzac Day the Australian 3rd Brigade made the initial landing, in darkness, just before 5 a.m. They expected to land at 'Z Beach', just north of the low promontory of Gaba Tepe, but as they approached the shore strong currents drove them 2 kilometres north of the intended site. Instead of a broad beach and an open plain, the troops faced a cove with a narrow beach. Above them rose steep, scrub-covered ridges scored with narrow, twisting gullies. As the Australians moved away from the beach they encountered increasingly strong groups of Turkish defenders and the impetus of the Allied attack was lost.

By 9 a.m. some 12,000 Australians had landed and the first New Zealanders began to reach the beach. The situation was confused. Numerous

gaps in the line waited to be filled, isolated groups remained forward of the main lines and men had become separated from their units. There was a critical shortage of artillery support and communication difficulties meant that only limited use could be made of covering fire from the Royal Navy guns out to sea.

Meanwhile the Turkish counterattack under Mustapha Kemal (Ataturk) gained momentum. The Turks repulsed scattered groups of Australians making their way up the crucial ridge from the height known as Baby 700 through Battleship Hill towards Chunuk Bair, one of the Anzacs' principal objectives.

After a long, slow climb from the beach, suffering casualties from artillery, machine gun and sniper fire, the New Zealanders arrived to find the Australian forces on the slopes beneath the summit of Baby 700 virtually wiped out. The line was open to fire from three quarters — the front, the

right and the right rear where Turkish snipers had infiltrated the Anzac positions. High scrub reduced visibility and increased tension. Enemies crept to within 20 metres of each other before being sighted and all movement had to be slow, low and careful; to rise was to offer a ready target for snipers. When the New Zealanders joined the surviving Australians they lay prone on the ground, grabbing what meagre cover they could. Sometimes the only protection was the body of a dead comrade. Casualties mounted rapidly. Reinforcements could not make it through the intense and accurate Turkish fire.

The troops who could have made a difference at this crucial stage — the rest of the Canterburys and the Otago and Wellington Battalions — remained on their ships. Between 12.30 amd 4.00 p.m. no soldiers were landed because the steamboats and lighters were ferrying wounded from the shore to the hospital ships. Aiding the wounded at the cost of landing reinforcements reduced pressure on the Turkish defence at a crucial stage and helped to ensure that the Gallipoli campaign would be bloody and protracted.

The invaders now contracted to close their line and braced themselves against the ferocity of the Turkish counter-attack. In the late afternoon the Anzacs fell back from Baby 700, bringing as many as possible of their wounded with them.

Three thousand one hundred New Zealanders crossed the beaches that first Anzac Day. Although the Turks had held the high ground and retained the strategic initiative, the Anzacs had fought heroically. In carving a tenuous foothold two young nations had created a legend.

The first day at Gallipoli set the pattern for the next eight months. By midnight the official estimate of the Anzac casualties stood at 2000; similar losses were attributed to the Turks. On 27 April the War Diary of the New Zealand Division noted that casualties to date stood at 931 — 241 men killed and 690 wounded or missing. In less than three days virtually one in every four New Zealanders at Gallipoli had become a casualty.

In the weeks and months that followed, Gallipoli settled into a deadly routine. Despite their best efforts, neither side could make significant headway. The Allies continued to cling grimly to their beachheads at Anzac Cove and Cape Helles while the

Quinn's Post during the erection of bombproofs. The chute is to carry sand from the mine workings. *Noel Hilliard.*

Turks met and repelled attempts to break through their defensive cordons. The Allied planners had few answers other than to commit more men and grind the enemy down in a war of attrition. It became a stalemate as both sides constructed strong lines of trenches facing each other.

The invaders held a front some 3000 metres long and only 1000 metres deep at its widest point. The sea was at their backs and on both flanks. Some 40,000 men were crowded onto a small beachhead, watched constantly by the Turks who not only held the high ground but could bring fire to bear on almost the entire area.

Both sides launched a succession of full-scale attacks. Casualties were so high by 19 May that a truce was arranged so that burial parties could take care of the health hazard posed by thousands of bodies swelling, bursting and rotting in the sweltering heat. As well as the fierce summer sun, poor diet, plagues of rats and flies and generally insanitary conditions added to the suffering. Malnutrition, gum sores, septic boils, skin infections and debilitating stomach and bowel disorders, especially dysentery, made many unfit for duty. Ten per cent of New Zealand's fatalities during the campaign (270 out of 2701) died of disease.

In late July Hamilton decided to make one more offensive, breaking out to the north of the beachhead,

scaling and seizing the heights of Chunuk Bair overlooking the Straits of Constantinople; this would clear the way for victory. The attack, involving 60,000 British and Anzac troops, began at 2.30 p.m. on 6 August. British and French forces at Cape Helles launched the first of two diversionary attacks. Three hours later in the southern sector of the Anzac beachhead the 1st Australian Infantry Division began a bloody assault on Lone Pine. Seven Victoria Crosses were awarded at the Pine in recognition of the Australians' bravery. In the south the British and French struggled towards the slopes of Achi Baba under constant bombardment.

After nightfall the Allied forces began moving north to take up their positions for a dawn attack. They moved out in two columns; the Australians, Indians and Gurkhas on the left were to attack Hill 971, while the New Zealand Infantry Brigade was bound for Chunuk Bair. Both columns had covering forces whose task it was to clear, silently with the bayonet, a number of Turkish posts dotted across the foothills of Chunuk Bair. The Right Covering Force consisting of the four Mounted Rifles regiments (Auckland, Wellington, Canterbury and Otago) and the Maori Contingent, encountered stiff opposition as they moved up the slopes. They had to attack again and again to secure the foothills, an effort Australian war correspondent C. E. W. Bean later described as a 'magnificent feat of arms . . . never surpassed, if indeed equalled, during the campaign'.

The plan, however, was two hours behind schedule and under pressure it began to break apart. At 4.30 a.m. on 7 August the 3rd Australian Light Horse Brigade clambered from their trenches at the Nek to launch themselves at the Turkish trenches some 30 metres away. Disastrously the Light Horse had failed to synchronise watches with the artillery and there was a gap of three minutes between the cessation of the preliminary bombardment and the signal to attack. The Australians, attacking in four waves, were mown down in a withering cross-

A makeshift Anzac operating theatre at Gallipoli. *Imperial War Museum.*

fire from Turkish machine guns on the Nek, Baby 700 and the Chessboard. Two regiments totalling 600 men had 234 killed and 138 wounded in little more than half an hour.

After the Mounteds' initial successes, the New Zealand advance ran into difficulties. Stubborn resistance from pockets of Turkish defenders and the rugged terrain forced detours and led to lengthy delays. It was 6 a.m. by the time the new leading Wellington Battalion reached the Apex, the point from which the final assault on Chunuk Bair was to be launched. It was long past dawn; the attack would have to be in daylight.

At this point the New Zealanders hesitated. The Auckland and Wellington Battalions were in position but the Otagos and Canterburys were still dispersed. The New Zealanders had no knowledge of the situation on either flank and they were under heavy fire from the crest of the ridge. In the opinion of the Brigade Major A. C.

Temperley, 'Prudence seemed to dictate a pause', and his commander, Brigadier F. E. Johnston, exhausted and ill himself, agreed. It was a fatal mistake. At 6 a.m. the Turkish defence on Chunuk Bair consisted of only an artillery battery and 20 infantry men. Within two hours reinforcements began arriving and by midmorning the position was heavily defended.

At 9.30 a.m. Godley issued a direct order to attack. Still the New Zealand commanders held back, wary of their exposed route to the rear along Rhododendron Ridge and suspicious of what the enemy on the crest of Chunuk Bair had in store for them. Finally at 11 a.m., in the cover provided by the Apex, the Auckland Battalion formed up to attack. Their line of advance was on a front of 60 metres up a narrow saddle to a small pinnacle some 100 metres away.

The soldiers advanced into the open. Before they had made 10 metres

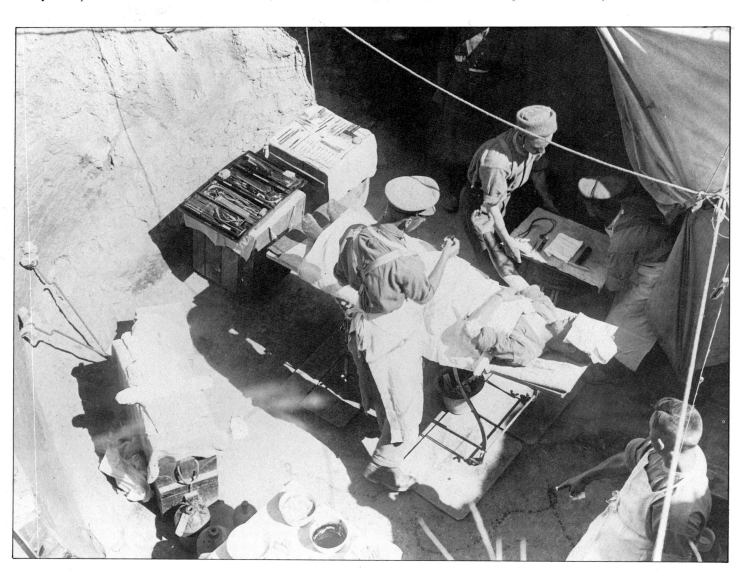

The **Wellington Mounted Rifles climbed this face of Table Top in the dark during the August offensive. Steps had to be cut with entrenching tools.** *Alexander Turnbull Library.*

they were hit by intense and accurate fire from the Turks on Chunuk Bair and on the ridges on either side of the Apex. Over 300 men fell, dead and wounded, as the attack shuddered to a halt. Down on Rhododendron Ridge the Canterbury and Otago Battalions were also under heavy fire. Movement forward or to the rear was suicidal so while their leaders planned the soldiers dug in to swelter in the sun.

In sharp contrast to the events at Lone Pine, the Nek and Chunuk Bair, the British landing at Suvla Bay proceeded with relatively little opposition. It was not going according to plan, however. The untried troops were landed in the wrong order and, again, at the wrong place, and men milled about on the landing beaches with little purpose or direction. Much of the problem lay with the indecisive and incompetent commander, General Sir Frederick Stopford. The Australians later accused the British of sitting on the beach brewing tea while the Light Horse attacked on the Nek.

At dawn on 8 August the New Zealanders launched another assault on Chunuk Bair. It opened with an intensive bombardment from the Anzac batteries and the Royal Navy's warships as the Wellington Battalion under the extremely capable command of Lieutenant Colonel W. G. Malone, moved forward through the decimated Auckland Battalion. They advanced on the Turkish trenches, meeting surprisingly little resistance. The initial objective achieved, the troops dug in as two raw Kitchener New Army battalions moved in on their flanks. Chunuk Bair was now in Anzac hands but the crest was vulnerable to Turkish fire.

The inevitable Turkish counter-attack began at 6 a.m. The slope of the ground on the Turkish side of the crest worked to their advantage. Much of their advance was over 'dead ground' (ground the New Zealanders could not fire at) and Turkish bombers were able to crawl to within 20 metres of the New Zealand trenches. Wave after wave of Turkish soldiers attacked, trying to push the invaders off the hill by force of numbers. Time and again the New Zealanders drove them back with steady and accurate fire and a succession of bayonet charges. By mid-morning more than half the Wellington officers lay dead or wounded and the situation was crumbling on both flanks. Most of the crest had been lost as the New Zealanders were forced to withdraw to their support

lines on the western (seaward) side of the slope. They still held the crest on their right flank and clung tenaciously to it until the late afternoon.

Behind the New Zealand trenches the ground was littered with wounded desperately seeking shelter from snipers, artillery, stray bullets and the blazing sun. It was suicidal to attempt to cross the exposed area between Chunuk Bair and the Apex or to move on Rhododendron Ridge. Corporal Cyril Bassett of the Divisional Signals Company spent the whole day tending the field telephone wires that kept Malone in touch with Brigadier Johnston, frequently repairing them under fire; he was awarded the Victoria Cross for his exploits. His bravery, though impressive, was not unusual for Gallipoli, yet that VC was the only one awarded a New Zealander throughout the whole campaign.

Water and ammunition were at a premium. Men in the front trenches searched their dead comrades for bullets and bombs, sucking pebbles in an attempt to ease their parched throats. The wounded cried continuously for relief from pain and thirst. Still the unrelenting Turkish attacks came. Godley, meanwhile, was making desperate plans to capitalise on the seizure of Chunuk Bair, the only success

of the day's offensives. He decided to abandon the attack on Hill 971 and direct all force towards strengthening the tenuous hold his troops had on that long sought after foothold, but even as he made his plans the moment was almost past.

By late afternoon the Wellington Battalion was in a critical condition. Its strength had been more than halved, it was short of officers and NCOs and those soldiers who remained were exhausted by 12 hours of hard fighting. The position had been under artillery attack all day and more than a few shells had come from the Allied seaward side. Part of the reason for this was the fact that artillery marker flags had themselves been blown away but, whatever the full explanation, it is clear that Allied artillery fire helped to make the Wellington position on the right flank of the crest impossible and forced them to withdraw to the seaward slope. At about the same time a shrapnel burst either from Navy guns or an Anzac howitzer killed Lieutenant Colonel Malone and wounded his second-in-command, Major W. H. Cunningham. Yet the battalion, with only three junior officers, held firm against their attackers.

At 8 p.m. under cover of darkness

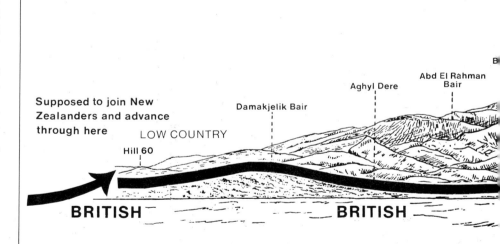

Supposed to join New Zealanders and advance through here

LOW COUNTRY

Hill 60

Damakjelik Bair

Aghyl Dere

Abd El Rahman Bair

BRITISH

BRITISH

from

KEY

N.Z. – New Zealanders backed by Gurkhas

N.S.W. – New South Welshmen

W.A.L.H. – West Australian Light Horse

British – 7th Gloucesters, 8th Welch Pioneers

The Otago's Attack. **A re-creation of a Gallipoli scene by Peter McIntyre.** *Queen Elizabeth II Army Memorial Museum.*

the Otago Battalion relieved the Wellingtons. A pitifully small party made their way down to the Apex; Bean described the scene 'of the 760 of the Wellington Battalion who had captured the height that morning, only 70 unwounded or slightly wounded men survived. Their uniforms were torn and their knees broken; they had had no water since morning; they could talk only in whispers; their eyes were sunken; their knees trembled; some broke down and cried like children'.

That was far from the end of the battle. The next day the New Zealand Mounted Rifles replaced the Infantry Brigade but, despite Godley's plans, the promise of Chunuk Bair was past. On the evening of the 9th the New Zealanders were replaced by two New Army Battalions — the 6th Loyal North Lancashires and the 5th Wiltshires. The now fortified positions the Aucklanders had created at the Pinnacle were taken over by the 6th Leinsters. These battalions bore the full brunt of Kemal's counter-offensive, involving three or four regiments, launched at dawn on 10 August.

They buckled and broke. The Turks

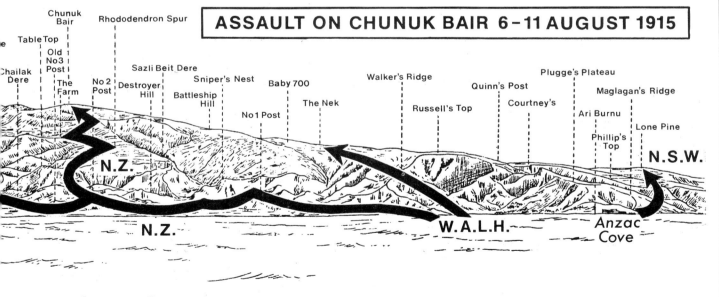

ASSAULT ON CHUNUK BAIR 6–11 AUGUST 1915

orama of Chunuk Bair
4·83km) south of Nibrunesi Point

n: A.E. Byrne, *Official History Of The Otago Regiment, N.Z.E.F. In The Great War, 1914-18* (J. Wilkie & Co. Ltd, Dunedin, 1921)

Anzac Cove from above the New Zealand Ambulance Station. *Noel Hilliard.*

swept down on the Apex, threatening to break right through the Anzac lines. They were held by New Zealand machine guns and New Zealand troops hastily moved up from their rest areas in the Chailak Dere gully. It was a fierce battle. A prisoner captured a few days later described the dead on the slopes south of Chunuk Bair as being like 'corn that has been reaped'.

By 11 August the broad battle ground to a halt. It was not that objectives had been achieved or defeats inflicted; both sides were simply exhausted.

The August offensives marked the effective end of the Gallipoli cam-

paign. The occupation of Suvla, Anzac Cove and Cape Helles dragged on for a further four and a half months but with little commitment. When the end did come it took the Turks completely by surprise. In stark contrast to the landing, the evacuation of Gallipoli proceeded in textbook fashion. Over three days and two nights thousands of men were spirited off the beachhead back to Mudros Harbour with only a handful of casualties.

It was not easy for the soldiers to leave. Many felt guilty, angry and frustrated at abandoning their dead comrades with the job uncompleted, but most also recognised the futility of persisting with the campaign. Of the 8556 New Zealanders who served on Gallipoli, 7247 were casualties — 2721

were killed. The offensives of 6-14 August accounted for over 2400 — one-third — of the total.

Yet amid the sorrow there was also pride. The New Zealand Army had been put to the test and, in meeting it, had created a legend. In fighting for King and Empire they had helped to forge a national identity. They could be confident of themselves and of their ability. They had shown courage, discipline, determination and commitment and some of them, for a brief moment on the crest of Chunuk Bair, had glimpsed the Dardanelles and the possibility of victory. New Zealanders at home knew that their sons had done them proud.

15. 1916 Te Mihaia Hou (The New Messiah): Tuhoe Prophet Rua Kenana is Arrested

NOT quite a year had elapsed since Maori and Pakeha Anzacs landed at Gallipoli when, on Sunday 2 April 1916, the last shots in the 50-year-old conflict between Maori and Pakeha within New Zealand were fired — at Maungapohatu deep in the isolated rugged Urewera country.

Against the background of World War One, anti-German hysteria was calling for the arrest of Rua Kenana Hepetipa. Rua, a charismatic Maori prophet, had built up a thriving community in the Urewera and was now refusing to allow recruitment among his people and was allegedly making pro-German statements. He also resisted any sale of land to the Pakeha and was known to be advocating equal application of the law in general to both races. Such advocacy was clearly seditious and the Ministers of Native Affairs (W. H. Herries) and Police (Alexander Herdman) had few qualms about sending 77 armed policemen to arrest the undesirable native on a sly grogging charge.

To the popular press Rua was some kind of guerilla leader holed up in a mountain fortress in the remote hinterland north-west of Wairoa, ready to take up arms on behalf of the Kaiser. This ignored the fact that he was in reality a pacifist, although also a Maori separatist who hoped that all Europeans would one day leave Aotearoa.

Mihaia. Rua stands beneath the wooden painted sign which marks the entrance to the eastern side of the pa enclosure. The King of Clubs, Rua's emblem, represented 'the Coming King', Rua the Messiah who would bring everlasting peace. *Auckland Institute and Museum.*

Police at Ruatahuna receiving arms and ammunition. *Auckland Weekly News.*

The police set out in disguise and under the leadership of Commissioner James Cullen, a man notorious for his role during the 1912 Waihi strike and who now, seemingly intent on retiring on a note of glory, invited along a newspaper reporter and photographer. It took the large party 3 days to reach the remote pa and on 1 April the group camped below it, fearing some kind of surprise attack from the 1000 or so inhabitants. Next morning Rua greeted the policemen warmly with offers of food, but Cullen rejected the offer, arguing that Rua had 'got away' before.

Rua had his people on the marae to offer a traditional welcome and now he instructed them not to resist. Cullen, ignoring etiquette, rode straight across the marae towards Rua, the rifles of his following mounted troopers glinting in the sun. Rua panicked and ran towards the safety of the village. Cullen immediately ordered his constables to seize the prophet; they rushed forward, threw Rua to the ground and handcuffed him.

A shot rang out. No one knows who was responsible: the Maori blamed a probably nervous and poorly trained constable, the police blamed the Maori. Deliberate or accidental, the shot was followed by 30 minutes of firing during which a constable was seriously wounded and Rua's eldest

son Toko was killed, along with his close friend Te Maipi Te Whiu. Thus were sewn the seeds of a still simmering bitterness. The official police report claimed that Toko was firing at the constables and was therefore shot in self-defence: Toko's wife Waereti Irohia maintained that her husband was already wounded and that he was hauled out from beneath a whare and shot in the back like a rabbit.

A careful reconstruction of the evidence by Judith Binney has not been able to confirm or deny either story, but it does seem clear that both Toko and Te Maipi were armed and did fire at the police; they were, however, in no position to have fired that first shot. Toko's weapon was a shotgun loaded with bird shot, lethal at only very short range. It seems likely too, that the fatal shootings would not have occurred had the policemen not broken ranks.

When the shooting was over Rua was marched out of the Urewera, handcuffed to another son, Whatu, for three days and then sent to Auckland by train. There a 47-day trial for sedition ensued. Rua's brilliant counsel, J. R. Lundon, pointed out that a person could be arrested on a Sunday for felony only and that sedition was not a felony. Furthermore, he succeeded in faulting police evidence sufficiently to persuade the jury that his client had committed nothing more serious than 'civil disobedience'. A verdict of not guilty on the charge of

sedition, and of 'moral guilt' in resisting arrest, was returned — much to the indignation of the press. Judge Chapman, however, overruled the jury and sentenced Rua to 12 months' hard labour and 18 months' reformative detention, despite protest by eight of the jury, who called for a commission of inquiry and published a case in favour of Rua. Their cry for mercy fell on deaf ears.

Rua was one of a long line of Maori prophets. He first attracted attention in 1906 when he spoke of one of his major visions, claiming that he had met an angel, who had led him to a secret place on the sacred heartland mountain of Maungapohatu. There he found the key to the salvation of the Maori people, a diamond which he would give to King Edward VII in Gisborne in return for the restoration of all Pakeha-owned Maori land. The Pakeha would then return across the sea to England, leaving the Maori in peace with their land legally restored to them.

Born in 1869, Rua was the posthumous son of one of Te Kooti's warriors. In the misty and magical country of the Urewera he became an active and devout member of the Ringatu faith. The founder of the religion, Te Kooti, had prophesied that he would be replaced by a chosen one, and Rua's powerful oratory, lifestyle and vivid visions helped to persuade the kaumatua (elders) and tohunga that he was indeed the prom-

Police in action at Maungapohatu, 2 April 1916. *Auckland Weekly News.*

The men, handcuffed. Maka Kanuehi, Pukepuke Kanara, Rua (with his left sleeve torn off). Whatu (Rua's son), Awa Horomona and Tioke Hakaipare. *New Zealand Centennial Police Museum.*

A Maori family in the Urewera outside a makeshift wharepuni, or sleeping house. Poor living conditions such as this led to increased sickness and disease. *Auckland Weekly News, 15 February 1906.*

ised saviour. Eria Raukura, an elder of part Tuhoe descent, baptised Rua as the Mihaia (Messiah) in front of a large crowd. Rua's claim to be the brother of Christ and son of the Holy Ghost was accepted naturally.

Rua offered the Tuhoe salvation at a time when they were on the brink of despair. Between 1896 and 1901 the tribe's population had fallen from 1400 to 1000, and they were desperately poor and unhealthy. Although they had land, they lacked money to develop it. The protection offered by the Urewera District Native Reserve Act of 1896 no longer seemed adequate to stop the Pakeha from coming in and snatching their land. Gold prospectors were allowed into the area in 1906. The state had already bought 3 million acres (1,212,000 hectares) of Maori land in other parts of the country and by 1906 total North Island land holdings had been cut to little over 8 million acres (3,232,000 hectares).

The recognition by Eria Raukura greatly enhanced Rua's mana and his popularity grew considerably. In 1906 he won many converts in the Urewera and the Bay of Plenty. The failure of King Edward to come to Gisborne that June Rua explained away by saying that he was in fact the King and that the millennium had been delayed. His

followers, now known as Iharaira (Israelites), grew into a highly disciplined group, strengthened by acts of faith healing. Alcohol and tobacco were banned. Iharaira were required to sell up their worldly goods and follow Rua into the interior to build the New Jerusalem.

Rua's increasing influence, in particular his moves to take Maori children away from schools to free them from European vices, led the government to pass the Tohunga Suppression Act of 1907. This move to curtail Rua's activities was supported by leaders of the Young Maori Party; reformers such as Te Rangi Hiroa (Peter Buck), Maui Pomare and Apirana Ngata felt that Rua was preventing Maori from enjoying the benefits of European civilisation.

To pay for the New Jerusalem land was sold — some 40,000 acres (16,160 hectares) for £31,000. Although this sale provided essential capital for development it also opened the floodgates to widespread alienation. More than half of Tuhoe's total landholdings would be sold between 1910 and 1921.

From the middle of 1907 about 1400 people followed Rua onto the sacred mountain of Maungapohatu. Like Te Whiti at Parihaka, Rua adopted only those aspects of European lifestyle which he thought would benefit his people. He placed great emphasis on hygiene, established a savings bank and general store, encouraged efficient farming and consolidated landholdings

under a co-operative form of ownership. At the same time he asserted the superiority of Maori traditions by removing his people from contact with Pakeha and keeping them in an environment rich in tribal associations.

Gradually the settlement began to prosper. Large quantities of top quality cocksfoot grass seed were sold to local farmers at good prices. Rua's cattle earned a sound reputation and the community grew potatoes, melons and maize. No one went hungry. Rua paid his followers standard wages; the savings bank operated as a communal pool of funds shared out according to family needs. Some of his people found the discipline too rigorous while others felt that the new prosperity was not evenly distributed. Malcontents drifted away at a steady rate but those who stayed seemed content with their very orderly, healthy community. It was certainly a big improvement over the misery and poverty of the past.

The focal point of Maungapohatu was the religious buildings set inside the fenced inner sanctum (wahi tapu). The Hiruharama Hou (New Jerusalem) was a two-sided house with separate entrances for each main tribe in the community. (Whakatohea, from the Opotiki area, was also represented in the village.) Playing cards painted to represent Old Testament history adorned the outside of the spectacular two-storeyed circular Hiona (Zion), known to Pakeha as Rua's 'temple'.

The Jewish Old Testament orientation of the religion practised at Mau-

Rua with some of his apostles. Rua and one of his wives stand together in the far upper right of the photograph. *National Museum.*

Rua's courthouse and meeting house. The top storey was used by Rua, his wives and two chiefs who at first formed a small council with Rua to judge on local disputes. The only entrance to this level was the outside stairs. The top storey measured 6 metres across and 4 metres high. The lower storey, 'the great court', measured 18 metres across and 6 metres high. The outside designs were borrowed from the ace of clubs and diamond suits of playing cards. *National Museum.*

The 'main street' of Rua's settlement, Maungapohatu, 1908. *Auckland Weekly News.*

ngapohatu was typical; Maori identified with the Jews because they were an oppressed yet chosen people. Theologically, Rua's religion was essentially an adaptation of Te Kooti's Ringatu. His taking of seven wives (eventually he had 12) had ample Old Testament authority but he added a Maori dimension by choosing one from each of seven hapu of Tuhoe, symbolising his attempt to unite a fragmented people.

By 1910 alcohol began to impinge on the tight discipline and order of life in the community. Rua found it impossible to stop his followers drinking something which was readily available to Pakeha, and he wanted Maori treated in the same way as Europeans in terms of access to alcohol. The issue symbolised the government's failure to administer the law impartially: Rua asked several times for a licence and became angry when it was refused. In a gesture of open defiance he sly grogged whisky to his followers, was fined but continued to use alcohol as a weapon against official discrimination.

Rua was gaoled for selling whisky in May 1915. The prison experience deeply disturbed the prophet and when he returned he cut off his hair as a symbol of a new start. He began to have more visions, prophesying that all the kings of the world, including the Kaiser, would soon come to the Hiona to usher in the millennium. Rua would have the highest throne of all, with the Kaiser and George V seated below him but above the lesser monarchs. This apparent pro-Germanism was compounded on 12 February 1916 by reports from local policemen Andy Grant and Denis Cummings of Rotorua that Rua was prophesying a victorious Germany which would allow him to become King of New Zealand. This was all the authorities needed and the police expedition was despatched.

Burdened with legal fees and costs, Rua returned from prison in 1918 to a shattered community overcome by debt. Because of damage to the settlement at Maungapohatu he moved to Matahi with a small core of his old following. Rua's lifestyle became more Europeanised; he even approved the establishment of a Presbyterian mission school. Yet he continued to lead his community and experienced many more visions. When he died in 1937 some 600 gathered, hoping for a miracle. They were disappointed.

All that remained of Rua's mission was the testimony of his life. His influence outside the Urewera was slight and even Tuhoe were divided about his leadership. His movement was, however, the last attempt to set up a separate Maori government in New Zealand and for some he provided the most vital ingredient for survival — hope. Without him the once proud Tuhoe might never have been able to fight back from the brink of despair. Rua was the product of a society confronted by rapid change. He was a traditional prophet and his careful emphasis on distinctively Maori symbols and heritage enabled an isolated tribe with little experience of the Pakeha and the best recorded folklore and mythology in Maoridom, to survive a severe crisis. Rua Kenana Hepetipa, Maori prophet, was thrown up by the circumstances of 50 years of ethnic confrontation.

Meanwhile another prophet, Ratana, was arising in the west. Rua not only hoped to end European domination but tried to renegotiate power relations within Maori society. Ratana shared Rua's aims but employed very different methods.

16. 1918 Repelling the Hun:
New Zealanders Plug the Gap During the German Spring Offensive

THE New Zealand Expeditionary Force arrived in France in April 1916. The New Zealanders now constituted a separate entity, the New Zealand Division, under the command of Major General Sir A. H. Russell, born in Napier, educated at Harrow, trained at Sandhurst. In May the New Zealanders had their first taste of warfare on the Western Front when they were asked to hold a sector of the line on the border between France and Belgium in the Armentières area.

On the Western Front massive armies confronted each other across low-lying areas. Both sides con-

Allied soldiers crossing a bridge of duckboards at Garter Point in October 1917. *Imperial War Museum.*

structed an intricate network of trenches which ran continuously for 720 kilometres from the Belgian coast to the Swiss frontier. For four years the trench lines remained much the same until the breakthrough in 1918. Barbed wire entanglements lay between the frontline trenches and 'No Man's Land' — a zone which averaged 225 metres in width but ranged from 20 metres to 800 metres across. The enemy sheltered behind its own barbed wire and was bedded in its own elaborate trench system.

Life in the trenches left an indelible mark on all who served in them. Existing in what was often a muddy, lice-ridden, rat-infested hole in the ground, waiting for a stray shell or a sniper's bullet, soon took its toll. The routines involved 'stand to arms' inspections, cleaning of rifles, repairing the barbed wire, digging and filling sandbags, observing the enemy lines.

Between major offensives raids were carried out on enemy lines to seize prisoners and inflict casualties. Daylight raids — carefully planned dashes across No Man's Land — came after a short artillery and mortar barrage. Night raids were much slower and more secretive. In trench warfare it was rare to actually see the enemy; it was easy to imagine the worst. The Germans were savages, Huns, beasts who raped women and bayoneted babies.

The soggy, low land near Armentières was quiet compared with some sectors but in just three months the New Zealanders staged 11 major raids and numerous patrols. Casualties totalled 2500 men, 375 of them killed. In early August the New Zealanders withdrew from the line to prepare for the 'second phase' of the Somme offensive, 65 kilometres to the south.

At dawn on 15 September the New Zealanders launched their first attack in the gigantic Battle of the Somme. Each man carried two gas masks, a rifle and bayonet, 200 rounds of ammunition in pouches and bandoliers, two bombs, two empty sandbags (to be used to fortify captured trenches), a waterproof sheet, a water bottle and a haversack containing a day's rations and an iron ration. Every second man carried down the centre of his back a shovel or a pick and every platoon had shared among its members smoke bombs and flares. Laden in this way they were expected to storm across No Man's Land, and fight the enemy in hand to hand battle in a maze of trenches and dugouts.

Behind an artillery barrage the New Zealanders advanced to seize two trenches. On 3-4 October they withdrew from the horror-filled swamp to count their losses; in just 23 days 1560 men had died and 5400 were wounded. The *Official History* summarised their achievements:

they had not merely performed the tasks set themselves, but on more than one occasion rendered effective help to formations on their flanks. Commencing on a frontage of under 1,000 yards, they were holding at the close a line nearly 3 times as long . . . they had achieved all but unbroken success, captured 5 miles of enemy front line . . . and fought their way forward for over 2 miles. Themselves losing under 20 prisoners, they had captured nearly 1,000 Germans, with many machine guns and war material.

In the following months the New Zealand Division built an impressive reputation as soldiers who could perform under all conditions. Their list of battle honours included most of the bitterly contested campaigns in the British sector — Messines, the Third Battle of Ypres, Polygone Wood, Passchendaele and Polderhoek Chateau — but their proudest achievements came in 1918, the last year of the war.

On 24 February 1918 the New Zealand Division moved away from the front for a long overdue spell of rest and retraining in the St Marie Cappel area 40 kilometres to the rear. Three months in the front line over a harsh winter, hard on the heels of six months of bitter fighting, had left everyone exhausted. For some, though, the relief came too late. On 3 March a private of the 2nd Battalion of the Otago Regiment shot and killed two officers and then committed suicide. The general verdict — he was 'presumably insane'.

For most of March the New Zealand Division rested and trained in the Etaples area. The combined effect of this rest and exercise was a tonic for the troops. The Divisional Medical Report for March and April noted 'a very noticeable improvement in the physical and mental condition of the troops'. The training also had its serious side, containing hints that a new, dramatically different assault was in the offing, a counter-assault on the German offensive which was expected at any moment.

A German offensive was virtually inevitable in early 1918. The war was going badly for Germany. Troops from the United States were starting to arrive in France in significant numbers and unless action was taken before the Americans came in force, Germany's chances of victory would be swept away. This would be their last chance to inflict a crushing defeat on the Allies.

The German offensive which began on 21 March 1918 was bold and innovative. The attack opened with a short (five-hour) ferocious artillery bombardment. (Almost half the entire German artillery strength on the Western Front was involved.) Much deeper than usual, the attack hit assembly areas, communication trenches, brigade and division headquarters and generally wreaked havoc on rear areas as well as forward defences.

New Zealanders being issued with their rum ration at Fleur
Imperial War Museum.

The intention was to demoralise and confuse the enemy rather than the usual aim of obliterating all defences. The infantry was left to neutralise any resistance offered.

The infantry also operated in new ways. In the lead came specially trained storm troops whose purpose was pure and simple: to move into the British lines as quickly and deeply as they could. They were to ignore and by-pass British defensive positions and simply keep moving forward. The troops following behind would mop up any remaining pockets of resistance.

On 21 March the German forces attacked along an 80-kilometre front from St Quentin in the south to Arras in the north held by the British 3rd and 5th Armies. It was against the latter's sector that the Germans directed their main thrust and their highest hopes. Outnumbered four to one, the 5th Army buckled and began to fall back. By 24 March the situation was desperate — the 5th Army had been smashed and their line was in tatters; it no longer existed on the Somme, in the south it maintained only tenuous con-

Frontline New Zealand headquarters covered in snow. *Alexander Turnbull Library.*

tact with the French and in the north it was also in retreat. Victory now lay within the Germans' grasp. Their main objective now was to break through between the 3rd and 5th Armies and wheel to the north-west to force the British back upon the Channel ports. They also wanted to capture Amiens, the vital railway town and British staging depot.

In the meantime, the New Zealand Division had moved south from its rest area to become part of the General Headquarters Reserve. Here they joined the 3rd, 4th and 5th Australian Divisions and the 32nd Division. On 25 March the New Zealand Division was ordered to Hédauville in the south of the 3rd Army area where a widening gap between IV Corps and V Corps left the way open for the Germans to break through in strength. Such a breakthrough could cause a general rout. It would split the British and French armies, forcing the British to pull back to the north to maintain access to the Channel ports while the French moved south to block the approaches to Paris.

The New Zealanders had to close the gap by establishing a line between the villages of Hamel and Puisieux, a distance of some 4 kilometres, over-

lapping with the 12th Division (V Corps) on their right and the 62nd Division (IV Corps) on their left. Any German advance parties were to be pushed back to the east, unless their strength made that impossible. In that event, the New Zealanders were to withdraw 1 kilometre to establish a line between the villages of Colincamps and Hébuterne. There was no provision for withdrawal behind this line.

As the orders to advance to Hédauville were received most of the division were on trains somewhere to the west of Amiens. The orders required immediate action, however, so as units arrived they discarded their packs, blankets and greatcoats and made ready for battle. No transport was available so everything had to be carried. Officers specified 'light fighting order' and each man loaded pouches and bandoliers with 220 rounds. Machine and Lewis gun crews were laden with as much ammunition as they could carry. At 10 o'clock that night, the first troops set out on foot to cover the 13 kilometres to Hédauville.

Although the roads were congested with refugees and military transport, all heading away from the front, the New Zealanders made good time. By

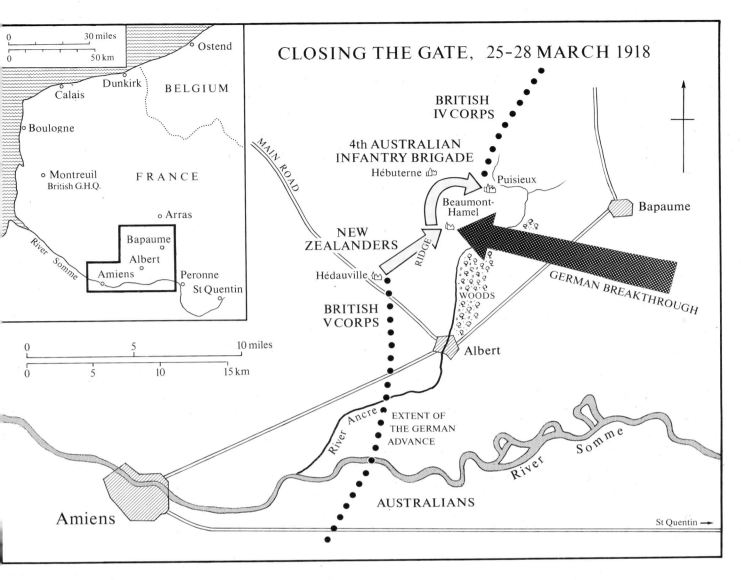

CLOSING THE GATE, 25-28 MARCH 1918

1.30 a.m., 26 March, Divisional Head-quarters had been established at Hédauville and in the succeeding hours more and more units arrived to be organised quickly into improvised brigades. In the interim the situation had deteriorated. The breach in the line was now 8 kilometres and the Germans were moving through in increasing numbers.

At 6.30 a.m. the New Zealanders began their own advance as the 1st Battalion of the 3rd (Rifle) Brigade moved north-east from Hédauville seeking to establish contact with the left of V Corps. This would secure the New Zealand Division's right flank and allow the main advance to take place along the line of the road running northward from the village of Beaumont-Hamel to Hébuterne. The intention was to pivot the division on its secure right flank, literally and figuratively shutting the gate on the Germans who would be driven back before the advance. At Hébuterne the

New Zealanders would link up with the 4th Australian Infantry Brigade which had been detached from its division and sent to IV Corps specifically to anchor that end of the line and assist the New Zealanders in closing the gap.

The manoeuvre was more easily planned than executed. The New Zealand advance was hindered by continued uncertainty as to when units would be available to be committed to the line. It also proved more difficult than expected to secure the right flank. The Germans were coming forward in increasing strength and proved difficult to hold, let alone repulse. For one very unpleasant period in the early and mid-afternoon the New Zealanders, taking cover in open ditches, fought a pitched battle against a superior number of Germans whose machine guns occupied the local high ground. The New Zealanders' vulnerability was increased because they had not made contact on either flank.

Fortunately they were not outflanked and as the day progressed more New Zealanders arrived to extend and consolidate the line.

By nightfall the New Zealand Division had made contact with V Corps, their right flank was secure and they occupied a strong and 'practically continuous' line of some 5 kilometres from just west of Hamel to north of the Serre road. In the south the gap had been closed but progress at the northern end was temporarily halted. The pause was necessary to avoid stretching the line too thin but the remaining New Zealanders had finally reached the front. Their journey had not been easy. The troops had been two nights without sleep and were tired and footsore after a forced march of 32 kilometres.

At 1 a.m. on 27 March they moved up to the line to bridge the last section of the gap. Against heavy machine gun fire they advanced rapidly, pushing the enemy before them and establishing

137

Allied soldiers, gas masks on, bayonets fixed, prepare for an attack. *Imperial War Museum.*

contact with the Australians at 6.30 that morning. The Anzacs then immediately pushed forward to establish a more secure line. The Germans hit back throughout the day and into the evening of the 27th, but the Anzacs held fast.

This pattern was repeated up and down the line. The 3rd Army, with the breach in its line eliminated, held firmly to its positions, resisting German pressure, while in the 5th Army area in front of Amiens the 3rd and 4th Australian Divisions halted the German troops within sight of the city's spires.

North of the Somme the immediate danger had passed and the New Zealanders and Australians set about the process of 'maintaining the offensive spirit' and 'establishing moral superiority over the enemy' by undertaking raids and 'minor operations'. On one raid on 30 March the New Zealanders attacked on a 1-kilometre front, captured 230 prisoners and 110 machine guns and, most importantly, seized the high ground in the centre of their line. From here they could view the German positions and movements well to the rear. This success was so against the trend it was seized on as a welcome tonic to the general gloom and the division received messages of congratulations from a number of divisional, corps and Army commanders.

The New Zealand Division remained in the line in the Hébuterne area until 7 June but faced only one

A New Zealander inspects the ribs of an unfinished German pillbox in the midst of a sea of mud. *Alexander Turnbull Library.*

Ambulance crossing the Selle River on a bridge built by New Zealand engineers. *Alexander Turnbull Library.*

more major German attack on 5 April. With the failure of that attack the Germans switched their effort to the Lys area to the north but their chance had passed. By the end of April the offensive had staggered to a halt. Its 40-day fury had cost over 500,000 casualties; 239,793 on the British side, 348,300 on the German.

The German Army had come close to success. They had opened a number of gaps in the Allied lines and for a short while had a chance to inflict a comprehensive military defeat that might have turned the war conclusively in Germany's favour. In large part the Germans' failure was of their own making. They should have moved against the weaker line of resistance to the south of the Somme. Nevertheless they would still have succeeded if it had not been for a handful of British, Australian and New Zealand Divisions who moved against the tide of battle to close those gaps, restore the line and deny a German breakthrough.

The halting of the offensive on the Somme marks a genuine turning point in the war. Never again would the Allied lines be subjected to the same threat. A few months later a flood of men and material from the United States would tip the balance of power decisively in the Allies' favour. Now they could launch their own offensive.

From the beginning of the offensive in early August until the declaration of the Armistice on 11 November 1918, the New Zealanders played a leading role. As shock troops they were involved in constant fighting. Against stubborn rearguard actions the New Zealanders made constant progress. By the end of August, for example, after six weeks of fighting, the New Zealand Division had taken 2521 German prisoners and had captured a total of 32 field guns, 527 machine guns, 29 trench mortars and two tanks. The cost: almost 3000 casualties.

Although losses were heavy, the attack succeeded spectacularly on a number of fronts. The Hindenburg Line was conclusively breached by the Australian 2nd, 3rd and 5th Divisions and the United States II Corps on 29 September. During this time the New Zealanders played a vital role in the series of attacks by which the 1st and 3rd Armies turned the flank of the line and advanced on Cambrai.

Despite successive defeats the Germans remained a force to be reckoned with. After a week in a rest area in the middle of October the New Zealand Division returned to the front and continued the advance towards the Sambre River.

The division ended the war on a high note, capturing the medieval fortress of Le Quesnoy, ringed with 18-metre ramparts and full of civilians. Under covering fire a platoon used a single scaling ladder to climb the ramparts and overpower two machine guns. The garrison surrendered soon after. The infantry were relieved at midnight on 5-6 November. Five days later the war ended.

New Zealand had sent over 100,000 men to serve overseas — 10 per cent of the population, a third of eligible males. The figure was exceeded in the Empire only by Britain. Although conscription had been introduced in 1916, over 70 per cent of New Zealand's fighting men were volunteers. Altogether there were 58,014 casualties — 16,697 killed, 41,317 wounded. In the Empire only Australia's horrific 65 per cent casualty rate exceeded New Zealand's 59 per cent.

17. 1918 The Black Scourge: The Great Influenza Epidemic

ON 11 November 1918 the 'war to end all wars' ended and jubilation and relief swept the Western world. New Zealand enthusiastically joined in the celebrations, although the small colony of little more than a million people had suffered horrendous losses: over 17,000 soldiers had been killed and over 40,000 were seriously wounded. But the seemingly endless slaughter had finally stopped.

Bands played, soldiers marched and crowds gathered to listen to endless speeches. Cheering and singing went on through the day and into the night. Liquor flowed liberally and men and women hugged and kissed with abandon. A week later the kissing had to stop when it became clear that a minor outbreak of influenza had heralded the arrival of a major epidemic.

It seemed as if a perverse deity was intent on stopping a war weary world from enjoying the first fruits of peace. The 'Great Flu' of 1918-19 was the worst pandemic since the Black Death of the 14th century. This particular strain of influenza killed more than 25 million people, well in excess of the 9 million killed in the First World War. Sometimes called the 'plague of the Spanish lady' (because of the havoc it wrought in Spain) or the 'Black Flu' (because victims sometimes turned black after death, reminding people of the Black Death) the pandemic began in Europe in April 1918. It spread rapidly, killing 250,000 in Germany, 375,000 in Italy, 170,000 in Spain, 160,000 in France and 250,000 in Great Britain. From there it moved on to Asia and the United States where it claimed over half a million victims. Distance provided no protection and Australia succumbed in October.

Contemporaries blamed the introduction of the virus to New Zealand on the arrival of the SS *Niagara* on 12 October 1918. That Prime Minister Massey and Finance Minister Ward

Patrons waiting to use the inhalation sprayer at the Health Department's Auckland office, November 1918. A spray of zinc-sulphate solution was supposed to kill flu bugs. It was useless but gave the appearance that something was being done. *Weekly News*.

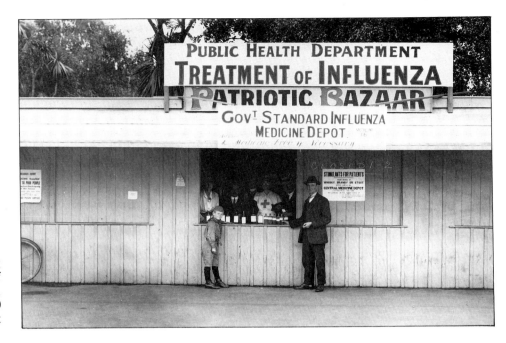

who were on board proved ready scapegoats tells us more about the growing unpopularity of these politicians than about the reasons for the flu's arrival. The deadlier second wave virus was in fact already active in New Zealand before the *Niagara* arrived. The ship did, however, pass the virus on to another steamer, the *Talune*, at Auckland which in turn carried the disease to Samoa, with devastating effects. Some 8500 people, a fifth of the islands' 37,000 inhabitants, died; the death rate of 229.7 per 1000 population was one of the highest anywhere.

The flu spread rapidly through New Zealand. It peaked in the third week of November and dwindled away by the end of December. Special inhalation chambers set up to check the spread of the 'great scourge' proved totally ineffective, as did the closing down of hotels and all places of popular entertainment. If anything, the chambers, which 'treated' up to 30 people at a time, accelerated the spread of what was a droplet infection. Bizarre-looking face masks were equally ineffective. Formalin and gauze proved no match for this virulent virus. By the time the pandemic passed it had claimed at least 6600 'official' victims.

This figure is conservative. It refers only to deaths directly attributable to influenza and excludes many victims who finally succumbed to pneumonia or heart failure. The virus literally killed its victims by flooding their lungs and drowning them. Often pneumonia finished them off. Geoffrey Rice's recent research estimates that the true figure is 8573 out of a population of 1,165,000, or a national death rate of 7.4 per 1000. Australia's rate, by comparison, was 2.3 per 1000.

The flu in New Zealand first reached epidemic proportions in Auckland. New Zealand's largest city suffered at least 1128 deaths, a rate of 7.57 per 1000. Rural areas in the north fared slightly better. As the epidemic spread south it wreaked havoc in some small towns and Maori pa. Towns like Taihape and Taumarunui experienced what is still remembered as 'the black fortnight'; at least 63 people died of influenza in the Taumarunui Hospital

Board area alone. These smaller settlements became instant ghost towns as most families went down with the flu.

Things were even worse for the Maori. Official figures put Maori deaths at 1130, a rate four and a half times higher than for Europeans. This understated the true position. Rice calculates that 2160 Maori died and this rate of 42.3 per 1000 was eight times the European rate. The isolation of most pa meant that many Maori deaths were simply not recorded. Maori seemed more likely to die from infection. The case fatality rate for Maori troops (that is the proportion of those infected who died from the flu) was 10 per cent as against 4½ per cent for European soldiers. Growing Maori immunity to introduced diseases, sometimes referred to as holding the key to the so-called 'Maori Renaissance', suffered a severe setback. A steady population increase since the low point of 1896 slowed significantly. Maori population rose from 52,997 in 1916 to only 56,987 in 1921.

Wellington was affected nearly as badly as Auckland. Some 757 deaths were attributed to influenza. Cook Strait did not act as a barrier although Nelson, Christchurch and Dunedin fared better than the major northern centres. Nelson had the lowest rate of any province, escaping lightly with 53 deaths. Some 447 deaths were re-corded in Christchurch where Show Week, held during the height of the epidemic, helped to spread the virus throughout the province.

Dunedin was the most mildly

affected of the main centres despite its notoriously fickle climate, but even so 273 deaths were officially attributed to the flu. Rural Southland was the worst hit South Island area; some 491 deaths in the province were attributed to flu, a higher figure than for more populous Otago province (436). Small towns such as Mataura and Gore suffered similar devastation to Taumarunui. The flu has remained an integral part of Southland folklore.

There were several distinctive features about the victims claimed by the epidemic in New Zealand. Generally pandemics kill the weak — the very old and the very young — but the Great Flu generally killed young adults. The 21 to 40 age group experienced by far the highest death rate. Christchurch differed slightly from the national pattern in that a higher proportion of babies and elderly died than in other centres. This discrepancy possibly reflected the higher rate of respiratory diseases in the garden city. Even in Christchurch, however, few children died.

Strangely, in New Zealand almost twice as many men died as women, the reverse of what happened internationally. Men aged between 30 and 40 succumbed far more often than any other group. The apparently healthy and strong were heavily over-represented among victims. Military camps were particularly hard hit; some 284 out of 7561 soldiers in training died, a death rate of 37.56 per 1000.

No one has adequately explained the high number of male deaths. One contemporary explanation suggested

Temuka Influenza Hospital. Men washing the 'infected' linen and garments. *Courtesy Mrs S. M. Mills, Dunedin.*

that the larger the chest cavity the lower the resistance. Others feared that here was further evidence of the generally poor health of New Zealand males which had been revealed by the high rejection level of military recruits on grounds of unfitness. Both explanations seem farfetched. It is more likely that women fared better because relatively few were in the workforce and so were less exposed to infection.

Whatever the reasons, the influenza epidemic caused much distress because it struck down so many parents with young families. Rice's Christchurch study shows that over half the victims were married people with children; in Dunedin over a third of the victims were parents. The flu dealt a double blow by leaving behind many solo parents, swelling the number of widows left by the slaughter on the Western Front. The official government report on the epidemic revealed that 828 widows had been left, along with 2323 dependent children. Far fewer widowers (89) were left to support 366 children by themselves.

Orphans who lost both parents were less common (19 in Christchurch and 12 in Dunedin). Generally the flu took the breadwinner, leaving families dependent upon the state. Remarriage was difficult because of a shortage of men in the marriageable age group; few had in fact remarried by the time the 1921 census was taken.

Some epidemics are socially selective, striking down more people living in poor housing, for example, but the Great Flu, like the Black Death, hit rich and poor alike, claiming victims right across the social spectrum. In Christchurch professionals were slightly over-represented, as were men from the commercial, retail and financial sectors. Oddly, those working in factories, an environment conducive to spreading the disease, were underrepresented. The densely populated inner suburbs inevitably fared worse than the more sparsely peopled outer suburbs, but areas notorious for their inferior and insanitary housing did not seem to be worse affected. Auckland was different, however, in that such areas were worse hit. Subsequent inquiry revealed that many houses suffered from chronic overcrowding with up to six people jammed into one room.

The Dunedin pattern was different again. Unskilled factory workers and the self-employed were hard hit, along with professionals and white collar workers. The poorer suburbs on the South Dunedin flat fared worse than any other suburb or the central city area. Health workers also noted that substandard and unhygienic housing seemed to encourage the spread of the disease and people living in such conditions were more likely to be infected.

The epidemic revealed other problems. Many people seemed totally ignorant about basic hygiene and about how infection spread. One doctor reported that his stethoscope stuck to the chest of one woman because she had covered herself with treacle. Children were often found with camphor bags tied around their necks. In Christchurch Nurse Maude reported that both middle and working class

Blenheim Borough.

Epidemic—Influenza.

FIFTY non-trained common-sense women capable of running an ordinary home, are asked to place their names on the Bureau List for volunteer service if and when wanted.

An inhaling plant has been installed at the Council Offices for use by the Public.

All proprietors of hotels, restaurants etc. are asked to pass used eating and drinking utensils through boiling water.

Will parents see that their children are kept away from the centre of the town.

The Bureau will be open between the hours of 8 a.m. and 10 p.m. daily and all night if required.

JOHN JOSEPH CORRY,
Mayor.

Council Offices, Blenheim.
15th November, 1918.

One of the many public notices on the flu which appeared in the *Marlborough Express*, 22 November 1918. *Courtesy Geoffrey Rice.*

families failed to realise the importance of keeping infected family members separate from one another. The discoveries of Pasteur do not seem to have spread very far beyond the medical profession; many people still believed in the old miasmic theory of vapours, and when modern medicines failed some turned to traditional folk remedies.

Such revelations raised concern about both public health education and the state of city housing. Nurse Maude and other health workers called for reform and their demands were met by the new Health Act of 1920. The Health Department, which had been formed in response to the Bubonic Plague scare in 1901, was overhauled. More health inspectors were appointed, with increased powers, and many more school nurses, who had been introduced in 1912, were appointed to teach children elementary hygiene.

Both politicians and the public agreed something had to be done to improve housing standards. The discovery of 'slums' in 'God's Own Country' was as shocking as the revelations of sweating in 1889. The town planning and urban renewal movement suddenly became popular. Many new houses were needed and more generous loans were made available to low income families under the Housing Act of 1919. Electricity and sewerage were provided for many more houses. The noticeable improvement in the comfort of urban life during the 1920s owed something to the epidemic and what it revealed.

The impact upon the Maori community was even more obvious. Confusion among detribalised Maori increased and they turned to Ratana, the newest prophet and faith healer, for succour. Significantly the most important influence on Ratana's thinking, after the Bible, was J. H. Pope's (Te Popi) little red book *Health for the Maori*. In other areas leaders in a more traditional mould won a stronger allegiance than before. Princess Te Puea pushed the King Movement in new directions in the Waikato and developed Turangawaewae Marae at Ngaruawahia as a model pa. Both Te Puea and Ratana placed great emphasis upon improving water supply and sanitation. So, too, did Maori leaders like Ngata who were men of two worlds. Te Rangi Hiroa (Peter Buck), appointed as foundation director of Maori Hygiene in 1920, built up the cadre of nurses and revived the local health councils which had been established by Seddon's Liberal government.

The combined efforts of these different leaders began to bear some fruit

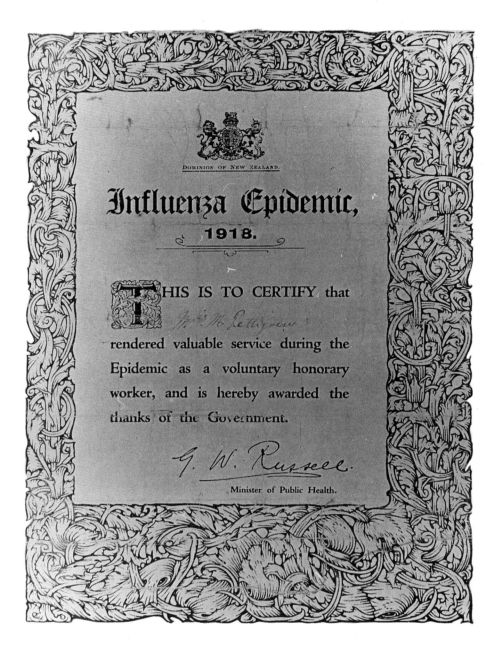

and the 1926 census showed that the Maori population had risen to 63,670. The increase was the result of a significant fall in infant mortality from 232 per 1000 in 1905 to 107 in 1926. Even though the birth rate had fallen many more Maori children were surviving the first year of life. Maori life expectancy also rose spectacularly over the same period, from 34 years for males to 47 years. Yet both rates still compared very unfavourably with those for Europeans. Infant mortality was more than twice as high (the European rate fell from 80 per 1000 to 45 over the same period) and European male life expectancy had risen to 63 by 1926. Maori leaders realised that many more improvements were required on a wide range of fronts.

The shock and trauma of the epidemic forced upon the European community a degree of co-operation never seen before in New Zealand. For a period of six weeks the bitter divisions engendered by the pressures of war seemed to be forgotten. Sectarian rivalry, anti-German hysteria, hatred of pacifists and fear and loathing of socialists and 'Bolshevism' were laid aside in the interests of survival. Some 228 doctors were still away on overseas service and so many of the remaining doctors and nurses were infected that people had to provide their own means of support. St John Ambulance, Red Cross, the Army and Services' Corps, the Women's National Reserve and Voluntary Aid Detachments all did sterling work, displaying heroic disregard for the risks involved. In Dunedin senior medical students helped to nurse patients in the hospital. Individuals from all walks of life, including children, helped to distribute medicine and tended the ill. Sometimes whole families were infected and had to be helped by neighbours or other volunteers. Inner city MPs such as Michael Joseph Savage added considerably to their reputations by working tirelessly through the worst weeks of November and December 1918. Many other acts of heroism went unnoticed as the community united to survive.

The Great Flu has left a very strong impression on the New Zealand folk memory. In a very direct way the flu affected between a third and half of the entire civilian population, whereas the war was fought by 100,000 soldiers on far away fields. And those soldiers tended to remain silent about their experiences; honest books about New Zealand soldiers' experience of the horrors of the Western Front did not begin to appear until 1935.

Anyone who was a child at the time of the epidemic still has vivid memories of deserted towns with their empty schools, closed shops, silent pubs and mournful churches. In contrast the war was a blur of endlessly marching feet, blaring brass bands, inevitable fêtes and assembling parcels of food and socks. Everyone has their story to tell about the flu and most are poignant because they are memories of trauma and disruption. Children whose parents died from the flu were generally very young and their sense of loss was profound. One man told how, as a seven year old, he was very proud to be asked to place a white flag in the family's mail box. He did not realise that this was the signal for volunteers to come and take away his mother's body.

Such experiences were multiplied many times. The fact that the 1920s in New Zealand was a time of sadness in which people concentrated on consolidation rather than a period of mad escapades and experimentation becomes understandable when it is remembered that most families in the small dominion had lost a member in either the epidemic or the war. This generation had every reason to be concerned with security from the cradle to the grave.

G.   R.

DEPARTMENT OF PUBLIC HEALTH

INFLUENZA

INSTRUCTIONS TO VOLUNTEER NURSES OR FAMILY ATTENDANTS.

PATIENT TO BE ISOLATED IN BRIGHT, WELL VENTILATED ROOM.
BE SURE WINDOWS OPEN FULLY

NO ONE EXCEPT THE NURSE OR ATTENDANT TO ENTER ROOM.

MILD CASES	SERIOUS CASES.	EXTREME
1. Keep chest covered with flannel, if patient has slight cough and pain in chest. DON'T OVER COVER.	1. Prop patient up in bed, if breathing is bad.	HAEMORRHAGE (or bleeding from the mouth).
2. Keep patient in bed for about a week; with open windows but no draughts.	2. Note colour of patient's face; if any blueness, report at once.	1. Send for the Doctor at once.
3. Give "standard influenza medicine" if feverish, and follow directions on bottle. (Medicine can be obtained from Depot.)	3. Keep chest and back well covered with cotton wool or flannel, RIGHT UP TO THE NECK.	2. Prop patient up high; then raise HEAD of bed by means of blocks or 2 strong boxes.
4. Gargle thrice daily with salt and borax (1 teaspoonful of salt, ½ teaspoonful of borax to 1 cupful of warm water).	4. If pain in back or side, poultice with linseed, or preferably with ANTI-PHLOGISTINE (carefully following directions on tin). On removing poultice, cover parts with wool.	3. Place a bolster under patient's knees, and tie each end of bolster to head of bed, to prevent patient slipping down.
5. Opening medicine, 1 or 2 pills at night, and, if necessary, salts before breakfast.	5. Give plenty of light drinks, such as barley water, lime juice, thin soups, beef tea, and milk and soda water.	4. Give ice to suck. (Ice can be had any hour by ringing 'phone 3708 day or night.)
6. Diet: If feverish, fluids only, every 2 hours.	6. Stimulant every 4 hours; either 1 tablespoonful of brandy or whisky in equal quantities of water.	5. Hot water bottle to feet (bottle well covered).
7. If temperature over 102, sponge with warm soapy water under blanket.	7. Hot sponge twice a day, UNDER BLANKET. DON'T EXPOSE PATIENT.	6. NO stimulants.
8. If faint, give sal volatile (½ teaspoonful in water every 4 hours).	8. Opening medicine nightly.	
9. DON'T GET UP TOO SOON.	9. IF URINE NOT PASSED IN 12 HOURS, REPORT.	DELIRIUM
10. Nurse to wear mask, and use disinfectants freely.	10. Fresh air essential, but screen patient from draughts.	1. Hot sponge patient under blanket.
11. Pieces of rag to be used for sputum AND THEN BURNT.	11. Keep notes of patient's condition for doctor.	2. Apply hot water bottle (well covered) to feet; then cold packs to head and back of neck.
12. No patient to go out of doors for 7 days nor to appear in public for 14 days from date of onset.	12. No patient to go out of doors for 7 days nor to appear in public for 14 days from date of onset.	

COPIES OF THE ABOVE CAN BE OBTAINED **FREE OF CHARGE** AT THE LOCAL DEPOTS OR ON APPLICATION TO THE DISTRICT HEALTH OFFICE, CHRISTCHURCH.

HERBERT CHESSON, District Health Officer.

THE TUG-OF-WAR.

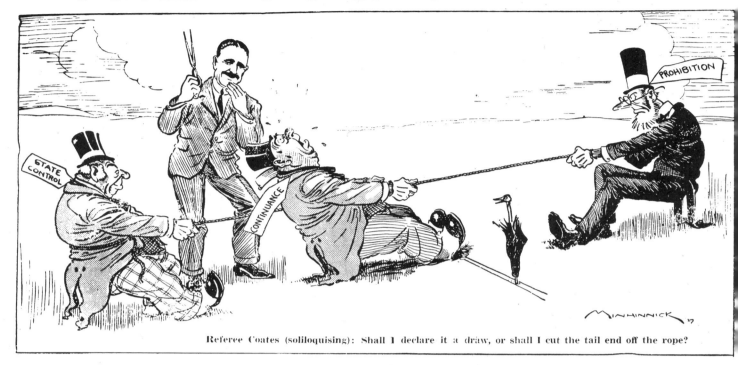

Referee Coates (soliloquising): Shall I declare it a draw, or shall I cut the tail end off the rope?

A temperance cartoon, 1927. In a 1919 referendum national prohibition came very close to succeeding. Thereafter, every three years voters were asked to choose between state control of alcohol, continuance and prohibition. *Alexander Turnbull Library.*

The co-operation engendered by the flu disappeared as soon as the flu epidemic passed. Divisions along sectarian, ideological and moral lines flared as the first year of peace degenerated into a bitter false dawn.

Soldiers who had hoped to return to a land 'fit for heroes' instead found civilians bickering among themselves. The Labour Party's decision to champion the cause of Irish independence aroused the ire of the Protestant Political Association and refuelled sectarian conflict. Massey extended the attack on Labour by emotively claiming all socialists were 'bolsheviks'; Labour's decision to nationalise land, banks and transport seemingly gave substance to the Prime Minister's claims. The formation of an Alliance of Labour made up of transport workers and miners revived the spectre of industrial militancy.

Soldiers' tolerance was strained when the good citizens of 'God's Own Country' voted for prohibition by a majority of 13,000 at a poll held in April 1919 and they expressed their displeasure by voting to reverse the decision. Reform won the 1919 or 'khaki' election easily on a 'loyalty' ticket — Massey's appeal to patriotism and tradition won the day. Reform took 46 seats to Labour's eight, while the Liberals were reduced to 19. Three independents made up a House which Massey would have little difficulty in controlling.

During the war years the New Zealand countryside experienced unprecedented prosperity when the British government commandeered all the meat, butter, cheese and wool the dominion could produce — and paid high prices. An international recession hit in 1921 and export receipts fell sharply. Public servants suffered 7 per cent pay cuts, unemployment rose significantly for the first time since 1909 and the rural boom ended abruptly. Many soldier settlers found it hard to meet mortgage repayments and by 1925 2200 of the original 9000 settlers had walked off their properties. (More marginal farmers were probably weeded out during these years than at any other time in New Zealand's history.) The small business bankruptcy rate between 1921 and

1923 was actually higher than during the 1930s depression.

One by-product of the recession was the decision of a conservative government to set up state-supported producer boards. Both the Meat Board (1922) and the Dairy Board (1926) were established to reduce farmer costs and improve marketing. Commodity prices picked up from 1924 and the New Zealand economy recovered as the American economy revived, but prosperity after 1926 was sustained only by heavy borrowing. Unemployment crept upwards and by the time the Great Depression hit with full force in the early 1930s, a quarter of export receipts were being absorbed by interest repayments on New Zealand's loans.

However, herd testing, machine milking, greater use of artificial fertilisers, improved pasture management and more scientific breeding saw the volume of dairy exports multiply three times in the 1920s. And motor vehicles, together with telephones and radios, helped to break down rural isolation.

Although agriculture remained the lifeblood of the New Zealand economy, it was no longer the major employer. Manufacturing, unlike in Australia, made little advance in the 1920s; rural people drifting into the cities found work in the rapidly expanding service sector.

Unlike Australia, New Zealand was not made more nationalistic by the horrific experience of the First World War. Foreign policy developed the British connection and New Zealand earned the title of 'Britain's dutiful daughter' during the 1920s. Yet despite Massey's misgivings New Zealand was represented in the League of Nations and access to the London market was retained despite the growing opposition of English farmers.

New Zealand reluctantly took up a League mandate over Western Samoa, a former German colony. Inept and oppressive as a colonial administrator, the New Zealand government encountered a long period of Samoan resistance from the Mau self-government movement.

More interest was taken in Maori affairs once Gordon Coates became Minister of Native Affairs in 1921. He settled several land grievance claims and founded the Maori Purposes Fund to support educational, cultural and social activities. After Apirana Ngata became Minister of Maori Affairs in 1928 government aid was given to Maori farmers for the first time. Nevertheless Maori and Pakeha continued largely to live in separate worlds.

The 1920s saw the rise of another prophetic movement based on the teachings of Tahupotiki Wiremu Ratana, whose spiritual mission was inspired by a vision which came to him in 1918. While seated on the verandah of his house he saw a cloud stop before him and the voice of God spoke from the cloud: 'I have travelled around the world to find the people upon whom I can stand. I have come to Aotearoa to choose you, the Maori people . . . cleanse yourself . . . unite the Maori people, turning them to Jehovah of the thousands.'

Ratana began to preach that Maori should unite as God's chosen people. His faith healing won attention and it was not long before a settlement, known as Ratana Pa, grew up around his house, as the new prophet assumed the mantle of mangai (mouth of God). Ratana was of low birth and his beliefs

Coaches, pictured here running the dramatic route linking the West Coast to Canterbury, were an important form of transport in many parts of New Zealand. This particular shot was taken in 1904 but the Otira to Arthur's Pass section ran until 1923 and was one of the last coaching services in New Zealand. *Canterbury Museum.*

Diggers cleaning and scraping their harvest of gum. *Auckland Public Library.*

appealed particularly to those of lower status — poor farmers and workers — whom he called the Morehu. Ratana's rejection of tribalism and denial of the importance of whakapapa gained him much support among the growing number of Maori alienated from their tribal lands. Many uprooted Maori found Ratana's promotion of hygiene and condemnation of superstition, sorcery and social hierarchy especially appealing.

In 1922 Ratana moved into politics and circulated a petition calling for the ratification of the Treaty of Waitangi. It won over 30,000 signatures. His son, Tokoura, came within 800 votes of winning Western Maori in the same year. Then in 1928 the mangai declared the end of his spiritual mission and the beginning of his temporal mission as he determined to win all four Maori parliamentary seats with his candidates whom he called the 'four quarters'.

Ratana began negotiations with Labour leaders Michael Joseph Savage and Peter Fraser in 1931 and an informal alliance was established for the election. When Eruera Tirikatene won Southern Maori for Ratana in a by-election in 1932 he was accompanied to his seat by the Labour whips.

Tirikatene was joined by Tokoura Ratana who won Western Maori in 1935. After the election the prophet visited Savage and a verbal agreement of support was formalised.

Ratana candidates continued to stand as independent Ratana. Paraire Paikea took Northern Maori in 1938 and Tiaki Omana unseated Ngata in Eastern Maori in 1943. Tirikatene became a cabinet minister in 1947. The Labour-Ratana alliance completely dominated Maori parliamentary politics down to 1963 when Puti Tipene Watene became the first Maori who was not a member of the Ratana church to win one of the four seats since 1938. The Ratana church peaked in influence in 1936 claiming 20 per cent of Maori religious adherents, second only to the Church of England. The percentage of Maori belonging to the Ratana church has steadily declined since the Second World War from 15 per cent in 1946 to 11.21 per cent in 1981. This places Ratana below Roman Catholics and Anglicans, but well ahead of the Ringatu faith to which a mere 2.1 per cent of Maori claim adherence.

The 1920s also witnessed the emergence to national prominence of one of New Zealand's most influential women — Princess Te Puea.

Born in 1883, Te Puea Herangi first came to occupy a leadership role in the King Movement in 1917 when she led a campaign against conscription of Waikato Maori in the First World War. Te Puea never forgot the grievances felt by her people when the New Zealand government confiscated Waikato land in the 1860s and opened it up for European farming and settlement. She followed the pacifist teachings of her maternal grandfather, King Tawhiao, the second Maori King.

After the war Te Puea helped nurse her people through the horror of the influenza epidemic and worked to bring about dramatic improvements in Maori health. In 1921 she set about building Turangawaewae Marae at Ngaruawahia as a central place where the Waikato people could rebuild their mana and find identity and self-respect. Eventually it became the largest marae complex in the country.

She fought hard to win compensation for Maori land unjustly confiscated. An alliance with Sir Apirana Ngata led to the introduction of land development schemes in the Waikato. Te Puea helped many local Maori to become successful farmers on the land of their ancestors. She encouraged a whole range of cultural activities from plaiting to carving to show that communal living was possible in the modern world. Turangawaewae became a national meeting place from the late

920s onwards and the old divisions between the Kingite Maori and other tribes slowly began to break down.

Like Mahatma Gandhi, Te Puea believed in the capacity of traditional societies to cope with the challenge of modernisation. She built on traditional Maori strengths and rejected outright Maui Pomare's idea that Maori could only progress by rejecting their own culture. Her emphasis on the importance of whakapapa and chiefly authority (rangatiratanga) made her suspicious of both Ratana and Labour. She was a close ally of Gordon Coates, knew George Forbes and Michael Joseph Savage and, despite initial misgivings, became a supporter of Peter Fraser. Her respect for Fraser was demonstrated by her decision not to actively oppose recruitment of the Maori Battalion.

Te Puea died on 12 October 1952, having won acceptance for the King Movement among both Pakeha and Maori. Even more important, she had shown the post-war generation of Maori that their own culture had the strength and flexibility to adjust to such new challenges as urbanisation.

Economic uncertainty, social anxiety and an unclear cultural identity were reflected in the confused politics of the 1920s. This was a decade of many parties. Reform, Liberal (which changed its name to National in 1925) and Labour were the most important but there was also a Country Party formed in 1922 and independents remained an important group within the House.

Labour made great advances in 1922 because of the serious impact of the recession upon inner city areas. They won 17 seats, threatening the Liberals as the official opposition. Temporary prosperity soon undermined those gains and New Zealand's first native born Prime Minister, Gordon Coates, easily won the 1925 election. Reform won 55 seats to Labour's 13 and National's 12 seats.

Coates soon lost support. His attempt to fix butter prices through the Dairy Board and the introduction of family allowances of 2 shillings per week for families with over two children where the breadwinner earned

under £4 per week, were seen by the business wing of the Reform party as insidious socialism. They broke away to form a new right wing party with the remnants of the Liberals late in 1927. The new party was known as United.

At the same time Coates continued to lose farmer support because of dissatisfaction with low butter prices. Labour meantime decided that its policy of land nationalisation, known as useohold tenure, would have to be dropped if they were ever to win rural seats. Otherwise they offered a good dose of socialism and held out hopes for an upset victory in 1928. They could not, however, defeat a geriatric Sir Joseph Ward, who came out of retirement to lead the United Party. The new party was returned with 26 seats and the support of four independents as against Reform's 29 and Labour's 19 seats.

Ward's return was inglorious and shortlived. He seemed to be trapped in the 1890s and his old solutions did not solve new problems. The Wall Street Crash of 1929 did not hit New Zealand immediately but by early 1930 New Zealand was in the grips of a major international depression. Ward resigned in May 1930 and died in July

Crowds gather outside Wellington's *Evening Post* office to view the 1931 election results. The election returned the Coalition (United and Reform) with 51 seats. Labour won 25, the Country Party one, independents four. *Alexander Turnbull Library.*

before the full force of the Great Depression struck.

The savage Hawke's Bay earthquake of 3 February 1931, which killed 256 people, added to the gloom and increased the need for government to provide relief. Orthodox policies in the form of two wage cuts of 10 per cent could not stop unemployment rising to 50,000 by mid-year. Ward's successor, George Forbes, lacked imagination and no one else in his party seemed to have any idea as to what to do. In desperation Forbes followed British precedent and formed a Coalition government with Reform in September. This makeshift conservative government won the December election by the comfortable margin of 51 seats to 25 as Labour became the official opposition. New Zealanders still hoped that the hard times would pass without their having to make any large-scale changes.

18. 1932 This! In God's Own Country!: Riots Break Out in Dunedin Auckland and Wellington

THE new Coalition government proved as incapable as the United Party of stopping the relentless downwards spiral of the depression. Unemployment climbed to over 50,000, 8 per cent of the workforce, in early 1932. The real rate was much higher; official figures omitted women and Maori.

For the first time since the 1880s the respectable lower middle class and skilled workmen began losing their jobs and office workers joined carpenters, brickies and general labourers in the soup queues. Even some professionals, including lawyers, accountants, dentists and teachers were laid off. Seasonal or intermittent unemployment was commonplace for unskilled workers but long-term unemployment, for more than two years in some cases, was new. Unemployment of any kind was a shock for white collar workers who assumed that safe work was their right.

Anger and confusion were intensified by the government's philosophy of no pay without work. Increasing numbers of married and single men were sent to isolated public works camps under Scheme 5. There married men were paid 14 shillings a day for a four-day week if they had more than two children. After April 1931 the rate of pay was reduced to 12 shillings per day for married men and 9 shillings per day for single men who were also limited to a two-day working week. In April one stand down week in four was introduced.

Still, despite having to work in appalling conditions during the harsh winter of 1931, the men of Scheme 5 at least felt they were doing something useful. They built roads, put through the Homer tunnel and planted the massive pine forests of the central North Island. Some men on urban relief work improved parks and school grounds; others dug holes and filled them in again.

Driven by continuous unemployment and near starvation living conditions, normally apathetic New Zealanders began to take desperate action. Large public protests organised by the Unemployed Workers Movement (UWM) had become a feature of

A cartoon history of the depression by Minhinnick. *Courtesy Sir Gordon Minhinnick, New Zealand Herald.*

Dunedin life by January 1932. Resentment among the unemployed grew as the government continued to suggest that everyone could get by if they 'ate a little less'. The Labour Party leader, Harry Holland, warned that some kind of popular uprising was imminent. Most, however, dismissed such talk as wild political rhetoric and when violence did erupt in April the UWM seemed as surprised as the authorities.

The closure in March of the Dunedin relief depot was an unpopular move, but the bureaucracy surrounding the distribution of relief caused even more irritation. Some men were supplied with relief only during their stand down weeks and their wives could not collect relief until husbands returned from the work camps. This meant families were often left without adequate food. The onset of winter further blackened the mood of the unemployed. The city had become a world of 'us and them'.

The flamboyant Labour MP for

This Labour Party handbill of 1931 shows Seddon watching relief workers dragging a chain harrow. It points to the uselessness of much of the relief work. *Alexander Turnbull Library.*

Grey Lynn, John A. Lee, returned to his native Dunedin and spoke to a crowd of 7000 on 3 April. In pouring rain Lee held the crowd spellbound. He declared 'war against those who are trying to drag the people down to degradation and poverty'. The crowd roared their approval and Lee wrote confidently to his wife Mollie that 'the revolution is here'.

His prediction of social explosion was confirmed on Friday 8 April when the new women's branch of the UWM led a march to the St Andrew Street depot to demand more relief. Out in front four women pushed prams emphasising the peaceful intentions of the demonstrators. Mayoress Helen Black was already unpopular for distributing food in her finest clothes. Her habit of handing out parcels in elegantly gloved hands was viewed as particularly insensitive by people who owned only one set of clothes and a pair of worn out, hand me down shoes. When she refused to distribute more food, claiming that each case had to be considered individually, the crowd erupted. Protesters smashed windows and overturned a taxi in which the mayoress had attempted to escape.

Dunedin remained tense and divided throughout the weekend. On Monday 11 April a crowd of single men met in the botanical gardens to organise a strike of relief workers. They then rampaged through the centre of town, breaking the windows of Wardell's large grocery store. Looting followed. Death threats were made to the mayor and the mayoress was warned that her home would be attacked. One group of men tried to storm the Harbour Board but were dispersed by police wielding batons. The UWM then called a meeting to declare a strike of relief workers.

The protesters had gone too far and alienated support. Six leaders of the UWM were arrested and the strike collapsed. Mark Silverstone, a Labour councillor, seized his chance and wooed the unemployed away from the now discredited UWM to the Labour Party. The stand down week was abolished in the cities and new work schemes were introduced.

Large-scale rioting in Auckland followed a few days after Dunedin. On 14 April a major blow up was narrowly

"THIS! – IN GOD'S OWN COUNTRY!"

Relief Workers Cheaper
THAN HORSES!

" So far as men engaged on Roadwork are concerned, the ideal " must be to move them ' over the fence ' on to the land."

THUS spoke the Rt. Hon. J. G. Coates, who with the Rt. Hon. G. Forbes is joint leader of the Government in Parliament. The above photograph is of relief workers working under his department, and shows what he means.

Women of New Zealand!
WILL YOU STAND FOR THIS?

This Government professes to save your country, but reduces your sons, your husbands, your brothers to the cheapness of horses. It is in YOUR power to effect a change in Government by voting LABOUR and let New Zealand be once again " God's own Country."

avoided when a truck provocatively pushed into a crowd of thousands of demonstrators protesting against conditions in the work camps. Incensed, the crowd moved to attack the vehicle. Jim Edwards, leader of the UWM in Auckland, jumped on the tray of the truck and called for order. His commanding voice calmed the crowd. Even the usually hostile local press were impressed by Edwards's nerve and conceded that the crowd had been well behaved.

The next night a procession of Post and Telegraph workers gathered in

Queen Street to protest the wage cuts. Thousands more joined the march to the Town Hall and numbers swelled to 20,000. Banners were unfurled; they carried stark messages like 'Close the Slave Camps'. Some began to sing:
    Hallelujah I'm a bum
    Hallelujah bum again
    Hallelujah give us a handout
    To revive us again.
Others chimed in:
    Why don't you work like other men do?
    How the hell can we work
    When there's no work to do.

No one was armed but a few windows were smashed.

News spread to the marchers that the 3000-seat town hall was full and that the police had shut the front doors. Jim Edwards ordered the marchers to try and enter through the side doors. These too were locked. Some of the men with Edwards thought they had been locked out and tempers flared.

One group ran back to the front doors and threatened to attack the police guarding the main entrance. Edwards tried to calm the crowd. An overeager policeman, mistaking Edwards's efforts at keeping the peace for an incitement to riot, batoned the UWM leader. Panic followed and the crowd, thinking Edwards had been killed, pressed forward. The police retaliated with a baton charge and mounted policemen rode in among the

milling throng.

Suddenly Edwards appeared on the balustrade of the town hall, his head dripping blood. Holding up a megaphone, he instructed the crowd to pack around the police to stop them using their batons, but he also begged his supporters to abstain from violence. His words probably came too late; when he was batoned again rioting was guaranteed.

Angry demonstrators armed themselves with pickets taken from Colin Scrimgeour's Central Methodist Mission. Open brawling followed and then the crowd surged down Queen Street smashing windows and looting. Most of their pent-up frustration was taken out on the shops rather than the police. The police themselves had been severely affected by the pay cuts and were reluctant to fight. People were more interested in protesting

than in stealing. One man pointedly wound up every alarm clock in a jeweller's shop but stole nothing.

Rioting continued for two hours. The fire brigade were brought in but refused to use their hoses and order was not restored until ratings were brought in from HMS *Philomel* tied up at Devonport Naval Base. Specials were also sworn in immediately to help the ratings.

The calm did not last long. A riot broke out in Karangahape Road on the night of 16 April. Over 50 plate glass windows were smashed and 50 people were injured. Yet there was no looting. In this instance bystanders taunted the new special police, many of whom had been brought in from country districts. The ill-disciplined and rather intoxicated specials responded by attacking a section of the crowd.

The Karangahape Road incident signalled the end of the Auckland riots. Edwards went into hiding but later turned himself in. He was imprisoned for two years for inciting the Queen Street riot.

A repressive Public Safety Conservation Act was passed immediately after the Auckland riots, greatly increasing police powers. Regulations were also introduced to prevent the entrance into New Zealand of anyone who had visited a communist country in the last three years. The stand down week was dropped and rates of pay under Scheme 5 were increased a little. This mixture of coercion and concession could not stop another outbreak of trouble in Wellington on 10 May.

A crowd of about 3000 relief workers who had come out on strike gathered in the Basin Reserve to listen to fiery speeches. They then marched on Parliament and sent in a deputation to meet the Minister of Employment, Gordon Coates. By the time Coates agreed to give special consideration to the grievances of Wellington relief workers, one group had grown restless and rampaged down Lambton Quay, away from the police guarding Parliament. They smashed many windows and looted much more systematically than the Auckland rioters.

This reckless and somewhat cowardly action annoyed the respectable citizens of Wellington and many enlisted as special constables to prevent a

Armed sailors stand guard while a shop- keeper clears away the damage caused in the riots. *New Zealand Herald.*

repeat of any further nonsense. They got their chance to prove their mettle on the evening of 11 May when a group of striking relief workers met at a vacant section in Cuba Street. After a very brief time the inspector in charge of the small group of mounted and foot police ordered the speech making to stop. The relief workers shouted angrily at this seemingly un- necessary intrusion. Undaunted, the specials set about silencing the speak- ers. They were greeted by a hail of stones so they charged the crowd with batons drawn.

The meeting broke up in a wild stampede. Contemporary photographs make it look like a scene from the Russian Revolution; only the ever present felt hats suggest that this conflict happened in quiet, peaceful New Zealand. The protesters re- grouped at the corner of Vivian and Manners Streets and the specials came in for a terrible tongue lashing from the large crowd. This time there was no fighting. The next few days were very tense but the riots had come to an end. Christchurch was the only major city to escape outbreaks of violence even though much tension was gener- ated by a tramwaymen's strike in late April.

The press blamed the disturbances on communists and hooligans, the Labour Party blamed them on the UWM and the Coalition blamed Labour. All missed the point: the riots were nothing more than unplanned outbursts of sheer frustration. As Johnson, the narrator in John Mul- gan's *Man Alone*, puts it: 'To them it was the releasing of accumulated de- sire, a payment for the weeks and months of monotony and weariness and poverty and anxiety that could be satisfied . . . in a few moments of freedom and destruction.'

The longer term consequences of the riots were far more important than the riots themselves. Thereafter both direct action and the UWM were discredited and the unemployed turned to the Labour Party as their saviour. Both Lee and Michael Joseph

Perhaps the most famous scene of the riots. Mounted and foot police using batons charge into a crowd who had gathered on a vacant lot at the top of Cuba Street, Wellington. It was first shown in the *Dominion***, 12 May 1932.** *Alexander Turn- bull Library.*

153

One of the camps provided for unemployed relief workers on the Pakiri Block, near Wellsford in 1933. *New Zealand Herald.*

Savage, who became leader of the Labour Party in 1933, feared that further outbreaks of violence would accompany greater government repression. But this did not happen. The unemployed instead chose moderate political solutions and flirted with the cheap credit ideas of Social Credit rather than the Fascist alternative which proved so popular in Europe.

The revolution that resulted from the riots was a revolution in attitudes. For the first time people blamed unemployment on an unfair economic system rather than on personal failings, and once this change in outlook occurred among many members of the middle classes it became possible for Labour to become the government. Now a group who once seemed wild, disreputable and dangerous appeared the only party capable of solving the depression. The elevation of the mild, kindly Savage to Labour's leadership

also helped to convince many that Labour was the only responsible alternative. It came as no surprise when Labour won by 55 seats to the government's 19, with independents securing the remaining six electorates.

Even though the riots only added up to six days in total they became a central part of the powerful depression mythology which shaped the lives of nearly two generations of New Zealanders. The riots came to represent the desperate outburst of a decent people against an unfair economic system, an expression of disgust at the absurdity of starvation in a land of plenty. Like the depression itself they have been celebrated in several major works of literature written by both contemporary and later authors. Many New Zealanders believe that the riots, like the Great Depression, were a bad thing. All kinds of major changes, including the creation of the welfare state, the promotion of economic insulation and interventionism by the state, were readily accepted as the means of preventing such a catas-

trophe from ever happening again.

Yet a more objective assessment suggests that the New Zealand experience was not especially severe by world standards. Unemployment peaked at around 100,000 in 1933, or about 15 per cent of the workforce. This rate was typical of most agricultural producers but well below the third of the workforce who lost their jobs in such heavily industrialised areas as the Clydeside in Scotland, north-east England, south Wales, the Ruhr Valley in Germany and the north-eastern United States. Even in Sydney and Melbourne about a quarter of the workforce were unemployed in the early 1930s.

Probably about half of the population suffered real hardships and experienced tangible losses. Women and the unskilled were hit very hard. Maori fell back on patterns of traditional subsistence. Those individuals lucky enough to keep their jobs got by despite the cuts. It must be remembered that the depression was all about deflation and that prices fell along with

Relief workers working on the approaches to the building of the Dominion Museum and Carillon in Wellington. *Alexander Turnbull Library.*

Women and children bore much of the brunt of the depression years. *New Zealand Herald.*

wages; basic necessities actually became cheaper. Middle class people had to make sacrifices too, but they were usually of a much milder kind. Some more well to do families were forced to dismiss a servant, to put the car up on blocks or to shut off the telephone. Car ownership fell away and the number of homeowners declined significantly as families were forced to move back into rental accommodation.

The despair of the unemployed is understandable. But why did so many white collar workers cut their ties with older conservative parties and become radicalised when they did not lose their jobs? The experiences and the sense of injustice promoted by unequal suffering provides part of the answer.

Country school teachers learned to allow their exhausted and malnourished pupils to sleep in class. They knew that these children had been working since dawn and would have to work until dusk after leaving school. Teachers in central city schools were even more aware of problems caused by malnutrition and jobs outside school hours. Employment of cheap child labour increased during the depression as older men were laid off.

Labour's promise to end youth rates and introduce free milk in schools had a very practical appeal to many teachers. Nearly everyone was shocked when the school entrance age was raised from five to six and teachers' colleges were closed down.

Office workers watched in shocked silence as respected colleagues were dismissed for no apparent reason. Respectable suburban homeowners were equally shocked when bailiffs came to remove the furniture and prized possessions of long-settled neighbours.

Some dairy farmers saw neighbours walk off their land after the stock and station agency had refused to allow their clients to spend money on underwear for their wives or toothbrushes for their children. Many of the men who clung tenaciously to their heavily indebted farms were conservative by nature but this did not stop them feeling angry with a government that allowed honest, hardworking and efficient farmers to be forced to throw away a lifetime's work. The progressively minded Coates responded with moratoriums on mortgages and devalued the New Zealand pound, but it was too little, too late. Labour's promise of cheaper credit and guaranteed prices proved more attractive and some dairy farmers took the unprecedented step of voting in Labour members in the so-called 'butter seats'.

The Coalition was an obvious scapegoat on which to blame the depression. The government seemed, in Tony Simpson's telling phrase, to have 'institutionalised misery'. In fact the Coalition did more than most contemporaries realised. They set up a Reserve (or central) Bank in 1933 and actually left a healthy balance of payments with which the new government was able to fund its experiments. The majority of New Zealanders did not view things so kindly and never forgave the Coalition for making the impact of the depression worse. They expressed their anger through the ballot box in 1935.

Yet more than the uneven sharing of hardship was involved in the radical change in attitude towards the unemployed and the switch to Labour. The majority of New Zealanders felt cheated by the depression. Survivors

Unemployed workers on a roadmaking gang, possibly in the Akatarawa, in March 1932, *New Zealand Herald.*

still blame their failure to do more in life on the grey years of the 1930s. All the very real gains which had been made since 1890 counted for nought. Swaggers stalked the countryside for the first time in the new century.

The 1920s was a time of rising expectations. By 1930 most New Zealanders had come to believe that they were sharing in the New Zealand dream of a prosperity divided fairly evenly among all hardworking citizens; they had a long way to fall. When they or their children fell it was a chilling experience, one they would never forget.

19. 1938   From the Cradle to the Grave:

The Passing of the Social Security Act

ON 2 April 1938 Prime Minister Michael Joseph Savage broadcast to the nation his government's plans for the introduction of a new comprehensive scheme of social security. He told his audience that all pensions paid out since 1898 would be consolidated and replaced by a new means-tested old age pension of £78 a year (30 shillings a week) at the age of 60. This new pension superseded the existing payment of £58 10s made to women over 60 and men over 65. Furthermore at 65 all citizens would be entitled to a national superannuation of £10 per annum rising by £2 10s each year to reach the level of the old age pension. The pension, therefore, would meet immediate need whereas the superannuation was the right of everyone.

Existing allowances for widows, orphans, the unemployed, the disabled, war veterans and miners suffering from pulmonary tuberculosis would be continued and, in some cases, increased. Even more important, a universal system of free medicine, including free hospital treatment, free medicine and a free general practitioner service, was also to be introduced. The whole scheme would be administered by a new Social Welfare Department and would provide social security from 'the cradle to the grave'. It was to come into operation on 1 April 1939 and was intended, in Savage's words, to provide 'a condition of social security unsurpassed in any

Savage radiated an image of warmth, humanity and commonsense. This allowed him to allay fears that Labour was a party of radical socialists. Thousands of Labour supporters hung this portrait of 'Uncle Joe' on their walls. *NZLP.*

other country in the world'. The Labour government had made clear its determination to establish a fully fledged welfare state.

The scheme would be funded by raising the existing unemployment tax on wages from 8d in the pound to 1 shilling and by continuing the levy of £1 on every male over 20 years of age. General revenue would contribute an equivalent sum to these two sources. Savage pointed out that the scheme had been carefully costed and that the country could easily afford it. He stressed that it built on the fine tradition of Richard Seddon and the Liberal government and downplayed its radicalism and socialist implications. He proclaimed that the stigma should be removed from charity. As he put it in a speech to Parliament: 'It was the inalienable right of every person to be secured against distress in any form.' An ebullient John A. Lee claimed that New Zealand could afford a system to provide security from 'erection to resurrection'.

Labour Party delegates gathered in the Wellington Town Hall went wild when Savage completed the broadcast, as did many ordinary people throughout New Zealand. Janet Frame recalls that when the Social Security Act was finally passed on 14 September 1938 her father, who regarded the election of a Labour government like a 'Second Coming', 'removed the [medical] bills from behind the clock and taking the poker from its hook by the stove, lifted the cover and thrust all the bills into the fire.' Many other families shared these mixed emotions of relief and triumph.

The political opposition, reformed into the National Party in 1936, criticised the measure as irresponsible and asked how the country could afford it in bad years as well as good. The conservative press echoed these concerns. Savage and Walter Nash countered such criticisms and turned them to the government's advantage. Nash quoted what sounded like current newspaper editorials and then revealed that he was in fact reading speeches made against Seddon's Old Age Pensions Bill in 1897 and 1898. Savage pointed out that Labour was continuing the Liberal reforms and argued that he had inherited the man-

Labour's policy has brought to every wife and mother happiness and prosperity in her home and for her children.

The woman in the home knows that the Savage Government has made secure the future of her children, her husband and her home.

How the National Party threatens Your Home!

RT. HON. G. W. FORBES: "Had not costs been reduced, the number of unemployed would be greater. IF THE OCCASION AROSE I WOULD DO THE SAME AGAIN."—("Evening Post," 19/9/35.)

MR. W. P. ENDEAN, M.P.: "We have Savage & Co. fiddling with a super pension scheme. . . . We are going to put a stop to this sort of thing when we get into power"—("Rotorua Post," 24/5/38.)

tle of Seddon rather than of some more socialist leader. He described social security as 'applied Christianity'. National's Sid Holland said it was 'applied lunacy' but only earned himself the displeasure of the public.

Criticism from the 'left wing' of the Labour Party posed more problems than the opposition of the National Party. Some of the younger, better educated and more radical members of caucus, including Dr D. G. McMillan and the Reverend Arnold Nordmeyer, felt that the government had not gone far enough. They were concerned that Savage had backtracked in means testing the old age pension, and they feared that Fraser would give in to the

powerful British Medical Association by limiting free medical services to the poor. Any such action would undermine Savage's efforts to remove stigma and discrimination from free medical treatment.

When the select committee reported on the social security scheme in late May it called for superannuation to include as many people as possible. The majority report recommended once the scheme was in operation that the income limit should be gradually increased until superannuation became truly universal.

This compromise satisfied the radicals in caucus and they claimed it as the direct result of their influence. In fact

THE NATIONAL PARTY WILL
ABOLISH OUTSIDE DOMINATION
OF PARLIAMENT!

Change the Government

National advertising in the 1938 election claimed the parliamentary Labour Party was being manipulated by the unions. *NZLP.*

ernment and moved even the mild-mannered Savage to wrath. A bitter war of words ensued, with Savage accusing the doctors of engaging in a 'sit down strike'. The BMA was not able to stop the introduction of social security in 1939 but it did force major compromises in 1941.

Savage was, of course, motivated by more than altruism in delaying the introduction of social security until after the 1938 election. Social security was as central to Labour policy as full employment and economic insulation and Savage wanted the law on the statute books before the election. But it was also a clever move which virtually guaranteed re-election. Savage knew that the 1935 election had not been as conclusive as it appeared to the public. A majority of New Zealanders had voted against Labour and the conservative vote had been split between the Coalition, the Democrat Party and various independents. This time there would be straight-out contests in 68 of the 76 European seats. Some 22 seats had also been won on a minority vote in 1935 and the new National Party was much better organised than the Coalition.

Savage's ploy paid off handsomely. The 1938 election produced the biggest mandate in New Zealand's history — 56 per cent of electors voted Labour. Labour lost nine seats, including four butter seats, but won seven new seats. National gains were also offset by the fact that Labour increased its hold over the marginals. Fifteen of the 22 candidates elected on a minority vote in 1935 were returned with absolute majorities while an alliance with the Ratana church gave Labour three of the four Maori seats. The final result read Labour 53, National 25 and Independents 2. This was an undisputed victory against a united rather than a divided opponent.

Obvious parallels can be drawn between the Labour victories of 1935 and 1938 and the Liberal triumphs of 1890 and 1893. In each case definite government action in the form of social security and the purchase of the Cheviot estate won an indisputable mandate. New Zealanders responded warmly to governments who kept their promises. Despite his benign appearance, Savage possessed much of Seddon's hard-headed political skill.

their agitation actually helped Savage achieve what he had wanted since he introduced his first pensions bill in 1920. The Prime Minister had always opposed the idea of any contributory scheme and was much more hostile to the medical profession than Fraser. He had been a consistent advocate of a free medical service since 1920 and was not as slow in realising this ideal as Lee and other impatient younger colleagues tried to make out.

Opposition from the insurance industry was eventually overcome with relative ease after a long discussion. On 12 April 1938 the British actuary G. H. Maddex reported to the parliamentary committee that the scheme would cost £17.85 million to implement in its first year. Some £9.85 million had to be found from general revenue or £2.355 million more than annual expenditure on existing social services. It was affordable.

The sternest opposition came from the New Zealand branch of the British Medical Association and its intransigent leader Dr James Peter Speid Jamieson. The BMA put up an alternative scheme whereby the population was divided into four classes, based on income and need. Jamieson stressed the special relationship between doctor and patient and freedom of choice. His unco-operative attitude incensed the gov-

UNEMPLOYMENT

Under *NATIONAL* Rule	Under *LABOUR* Rule
A total of 35,979 registered unemployed in November, 1935. Only physically fit allowed to register. Old clothes drives and soup kitchens. Sustenance rates: Single men averaged about 10/- weekly; married men, seven children, about 30/- weekly.	Unemployed reduced to 16,367, and of these 8,000 are physically unfit for work, although allowed to register for sustenance. **Actual unemployed as at February 12, 1938, only 7,241.** Sustenance and relief payments greatly increased.

LET LABOUR FINISH THE JOB

PENSIONS FOR THE NEEDY

Under *NATIONAL* Rule	Under *LABOUR* Rule
Miners' phthisis, war, veterans', blind, etc. pensions were reduced as much as 29 per cent. in some instances. The aged and the infirm were generally dependent on charity to supplement their meagre resources.	Pension cuts restored and increases made. Residential period reduced. Amount paid to Old Age Pensioners has more than doubled since 1935. Deserted wives' pensions instituted. War and veterans' pensions show an increase of over £400,000 yearly. Widows are receiving £188,000 more. Total cost of all pensions £6,769,423.

LET LABOUR FINISH THE JOB

Labour's 1935 manifesto had promised security and prosperity for all. In 1938 they wanted a chance to complete the task. *NZLP.*

Many historians have labelled the Social Security Act the most important piece of legislation in New Zealand's history. With its passing New Zealand resumed its place as one of the most progressive nations in terms of social policy; only the Scandinavian countries developed similar schemes at this time.

The Social Security Act represented the high point of evolutionary socialism in New Zealand. When combined with exchange controls and import licensing (admittedly adopted as emergency measures aimed at staving off a financial crisis), the Social Security Act completed the transition to a mixed economy. The Reserve Bank had already been nationalised in 1936 and marketing departments replaced the older boards. Power shifted from the localities to Wellington as centralised planning replaced ad hoc private sector development. After December 1938 the state became economic manager rather than assistant to individual effort. The mildly state interventionist impulses of the Liberals which were intended to help people help themselves were replaced by a system which became something of a prototype for many of the West European economies which emerged after the Second World War. The year 1938 was an economic, political and social watershed which placed New Zealand in the vanguard of international developments.

Social security brought real gains to many. By 1939 New Zealand could boast the third highest standard of living in the world. A safety net had been placed under most citizens to stop them falling into the gutter and nearly everyone felt more secure. A clear majority of the electorate were quite prepared to pay higher taxes in return for guaranteed protection against accident or ill health.

Despite its enormous popularity the scheme continued to be criticised from both right and left. Conservatives complained that the new system discouraged thrift and pulled everyone down to the same level, encouraging mediocrity. The government countered that they had not pulled down the old order but had lifted many people out of poverty and despair.

The first Labour government contained some intelligent politicians. Fraser, Savage, Nash and Lee, although self-educated, were extraordinarily well read. Not surprisingly education was an important priority.

Fraser proved an effective and innovative Minister of Education. The school leaving age was raised to 15 in 1944 and bursaries were introduced for university students. In 1939 Fraser appointed a radical young reformer, C. E. Beeby, as Director General of Education. Curriculum changes followed at all levels, intended to make education more enriching and to promote greater educational opportunity.

Adult education was extended by revitalising the Workers' Educational Association and an Adult Educational Council was established in 1938. A National Library Service was also founded in the same year, with the help of a Carnegie grant. Education and good books were taken outside the ivory towers of the universities and the cities and made available to ordinary New Zealanders living in more remote centres.

Labour's achievements in other cultural areas were equally impressive. A Dominion Art Gallery and Museum were built in 1936, realising a dream of the Reform Party. The National Broadcasting Service was set up in 1936, with rigorous standards, modelled on the BBC, imposed on the non-commercial sector. The 1940 Centennial Celebrations stimulated New Zealand writing and painting and quickened the search for a distinctive

THIS IS THE HOUSE THAT GREED BUILT.

THIS IS THE MAN, ALL TATTERED AND SHORN, WHO LIVED IN THE HOUSE THAT GREED BUILT.

THIS IS THE MAN, NOW ALL FORLORN, WHO SHEARED THE MAN, WHO LIVED IN THE HOUSE THAT GREED BUILT.

THIS IS THE COW WITH THE NOISY HORN WHO MOOS AND MOANS AND GROANS FOR THE MAN, WHO SHEARED THE MAN, WHO LIVED IN THE HOUSE THAT GREED BUILT.

AND THIS IS THE MAN WITH HIS HOUSING PLAN, WHO'S QUEERED THE PITCH OF THE MAN WHO WAXED RICH BY FLEECING THE MAN. WHO LIVED IN THE SHACK NOW PULLED DOWN BY JACK AND REPLACED BY THE HOUSE THAT JACK BUILT.

national identity. In 1941 the National Film Unit was established. It brought the reality of the war home to the civilian population in a way that had not been possible during the First World War. The New Zealand Symphony Orchestra was formed in 1946.

Despite these achievements some critics on the left felt that Labour's reforms fell short. Lee knew that the successful state housing programme had not reached all the poor and he found that social security did little to address the problem of poverty among the middle aged and low income families. Old age poverty, on the other hand, was largely eradicated.

Savage and Fraser were also concerned with improving Maori living standards. Family benefits helped more than superannuation because there were few Maori aged over 60. More money was made available for land development schemes but the isolation of many pa and the appalling standard of Maori housing limited the impact of the 1938 reforms. A more comprehensive reform was required and the Maori Social and Economic Advancement Act of 1945 directed more funds towards improving Maori health and education.

Savage had always been a strong advocate of equality for women but his legislative reforms did little to promote greater equality of women or to extend their more traditional roles. On the other hand widows faced fewer financial worries after the 1938 Act.

Caucus members like Lee and Frank Langstone, who favoured Douglas Credit type solutions for providing more and cheaper money, felt that Nash's financial management was too orthodox and that the government was too soft on the rich. They felt that Savage, by his own admission, was a

humanitarian rather than a socialist. Later socialists have echoed these criticisms by arguing that all Labour's reforms did was give capitalism a human face; Labour failed to turn New Zealand into an independent socialist state.

Such criticism is unfair. New Zealand was — and still is — a small country living in a capitalist world, on which it was dependent for its markets and its capital. The public were wary of the very word socialism, despite Lee's extravagant claim that New Zealand's evolution had followed socialist lines. Savage's view, that New Zealanders were traditionally conservative, was more realistic. Even if critics such as Lee were right, New Zealand did not have the resources to stand up as an independent socialist state. As it was, Savage's reforms and regular Social Credit-like utterances about costless credit drove capital out of the country and frightened British investors. Only some desperate diplomacy from Nash in 1938 and 1939 saved New Zealand from bankruptcy.

There is no doubt, however, that it was doctors and dentists, not pensioners, war veterans or widows, who gained most monetary benefit from the creation of the welfare state. Free maternity care took some time to arrange and the final agreement over the general practitioner service was not hammered out until October 1941. Fraser, Nordmeyer and the BMA agreed to introduce a fee for service scheme in place of free visits to the doctor. The state guaranteed to pay 7s 6d per visit, or 12s 6d for home visits, a sizeable sum when the average wage was about 90 shillings a week. Doctors were then left to charge a token fee of around 3 shillings from the patient or to claim a refund from

A cartoon from the *Standard*, 11 March 1937. Labour's philosophy was that every New Zealander had a right to decent housing. In 1936 they set up a department of housing construction to build state houses. John A. Lee was responsible for carrying out housing policy. *Auckland Public Library.*

the Social Security Fund. This caused some confusion until the 1949 Social Security Amendment Act allowed the patient fee to rise while the state's payment continued at 7s 6d, that is, as an ever decreasing subsidy. This system boosted and guaranteed doctors' salaries. It provided them with the best of both socialised and private medicine and prevented the establishment of a National Health Service like that in Britain.

Even though the New Zealand Dental Association was not as powerful as the BMA and was not backed by a British parent organisation, it, too, succeeded in preventing the introduction of a free dental service. Instead primary school children continued to be treated by a much larger number of dental nurses while the adolescent scheme was introduced in 1947 to meet the needs of secondary school children. Under this scheme young dentists were paid a subsidy to provide treatment free of charge for adolescents. It worked so well that many young dentists were able to set themselves up in private practice on the basis of a few years of treating adolescents. Once again they had the best of private and socialised dentistry with adults being left to pay for their treatment.

Who was most responsible for the introduction of social security? It is probably most accurate to say that it was a team effort guaranteed success by Savage's inspiration of delaying its

161

Economic
1936 Nationalisation of the Reserve Bank. Introduction of a basic wage for those on work schemes as well as the 'permanent' workforce. Introduction of the 'guaranteed prices' for butterfat. Compulsory unionism introduced. Eight-hour day and 40-hour week made standard.

1938 Exchange controls and import licensing introduced.

1939 Raises New Zealand's standard of living to the third highest in the world. Completes the construction of 5500 homes.

1945 Nationalisation of the Bank of New Zealand.

1945-49 Operates a successful rehabilitation scheme for ex-servicemen.

Social
1937 Free milk supplied to school-children.

1938 The Social Security Act of 1938 provides for a free health system, universal superannuation and dramatically widens the scope of the welfare state.

1943 School Dental Nurse Scheme is upgraded.

1944 School leaving age raised to 15.

1945 The Maori Social and Economic Advancement Act establishes the Department of Maori Welfare.

Cultural
1936 New Zealand Broadcasting Service set up. Dominion Museum and Art Gallery completed.

1938 National Library Service established.

1940 Centennial celebrations.

1941 National Film Unit set up.

1946 State Literary Fund established to encourage local writers.

1946 New Zealand Symphony Orchestra established.

Political
1935-40 Michael Joseph Savage Prime Minister.

1940-49 Peter Fraser Prime Minister. Fraser's defeat by National in 1949 marks the end of 14 years of Labour rule, the second longest term of power for any New Zealand government.

---

introduction until after the 1938 election. Above all the Social Security Act represented a collective act of faith on the part of the Labour Party — everyone committed themselves to a belief in the capacity of the New Zealand economy to carry such a scheme in perpetuity. This commitment explains in part why the Social Security Act became a sacred cow almost beyond criticism, which has not been subjected to continual amendment, improvement and extension like its Scandinavian equivalents.

By the time Labour became the government its leaders had already used up much energy during their long period in opposition. The cabinet, with an average age of 57, soon experienced serious burnout; most remaining energy was sapped by the war effort. When the one young hopeful, John A. Lee, was expelled from the party in 1940 for criticising the leadership, an opportunity for revitalisation was lost. Lee's arrogance and insensitivity did not help his case but the party could ill afford to lose a man with such flair, talent and drive. By 1946 Labour was tired and largely devoid of fresh ideas.

Labour did not so much 'betray a vision' as historian Tony Simpson would have it, as fail to develop a vision with the breadth and flexibility to cope with the relentless march of history.

Cartoonist Minhinnick had no doubts Savage was responsible for Labour's decisive election victory in 1938. *Courtesy Sir Gordon Minhinnick, New Zealand Herald.*

Link: From Social Security to War

Michael Joseph Savage, an Australian of Irish Catholic parentage, was reluctant to involve his people in fighting yet another war for Britain. He had to be cajoled into making his famous speech: 'Where she [Britain] goes, we go, where she stands, we stand.' Other Labour leaders were more enthusiastic because, unlike 1914, there was an identifiable enemy — Fascism. Men like Peter Fraser and Bob Semple, who had gone to gaol for their opposition to the First World War, felt they were quite consistent in committing themselves to fight Hitler and Mussolini. Some of the public were less convinced by Fraser's about-face although a large majority supported New Zealand's involvement.

Men enlisted with more muted excitement and less jingoistic fervour than in 1914 after New Zealand declared war on Germany just before midnight on 3 September 1939, 12 hours before Britain because of the time difference. Recruiting began on 12 September. On that first day 4419 enlisted and within the first week 12,000 men had signed up. They were the usual mixture of youthful adventurers, men escaping unhappy marriages and ordinary citizens determined to do their duty.

Voluntary enlistment flagged a little in 1940 so the age limit was raised from 35 to 40. By the time conscription was introduced on 23 July 1940 59,664 men had volunteered for active service. Relatively few members of the public seemed particularly bothered by the irony that conscription had been introduced by a party who, in 1916, had come into being in opposition to conscription. There seemed to be little choice and few voices were raised against this action.

The Expeditionary Force which sailed for Egypt on 5 January 1940 was different from its 1914 equivalent in that it was a separate unit under its own New Zealand command, headed by the dental mechanic turned Major General, Bernard Freyberg. A new Maori Battalion was also formed with its own command. Unlike the Pioneer Battalion of the First World War, Maori troops did not have to fight under Pakeha officers and were entitled to fight in the frontline as well as support actions.

The majority of these soldiers, both Maori and Pakeha, were also a little less naive than the young men of 1914;

Freyberg commanded the 2 (NZ) Division through campaigns in Greece, Crete, North Africa and Italy for a remarkable six years. *Courtesy Peter McIntyre.*

they too were excited and hoped for adventure but this time they knew that war was hard. They also had a high reputation to live up to and this made departure a much more sombre moment than in 1914. There were more tears than cheers as the men sailed away to Cairo.

Soldiers who fought under the New Zealand command, from whatever echelon, and in whatever battalion, experienced very mixed fortunes. Their first major action was in Greece between March and May 1941, where the New Zealanders fought heroically against overwhelming odds. At times their inexperience in battle told against them, as did some clumsy decisions taken by the higher officers, but in the long run pistols proved no match for tanks supported by stukas. New Zealand soldiers began the Second World War as they had begun the First — by suffering a heavy

defeat. Losses were heavy, with 291 killed, 599 wounded and 1614 taken as prisoners of war. The New Zealanders nevertheless acquitted themselves well, and played a part in slowing the relentless German advance. As every New Zealand tourist to Greece knows, the efforts of our soldiers were deeply appreciated by the Greek people. Yet this inauspicious beginning did not win the glory of Gallipoli.

Worse followed in Crete. There the tired and ill Kiwis joined some Australians and Greeks between 20 and 27 May in defending the island against what was at that time the greatest airborne invasion in history. Some critics have suggested that a more aggressive approach by Freyberg and

Crete Sketches. After withdrawal from Greece 4 and 5 Brigades were sent to Crete. A relentless German airborne assault resulted in another major defeat and heavy casualties. *Courtesy Peter McIntyre.*

his commanders could have repulsed the German attack, but what these armchair strategists forget is the chaos that reigns in any battle, especially where a new technology or strategy is used. The New Zealanders were also heavily outnumbered, they lacked adequate transport, were short of field guns and had no air support. The bravery of the Kiwis was evident on many occasions. The fierce charge of the Maori Battalion made in an endeavour to retake Malerne aerodrome was especially memorable. Charles Upham won the first of his two Victoria Crosses by clearing several houses of German soldiers. Even the severest critics were forced to admit that so many paratroopers were killed that the Germans never used them again in the war.

Casualties were very high, with 634 New Zealanders killed and 2217 taken prisoner. A further 967 of those taken off the island were wounded. The casualty rate was over 50 per cent. This heroic but futile resistance hardened the resolve of the New Zealand troops but many could not help feeling that Winston Churchill and British high command were once again responsible for the unnecessary slaughter of New Zealand soldiers.

Prime Minister Fraser was persuaded to keep his troops in Europe and retain Freyberg as his chief of staff because of glowing testimonials made by Churchill and several British generals. Fraser, however, insisted that the New Zealanders should not be wasted on any more futile holding operations. He had his way and the fortunes of the Kiwis changed in the deserts of North Africa. Initially they found themselves engaged in supportive operations against the demoralised Italians but from February 1942 they fought against the formidable Afrika Korps commanded by the legendary General Erwin Rommel.

The highly mobile nature of desert warfare seemed to suit the Kiwi troops. Carelessness occasionally cost them dearly but generally they displayed speed and stamina. The fighting was rather indecisive until the massive assault launched at El Alamein in October 1942. New Zealanders distinguished themselves in this major advance and helped General Montgomery and the Allies to push home the advantage until the Germans finally capitulated in May 1943. The Maori Battalion became especially promin-

ent during this final phase of the desert campaign. Moana-nui-a-Kiwi Ngarimu won a posthumous VC for his part in taking a heavily armed fort, while Arapeta Awatere became especially feared for his aggressive attitude and rose rapidly through the ranks. By the end of the fighting in North Africa the Maori Battalion had won the respect of German foe and British and Pakeha New Zealand troops alike. Any doubts that may have been harboured about the Maori capacity to sustain long campaigns had been removed in the most convincing fashion.

The tide of the war turned once the Afrika Korps surrendered. But the costs of victory had been high. New Zealanders lost more men in the desert than in any other theatre of the Second World War. Some 2700 were killed and 6000 wounded; a further 3600 were taken prisoner. The only compensation was the fact that there seemed some point in sustaining such losses. Final victory now seemed

The Infantry, Sidi Rezegh (Libya). Fighting in North Africa over thousands of square kilometres of open flat desert with no frontline called for new battle skills. *Courtesy Peter McIntyre.*

assured and confidence grew because the Kiwis had once again proved their worth as soldiers. A high percentage of the long-serving echelon were sent home on leave and some refused to return to combat, arguing that they had done enough.

The New Zealanders left behind in Egypt entered the Italian campaign from September 1943 with some enthusiasm because they believed Italy could be taken with relative ease. The Kiwis knew that they had once again been diverted into a sideshow; the main Allied thrust would obviously have to be made in France. They were, nevertheless, determined to hasten the end of the war and a large group of keen new recruits from New Zealand brought a renewed vigour to the task.

20. 1943-45   Learning the Hard Way:
The Italian Campaign

A New Zealand infantryman fires his bren-gun from behind a wall of sandbags on the Via Emilia just before the crossing of the Senio River in Italy. *G. F. Kaye.*

OVER 14,500 troops of the 2nd New Zealand Division began to join the 8th British Army and the 8th Indian Division at Taranto on the heel of Italy from 9 October 1943. The New Zealanders, better equipped than ever before, were also supported by 150 Sherman tanks. They were, however, a far less experienced group than the division which had fought in the desert — nearly half were new recruits or had fought in North Africa for only two months, while some 5500 battle-hardened soldiers had been sent home on furlough, leaving the division short of seasoned middle and lower rank officers.

Most of the Kiwis had arrived from Egypt by mid-November and they moved up the Adriatic coast to join British scouts who had reached the Sangro River on 8 November. The longer serving soldiers were delighted to be out of the desert and found the sight of farmland, olive groves and vineyards pleasing. They also thought the stone houses picturesque. They soon learnt, however, that these 'casas' were as liable to contain heavily armed German troops as welcoming Italian families.

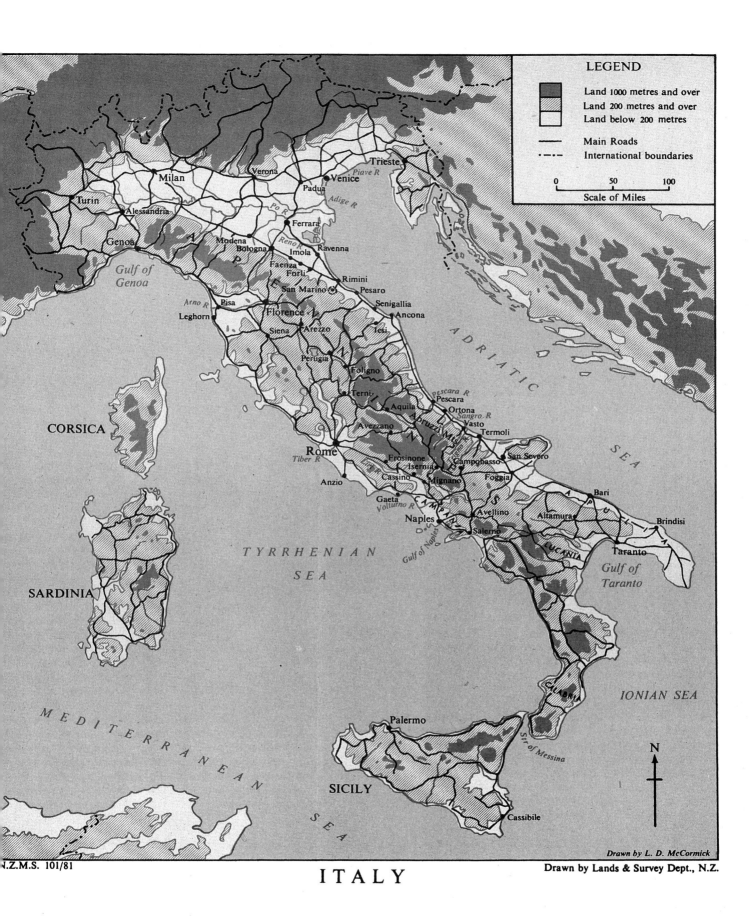

LEGEND

Land 1000 metres and over
Land 200 metres and over
Land below 200 metres

Main Roads
International boundaries

0   50   100
Scale of Miles

Milan
Turin
Alessandria
Genoa
Verona
Venice
Padua
Trieste
Piave R
Adige R
Po R
Ferrara
Modena
Bologna
Reno R
Imola
Ravenna
Faenza
Forli
San Marino
Rimini
Pesaro
Senigallia
Ancona
Arno R
Pisa
Leghorn
Florence
Siena
Arezzo
Iesi
Perugia
Foligno
Terni
Pescara
Aquila
Ortona
Pescara R
Sangro R
Avezzano
Vasto
Termoli
Rome
Tiber R
Frosinone
Isernia
Campobasso
San Severo
Anzio
Cassino
Mignano
Foggia
Gaeta
Volturno R
Naples
Avellino
Bari
Altamura
Brindisi
Salerno
Taranto
Gulf of Naples
Gulf of Taranto

Gulf of Genoa

ADRIATIC

SEA

CORSICA

TYRRHENIAN

SEA

SARDINIA

MEDITERRANEAN

SEA

IONIAN SEA

Palermo

SICILY

Str of Messina

Cassibile

N

Drawn by L. D. McCormick

N.Z.M.S. 101/81

ITALY

Drawn by Lands & Survey Dept., N.Z.

German prisoners captured near the Sangro River, Italy. *G. F. Kaye.*

As they moved north it became clear that many things, including the climate and the geography, were very different from North Africa. The idea promoted in tourist brochures that Italy was blessed by a balmy, sub-tropical climate were dashed when the weather turned intensely cold. Coastal plains soon gave way to the mountain spine of central Italy where narrow, twisting roads slowed progress and tanks frequently became bogged in the mud. Even if the Germans capitulated quickly Italy itself was not going to be the picnic many New Zealand soldiers had imagined.

The country around the Sangro River reminded the troops of New Zealand. It was high and rugged and rose on the far side of the river into snow-capped mountain passes which could be easily defended. The river itself was a series of braided streams not unlike the wide gravelly rivers of Canterbury. It was in flood and flowing swiftly. Colonel John Male recalled 'white stones in the riverbed, mountains leaning over us and the Sangro itself, an angry snow-fed stream which might have tumbled down from the Southern Alps.'

The New Zealanders who looked across the river from the safety of olive groves could see that the river itself would cause more problems than German defenders who had retreated further into the mountains. It was, in the words of Neville Phillips, official historian of the early part of the Italian campaign, a 'capricious' river. Several soldiers drowned in it and it proved a nightmare to patrol. Sappers (en-gineers) had to work extremely hard (as they would throughout the rest of the Italian campaign) to enable trucks and tanks to cross. German mines which had been laid in large numbers also proved a problem; they would do so again and again.

Before the river could be crossed one last German-held village south of the Sangro had to be captured. Fighting for the New Zealanders began on 13 November and culminated in an attack on Perano on 18 November. This action, undertaken with the Indians on the New Zealanders' left flank, represented the first use of tanks by New Zealanders in warfare. (On previous occasions they had always fought in support of British tanks.) The village was taken after a hard fight and the tanks proved alarmingly cumbersome on the soft ground.

The various New Zealand battalions crossed the river between 23 and 28 November. Some encountered problems with trucks getting stuck in the water and others engaged in some light skirmishing. But for the 23rd Battalion it proved relatively easy; Angus Ross remembers it being rather like a Sunday afternoon hike in back-country Otago. Once across the river the Kiwis had their first men killed in Italy when a group of Germans struck suddenly against a patrol which wandered too far from its support. The New Zealanders responded by taking the village of Castelfrananto. Neville Phillips remembers jubilant scenes between liberators and the liberated. At this stage the Kiwis were, in Angus Ross's words, full of 'cheerful optimism'.

This optimism continued for a few days as the Kiwis made steady progress against the ill-disciplined 65th German Division. But things changed after 2 December when the New Zealanders were ordered to take the village of Orsogna and then break through the 'winter' line and fight their way to the Adriatic coast to join the Canadians and British at Ortona.

Orsogna was a natural mountain fortress easily defended by tanks. Plunging gullies surrounded it on all sides, giving the defenders a superb view of all quarters. There was no easy access from the south, making the use of tanks very difficult. And it was defended by the elite 26th Panzer Division, crack troops who were fresh, fit and ready to fight. The New Zealanders actually held the village for a few hours but their lack of armoured support made them vulnerable and they were driven out on 3 December. They attacked again on 6 December only to find that the 65th had been joined by the equally formidable 90th Panzer Grenadier Division. German sappers planted mines all around the outskirts of the town to great effect and blew up buildings.

The Kiwis attacked twice more in Operations Florence and Ulysses but were repulsed by the determined Germans who had been joined by the III Battalion 4 Parachute Regiment. The few New Zealand tanks brought into the action were mauled by the well-placed German artillery and tanks. By Christmas 1943 heavy snow covered the area and a stalemate had been reached. The freezing weather wrought havoc among the troops — hypothermia became a common problem and a few suffered from frostbite. One way of coping with the cold was to leave slit trenches and huddle around fires in deserted houses. These houses were, however, much more dangerous than the trenches because they were frequently shelled by German artillery and sometimes had been booby-trapped by retreating German engineers. Frozen men do not make efficient soldiers and the rate of respiratory infection increased alarmingly when men chilled themselves by rushing out of heated houses into the intense cold.

The rugged terrain defeated several Kiwi attempts at co-ordinating tank and infantry attacks. Orsogna seemed impregnable and earned itself the title

of 'Stalingrad of Arbizzi' (the name of the local mountain range). In late January the weary and disappointed Kiwis handed over to the 4th Indian Division and retreated to Naples where they regrouped. Casualties resulting from the bitter fighting were the worst in a long time with 413 killed and 1150 wounded, higher in fact than they would be at the notorious Battle of Cassino. After Orsogna it became clear to most New Zealand soldiers that quick and easy victories were illusions which existed only in the minds of military strategists and politicians. A long, hard and dangerous slog up the heavily defended 255-kilometre-wide peninsula lay ahead. The Sangro became a kind of Rubicon for the New Zealanders across which they advanced into military maturity and the fiercest fighting of their war. The concluding lines of Les Cleveland's poem *Winter 1944 Melodrama Orsogna* catch the frustration and disillusionment induced by the failure of the first major action in Italy:

The patrol wavers, insect like
Then step-by-step minutely back-tracks
Leaving a faint question traced in the snow.

The Americans and British troops to the New Zealanders' left and the Canadians to their right at Ortona had also suffered heavy casualties in advancing up the peninsula. Yet Churchill remained determined to end the stalemate in Italy. He and General Dwight Eisenhower decided that the Allies should concentrate on breaking through the Gustav Line at Cassino and proceed up through the Liri Valley and on to Route 6 which led directly to Rome.

This long drawn-out action confirmed the growing feeling among the Kiwi soldiers that war was hell and that their winning streak had come to an end. The English Field Marshal, Bernard Montgomery, and the American Commander, Lieutenant General Mark W. Clark, began the battle to take the ancient Benedictine monastery at Monte Cassino in January 1944.

Cassino, Italy, in the early stages of the assault. The town's famous monastery which General Freyberg ordered bombed can be seen isolated on a hill above the town. *Alexander Turnbull Library.*

Fighting continued until 18 May when the Germans finally withdrew. It seemed that these commanders, especially Clark, became obsessed with taking the monastery even though it was of relatively little strategic importance. The Allied advance was delayed to a serious extent as wave after wave of American, British, French, Indian, Polish, Canadian and New Zealand troops threw themselves against well-equipped Panzer divisions.

At Cassino the New Zealanders and Indians were used as shock troops in much the same way as they had been in World War One. The New Zealanders were engaged in two desperate battles against heavy odds. The first major advance made by the New Zealanders, known as the 'second battle' of Cassino, followed on from a month of unsuccessful assaults carried

out by the Americans and British. Casualty rates during the 'first battle' had been as high as 50 per cent; New Zealand soldiers still remember seeing bodies of American troops floating down the Rapido River. By the time the Kiwis were ordered to attack on 15 February 1944 the ancient monastery had, in the words of Neville Phillips, become 'a phobia and obsession'. New Zealand soldiers were relieved to hear that Freyberg had ordered the monolithic structure to be bombed in an endeavour to get the Allies moving again.

What the troops did not know was that both Freyberg (who was now a corps commander) and his divisional commander, Major General H. Kippenberger, were very worried about Operation Avenger. Freyberg's normally democratic method of consulting with his battalion commanders had also broken down under the pressure and the corps commander was tending to make decisions in isolation. Both he and Kippenberger were concerned that they would not be able to concentrate enough infantry and tanks in the difficult country around Cassino. They were supposed to throw a bridgehead across the Rapido River, take the railway station and move tanks along the railway embankment. The tanks would then be able to advance to Route 6 while the Indians diverted the German defenders by attacking the massif below the monastery.

In reality the plan was incredibly difficult to execute because the mountainous country around Cassino severely limited the number of tanks that could be used. Large groups of infantry could not be massed in any one place and supplies and ammunition had to be brought in by mule. Matters were made worse by the fact that recent heavy rains had caused the Rapido to flood. Operation Avenger bordered on the impossible.

The Kiwis' spirits were raised, however, at 9.30 on the morning of 15 February when a large squadron of bombers pounded the monastery. Their hopes were soon dashed when it appeared that the mountain fortress was still largely intact and that the bombing had caused nearly as many casualties among the Allies as it had among the Germans. A critical eight-hour delay followed before the attack by British and Indian troops began, giving the highly disciplined paratroopers time to regroup.

The Maori Battalion commenced their attack at 9.30 on the night of 17 February and by midnight they had taken the railyards. They were joined at 2 a.m. by engineers, already two hours behind schedule, who set about repairing craters in the embankment so that the tanks could advance. Unfortunately, the moon became very bright around 3 a.m. and exposed the sappers to heavy crossfire. Their work was not completed by dawn and they withdrew, leaving the Maori to hold the station until the following evening. The Maori were almost completely surrounded by the Germans by early morning. An Allied smokescreen did not prevent the enemy from pumping heavy artillery and small arms fire into the station area and fierce hand to hand fighting followed soon after. A supporting company was caught in heavy artillery fire and was unable to relieve the men in the station. Then the Germans brought up tanks against men whom they knew were not equipped with anti-tank weapons. After a day of desperate fighting, the Maori were forced to withdraw at 4 p.m. Only 76 of the original 200 men returned; 22 had been killed, 24 were missing and 78 were wounded. The Indians fought with equal gallantry but also failed to take their objectives.

Morale fell after Operation Avenger because the heavy losses had been to no avail; the Maori had failed to gain a single advantage. The cold and wet weather also continued to cause problems and outbreaks of diarrhoea became all too common. New Zealand soldiers experienced their highest levels of psychiatric breakdown for the entire war.

There was a sense of relief when the Kiwis were given another 'crack at the Hun' a month later. This time the 24th, 25th and 26th Battalions were instructed to take the town of Cassino after the area had been subjected to one of the biggest saturation bombing operations of the war. Some 280 heavy and 180 medium bombers were instructed to drop 1000 tonnes of 1000-pound (450-kilogram) bombs on the Cassino area for three and a half hours, commencing at 8.30 a.m. on 15 March. The bombing was to be followed by an eight-hour artillery bombardment carried out by 200 guns. The idea was that the Germans would be blown into submission.

Yet Freyberg was still worried. He had doubts about the effectiveness of saturation bombing and still wondered if he could concentrate enough infantry on the town. He also did not want to lose large numbers of men. Major General G. B. Parkinson, who had taken over from the wounded Kippenberger as divisional commander, seemed less concerned.

The bombing itself was truly awesome, flattening both the town and the monastery, its results reminding one German commander of the Somme. A corporal in the 25th Battalion thought

Cassino had become 'a vision of the end of the world'. Yet appearances were deceptive because most German soldiers survived in their deep-set bunkers and the bombing only hardened their resolve to fight. Allied troops were also caught in the destructive blast and 15 members of the Maori Battalion were killed. Even worse, the town was reduced to a series of bomb craters and ruined houses. The craters made the use of tanks impossible and the rubble provided ideal defensive positions for the Germans.

On 15 March the New Zealanders began their attack with considerable enthusiasm but they soon ran into problems as only one road leading into the town was passable by tanks. Still there were initial successes as D Company of the 25th captured the castle on Castle Hill but a communication failure meant that the Indians delayed their attack on the monastery for two hours, waiting for this news. The post office in the town was taken by 3.30 in the afternoon.

Thereafter everything went wrong. The New Zealanders, unaccustomed to street fighting, failed to take either the heavily fortified Continental Hotel or the Hotel des Roses. Progress ground to a halt and tanks could not be brought up to support the men; Freyberg had great difficulty in getting in reinforcements. Even the Maori Battalion could not match the ferocity of the German paratroopers. The advance soon came to be measured in centimetres rather than metres and one group of New Zealanders actually spent three days in the same house as a group of Germans, both sets of soldiers pinned down by the deadly covering fire. Bulldozers were unable to clear the rubble and when the 23rd Battalion joined the action on 20 March they could not even see the well-entrenched Germans.

The New Zealanders were forced to withdraw by 23 March with men beginning to suffer from battle exhaustion. Supplies of food and medicine had been hopelessly inadequate and sleep was impossible. Casualties had been high with 206 men killed, 1085 wounded and 101 missing, a rate of 36 per cent for the six battalions who had fought in this action. Gains were non-existent and the only compensation was the knowledge that they had inflicted heavy losses on the Germans

— the resolute paratroopers had suffered a casualty rate of 62 per cent. The New Zealanders still felt bitter disappointment at their failure to make any advance. One anonymous soldier caught their mood when he said: 'The name that is most generally applied to the New Zealand Division both individually and collectively, is Kiwi . . . One version of the derivation I have heard goes like this: "Like the bird we can't fly, we can't see, and we are rapidly becoming extinct".'

At Cassino it seemed as if the clock had been turned back to the First World War. The mobility which had characterised the North Africa campaign and the advance to the Sangro River was exchanged for a setpiece battle that brought tremendous losses. Casualties were high and the futility of the Western Front seemed to have returned; Freyberg summed up this feeling when he said, 'Reminds you of Passchendaele, doesn't it?'

All the New Zealand battalions enhanced their reputations for bravery and tenacity. The Maori Battalion proved once and for all that it could handle setpiece actions as well as the more free-wheeling form of desert warfare. The historian of Cassino, John Ellis, praises the New Zealand soldiers who 'had, as ever, done their best', but he is more critical of Freyberg for taking on missions that had a very remote chance of success. Glory was once again won at terrible cost: 343 men were killed, 1211 wounded and 42 taken prisoner. It was, in Ellis's phrase, a 'hollow vic-

tory' which achieved little but cost much.

The Kiwis did not share in the joy of liberating Rome. Instead they plugged on up the peninsula after they had completed a difficult withdrawal from Cassino. Time and again they ran into heavily fortified houses and canals as they inched their way forward. Yet morale gradually recovered as they were at least making progress. Fighting was especially bitter around the River Arno, near Florence, and ended in a pitched hand to hand battle. Fierce actions also occurred at Monte Lignano, Arezzo, San Michele, La Romola and in crossing the Senio. Sappers proved critical to the advance both as bridge builders and as defusers of miners. They also spent much of their time digging trucks and tanks out of the mud. The slowness of the advance meant that the Kiwis had to suffer through another particularly harsh Italian winter.

As the advance continued much of the dash of the troops disappeared. The war was clearly won and they became noticeably more cautious. On the other hand, experience welded them into a more effective unit. Air and ground strikes became much better co-ordinated and new weapons like the flame thrower were used to good effect. The improved co-ordination and greater professionalism was particularly obvious in the crossing of the Senio River on 9 April 1945.

This river was heavily defended by mortar and artillery on the far stopbanks, but a carefully planned four-

New Zealand infantry prepare to enter the frontline town of Faenza by crossing the Lamone River, November 1944, Italy. *G. F. Kaye.*

New Zealand infantry advance cautiously through the rubble of Faenza. *G. F. Kaye.*

Kiwi soldiers gather around to warm up inside the remains of an Italian house at Faenza. *G. F. Kaye.*

hour bombardment by fighter planes and artillery wore the enemy down. This time the infantry attacked immediately the bombardment ceased, before the Germans had gathered their composure, and flame throwers inflicted further damage before the New Zealanders stormed across the river in boats and on kapok bridges. Once the infantry had crossed the sappers threw bridges across the water to bring up tanks and support. The first bridge was in place within six hours of the attack and six were in place a mere eight hours after the fortified stopbanks had been taken. Casualties were light and the beaten enemy capitulated meekly.

After crossing the Senio the advance across the Italian peninsula was rapid. The Kiwis proceeded in a very efficient manner and suffered only light casualties, despite having to take heavily fortified canals and houses. Sometimes they avoided such barriers and sped around minefields. The reputation for speed and stamina won in the desert campaigns was shown in the last phase of the war as the Kiwis took Bologna on 21 April 1945 and moved on to Venice.

Freyberg was ordered to have his men race to Trieste to take the city as a military objective, not, as is popularly believed, to prevent the key port being taken by the Yugoslavs. The Kiwis completed the operation on 2 May and an uneasy truce prevailed. Discipline broke down somewhat after Germany surrendered on 8 May. Any major incidents were nevertheless avoided and Tito withdrew in June. So the European theatre of war came to a close.

The New Zealanders had lost 1825

A German Arado Ar 96 erupts in fire and smoke as it is shot down by New Zealand Wing Commander Evan Mackie flying a Spitfire. *Evan Mackie Collection.*

killed and 6632 wounded in Italy. Only 211 had been taken prisoner, a statistic that reflected both the ferocity of the German and New Zealand soldiers, and the fact that the Kiwis were part of an advancing army. Many soldiers felt a little cheated that they had missed out on the major theatre of action, yet they also realised that they had played their part in the Allied victory by tying up a few crack German divisions who could have been used in France or Russia. The Kiwis had also proven themselves as good as any other troops. As one respondent to a recent survey of soldiers who fought in Italy put it, 'they had fought above themselves.' Morale had held up surprisingly well despite the difficult conditions. Rates of desertion, refusal to go into battle and mental breakdown were lower than for the British and American troops. Despite a despondent period after Cassino, the New Zealand soldier had come of military age.

A recent book by John McLeod has queried the high reputation acquired by New Zealand soldiers in the Second World War. He suggests that the idea that the civilian New Zealander was somehow a 'natural' soldier who performed better than his allied counterparts is a myth developed by the Returned Services Association, politicians, the official war histories and fiction writers. McLeod's attempt at judging the performance in more objective terms was long overdue but like most revisionists he has overcorrected.

Few soldiers who fought in Italy or anywhere else made extravagant claims after the war except when full of booze on Anzac Day. The multi-volume official war history is hardly excessive in its glorification of the campaigns. Several of the historians who wrote these large volumes, including Neville Phillips, Angus Ross, Robin Kay and R. M. Burdon, later won a reputation for careful scholarship and balanced judgement rather than rhetorical excess. Dan Davin's prose has been praised for its sparse-

A German Focke Wulf is brought down by New Zealander Flight Lieutenant Tony Robson, flying a Spitfire in 485 Squadron RNZAF on 4 May 1942. This was one of the best photographic sequences of an enemy fighter being shot down taken during the war. *A. R. Robson.*

The German battleship *Graf Spee* after being blown up by its commander, 1939. The New Zealand ship HMS *Achilles* and the Royal Navy cruisers *Ajax* and *Exeter* inflicted heavy damage on the *Graf Spee*. The Germans took shelter in Montevideo Harbour in neutral Uruguay. After being asked to leave, the *Graf Spee* put to sea and the ship was scuttled rather than face battle with the waiting *Achilles* and other ships. *Gary Couchman.*

ness and his war stories catch the laconic and understated nature of New Zealand speech.

McLeod has invented something of a strawman to knock down. He assumes that the New Zealand public was extremely naive. Many citizens at home were themselves old soldiers who knew that soldiers sometimes got drunk, ran amok, visited prostitutes, engaged in fleeting liaisons, caught venereal disease and looted. The First World War had taught many civilians that this was all part of the business of war. Just because these problems were rarely talked about in public did not mean that most adults were unaware of their existence. The fact that 432 men of the 2nd New Zealand Expedi-

tionary Force refused to return to active service after being brought home on furlough in 1943 must also have alerted many civilians to the fact that there were problems with command and the manner in which the war was being fought.

All myths exaggerate and should be questioned from time to time. But debunking is a risky business. McLeod has made the mistake of lumping together all the faults and disasters of the New Zealanders without balancing them up against their successes. Churchill and British field marshals like Montgomery and Lord Alexander were lavish in their praise of all Commonwealth troops, yet Montgomery, Rommel and Anthony Eden, the British Foreign Minister, claimed that the New Zealanders were the 'best' unit in the 8th Army. Several military historians, including Englishmen Liddell Hart and John Ellis and Australian Alan Moorehead, endorse this high opinion. Even the 9th Australian Division paid the Kiwis the ultimate tribute by claiming that they were 'second only to the New Zealanders'.

New Zealanders made as big a

contribution in other services as they did in the Army. Over 9000 served in the Royal Navy on patrol work and 10,950 were pilots, navigators and gunners in fighter and bomber command in the RAF; 103 New Zealanders flew in the critical Battle of Britain. There were many superb individual efforts made by men such as Air Vice Marshal Sir Keith Park, Captain C. F. Gray and Commodore Deere. Over 3000 New Zealanders were killed while serving with the RAF.

The impact of the North African and European theatres upon New Zealand's home front and future strategic concerns was peripheral in comparison with the fall of Singapore on 15 February 1942. Distance no longer guaranteed immunity from attack and as the British Navy did not come to the rescue, New Zealand was forced to turn to new allies — the United States and Australia. When the Americans won the vital battle of the Coral Sea in May 1942 it became clear that New Zealand's defence would be reliant upon the emerging super power.

Once Singapore fell New Zealand

The Pacific campaign. 8th Brigade of the 3rd New Zealand Division land on Sterling Island at dawn on 27 October, 1943. *Alexander Turnbull Library.*

civilians were forced to face the reality of invasion for the first time. War suddenly affected everyone, not just the soldiers whom Fraser left in North Africa. The Australians recalled their troops at this time but New Zealand did not and the civilian population was left feeling very vulnerable.

Some 20,000 New Zealand troops of the 3rd Division were sent to fight in the uncomfortable and dirty Pacific war where they were devastated by disease. At various times they were supported by 5000 men from the Royal New Zealand Navy (formed in 1941) and 15,000 men from the Royal New Zealand Air Force (formed in 1937). Casualties were relatively slight with 2207 killed and nearly 3000 wounded. But those unlucky enough to be taken prisoner by the Japanese were subjected to far worse barbarities than men who were captured by the Germans. The Pacific division entered the war in November 1940 and disbanded in October 1944 once it was clear that the Japanese threat had been removed. Some troops later travelled from Italy to join in the occupation of Japan after the second of two nuclear

bombs brought Japan to its knees on 15 August 1945.

Between 1939 and 1942 New Zealand was defended by the ill-equipped Home Guard of 123,000 men who were either too old or unfit for service or engaged in reserved occupations and an Air Force which grew from 750 to 34,000 men. Then between 1942 and 1944 100,000 American servicemen poured into the country. Their arrival added a feeling of security but their greatest impact was social rather than military; the well-paid Americans swept many New Zealand women off their feet.

The reality of war was also brought home by the presence of over 800 Japanese prisoners near Featherston in the Wairarapa. When they attempted a mass escape on 25 February 1943, 40 were killed and 82 wounded. Most New Zealanders were shocked by the incident, especially as the prisoners had been well treated.

The government took a hard line against conscientious objectors; over 800 men were placed in an internment camp. In addition 3400 people were classified as enemy aliens and 200 were

interned on Somes Island in Wellington Harbour.

The emergence of a home front meant that the lives of New Zealand women were affected much more directly by the Second World War than by the First. With 194,000 men serving in the armed forces, or two out of three of those eligible, many more employment opportunities were made available for women. Such traditional male preserves as bus and taxi driving, sawmilling and baking were taken up by women. The number of women employed in industry rose from 21,000 to 38,000, including 2770 in the male-dominated metal and machine crafts. Over 2000 women worked in agriculture as land girls, while a further 8700 put on uniforms and joined the women's services in the Women's Army Auxiliary Corps (WAAC), the Women's Auxiliary Air Force (WAAF) and the Women's Royal New Zealand Naval Service (WRNS).

civil service and factories brought about the final collapse of domestic service as a major employer of women.

Japan's entry into the war, the failure of the Royal Navy to provide adequate protection and the biggest manpower contribution per capita outside the Soviet Union (over a quarter of the male workforce served in the armed forces) meant that New Zealand was exposed to the experience of total war even though the country was not invaded. Manufacturing was stimulated with the volume of production increasing by a third, yet New Zealand remained as dependent upon one market and three export staples in 1945 as it had been in 1939.

Some 11,625 men were killed in the Second World War and 17,000 were wounded, over 6000 of them seriously disabled. These losses were high but not as horrendous as those of the First World War because the 1939-45 war was a more mobile affair fought by machines as well as men. Consequently civilians often suffered greater losses than soldiers. Improvements in medical treatment also reduced the death rate from wounds. On a per capita basis New Zealand's losses were also double those of Canada and Australia. Nevertheless, because total losses were more modest and no influenza epidemic followed the peace, the 1950s were not a sad and despondent decade like the 1920s.

Finally, the Second World War had a greater stimulus on the development of New Zealand nationalism than the Great War, despite the ongoing strength of sentimental attachment to Britain. Necessity forced New Zealand to behave in a more independent fashion and reorientate towards America and Asia.

The first women police constables were also appointed in 1941.

The impact of the Second World War upon women should not be exaggerated, however, because the majority returned to more traditional roles once the war was over. Women continued to be paid far less than men and were forced out of higher executive positions once the troops came home. Still a range of clerical positions within the civil service were opened up for women and factory work became more acceptable. The shift into the

Link: From Peace to Waterfront Strike

New Zealanders wanted to relax and enjoy the good times they felt were sure to follow Japan's surrender on Sunday 2 September 1945. After so many years of hardship and controls they felt that they deserved to share in the good life introduced by the American marines. Fraser and Nash, however, seemed to have other ideas.

The two British born leaders continued wartime rationing and regulation to help Attlee's Labour government rebuild war-torn Britain. They also feared that inflation would run rampant if wartime controls were taken off too rapidly. Fraser and Nash remembered the problems that resulted when New Zealand switched suddenly from wartime conditions to the free market in 1920 and 1921 and they were determined to make a better job of rehabilitation than Massey's government. Even their severest critics conceded that they succeeded in achieving that goal, but a growing number of New Zealanders were becoming impatient.

The continuance of the wartime stabilisation policy did not satisfy many who wanted to build a better and brighter world. They longed for more than minor modifications to the welfare state, and resented the shortages of imported and consumer goods.

The dissatisfaction showed in the 1946 election when Labour was kept in power only by the four Maori electorates. The government was also helped by its decision to abolish the 'country quota', or 28 per cent weighting of rural seats. More controls were dropped in 1947 but it was not enough. Returned servicemen raising families struggled to find adequate housing.

In comparison with Labour's ageing Fraser and Nash, National's Sid Holland appeared young, dynamic and refreshing. He was also a New Zealander who had served as a soldier in the First World War. He modelled himself on Australia's new brash and ebullient conservative leader, Robert Menzies. Like Menzies, Holland was an ardent Empire loyalist, very pro-American and an outspoken critic of communism. His call to consolidate the gains made by Labour, while removing their socialist excesses, appealed to people who aspired to a safe job, a car and a comfortable bungalow equipped with an electric stove, fridge, water heater and washing machine.

The Labour government also lost

Prime Minister Peter Fraser and Defence Minister Bob Semple deeply split the Labour movement with their support for peacetime military conscription. The Peace and Anti-Conscription Federation published this cartoon in *Civil Liberty*.

some of its traditional supporters between 1946 and 1949. Once controls were removed prices ran ahead of wages and a growing number of unions became restive; even respectable white collar unions like the Public Service Association demanded more money. But the most troublesome unions were the watersiders and carpenters. Along with other left wing unions, they wanted an end to the government's policy of stabilisation and one of the tools of that policy, the Arbitration Court. Because direct confrontations with employers promised better wages and conditions, they engaged in a great deal of direct action between 1946 and 1949.

The dissatisfaction of the more militant unions was increased by the government's drift to the right in foreign policy as Fraser came under the influence of Cold War attitudes. Fraser, Defence Minister Bob Semple and the FOL began to see communists everywhere. The fact that a few watersiders were members of the very small New Zealand Communist Party made them even more suspect in the eyes of the Labour establishment. The militants in turn lamented the replacement of the bold independent foreign policy of the late 1930s with a pro-American stance. Most militants found it ironic that a man like Fraser, who had stood up to Fascism and advocated the rights of small nations when the United

Nations was established, should now turn into a Cold War warrior.

Disbelief turned to outrage when Fraser and Semple gave in to British and American pressure and introduced peacetime conscription. In the referendum Fraser held on 3 September 1949 three to one voted in favour but 37 per cent of the eligible population did not participate. It was ironical that two men who had gone to prison in the First World war for opposing wartime conscription should now introduce conscription in peacetime. Some, disenchanted, resigned from the Labour Party; others stayed away from the polling booths in 1949.

The Labour monolith fell with scarcely a whimper; the government lost the election by 46 seats to 34. Fraser seemed to be the only person who was genuinely surprised by the result, even though his own party organisers had warned him that Labour was suffering from a rapidly declining membership and hopelessly inadequate finances. Fraser died on 12 December 1950, disillusioned by the ingratitude of those whose interests he had worked so hard to defend.

21. 1951 Labour Self-Destructs: The 151-Day Waterfront Strike

THE years from 1946 to 1949 saw a rash of stoppages at the country's ports as the watersiders used strikes, go-slows and overtime bans to wring concessions from their employers.

Harold (Jock) Barnes, the president of the New Zealand Waterfront Workers' Union (NZWWU), was an able, ambitious, militant socialist who saw the unions as the conscience of the labour movement. Unions were much more than fighters for better wages and conditions — they were the voice of the working class who were entitled to a say in both domestic and international affairs. Toby Hill, the national secretary of the NZWWU shared Barnes's beliefs. Much of their agitation centred on their opposition to compulsory arbitration. The unions would, they argued, be stronger without the Arbitration Court which regulated disputes between workers and employers.

The Labour government tried to isolate the watersiders from the rest of the trade union movement dominated by the moderate and pro-government Federation of Labour. Barnes and Hill were targeted. Semple labelled Barnes 'a wrecker . . . ambitious for personal power . . . a real threat to the industrial peace and general welfare of the people.' The Labour government believed that its cradle to grave welfare state had made strikes unnecessary. Strikes also threatened its economic stabilisation policy and made elections more difficult in 1949.

The rift between the militants and the government and FOL created a field day for the National Party. Who was running the country, Holland and his Labour spokesman William Sullivan asked — the watersiders or the

government? National would restore industrial order and protect the arbitration system.

National easily won the 1949 election but spent a quiet first year in office; unionists seemed surprised by Labour Minister Sullivan's conciliatory approach. In February 1950 Fintan Patrick Walsh, the leader of the moderates within the FOL, attempted to force the NZWWU out of the FOL by asking the watersiders to join the other member unions in withdrawing from the pro-Moscow World Federation of Trade Unions. When, as Walsh hoped, Barnes refused, the FOL executive tried to expel watersiders. Other unions, however, decided that the action was unconstitutional. The issue could only be resolved by the annual conference in April, where Walsh repeated his demand. The watersiders withdrew, along with 60 other delegates representing some

A loyalty card issued to strikers who stood firm throughout the 1951 strike. *Ian Burnett.*

75,000 workers, and formed a rival Trade Union Congress on 18 April 1950.

By the time the TUC held its first conference in August it was essentially a watersiders' organisation. The wharf labourers had never, in the history of their union, been so isolated and vulnerable. Relations with the new government cooled from May when the TUC undertook industrial action to protest the removal of food subsidies, the lifting of price controls on cakes and groceries and increased rail and petrol prices. They also demanded a wage increase of 2 shillings an hour. Sullivan managed to persuade the watersiders to return to work but they came out again in June in opposition to a Waterfront Industry Commission

(WIC) decision to treat a ship carrying a particularly dirty cargo as 'preference', that is a vessel whose cargo had to be unloaded and loaded quickly.

Sullivan remained calm and got the watersiders back to work by offering more money for dirty jobs. The port employers were incensed and even the Labour Party lambasted Sullivan for being soft. It was clear that the new government could no longer afford to give in to the wharfies.

In July the Waterfront Industry Authority granted an increase of only 3d per hour rather than the 2 shillings the union had requested. The union declared that it wanted the WIA abolished and a return to direct bargaining between employee and employer. Inflation was rising and the National government had no intention of giving the strongest union in the country a chance to unleash a wage explosion through direct negotiation.

Barnes ignored the growing clamour to bring the watersiders into line and on 3 August called a strike over tea breaks. To the public this seemed a very trivial matter and newspaper editorials demanded swift and strong action. The *New Zealand Herald* pointed out that the government could use the Public Safety Conservation Act of 1932 to declare a state of emergency to get the wharves working smoothly again.

A showdown was averted, however, by the intervention of the FOL and a Royal Commission was promised to investigate the waterfront industry. The wharfies agreed not to strike while the commission sat.

Another dispute flared in September, however, over the loading of lampblack. The WIA granted an extra 1s 6d per hour for handling the dirty and dangerous material but the NZWWU claimed that the WIC had promised them 2s 6d back in June. Barnes blasted Judge Dalglish of the WIA and ordered his men to stop work if they were penalised for refusing to load lampblack.

Barnes's directive infuriated the shipping companies and port authorities, who retaliated by imposing penalties. Another strike was under way by 13 September and employers and the press called for government intervention. The FOL made strong government action easier by disassociating itself from the dispute, but the

government still feared that there might be some public sympathy left because lampblack was such a difficult cargo to handle.

Shipowners and port authorities then tried forcing the issue by ordering the watersiders back to work. Finally, on 20 September, Holland warned the watersiders that he would impose a state of emergency unless they resumed work. The Prime Minister also told the House that the dispute was part of the Soviet plan to undermine the Korean war effort.

The government actually declared a state of emergency but the Labour Party produced a last minute solution by persuading the government to call a compulsory conference. At this the NZWWU was promised that the appointment of the Royal Commission would be accelerated and two days later they were also awarded the 2s 6d extra for unloading lampblack. Jubilant wharfies returned to work immediately.

Overconfident, Barnes believed that he could wring even more concessions from this new 'Tory' government. In October he refused to co-operate with the Royal Commission because it was not investigating all aspects of the waterfront industry. The shipowners and port authorities responded by breaking off talks. Barnes continued to demand direct bargaining but the employers were only prepared to work through the WIA, the Arbitration Court or the Royal Commission. A showdown seemed inevitable.

By the end of 1950 the watersiders had alienated just about everybody. Anti-communist hysteria whipped up by the press meant that few people bothered to think about the failures of the shipowners. The FOL was unsympathetic and quite happy for the militants to receive a drubbing. The wharfies had turned themselves into a scapegoat for the nation's problems.

Holland got his chance in February 1951 after the FOL and TUC protested the Arbitration Court's 15 per cent general wage increase. Toby Hill thundered that the government was 'like the Bourbons — they have not heard the tramp of marching feet'.

The watersiders were not automatically covered by the Arbitration Court order. What would the militant watersiders settle for? Eventually they reduced their claim to 4s 10½d — a 15 per cent increase — but the employers offered 4s 7½d. To force the port employers to increase their offer Barnes declared an overtime ban on 13 February. The employers retaliated on 15 February by placing all men who refused to work overtime on a two-day penalty, cutting their working week from 40 to 16 hours. Barnes claimed a lockout; employers and newspapers screamed strike.

Acting Prime Minister Keith Jacka Holyoake called a compulsory conference on 16 February. He insisted that the dispute be taken to arbitration; Barnes replied that he would accept direct bargaining. The cabinet decided

"The Country is right behind the Government."

Cartoons from illegally published *Wellington Watersiders Official Information Bulletins*. **In spite of their great efforts their underground operations could not compete with the newspapers and radio to which emergency regulations denied them access.** *Ian Burnett.*

Prime Minister Holland's tough stand against the watersiders.
On 27 February 1951, the day after the emergency regulations had gone into force, he declared in a national broadcast:

- We could give in to the strikers — but we won't.
- We could capitulate to direct action — but we won't.
- We could let tyranny replace democratic government — but we won't.
- We could let down every worker who abides by the law — but we won't.
- We could let direct action pay better dividends than democratic methods — but we won't.
- We could shirk our plain public duty — but we won't.

that the only way out of the impasse was to enforce arbitration.

Holland, now known by the wharfies as 'the Senator for Fendalton', returned that night from America. He heightened tensions by telling a dinner audience that anyone 'who stands in the way of the country's preparation for defence to ensure peace . . . by limiting the handling of goods is a traitor'. The battle lines were drawn.

When watersiders arrived at work on Monday morning they were greeted by notices informing them they could continue only if they were prepared to work normal hours and overtime. Once again the NZWWU claimed that they had been locked out and work stopped on the wharves. The government was now under intense pressure from farmers, businessmen and newspapers to declare a state of emergency. No one in cabinet represented an urban working class electorate. There seemed little choice but to declare a state of emergency on 21 February. The watersiders were given until 26 February to capitulate.

This time there was no turning back. The government declared the strike illegal and deregistered the NZWWU. The emergency regulations were then implemented to remove freedom of speech, suspend Parliament and deny either trial by jury or right of appeal. Even though the Labour government had taken these powers in 1939, they had never applied them in full. Now Holland, a constant critic of Labour's totalitarian tactics, used these same powers to full advantage.

This single action removed all protection for the watersiders. The Labour Party was powerless to help them and a very uneven contest unfolded in what had become virtually a police state. Servicemen were brought in to work the wharves as the pattern of 1913 was repeated. It soon became clear, though, that there was much more skill involved in a wharfie's job than a critical public realised. Laid-off unionists jeered as servicemen struggled with heavy loads and dropped boxes of apples.

Both government and press had a field day now that the unions had no

During the strike servicemen were put to work on the wharves. *Auckland Star.*

means of answering back. No paper was allowed to print the watersiders' side of the story and a few illegal underground presses were no match for the deluge of hostile propaganda. There was no way of denying the charge that the militants were little more than agents of the Soviet Union. The fact that Barnes and Hill were not communists went unnoticed as hysteria swept the country.

This barrage of criticism also whittled away support from miners, seamen, freezing workers, harbour board employees and some hydro construction workers. Railwaymen and some drivers refused to handle goods unloaded by non-union labour but this campaign proved largely ineffective. Walsh and the FOL did their best to make it impossible for other unions to support the watersiders who, by April, were virtually on their own. The Labour Party was the only organisation which continued to demand a rational solution to the crisis.

Nash called for a compulsory conference but this appeal had little impact when Parliament was in recess and a total radio ban on his speeches further restricted his effectiveness. He also tried to keep open lines of communication with Barnes and Hill and earned himself the wrath of Walsh in the process. Nash, critical of the loss of civil liberties, became a victim of the regulations himself when he was refused permission to speak at the Auckland Town Hall in early May. Finally, on 13 May, he managed to speak to a crowd of 6000 in the Auckland Domain. There he made the unfortunate remark that Labour was neither for nor against the strikers. What he meant was that his party opposed the watersiders' refusal to come to arbitration but that they were equally alarmed by the government's use of undemocratic methods to crush an undemocratic action. Nash never lived down this faux pas.

As the dispute dragged on the families of some of the strikers began to experience real hardship. Under the emergency regulations it was illegal to

An illegal underground cartoon produced by the Wellington watersiders. 'Slippery Sid' is Prime Minister Sid Holland. 'Wild Bill Sullivan' is the Minister of Labour. 'Scabaxter' is the secretary of the Federation of Labour, K. McL. Baxter. *Ian Burnett.*

supply strikers or their dependants with food. This draconian ruling did not cause too many problems because many people ignored it and many wharfies found other work. Sometimes wives of wharfies went out to work and tightly knit communities like Port Chalmers proved remarkably supportive. Few wharfies scabbed and those who did were never forgiven by their former mates. There was, nevertheless, genuine hardship and much resentment and frustration.

Violence flared on several occasions. A general melee broke out in Auckland on 28 April when a new port union was formed and on 30 April explosives were found under a railway bridge near Huntly. The Auckland watersiders again tried to stop the new unionists working on 3 May. These actions gave the government an excuse to swear in more specials and tighten the regulations further. Police raids were carried out against the underground press and some wharfies countered by trying to intimidate 'free' labourers in their homes. The worst outbreak occurred on 1 June in Auckland when police batoned a crowd of men and women in a display of excessive zeal not seen since 1932.

After this incident the strike began to peter out and the 151-day strike ended on 11 July. The longest, most costly and widespread industrial battle in New Zealand's history was over. It had caused the loss of 1.1 million man days and cost the country at least £40 million. The once powerful national watersiders' union was replaced by 26 small port unions. Both the union movement and the Labour Party had been left bitterly divided.

With his popularity at an all time high Holland called a snap election for 1 September, dissolving the recently assembled Parliament on 11 July. The campaign was probably the dirtiest in New Zealand's political history. National declared that the election was a contest between 'The People versus the Wreckers'. Hackneyed old stories that Nash had once been a bankrupt were dredged up and his earlier visit to Russia was cited as proof of his communist leanings. Labour's counter that National were the party of depression made little impact on people experiencing record levels of prosperity. National won by 20 seats, taking 54 per cent of a low voter turnout.

A powerful mythology has developed around the 1951 Waterfront Strike which clouds the understanding of later generations. The wharfies themselves felt so isolated that the have exaggerated the heroism of thei stand and the extent of their suffering Few could dispute their claim, however, that they were involved in the greatest dog fight in New Zealand' industrial history. It is the hopeless ness of their cause which has led historians and authors to elevate rather pointless scrap into a battl between good and evil. Clair Matthewson has shown that severa novelists have portrayed the 151-day strike in similar terms. Maurice Shad bolt in *Strangers and Journeys* Maurice Gee in *Sole Survivor* and Kar Stead in *All Visitors Ashore* all impl that the strike was a bad thing which brought about the triumph of reactio and revealed the dark side of the Nev Zealand character for all the world to see.

The problem with such intellectua reinterpretation is that it confuses Hol land's heavy-handed treatment of the strikers with the justice of the water siders' cause. It should not be forgot ten that the watersiders had behaved unreasonably for seven years and had sorely tried the patience of both Labour and National. Had Labour been returned in 1949 they, too, would probably have been forced into showdown. Furthermore, the disput had more to do with the clash between Barnes and Walsh than between beleaguered union and an evil, grasp ing Tory government. All this does no excuse the excesses of the Holland government but rather suggests tha the wharfies were their own wors enemies.

The popular mythology associated with the 1951 strike has in fact had much greater impact on later develop ments than the contrived literary view New Zealanders learnt one thing above all else in 1951 — that politica excess of any kind is dangerous and ugly. Until 1984 National and Labou tussled for the middle ground, offering similar mixes of philosophy and policy There were no radical changes unti Roger Douglas became Minister o Finance in July 1984.

Link: From Holland to Te Maori

The period between 1951 and 1967 was the most conservative in New Zealand history, in every sphere of life. In the economic field many hydro dams were built and there was considerable development of forestry but little economic diversification occurred. Pastoral products still accounted for 90 per cent of export earnings in the mid-1960s. The numbers of farms and farmers actually increased in the early 1950s but aggregation of holdings in the 1960s saw this trend reversed. Manufacturing employed growing numbers of the workforce but made little contribution to exports. Horticulture and viticulture remained small in scale.

After the war New Zealand turned to the United States to replace Britain as a major ally. In 1951 New Zealand joined the United States and Australia to form the ANZUS pact, which, until 1987, remained the cornerstone of New Zealand's security arrangements.

One of the major reasons for the conservatism of this period was the widespread prosperity. There was a modest balance of payments crisis in 1957 and 1958 but otherwise these were good times. Unemployment was unknown and wealth was relatively evenly shared. New Zealand during the 1950s and 1960s boasted some of the lowest wage differentials in the world. Migrants were brought in from Holland and the Pacific Islands to make up the labour shortage as the baby boom created a new demand for houses, schools and public works.

A population increase from 1.7 million in 1945 to 2.6 million in 1966 produced other interesting sociological effects. The drift to the cities continued despite the ongoing dominance of pastoral farming. By 1961 over three-quarters of European New Zealanders were living in cities or towns. The majority of these city dwellers chose to live in the sprawling new suburbs as they strove to realise the old New Zealand dream of home ownership. This trend was most marked in Auckland where, by 1961, three-quarters of the population were living in outer suburbs. Nationally the move to home ownership was noticeable, with nearly 70 per cent of New Zealanders owning their homes by 1961, one of the highest levels in the world.

Whole areas were taken over by families of roughly the same age. Artificial communities with no older

Labour's Finance Minister Arnold Nordmeyer presents the 'black budget' on 1958. It brought increases in taxes on cigarettes, tobacco, beer and new cars. Labour never overcame the public resentment and was swept from office in 1960 after only one term. *Evening Post.*

citizens were thereby created and the 1960s produced a new problem — suburban neurosis. Many women found life extremely difficult in isolated suburbs poorly equipped with shops or facilities for their children. The very newness of the suburbs combined with the lengthy absence of husbands at distant places of work helped to make them into something of a wasteland until women learnt to develop their own networks of support.

Cultural development did not flourish in what Austin Mitchell later described as the 'half gallon, quarter acre pavlova paradise'. Writers and painters battled away against the odds but received scant support. Strong voices like those of the poet James K. Baxter were not stifled by the prevailing hedonism and Janet Frame startled international critics with the perceptiveness of her novel *Owls Do Cry* published in 1957. But artists generally

received little sympathy or support. Abstract painting was openly ridiculed and sport, especially rugby, remained king. Youth culture imported from the United States provided a small challenge to the conformity of adult New Zealand but its derivative nature limited its impact.

Little wonder, then, that the politics of this period were bland and dominated by conservative 'consensus' politics. Sid Holland and his National government were returned to power in 1954 with a considerably reduced majority; they won 45 seats to Labour's 35. Links with the United States and non-communist Asian countries were further strengthened in

Six o'clock closing ended in 1967; hotels were allowed to open until 10 o'clock. Here patrons at Wellington's Metropolitan Hotel celebrate the dawning of New Zealand's 'enlightened' drinking. *Evening Post.*

the same year when New Zealand joined the South East Asian Treaty Organisation (SEATO). Then in 1957 Walter Nash led Labour to a very narrow, two-seat victory.

The second Labour government is not remembered for its innovative policies but rather for the notorious 'black budget' of 1958 when austerity measures were taken to reduce the balance of payment deficit. New Zealand voters never forgave the wowserish Nash and Finance Minister Nordmeyer for putting up the price of their beer and 'baccy'. In 1960 National was returned with a comfortable majority of 12 seats.

Nash's efforts at stimulating industrialisation were soon forgotten, as Keith Holyoake, who took over as National's leader on Sid Holland's death in 1957, turned attention back to bolstering the traditional industries. Farming remained buoyant and the electorate was satisfied with Holyoake's relaxed style of leadership. Holyoake won easily in 1963 by 10 seats against Arnold Nordmeyer's Labour team and by nine seats against Labour's new leader Norman Kirk in 1966. Only limited efforts were made to find new markets or develop new products so long as the golden weather

continued.

In 1967 Britain sent shudders through the complacent New Zealand countryside by entering into serious negotiations with the European Economic Community (EEC). The 'golden weather' came to an abrupt end as New Zealand experienced its first large deficit on its balance of payments since the Great Depression of the 1930s, noticeably larger than in the 'black' year of 1958. It was also in 1967 that Robert Muldoon became Minister of Finance.

One of New Zealand's most peculiar institutions — 6 o'clock hotel closing — was finally voted out by referendum in 1967. Longer hours were just the boost that the local entertainment, restaurant and wine industries needed. The New Zealand fashion industry, too, was stimulated by the growth of a generic musical culture.

Live theatre also benefited from the happy conjunction that occurred when the children of the baby boom reached adulthood at a time when going out to be entertained was fashionable. Professional theatre companies sprang up in Auckland (The Mercury), Wellington (Downstage) and Christchurch (The Court).

University rolls exploded as the 'baby boomers' poured into tertiary education. The number of tertiary students doubled from 15,000 to 30,000 between 1961 and 1971. Massey Agricultural College was expanded into a full university in 1964 and

Waikato University came into being in 1968. By 1984 there were 160,000 students receiving tertiary education, 58,000 of them at university.

Poets and public controversialists flourished in the freer, more open social climate. Religion, politics and sex were no longer taboo subjects in conversation. James K. Baxter wrote a long, provocative ode on mixed flatting in 1967 and Dr Erich Geiringer worried parents by urging students to tear down the walls of single sex hostels. Permissiveness was also encouraged by the 'flower children' or 'hippie' movement emanating from California. The greater availability of contraceptives, particularly 'the pill', further promoted sexual freedom.

The restless younger generation found an outlet for their impatience in their protests against New Zealand's and the United States' involvement in the Vietnam War. The protest movement grew rapidly in the late 1960s spawned such radical groups as the Progressive Youth Movement and launched the careers of such high profile radicals as Tim Shadbolt. Large-scale marches became a feature of the early 1970s.

The radical and searching thrust of the late 1960s and the growth in tertiary education gave a real boost to every form of artistic endeavour. Writing reached a new maturity during the late 1960s and early 1970s, with Janet Frame, Frank Sargeson and Maurice Shadbolt enhancing already established reputations. Maurice Gee's *Plumb* (1976) won acclaim locally and overseas and remains the best intellectual history of New Zealand published to date. Much poetry of worth poured forth from the pens of poets such as Curnow, Baxter and Glover.

In painting, a more recognisable New Zealand art began to emerge in the late 1960s and an innovative film industry made its mark, although it began to run into serious money problems in the 1980s. New Zealand television became markedly more professional and local drama could be compared favourably with overseas productions. A craft boom in the 1960s saw thousands take up pottery, ceramics, weaving and other crafts on a full- and part-time basis. A growing interest in New Zealand history has seen New Zealand history courses in universities boom and books on the subject become bestsellers; New Zealanders are keen to know about their 'roots'.

Although New Zealand women won

greater gains from the Second World War than from the Great War, no really significant advances were made until the radical period of the late 1960s. The revitalised international feminist movement began to produce an impact in New Zealand as the pace of social change quickened.

Initially the feminist movement affected mainly well-educated and professional women, who set up collectives in the main centres and several smaller towns to spread the 'new' gospel. *Up from Under* (1970) was the first periodical established to promote the revitalised ideology and it was soon followed by the more militant *Broadsheet* in 1972. Regular conventions were held to raise consciousness and the movement probably reached its peak in terms of activity in the early 1970s.

Several significant victories were won in this period. In 1972 equal pay legislation was introduced for the private sector, equal pay having been legislated into the public sector in 1960. A Women's Electoral Lobby (WEL) was established in 1975 to promote women's issues in the male dominated world of politics and women also began to enter such traditional male bastions as the medical and dental professions; by the early 1980s women students in these schools were actually outnumbering their male counterparts. Much energy was also expended in the debate over abortion and fertility control. The Contraception, Sterilisation and Abortion Act of 1977 was, however, an unsatisfactory compromise which did not satisfy either the pro-life or pro-abortion lobbies and it incensed many feminists who believed that it was a woman's right to choose whether she should terminate an unwanted pregnancy.

Change began to percolate into a wider range of social groups from the late 1970s as more women moved into the workforce. (In 1951 there were 308 women in the workforce for every 1000 men; by 1981 there were 525 women for every 1000 men). Sonja Davies was the first woman elected to an executive position on the FOL in 1978. Two years later the Working Women's Charter to protect

the rights of working women was passed by the federation. More Maori women also became more prominent in the feminist movement which set out to change its white middle class image. In 1982 Sue Wood became the first woman president of a political party when she took over from National's George Chapman. Margaret Wilson became president of the Labour Party two years later. A record number of 10 women MPs was elected to Parliament in the 1984 election.

The appointment of Ann Hercus as the first Minister of Women's Affairs in 1984, however, suggested that there were still large areas requiring reform. Equal pay remained little more than a legal fiction with the average female wage still only something like three-quarters of the average male wage. Most chief executive positions in government, commerce and education

were still held by men and such male bastions as boys' secondary schools and sports clubs remained largely untouched by feminism. Whatever measure of women's position was used, New Zealand remained far behind the Scandinavian countries, Holland, Western Germany and the United States. Giant strides have been made since the 1960s but many more changes are required, especially in terms of male attitudes towards women and the part played by women in business. The feminist movement itself has tended to splinter into moderate and militant factions yet the more extreme fringes continue to provide the energy so vital to winning further reform.

The pace of change — cultural, social and economic — quickened after 1973 when Britain finally entered the EEC. New Zealand was thereafter

Rob Muldoon, one of New Zealand's hardest hitting politicians since the Second World War, adopts an aggressive pose in a friendly cricket match. Muldoon was Prime Minister between 1975 and 1984. *Evening Post.*

forced to face the reality of living in a post-colonial world. With the luxury of a large guaranteed market gone, new markets had to be opened and export products diversified in the interests of survival. Sentimental ties to Britain had been weakening for some time and younger Pakeha New Zealanders no longer viewed Britain as 'home'. New Zealanders of all races were beginning to realise that theirs was a South Pacific nation.

Despite the complaints made by politicians of all parties, the rate of diversification, both in terms of markets and products, has been rapid since 1973. Then Britain was still New Zealand's largest trading partner. Some 40 per cent of our exports were directed towards this traditional target. By 1984, however, Britain had slipped into fourth place behind Australia, Japan and the United States. Pastoral farming still remains central to our economy but its share of export earnings has declined from 84 per cent in 1973 to 50 per cent by 1984.

The ubiquitous sheep has been joined by growing numbers of deer and goats. Horticulture, viticulture and fishing have encountered problems but made significant progress. Apple exports alone passed the $200 million mark in 1986 and fish are earning record prices on the Japanese and American market. Timber continues to make a big contribution which will expand at the end of the 1980s as new plantings mature. Manufacturing became a major export earner for the first time after 1973. By 1984 manufacturing was responsible for winning 22 per cent of exports as against a humble 8 per cent in the early 1970s.

The number of Japanese and American tourists coming to the shores of Aotearoa has increased spectacularly. Tourism now rivals the woollen industry as the fourth largest earner of export receipts in 1985-86.

In total New Zealand has made more rapid progress in 14 years in breaking the patterns of economic

colonisation than most countries of a similar historical background. Argentina, Uruguay and Australia have tried to industrialise over a longer period of time but have achieved less and made fewer adjustments. The problems confronting this whole group of ex-colonies are, however, much the same since Britain entered the EEC and the oil shock of 1973 threw the world into confusion. All these countries have been plagued by inflation, unemployment and serious indebtedness.

Double-figure inflation levels of up to 18 per cent since 1973 have made things difficult for a trading nation like New Zealand when major trading partners have achieved low, single-figure inflation. But there has not been much difference between the Australian and New Zealand inflation rates.

Unemployment levels have risen from virtually nil in 1973 to Great Depression levels of around 80,000 or about 5.5 per cent of the workforce. This is a relatively low figure by international standards, but such relatively modest levels are taking their toll in a small country which experienced full employment for 37 years between 1938 and 1975. The unskilled Maori and women, now employed at the ratio of one to every two men in the workforce, have been worst hit, as in the 1930s.

Debt was not a serious problem under the careful management of Walter Nash and during the prosperous years of the 1950s and 1960s, but the oil shock of 1973 changed all that — New Zealand has run a balance of payments deficit in every year since. Robert Muldoon's 'Think Big' programme, devised in a desperate attempt to provide a heavy industrial base and insulation against future oil shocks via the Vogelite policy of heavy borrowing, exacerbated the problem. The $1 billion mark was reached in 1975 and climbed to over $9 billion in 1983-84. In 1986 the deficit topped $30 billion.

On the political front both National and Labour governments continued to hope that a sustained boom in exports would solve New Zealand's economic woes. National's Keith Holyoake stepped down in 1972 after 12 years in office, to be replaced by his deputy John Marshall. In the 1972 elections Labour, led by Norman Kirk, won a

Neither side looks particularly agitated as 1981 anti-Springbok tour protesters begin demolishing a security fence at Auckland Airport. Minutes later the fence was ripped to the ground. *Evening Post.*

Protesters turn away from police after an eyeball-to-eyeball confrontation in Cuba Street, Palmerston North, during the 1981 Springbok tour. *Evening Post.*

ularly to make adjustments. In June 1984 he surprisingly called a snap election for July. Muldoon faced a rejuvenated Labour Party led by David Lange and a new New Zealand Party led by property developer Bob Jones, which drew its core support from discontented National Party supporters. Labour won 56 seats, National 37.

The fourth Labour government, dominated by Finance Minister Roger Douglas, moved quickly to free up the economy and expose New Zealand to more international competition. The currency was devalued by 20 per cent and later floated. All restrictions on interest rates were lifted. Import controls were loosened, subsidies on agriculture largely removed and most export incentives scrapped. To make them more efficient, government trading departments are being (1987) replaced by corporations which are expected to compete and earn their keep like private companies.

By New Zealand standards the changes initiated by Roger Douglas amounted to a virtual economic revolution. In social welfare there was a marked move away from Labour's traditional philosophy of 'universality' as welfare benefits were targeted more specifically at those in need.

In foreign affairs, the Lange Labour government adopted an equally radical stance. Its nuclear-free policy banned the visits of nuclear armed ships and in retaliation the United States withdrew its security guarantees, effectively rendering the ANZUS pact inoperative.

Today New Zealand is unrecognisable as the nation which Austin Mitchell in 1972 called the 'world's most stable and, probably most conservative society'. In the 1890s it was viewed by foreign intellectuals as a social laboratory; today it is an economic laboratory engaged in high risk experimentation. In the meantime New Zealanders are continuing to search for a national identity which marks them out as a distinctive South Pacific people.

landslide victory and this government spent freely on social programmes. When the charismatic Kirk died suddenly in 1974, he was replaced by former Finance Minister Bill Rowling.

In the meantime an aggressive Rob Muldoon had replaced 'Gentleman' Jack Marshall as National's leader. In 1975 he reversed the 1972 election result and took over as Prime Minister and Finance Minister for the next eight and a half years.

Like Kirk, Muldoon immediately cut back on spending but then, as unemployment rose, allowed government spending to rise sharply again. In 1976 he introduced a national superannuation scheme which gave every citizen a sizeable pension at the age of 60. The 1978 election saw Muldoon

lead National to a 51-seat win over Labour's 40. Although in 1981 Labour under Rowling again collected more votes than National under Muldoon, National won more seats to hold a slender two-seat margin over Labour and Social Credit combined.

Some commentators believe that the violence that had erupted during the 1981 South African Springbok rugby team tour of New Zealand was responsible for National holding onto some key marginal seats such as Invercargill. The tour saw seven weeks of sustained protest, the cancellation of a game and previously law-abiding citizens battling with police.

As Minister of Finance, Muldoon continued to use economic controls and regulations and intervened reg-

22. 1984-96 The Rogernomics Revolution to MMP

WHEN I completed the first edition of this book, the impact of the radical reforms initiated by the Fourth Labour Government was unclear. Eight years later it is obvious that they constitute the most important change of direction in New Zealand's history since the 1890s. Whereas the First Labour Government built upon and expanded the state supported reforms of the 1890s, Roger Douglas rejected 90 years of experimentation and pushed New Zealand in a completely different direction. Historians do not claim to be good at prediction, but I have been proved right about the high risk of his experiments. The costs as well as the gains have been enormous. What we could not forsee in 1988, however, was that National under the influence of Ruth Richardson would push the country even more rapidly down the path opened up by Labour. Whatever we label this change, and the shorthand 'New Right' has its limitations, it is clear that the years 1984-1996 witnessed the most dramatic changes in this country's history. During this time the captains of the ship of state stopped the normally cautious weaving around a centrist track and swung the helm wildly to starboard.

A conjunction of factors caused the revolution known colloquially as 'Rogernomics' (and later 'Ruthanasia'). The most important factors were concern over mounting debt and the emergence of a new generation of politicians with a different vision of New Zealand than that of the Welfare State. Within days of taking office the young Cabinet, with an average age in the low

David Lange and Geoffrey Palmer stride to power 15 July 1984. *New Zealand Herald.*

40s rather than the traditional 50s, learned that New Zealand would have to default on paying the interest on its debts unless government took drastic remedial action. The Reserve Bank, working in conjunction with the World Bank and the International Monetary Fund, may have exaggerated the seriousness of the situation, but their dire predictions provided Roger Douglas with ample justification for implementing a radical shift in economic policy. Douglas had virtually a free hand as the other leaders concentrated on foreign policy, race relations, gender and environmental issues. Furthermore, Labour's economic policy in 1984 had been vague and he was not tied by election promises.

Douglas devalued the dollar by 20 per cent and removed controls on prices and interest rates. By March 1985 he had floated the New Zealand dollar, removed all farming subsidies and eased back tariffs on manufactured goods. Richard Prebble applied similar medicine to the Railways Corporation, sacking thousands of employees. Air New Zealand's traditional local monopoly was also thrown over in 1987 when

government granted Ansett, an Australian company, flying rights within New Zealand.

In 1986 Douglas introduced a new indirect tax known as the Goods and Services Tax, set at 10 per cent on all transactions. Various lobby groups sought exemptions, but Douglas applied the measure universally and reaped a substantial increase in the tax take as a result. In return he lowered the top tax rate to 33 cents in the dollar. He removed all other rungs on the progressive table except for 24 cents in the dollar applied to all citizens, no matter how poor. He also applied a surcharge to super-annuants when he discovered that the taxpayer contribution to superannuation equalled the proportion of tax directed to health and education combined. New Zealand simply could not afford Muldoon's 1975 election bribe. Even so, he horrified traditional Labour Party supporters by this shift away from the principle of 'each according to their means'.

Treasury and big business, represented by a new pressure group known as the 'Roundtable', backed Douglas's reforms and the process gained

Roger Douglas reads the first of his revolutionary budgets, 8 November 1984. *Dominion.*

Above: Douglas Myers, brewing magnate and chairman of the Roundtable, stands behind his product, 1990. *New Zealand Breweries.*

momentum. Douglas justified the changes, saying that the government could no longer maintain 'fortress New Zealand' because the communications revolution brought about by advancing computer technology enabled capital to flow around the globe at extraordinary speed. The 'third industrial revolution' ruled out a 'fortress economy' as a viable option. The economy could only survive by becoming as efficient and as entrepreneurially innovative as possible. Douglas's arguments also reflected current economic fashion which saw a move away from Keynesian style intervention to a more free-market approach. England practised 'Thatchernomics' and the US 'Reaganomics'. New Zealand fell into line with 'Rogernomics'. International investors poured money into New Zealand and the international economic press, especially the influential *Economist*, applauded Douglas. New Zealanders remained less convinced as inflation rocketed to 17 per cent and unemployment rose relentlessly.

The electorate gave Labour another opportunity in 1987, this time anticipating a more balanced approach. Instead Douglas increased the rate of reform. Richard Prebble joined in by selling off state assets at an accelerated rate, including all 423 post offices during 1988. The spectacular sharemarket crash of October 1987 added to the public's growing sense of unease, especially when it was learned that the scale of damage was considerably increased by New Zealand's lack of controls over commercial activity. The extremes of interventionism and bureaucracy seemed to have been replaced by a free-for-all within the world of stocks and shares.

David Lange tried to temper these moves and restore calm by talking about the need for a 'cuppa', or a breather, from the relentless pace of reform. He cited the massive 1988 report of the Royal Commission on Social Policy as providing a humane vision on how the country might overhaul the Welfare State. He also oversaw reform of school management through the Picot Report. Instead of expanding welfare operations, however, government reduced spending by trying to target those most in need. 'Tomorrow's Schools' also involved setting up parent-dominated Boards of Trustees in 1989 in an attempt to increase parent control of school management and to enable the education system to produce a more skilled workforce capable of handling the demands of modern technology.

Treasury warned that teachers had 'captured' the school system and were protecting inefficient methods. Cynics believed that the experiment was nothing more than an attempt to reduce management costs. Instead of creating achieving equity, however, it seemed that the new system brought some big advantages to schools in wealthy areas while disadvantaging those in poorer areas. The vision of education as a 'public good' seemed to be replaced by the idea that education brought private advantage.

Disillusioned by the failure of such rapid change to bring 'gain' rather than 'pain', Lange forced Douglas from the post of Minister of Finance in December 1988. Richard Prebble followed voluntarily. When this drastic measure failed to stop the juggernaut, in August 1989 an exhausted Lange resigned his post to the solid but colourless Geoffrey Palmer. Lange left New Zealand quite different from the country envisioned by the First Labour Government. Gains could be discerned in terms of lifestyle and choice with the emergence of a cafe society in the main cities and a resurgence of the arts, but unemployment rocketed to a record high of over 100,000, or more than 7 per cent of the workforce. Crime rates, especially those relating to violent crime, rose even faster. Productivity still remained low and debt continued to rise. In a desperate effort to contain rampant inflation, Labour had passed a Reserve Bank Act in 1989 to keep inflation rates below those of our major trading partners. This strict control lowered inflation but kept interest rates and the dollar higher than exporters wanted. Jim Anderton protested Labour's refusal to change direction and when Douglas rejoined Cabinet in October 1989 he broke away to form the New Labour Party. More drastic measures were taken from late 1989 as Labour raised GST to 12.5 per cent and privatised New Zealand Steel, Coal Corp, State Insurance and Post Bank. In 1990 Labour also sold Telecom to a United States-dominated overseas consortium. Mike Moore came in as a late replacement as leader in September. Even his more populist style could not stop a disgruntled electorate punishing at the 1990 election what seemed to be a very arrogant Labour government for going too far, too fast.

Jim Bolger led National to a sweeping victory on the promise of establishing a 'decent society'. His Finance Minister, Ruth Richardson, however, dreamed of an 'enterprise society'. Realising that

Labour had made hard changes which National had never had the courage to implement, Richardson decided to push reforms even further. The traditionally pragmatic National Party fell under control of ideologues. This became clear in December 1990 when Richardson reduced benefits, only to reduce them further by over a billion dollars in her first full budget of July 1991. This 'minimalist' approach was intended to break dependency on welfare but only stimulated the growth of an alarmingly criminal underclass. By reducing the purchasing power of beneficiaries, it also hurt small businesses. In 1991 National dealt a further blow to an already weak Trade Union movement by passing the Employment Contracts Act to make unionism voluntary and thereby providing employers with greater flexibility in setting wages. Government also raised charges for Accident Compensation and made the system less generous. Language changed too as government and Treasury tried to impose the business model on every facet of New Zealand life. Vice-Chancellors became 'chief executives', university and school staff were renamed 'resources' and students were referred to as 'clients' or 'stakeholders'. Meantime unemployment climbed to over 200,000, or about 12 per cent of the workforce, reviving memories of the Great Depression.

Government added to their unpopularity in 1992 by substantially increasing fees for tertiary education (stepped up by Phil Goff in 1989 to an average of

A rather pensive Ruth Richardson defends her 1992 budget. *Otago Daily Times.*

$1,100), basing these fees on a loans scheme with steep interest rates. They sold the Bank of New Zealand to National Bank Australia in the same year and sold the now efficient New Zealand Rail to the Central Wisconsin Transport Company in 1993. Richardson and Cabinet, without consulting health professionals, replaced Labour's elected Area Health Boards with appointed Regional Health Authorities and converted hospitals into Crown Health Enterprises. This funder–provider split was intended to reduce the burgeoning health bill by running the whole system along business lines. Instead costs have blown out wildly and the public has become disillusioned with declining standards of health care. John Luxton as Minister of Housing also raised state housing rentals to market value and suddenly New Zealand's welfare, health, education and housing policies appeared much closer to those of the United States than those of the social democracies of Scandinavia.

Winston Peters, longtime gadfly of the National Party, argued that such extremism broke election promises. Scenting corrupt manipulation by big business, he became a thorn in the side of his own government. In October 1991 an exasperated Jim Bolger sacked him from the post of Minister of Maori Affairs and the National Caucus expelled him in October 1992. A furious Peters responded by resigning and won a by-election for the Tauranga seat in April 1993. He rubbed salt in National's wounds by forming his own party, New Zealand First, in July 1993. Then, just as things seemed hopeless, the economy began to turn around and National cleverly orchestrated a good-news campaign to convince New Zealanders that gains had finally been made.

A budget surplus achieved in 1993 and the indifferent performance of the Opposition enabled National to scrape back into power. Significantly, 53 per cent of New Zealanders also voted at this election to change the First Past the Post electoral system to Mixed Member Proportional representation. Dual voting made it possible for the first time in New Zealand's history to split votes between candidate and party. Coalitions seemed the most likely outcome of the system already in use in Western Germany. New Zealand voters thereby made clear their desire to slow down the pace of change.

Rather than heeding the warning from the electorate, the National Government went on with the business of 'reform'. Bill Birch replaced Richardson, but initially proved just as hard-nosed. Government increased medical and tertiary education fees and continued to sell off assets. Jenny Shipley as Minister of Health pushed on with reform of health administration despite continual protest from health professionals. Lockwood Smith as Minister of Education brought considerable advantage to private schools by integrating them into the state system on extremely favourable terms. He continued to push for bulk funding of schools. Under this system boards of trustees rather than central government would be responsible for teacher salaries. This time an alliance of teachers and parents, unanticipated by government and Treasury, generally opposed such a change. The Post Primary Teachers' Association stood firmly against National's scheme and went on strike several times before winning a modest salary increase.

Birch and his government only began to behave in traditional fashion in the election year of 1996 when they offered modest income tax cuts as reward for a decade of pain. Government also made extravagant claims that the Employment Contracts Act had stimulated growth and lowered unemployment to around 100,000, or about 7 per cent of the workforce. Academics who have studied the impact of this legislation, however, cannot find any hard evidence to support these claims and the old problem of low productivity remains unresolved. Improvement in economic performance has probably resulted from diversification, greater efficiency, higher skill levels in the workforce and improved marketing of our products. Tight fiscal control under the Reserve

A determined Winston Peters launches the New Zealand First Party in July 1993 stressing the nationalistic imagery of an oversized New Zealand flag. *Otago Daily Times.*

Bank Act has also kept inflation low but the impact of this policy remains contentious.

By 1995 many New Zealanders were deeply concerned over increasingly grim crime statistics, male violence towards women, a mounting drugs problem, and the highest rate of suicide amongst teenage boys in the developed world. Government planners got their sums wrong on population growth and schools found themselves short of teachers. Women had made steady gains in most areas of New Zealand life but, as a group, remained seriously disadvantaged in competition for top jobs. Family breakups still continued to financially hurt women much more than men and the promise of second-wave feminism remained unfulfilled. Food, wine and coffee improved dramatically in the early 1990s, but the Homosexual Law Reform Act of 1986 did not make New Zealand a noticeably more tolerant society. Problems afflicted the countryside as well as the city when a sustained fall in beef and lamb prices also hit traditional farming districts hard. It had become clear by election year that rural education and health services were being run down in an alarming manner. Some also feared that the 'economic recovery' existed more on paper than in reality, because no new set of base industries had emerged to replace the declining farming sector. Winning the America's Cup in 1995 and performing well at the 1995 Rugby World Cup could not hide the fact that New Zealand faced serious problems.

National, nevertheless, dominated the polls through most of 1995 as their good-news machine continued to dominate the media. Labour's new leader, Helen Clark, who replaced Mike Moore in a messy coup in late 1993, seemed unable to fire the imagination of the electorate. The government also gloated as the Left continued to squabble amongst themselves. But despite the tax cuts this popularity did not last. Winston Peters chipped away at government involvement in questionable tax deals in the Cook Islands, whipped up fear over rising levels of immigration from Asia, and won a powerful support base amongst Maori and superannuitants. His fortunes continued to soar despite the resignation of new recruit former National Party maverick Michael Laws in response to charges of improper

conduct in local-body elections. University students, tired of relentless fee increases, occupied registries around the country. Medical services came under intense scrutiny and RHAs became extremely unpopular. Many expressed concern over selling off several North Island forests. Disenchantment grew throughout 1996.

Helped by Mike Moore's first pledge of undivided loyalty in three years, Helen Clark pulled off a remarkably effective election campaign. Special coaching in how to handle the media enabled her to win back public support eroded by internal squabbling and memories of the damage caused by Rogernomics. She also focused effectively on the key problem areas of health and education. This time her party produced convinc-

ing policies which seemed noticeably different from those of the government. Her personal recovery and a return of support from women throughout the electorate saved New Zealand's oldest political party from what seemed like almost inevitable oblivion.

The first MMP election produced a fascinating result. Voters expressed satisfaction with overall economic policy, with 75 per cent voting for parties advocating a continuation of current free-market-oriented economic policies (National won 34 per cent of the vote, Labour 28 per cent, New Zealand First 13 per cent). Only 10 per cent voted for the more interventionist approach of the Alliance, while 8 per cent voted for ACT (Association of Consumers' and Taxpayers), led by

Richard Prebble and formed in 1994 by Roger Douglas to push his free-market reforms even further. Nevertheless, intelligent use of vote-splitting revealed deep dissatisfaction with health and education policies. Superannuitants also seemed annoyed at the continued surcharge and asset-stripping of the elderly who spent their final years vegetating in expensive nursing homes. Some 51 per cent of the electorate voted against the status quo on these policies although they generally supported the thrust of economic policy.

Much to the horror of tertiary students, their parents and many elderly voters, Peters finally settled on a coalition with National, thereby retaining the right of centre direction developed by National. He won the combined position of Deputy Prime Minister and Treasurer. This left him in a very powerful position as the role of Treasurer as developed in Australia is superior to that of Minister of Finance. Labour refused to concede financial control. This suited Peters, who argued that it was easier to deal with one party than two and that the Alliance could not be trusted. He also seemed more comfortable with his former conservative allies than with the Left.

National promised to abolish the RHAs and the surtax on superannuation, to end privatisation, to increase social spending, and to grant major concessions to Maori. In return, Peters accepted continuance of tight control of fiscal policy through the Reserve Bank despite his condemnation of this institution throughout the campaign. National hoped that Peters' concession on this key control mechanism guaranteed the continuance of orthodox financial management and free-market

Richard Prebble goes on the attack during the 1996 election campaign. He succeeded to the point where the free market ACT party won 8 seats in the new parliament. *Otago Daily Times.*

policies. National was discarding its more ideological garb of recent years and returning to its old pragmatic self. Jim Bolger showed once again that he was an adroit political survivor. His ability to compromise and negotiate will ensure that historians portray him as one of our country's most shrewd Prime Ministers.

Unlike the pragmatic National Party Labour stuck to its principles – but remained in Opposition. Helen Clark thereby missed the opportunity to become New Zealand's first woman Prime Minister.

Descent into such trivial concerns as the price paid by government members for underpants soon dashed New Zealanders' high hopes for better government associated with the introduction of MMP. Obvious strains between National and New Zealand First increased as MMP failed to slow the implementation of ever more extreme 'New Right' reforms such as tariff reductions and asset sales. By 1998 National had sold off over $6 billion worth of assets, including the Housing and Forestry Corporations, as against the $9 billion sold off by the Fourth Labour Government. Car assembly came to an end in 1998, lowering the cost of new cars but laying off at least 1,500 workers. Government made no attempt to retrain these workers, leaving them with little prospect of finding alternative employment.

As the juggernaut relentlessly ground on, the two old main parties compounded a growing sense of unease by displaying little capacity for behaving in a more consensual manner. Only Jim Bolger's powers of conciliation kept the coalition together. Once Jenny Shipley replaced Bolger on 8 December 1997 after a relatively bloodless coup in November and became New Zealand's first woman Prime Minister, the Coalition disintegrated and ended in late August 1998.

National continued as a minority government propped up by the New Zealand First mavericks who relabelled themselves 'independents'. Alamein Kopu, originally elected as an Alliance list MP, also supported the government after leaving the Alliance to form her own Maori women's party. Peter Dunn, sole survivor of the United Party, pledged his vote and ACT generally supported the government's agenda, especially the introduction of tax cuts in 1996. Tau Henare later formed Mauri Pacific but remained as Minister of Maori Affairs, insisting that he could achieve more for Maori by serving in government than by joining the Opposition.

The economy meantime remained as fragile as ever despite government attempts at 'spin doctoring' a recovery and belatedly forcing interest rates down in 1998. Remarkably, the serious Asian financial crisis of 1997/8 seemed to have little obvious impact, but superficial resilience meant little as overseas debt climbed relentlessly to $100 billion. New Zealand slumped to twentieth position on the OECD ratings by per capita income, below such maligned interventionist states as Australia, Ireland, the Netherlands and all the Scandinavian countries. By early 1999 a serious balance of payments crisis emerged as it became obvious that we were importing more than we earned from exports.

Commentators blamed low commodity prices, but no party seemed able to devise policies which would help the struggling ex-colony find a major means of supplementing the decline in the earnings of traditional farming industries. Wool had collapsed as an export earner to win a mere four per cent of export income by 1998, and meat had fallen to a modest 13 per cent. Only dairying continued to hold its export share at 17 per cent. Manufacturing continued to slide as government removed tariffs, and even the growing tourist industry failed to compensate for the downturn in earnings from agricultural and timber-related products. Unemployment remained steady at around seven per cent as tourism generated part-time and low-wage jobs, but the regions suffered ever greater decline while Auckland grew ever larger. Both growth and productivity figures stayed well below those of most developed economies. Whereas the United States managed growth rates of over four per cent per annum throughout the 1990s, New Zealand struggled to achieve 2.6 per cent. Worse, while a re-unified Germany managed to increase productivity by more than four per cent per annum through the 1990s, New Zealand did not even manage one per cent per annum. Even sympathetic economic journals such as the *Economist* now admit that little 'gain' other than control of inflation has occurred after 15 years of 'pain'. Yet New Zealand persists in following the American model

A somewhat bemused New Zealand public watch Winston Peters make Jim Bolger and Helen Clark jump through the hoop. *Otago Daily Times.*

and ignores alternatives offered by smaller societies such as Scandinavia and Ireland.

Government 'reforms' in health and education became increasingly more unpopular. Student loan debt soared and waiting lists worsened but the 1999 Budget did little to address these problems. Labour moved ahead in the opinion polls despite producing little policy to distinguish it from National. Indeed, by mid-1999 it seems that the main difference between the centre parties lies in the area of taxation, with National offering small reductions and Labour small increases.

Labour is also talking of pursuing the so-called 'third way' after Tony Blair's British Labour government, whereby the state will become directly involved in promoting enterprise and in assisting research and development. Labour's other trump card may be promotion of cultural nationalism on the basis that Ireland has turned its economic performance around by promoting its cultural activities. Labour has reached an agreement with the Alliance just as ACT sided with National, because whoever wins the election seems certain to be forced into coalition.

Whether or not the electorate finds Labour's polices sufficiently inspiring remains to be seen, but inept management by the government of large compensa-

tory payouts to sacked members of the Tourism Board and unpopular Fire Service Commissioner Roger Estall have helped Labour's cause. Unless Prime Minister Shipley regains her poise, National may well may lose the election rather than Labour win it.

Much depends, of course, on the performance of the minor parties, with ACT only scoring around five per cent and New Zealand First polling below the margin of error. It seems that New Zealanders are reverting to their more traditional patterns of allegiance in both general and Maori electorates.

Whoever wins the 1999 election, the MMP experiment is destined to come to an abrupt end unless the new government can secure more broad-based support for its policies and restore some degree of more widely shared prosperity. A return to the relatively stable patterns of the mid-twentieth century remains highly unlikely. At the dawning of a new millennium, New Zealanders are once more seeking new solutions to old problems, and the country seems likely to continue as a social laboratory for some considerable time.

22. 1986 Te Hokinga Mai (The Return Home):

Te Maori and the Cultural Renaissance

WHEN the Te Maori exhibition opened in Wellington on Saturday 16 August 1986, after a hugely successful year-long tour of the United States, it raised unprecedented interest in the taonga (treasures) of the Maori people. A record 186,000 visited the National Museum to view the artworks of the tangata whenua. Rave reviews by critics in New York, St Louis, San Francisco and Chicago persuaded many adult Pakeha to look again at objects to which, as schoolchildren, they had been dragged to museums to view.

In the past most museums had presented Maori artefacts housed in peculiarly European institutions, museums, as dead objects. Te Maori showed them as living things reflecting the creative spirit of a people; it persuaded many New Zealanders to remove the filters of prejudice and see for the first time that the indigenous art of Aotearoa had unique beauty and spiritual power.

Te Maori is both a lament and a celebration. It expresses the pain experienced by the Maori people as Europeans have tried to colonise their culture and history. It portrays the sense of loss of the land and traditional values. Yet it also displays a new found pride in Maori heritage. Te Maori is the most positive by-product of the second great Maori cultural renaissance which began in the 1960s.

This renaissance took many forms. Traditional Maori carving, plaiting

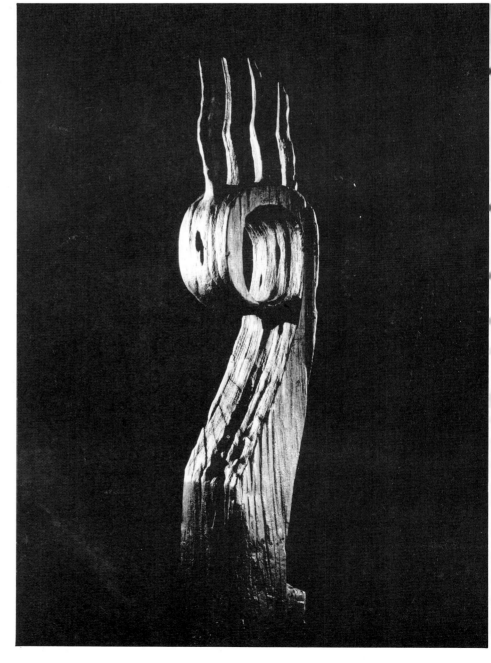

Uenuku, one of the Te Maori exhibits. This carving represents a tribal god of the Tainui people. Carved between 1200 and 1500, it resembles some Hawaiian carvings. Photograph by Brian Brake. *Courtesy Te Maori and Mobil.*

196

and weaving underwent a resurgence, while motifs and forms inspired a new generation of painters, craftspeople and designers to explore new ways of expressing their Maoritanga.

A distinctive school of Maori writing emerged. Perhaps the best known poet is Hone Tuwhare whose *No Ordinary Sun*, first published in 1964, is one of the best selling poetry books published in New Zealand in the last 20 years. In the early 1970s Witi Ihimaera's prize-winning short stories and novels provided a boost to a burgeoning group of Maori writers. His early work concentrated on rural Maori life, but as his confidence grew he widened his scope and vision. In 1986 his novel *The Matriarch* won the Wattie Book Award. Patricia Grace's short stories and novels on Maori themes have enjoyed similar acclaim. *Waiariki*, published in 1975, was the first collection of stories by a Maori woman writer.

The greatest international recognition came in 1985 when Keri Hulme won the prestigious English literary award, the Booker Prize, for her novel *The Bone People.*

In part the renaissance was a reaction to the loss of identity and alienation that had followed the progressive loss of Maori land (see chart, p.194) and their population movement from rural communities and marae to the towns.

Within the generation between the end of the Second World War and 1971 the Maori changed from a rural to an urban people, a transition which took Pakeha four generations. In 1945 88 per cent of Maori lived in country areas; by 1981 over 80 per cent lived in towns and cities. From the 1920s onwards, mechanisation of agriculture removed employment opportunities and a people who had been reduced to little more than a rural proletariat were forced out of their isolated pa to search for work in the towns.

Some returning soldiers were excited by what they had seen overseas and wanted to leave tiny settlements where nothing much seemed to happen. The standard of housing in the

The future of the Maori language depends upon the likes of this young speaker in the Korimako National Speech Contest. *Evening Post.*

more remote settlements was also appallingly low. A 1951 official review conceded that a third of Maori houses were little more than 'shacks' lacking even the most basic amenities. A move to a town offered prospects of more convenient and hygienic accommodation and better schooling. Maori parents wanted to share the same dream most Pakeha held after the Second World War — a secure, comfortable lifestyle.

Of all the cities Auckland, with its industrial base and jobs, held the greatest attraction. By 1986 90,825 Maori lived there. As in the days of pre-European settlement, two-thirds of all Maori live in the northern half of the North Island.

In the towns and cities traditional Maori values came under pressure. Tribal bonds were harder to maintain. The marae was no longer the central focus of community life.

The use of Maori language had already been declining because Pakeha educational authorities insisted that only English be spoken in schools. But as Maori urbanisation increased, the decline accelerated until the extinction of the language became a real fear. And the battle for survival in the cities was made more difficult by the fact that Maori often lacked the qualifications and money needed for good jobs and housing. Moreover, schools, courts and other institutions all seemed to be geared for the Pakeha majority.

Few Maori seemed to relate to the European education system. Maori underachievement became a major social problem. In 1985 61 per cent of Maori left secondary school without any formal qualifications. In universities and polytechnics Maori student numbers remain low despite generous bursaries and scholarships. The lack of qualifications mean that Maori are not breaking into the professions; the pattern of heavy representation in low paid, low status and less secure jobs is repeated.

Unskilled Maori teenagers found it difficult to find jobs as unemployment increased in the 1970s. Maori youth unemployment figures were up to five times higher than for Pakeha youth. Bitterness, resentment, frustration and boredom saw increasing numbers of Maori teenagers come before the courts. Today Maori make up 55 per cent of the prison population.

Large urban gangs surfaced as alienated young Maori sought some form of group identity in a detribalised world.

To some extent a high number of youth related problems among Maori is to be expected since the Maori population has a much younger age profile than the European population. In 1985 only 4.4 per cent of the Maori population was aged over 60, as against 15.6 of the non-Maori. Youth, then, have the numbers in Maori society at a time when the elderly are absorbing more of the welfare vote in European New Zealand.

As the gulf between Maori and Pakeha in schooling, jobs and housing seemingly widened new urban protest movements began emerging in the late 1960s. Modelling themselves on the American black civil rights movement, groups such as Nga Tamatoa hit out at New Zealand's record in race rela-

tions. At first Pakeha felt insulted but vocal leaders such as Syd Jackson and Dun Mihaka won the sympathy of some younger Europeans. For the first time Maori radicals had an audience who seemed prepared to listen.

Maori grievances focused on the loss of land and the Treaty of Waitangi. Some wanted the treaty ratified and past injustices rectified; others dismissed it as a fraud. All were alarmed that Maori land holdings had been reduced to little more than 3 million acres (1,212,000 hectares) by the early 1970s.

The increasingly vocal and high profile movement attracted considerable media attention and won promises of action from Maori Affairs Minister Matiu Rata and the new Labour government in 1972.

In 1975 protest action centred on a 1120-kilometre land march from Te

Mrs (later Dame) Whina Cooper aged 80 led the 1975 Maori land march from Te Hapua in the far north to Wellington. *Evening Post.*

Hapua, near Cape Reinga, to Wellington. Led by 80-year-old Whina Cooper, several thousand joined in to demand that 'not one more acre' of Maori land be alienated. A Memorial of Rights calling for the protection of Maori land and culture, signed by over 60,000 people, was presented to Parliament. The government made sympathetic noises but no specific promises.

In January 1977 young Ngati Whatua activists occupied a block of Auckland Crown land called Bastion Point. It was the last remnant of their once large Auckland ancestral lands and they wanted it returned, whereas the government had plans to sell it off for luxury housing. In May 1978, after a 17-month occupation, the largest formation of police ever assembled in New Zealand removed leader Joe Hawke and his supporters.

Meanwhile Eva Rickard, in February 1978, set up camp with 150 people on the Raglan golf course to protest at Maori land which had been compulsorily acquired by the government during the Second World War, being leased to the golf club. After a sustained protest the land reverted to the Maori owners.

Many Pakeha have found it hard to appreciate the strength of Maori feeling over land. The New Zealand Maori Council summarised much of the contemporary Maori feeling on land when in 1983 it argued in *Kaupapa: Te Wahanga Tuatahi:*

> Maori land has several cultural connotations for us. It provides us with a sense of identity. It is proof of our continued existence not only as a people, but as the tangata whenua of this country. It is proof of our tribal and kin ties. Maori land represents turangawaewae.
>
> It is proof of our link with ancestors of the past, and of generations yet to come. It is an assurance that we shall forever exist as a people for as long as the land shall exist.
>
> But also land is a resource providing even greater support for our people — to provide employment — to provide us with sites for dwellings — and to provide an

October 13, 1975. The long queue of Maori land marchers stretches along the Porirua motorway on the last stage of an arduous trek from Northland. *Evening Post.*

199

income to help support our people and to maintain our marae and tribal assets.

Alienation and growing frustration saw a growing mood of Maori separatism develop. Matiu Rata reflected this when he split from the Labour Party in 1979 to form Mana Motuhake (separate identity, or Maori sovereignty). The party promoted exclusively Maori interests and challenged the long association between Ratana and Labour established in the 1930s. In the 1981 and 1984 elections Mana Motuhake ran second to Labour in the four Maori electorates.

In her book *Maori Sovereignty*, published in 1984, Auckland psychologist Donna Awatere, one of a growing band of articulate, high profile Maori women, called for the creation of a Maori state.

Since the late 1970s the Waitangi Day celebrations have been a focal point of protest. Some progress was made in 1975 when the Waitangi Tribunal was set up to consider claims relating to the practical application of the principles of the Treaty of Waita-

ngi. However, it excluded grievances arising prior to 1975. In 1985 the powers of the tribunal were widened so it could make recommendations back to the treaty's enactment in 1840.

The first signs of real progress came in the mid-1980s as the courts began to acknowledge that the treaty had legal status especially in cases involving resources. In 1986 the High Court quashed a conviction of a Ngati Porou man for taking undersized paua on the basis that he had a customary right to take shellfish.

The real breakthrough came in 1987 when the Maori Council won a victory in a legal fight to stop disputed Crown lands being transferred to the newly created state owned enterprises. In a landmark decision to the Court of Appeal ruled that 'the principles of the Treaty of Waitangi override everything else in the State Owned Enterprises Act.' Moreoever 'those principles require that Pakeha and Maori treaty partners [are] to act towards each other reasonably, and with the utmost good faith.'

Maori Council chairman Sir Gra-

Police ring demonstrators at Bastion Point in 1978. *Auckland Star.*

ham Latimer hailed the decision. 'It's a tremendous boost', he said. 'It means we can have faith in the judicial system of this country . . . We were very fast losing all types of confidence in the judicial system. It seemed like we always ended up at the wrong end.'

As Maori unemployment increased through the late 1970s and into the 1980s there were renewed demands for Maori to control their own economic future. At the Maori Economic Development Summit Conference held at Parliament in 1984 there were calls for government funds to be channelled through Maori tribal organisations and for the creation of a Maori investment bank.

The fight to save the Maori language from extinction has made significant progress. Pre-school Kohanga Reo (language nests) were established. In 1986, 441 such nests catered for over 8000 children. Several bilingual (Maori-English) primary schools have been established and Taha Maori

The Decline of Maori Landholdings

1840 Treaty of Waitangi signed. 66,400,000 acres (26,825,600 hectares) in Maori hands.

1844 Crown's pre-emptive right to buy land from the Maori waived by Governor FitzRoy. Private sales between Pakeha buyers and Maori sellers allowed.

1846 Crown pre-emption resumes. Between 1846 and 1853 Grey purchases 32 million acres (12,928,000 hectares) under Crown pre-emption for £50,000, including most of the South Island.

1852 Approx. 34,000,000 acres (13,735,000 hectares) still in Maori hands.

1860 Pakeha population at 79,000 surpasses declining Maori population. The New Zealand wars began. 21,400,000 acres (8,645,600 hectares) still in Maori hands.

1864 Confiscation of 3.25 million acres (1,313,000 hectares) in North Island begins. Approximately half of this is later returned.

1865 Main campaigns of the wars finish. Native Land Courts established. Crown pre-emption ceases, private sales begin again.

1891 Liberal government gains power. 11,079,486 acres (4,476,000 hectares) still in Maori hands – 10,829,486 in the North Island, 250,000 in the South Island. The Liberal government buys 3.6 million acres (1,454,400 hectares) between 1891 and 1911.

1896 Maori population reaches lowest point in 19th or 20th centuries (42,113). Pakeha population now 701,101.

1911 7,137,205 acres (2,888,430 hectares) approximately remain in Maori hands.

1920 4,787,686 acres (1,934,000 hectares) remain in Maori hands.

1936 Maori population double that of 1896 (82,396). Pakeha population 1,491,486.

1939 4,028,903 acres (1,628,000 hectares) remain in Maori hands.

1961 Maori population doubled again from 1936 – now 167,086.

1975 Waitangi Tribunal formed to make recommendations on claims relating to the practical application of the principles of the Treaty of Waitangi, but excluding grievances arising before 1975. Maori Land March. 3 million acres (1,212,000 hectares) remain; the remnants of tribal estates.

1985 Waitangi Amendment Act passed, allowing the Waitangi Tribunal to recommend on claims dating right back to the Treaty's enactment in 1840.

1996 Area of Maori land is increasing with the settlements.

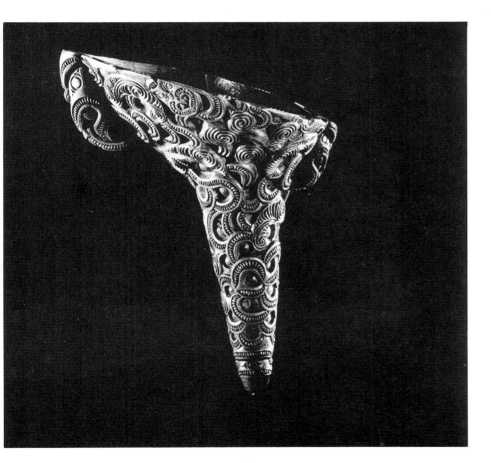

A Ngapuhi feeding funnel or korere exhibited at Te Maori. This funnel was used to feed a chief when his face was being tattooed. A chief's face was very tapu. If cooked food touched the lips when they were still raw from tattooing, it would remove the tapu from the work and cause it to fail. Photograph by Brian Brake. *Courtesy Te Maori and Mobil.*

(Maori language and culture) is becoming an increasingly important part of primary and secondary school programmes.

The calls from Maori for Pakeha to share their power and resources and work in partnership with Maori will very likely grow in intensity. On the positive side the Education, Justice and Social Welfare Departments have made strong moves to view their services from a Maori perspective. Maori are receiving a more sympathetic hearing than at any other time in New Zealand's history but Maori relations nevertheless remain highly volatile. Maori frustration is still high. It is, as former Race Relations Conciliator Hiwi Tauroa puts it, 'a race against time'.

Since the first edition of this book the so-called 'Maori Resurgence' has gathered speed and momentum. Maori cultural influence has never been higher in general New Zealand life. Kura kaupapa, or total immersion schools, championed by the dynamic Dr Pita Sharples, and a growing number of Maori radio stations have probably saved the Maori language. Particpation in tertiary education has increased and Maori Studies Departments are thriving at all the Universities. On the other hand, Maori representation on television remains slight, many Pakeha are still woefully ignorant of Maori history and culture, and youth unemployment remains alarmingly high. Even so, real gains have been made through Treaty claims

initiated by the Labour government in 1985. As far as the general public and some politicians are concerned, these claims appear to have only been settled slowly because of the time-consuming historical research required to sustain them, but this massive effort by iwi produced tangible results in 1995 (Tainui) and 1996 (Taranaki, Whakatohea and Ngai Tahu settlements).

Real gains where first made in the area of fishing in 1989 when Maori were granted 10 per cent of the fishing quota. This reparation infuriated many Pakeha fishermen and they protested vociferously. These dissident voices died away at the public level fairly quickly, however, leaving a much more complex set of negotiations to iwi representatives. Ngai Tahu appeared to gain most in 1992 when they won monopoly over South Island coasts under the Sealord deal. The Maori Fisheries Treaty of Waitangi Act of 1992 also strengthened tribal claims against those of government and private corporations.

The fisheries victory boosted Maori confidence and they threw even greater energy into securing settlements worth $187 million, $135 million, $44 million and $170 million for Tainui, Taranaki, Whakatohea and Ngai Tahu respectively. Indeed Treasury became so alarmed at the drive to complete claims that they recommended capping Treaty settlements at one billion dollars in 1995. Maori rejected this notion unanimously, pointing out that reparation should be ongoing as iwi tried to work out how best to use their settlements for the good of all their members. Minister of Maori Affairs Doug Graham and the National Cabinet refused to listen

to this council and ran into an embar rassing rejection of the idea of a 'fisca envelope' from one end of the countr to the other. Some commentators, an many Maori, also felt that governme had moved funding out of Mao development and into underwriting Treat settlements.

Final solutions may appear possibl to economists, but Maori and man other New Zealanders realise tha something as complex as reparation fc past grievances will take a long time t settle. Each problem solved has als generated new problems, with 27 leasehold farmers on the West Coa of the North Island, for example, angr at what they see as inadequate comper sation for using their farms as part c the Taranaki settlement. Apologies fro Government for past wrongs, especiall over Raupatu or confiscated land, hav been appreciated, but many mor improvements are required in th provision of jobs, health and educatic services before the matter is settle Far too many Maori children ar suffering childhood diseases such a Hepatitis B and Reumatic Fever at leve comparable to those of the unde developed world. Far too many youn Maori are still underachieving educa tionally and coming up against the law and far too many Maori women ar still dying of obstetric problems an lung cancer for any kind of fina settlement to be imminent.

The drive to securing Treat settlements has gone hand in hand wit a move towards greater iwi autonom Labour stimulated a process which wa already under way by holding hu through 1987 and 1988 to learn wha Maori wanted. These consultation resulted in the closing of the old Mao Affairs Department in 1989 an replacing it with an Iwi Transitio Agency or Te Tira Ahu Iwi, and a ne Ministry of Maori Affairs, or Manut Maori. The National Council of Tribe was established in 1990 to ensure tha greater tribal autonomy did not unde mine Maori representation at the nation level. Then Winston Peter's derailed th process somewhat by phasing out th Iwi Transition Authority two years earl and replacing it with a Ministry of Mao Development, or Te Puni Kokiri, i 1992. Despite its being launched wit much fanfare as 'Ka Awatea' (A Ne

A resolute Bob Mahuta, Tainui leader, before finalisation of the Tainui claim. *Waikato Times.*

Prime Minister Jim Bolger is drawn as clown for refusing to accept rejection of th 'fiscal envelope' proposal by moderate well as radical Maori representatives. *Ne Zealand Times 1995.*

Day), government did not fund this new body very generously and it soon became extremely unpopular with both Maori and some members of Cabinet. Matters came to a head in October 1991 when Bolger sacked Peters from Cabinet and the National Caucus expelled him from the Party in October 1992. Peters responded by forming his own party, New Zealand First, nine months later in July 1993, which targeted Maori amongst other voters. His initiative succeeded to the extent that Tau Henare, son of a family of great mana, won Northern Maori from Labour at the 1993 election.

Tribes continued to show deep distrust of any state control. Ngai Tahu, led by the charismatic Sir Tipene O'Regan, carried this further when they forced the Runanga o Ngai Tahu Act through Parliament in 1996. The Alliance's Sandra Lee, who is of Ngai Tahu descent, opposed the measure but it passed easily. As a result Ngai Tahu have now established a distinct legal identity. They will either sink or swim under their own control. Several other tribes seem likely to follow this model. Tino rangatiratanga has been achieved at the tribal level at least. Whether or not they will be better able than nation states to resist the growing control of the international economy by multinational corporations remains a moot point and O'Regan's faith in the strength of what he calls 'collective capitalism' will be sorely tested. Some conservationists also remain sceptical that group ownership will protect the environment more effectively than private ownership by Pakeha or overseas investors. Naturally Ngai Tahu counter they that they will do better and that recreationalists have nothing to fear.

The rather conservative Maori Congress has been promoting the old Kotahitanga idea of establishing two equal Parliaments throughout the 1990s, but the idea has gained little currency outside Maoridom. More strident calls for full tino rangatiratanga at the national level from radicals such as Ken Mair have received an even more mixed reception. Mair, great-grandson of a famous soldier who fought against Maori in the wars of the 1860s, led an occupation of Motua Gardens in Wanganui for several months in 1995. Although very real historical grievances underlay his actions, the media reported his protest in a very sensational fashion and this stand won little support for Maori sovereignty. Burning down the historic Takahue school near Kaitaia in September 1995 further damaged the radical cause. Such apparently senseless actions also added support to critics from within Maoridom such as Alan Duff who urged that Maori end their dependency on the state through adopting policies of self-help. Lee Tamihore's powerful movie version of Duff's novel about a dysfunctional urban Maori family, *Once Were Warriors*, added fuel to Duff's arguments.

Apart from ongoing disruption of Treaty celebrations at Waitangi, Maori appeared to learn that direct confrontation secured few tangible gains and changed tactics. They not only pursued Treaty claims with renewed energy but strengthened ties with New Zealand First. Peters toured all the major iwi to choose candidates in the Maori way, whereas Labour and the Alliance still continued to choose them in orthodox Pakeha fashion. This tactic proved extremely successful, with New Zealand First taking from Labour all five of the

Tipene O'Regan, champion of tribal tino rangatiratanga, explains the Sealord and fisheries deal to a media frequently bemused by his astute leadership. *Otago Daily Times.*

new Maori seats created for the MMP Parliament. Suddenly Maori held the balance of the power for the first time since the 1850s. Furthermore, the high-ranking Te Heuheu family are now represented in National, the flamboyant former radical Donna Awatere has moved right across the political spectrum to join ACT, and the Mahutas are found in Labour's ranks along with the Ngati Whatua and Bastion Point leader Joe Hawke. All in all there are 15 Maori MPs in the new Parliament, a level of representation in proportion to their numbers in the population. Whether this makes much difference to power relationships in New Zealand and the survival of Te Reo and Maori culture remains to be seen, but Maori have now manoeuvred themselves into their most powerful position since before the wars of rangatiratanga of the 1860s. There is now unprecedented opportunity to confront the problems of oppression, inequality and unfairness. A social revolution equal in magnitude to the economic revolution of 'Rogernomics' was now a real possibility.

The 1996 election result really did promise much for Maori. Sadly, little of that promise has been realised. Maori MPs have generally worked against one another rather than as a powerful block and the statistics concerning unemployment, poor health and crime are as bad as ever. Te Reo also seems to be under threat since government had failed to establish a full-time Maori television channel. Some 62 Kohanga Reo have closed in these last years of the century, complaining of underfunding and bureaucratic interference. Recently mass resignations have beset the Maori Language Commission, again in protest at chronic underfunding. On the other hand, Maori have raised their public profile and continued to secure advances in the cultural area despite generally negative publicity.

Maori music, arts, literature and film have continued to grow in strength despite the absence of media quotas. Anyone watching televised talent shows must be impressed by the extraordinary depth and range of talent amongst Maori and Polynesian contestants. The commercial success of the likes of Bic Runga, Mahinirangi Tocker and Emma Paki reinforces this impression as does the extraordinary fine singing which accompanies Michael Parmenter's dance opus 'Jerusalem'. In the classical field Deborah Wai Kopaha seems destined to become another Kiri Te Kanawa. Witi Ihimaera and Patricia Grace have produced powerful new novels (*The Dream Swimmer* and *Baby No Eyes* respectively) and new writers are emerging to reinforce their talents. Alan Duff's novel *What Became of the Broken Hearted?* has been made into a fine movie sequel to *Once Were Warriors* and Briar Grace-Smith and Apirana Taylor are producing some powerful new plays. The standard of waiata, poi and haka at cultural competitions continues to lift although few Pakeha notice. Generally Maori talent is helping to build a stronger sense of national identity.

Maori protest also seems to have changed its style somewhat. Tame Iti of Tuhoe, after achieving notoriety for spitting at the Governor General Kath Tizard, has recently turned to satirising government hypocrisy in his paintings. 'Borrowing' Colin McCahon's famous painting of the 'Ureweras' tested Pakeha patience more, as did establishing a separatist 'Tuhoe nation' park. Like Mike Smith and Ken Mair, Iti seems to have become more adept at manipulating the media. Mike Smith infuriated some Aucklanders by attempting to cut down the 'one tree' atop Maungakiekie, but the symbolism caught the imagination of other New Zealanders. Many detected the irony of this action on the hill which still houses Logan Campbell's misguided memorial to the 'dying' Maori race.

On the more positive side of the ledger it is clear that the Ngai Tahu and Tainui settlements have been carried through successfully by Sir Douglas Graham, Sir Tipene O'Regan and Sir Robert Mahuta. But other settlements are still in disarray. Several Whakatohea hapu rejected their settlement outright and Taranaki iwi are arguing over how best to use their settlement. Further north the several tribes and subtribes involved in the Muriwhenua claim still seem far from agreement.

Recent, more controversial Tribunal recommendations concerning the Wanganui River and air waves have startled mainstream Pakeha opinion and lost some goodwill within the Pakeha world, especially when settlement monies are diverted to cutting down more native trees as in the Catlins area inside Ngai Tahu territory. Increasing clashes seem certain between mainstream conservationists, dubbed 'irridescent greens' by O'Regan and iwi set on redeveloping their economic base.

Another major challenge has emerged within Maoridom in a newly assertive urban group lead by John Tamihere. Younger Auckland-based Maori represented by Tamihere are arguing that they too deserve to be classified as iwi who should share in gains ensuing from settlement of Treaty grievances. To make the point Tamihere has challenged the Fisheries settlement of 1992 by engaging 20 lawyers to fight the matter out before the Privy Council in London. Such litigation is placing enormous strains on the resources of both the new urban groups and the older land-based iwi and seems to be principally benefiting lawyers.

This split between the older leaders – sometimes labelled 'the Brown Table' (a term employed by journalists to suggest that they are the Maori equivalent of the wealthy financiers in the Round Table) – and the new urban radicals is destined to become a major feature of the new millenium. Labour scored something of a coup in running Tamihere in Hauraki, a move which could win back support after the devastating losses to New Zealand First in 1996.

At the dawn of the new millenium, Maori society remains as competitive and as dynamic as ever. It may yet play a major part in challenging the excessive 'reforms' of the last 15 years because Maori, more than any other group, seem determined to assert their sovereignty against the powerful tide of globalisation. They may also have to adjust their strategies if they hope to take advantage of the new ethnic profile of New Zealand. Despite the silence of politicians, demographers estimate that in 2020 Pakeha will constitute less than half the population, while Maori will stand at nearly a quarter and Asians at around 15 per cent. Pacific Islanders will be outnumbered by Asians after 2006, but they will still make up over ten per cent of the population in 2020. New Zealand's population is becoming more Polynesian than at any time since 1856, but this new multi-cultural society will have much stronger Asian representation and a European element with much stronger links to Aotearoa than to the old homelands of Britain. The long-standing Maori capacity to adapt to, survive and resist rapidly changing circumstances will be tested again by these big shifts.

Chronology

Key Events: Maori History and Race Relations

750-800 AD First Polynesian sailors discover Aotearoa.

1000 By now most of coastline and parts of inland had been explored.

1200-1500 Period of expansion and rapid change. Population increases beyond 50,000 and a distinctive Maori culture emerges.

1400 Extinction of most species of moa.

1500-1769 Classical period. Slowing down of the rate of change. Fortified pa built.

1500-1800 Climate cools and storms increase. Diet becomes more limited and long distance voyaging ceases.

1642 December 13 Abel Tasman rediscovers New Zealand.

1769 October 6 Lieutenant James Cook confirms Tasman's rediscovery.

1807? Battle of Te Kai-a-te-Karore in which Ngati Whatua defeat Ngapuhi.

1814 Establishment of the CMS mission at Rangihoua.

1820 December 22 Hongi Hika sails for England.

1821 October Hongi begins the musket wars.

1821-23 Te Rauparaha leads a migration of Ngati Toa from Kawhia to the southern North Island.

1823 Arrival of Henry Williams at CMS mission.

1823 Establishment of Wesleyan Methodist Mission Society mission at Whangaroa.

1828 March 6 Death of Hongi Hika.

1830 Te Rauparaha traps Te Maiharanui of Ngai Tahu.

1832 Te Rauparaha takes Kaiapoia pa and decimates Ngai Tahu.

1835 Declaration of Independence signed by James Busby and Bay of Islands and Hokianga chiefs.

1835 Establishment of the Aborigines Protection Society.

1837 Report of Parliamentary Committee on treatment of Aboriginal peoples.

1838 Arrival of Bishop Pompallier and the Roman Catholic Mission.

1839 August 14 Captain William Hobson despatched with final instructions.

1839 September-December Colonel William Wakefield 'purchases' 20 million acres (8 million hectares) of land.

1840 January 29 Hobson arrives in Bay of Islands.

1840 February 6 Signing of Treaty of Waitangi.

1842 September 10 Death of Governor Hobson.

1843 June 17 Wairau 'incident' occurs in which 22 Europeans and six Maori are killed.

1843 December 23 Arrival of Governor Robert FitzRoy.

1844 March 26 Abolition of Crown preemption.

1844 July 8 Hone Heke chops down the flagpole at Kororareka.

1844 July 31 Sale of the Otago block.

1845 Emergence of Papahurihia in Hokianga area.

1845 January 10 Hone Heke chops down the flagpole again.

1845 March 11 Hone Heke and Kawiti sack Kororareka.

1845 May 8 Hone Heke and Kawiti defeat Colonel Hulme at Puketutu.

1845 July 1 Hone Heke and Kawiti defeat Colonel Despard at Ohaeawai.

1845 November 14 Arrival of Governor George Grey.

1846 January 11 Despard takes Ruapekapeka for Grey.

1846 July 23 Grey kidnaps Te Rauparaha.

1847 Grey overcomes resistance near Wanganui.

1848 September Grey makes peace with Te Rangihaeata.

1848 Purchase of Ngai Tahu block (Canterbury) of 20 million acres (8 million hectares).

1852 Constitution Act signals policy of political amalgamation.

1853 Grey departs having bought most of the South Island and succeeded in changing a bicultural policy into one of amalgamation.

1854 Movement to stop landsales gathers momentum.

1856 Responsible government and dual control of Native Affairs introduced.

1858 King Potatau I (Te Wherowhero) crowned at Ngaruawahia.

1859 March Governor Thomas Gore Browne accepts Teira's offer of land at Waitara and incenses Wiremu Kingi.

1860 March 17 Hostilities break out in Taranaki.

1860 June 27 Colonel C. E. Gold defeated at Puketakauere.

1860 November 6 Ngati Haua defeated at Mahoetahi by Major General T. S. Pratt.

1861 April 8 Governor Gore Browne and Wiremu Tamihana secure a truce in Taranaki.

1861 September George Grey recalled as Governor.

1862 Maori Schools established.

1863 April 4 Grey reoccupies the Tataraimaka block.

1863 May 4 Rewi Maniapoto ambushes the blockade at Tataraimaka.

1863 May 11 Grey declares in favour of Wiremu Kingi's claim to land at Waitara.

1863 June 4 Grey retakes Tataraimaka.

1863 July 12 General Cameron leads 4000 troops across the Mangatawhiri Stream.

1863 November 21 Maori defeated at Rangiriri.

1864 February 1 Burning of supply village at Rangiaowhia.

1864 March 30-April 2 British defeat Rewi Maniapoto at Orakau.

1864 April 24 Ngai Te Rangi and Kingite forces defeat the British at Gate Pa.

1864 June 21 British avenge Gate Pa at Te Ranga.

1864 Grey confiscates Maori land.

1865 Establishment of a Native Land Court.

1867 Establishment of four Maori seats in Parliament.

1868 November 10 Matawhero 'incident' involving Te Kooti.

1868 November 13 Te Kooti's killing avenged by Europeans near Gisborne, at Ngatapa Hill.

1872 Cessation of hostilities as Te Kooti escapes into the King Country.

1873 Repudiation Movement in the Hawke's Bay leads to appointment of a Commission of Inquiry into Alienation of Native Lands in the Hawke's Bay.

1880 James Pope appointed Director of Native Schools.

1881 Te Whiti arrested.

1884 King Tawhiao visits Queen Victoria in London.

1885 Kotahitanga (union) Movement appoints a committee of 30 to check the progress of legislation in Wellington.

1892 Kotahitanga formally constituted at Waitangi, form own parliament.
King Tawhiao goes to Waikato.
John McKenzie increases Crown monopoly over Maori land sales.

1893 King Tawhiao banishes Europeans from New Zealand.

1894 King Movement establishes its own parliament (Kauhanganui or Great Council).
Native Rights Bill defeated in Parliament.
John McKenzie steps up Maori land-buying programme.

1896 Native Rights Bill defeated again.

1897 Te Aute Students' Association formed.

1900 Seddon passes Maori Councils Act. Ngata appointed organising secretary.

1902 King Mahuta appointed to the Legislative Council.

1905 Apirana Ngata elected for Eastern Maori.

1906 June The prophet Rua Kenana waits for King Edward in Gisborne.

1907 Stout-Ngata Commission.
Tohunga Suppression Act.

1908 June 23 Rua meets Premier Joseph Ward at Whakatane.

1909 Te Rangi Hiroa (Peter Buck) elected MP for Northern Maori.

1911 Maui Pomare elected MP for Western Maori.

1912 Pomare joins the cabinet of William Massey.

1916 Establishment of the Pioneer Battalion.

1916 April 2 Rua Kenana arrested in the Urewera.

1917-18 Ngata recruits Maori for the Pioneer Battalion while Princess Te Puea opposes both voluntary enlistment and conscription in the Waikato area.

1918 November The prophet Ratana has a vision as the influenza epidemic decimates the Maori population.

1919 Te Rangi Hiroa appointed Medical Officer for Maori Health.

1921 Te Puea builds model pa at Turangawaewae Marae, Ngaruawahia and Gordon Coates becomes Minister of Native Affairs.

1922 Ratana calls for ratification of the Treaty of Waitangi.

1925 Gordon Coates become Prime Minister.

1926 Sim Commission recommends compensation for confiscation of Waikato and Taranaki lands.
Maori Purposes Fund established and Maori Arts and Crafts Act passed.
Inter-tribal Carving School opened in Rotorua.

1928 Ratana concentrates more on politics.
Ngata becomes Native Minister in United government.
F. A. Bennett appointed as Anglican Bishop of Aotearoa.

1929 Te Puea opens Mahinarangi meeting house. Ngata wins state funding for Maori farming.
1931 Agreement between Ratana and the Labour Party secured.
1932 Eruera Tirakatene wins Southern Maori.
1934 Ngata resigns as Native Minister.
1935 Tokouru Ratana wins Western Maori.
1936 Otaki hui of all tribes called by Ngata.
1937 Waitara transtribal hui.
1938 Paraire Paikea wins Northern Maori. Ngaruawahia hui of Kingite and non-Kingite Maori.
1939 Maori Battalion formed under its own command.
1941 March-May Maori Battalion serves with distinction in Greece.
1941 May 20-27 Maori Battalion puts up fierce defence of Crete.
1942 February-1943 May Maori Battalion earns fine reputation in the desert area in North Africa. Tiaka Omana takes Eastern Maori and so secures the 'Four Quarters' for Labour. Maori War Effort organisation established.
1944 February-March Maori Battalion earn special praise at Cassino.
1945 Maori Social and Economic Advancement Act passed.
1946 Peter Fraser becomes Native Minister.
1947 'Maori' replaces 'native' in official usage.
1951 Maori Women's Welfare League established.
1960 Small opposition to All Black tour of South Africa. New Zealand Maori Council established.
1961 Hunn Report and Maori Education Foundation set up.
1967 Maori Affairs Amendment Act accelerates alienation of Maori land.
1970 Nga Tamatoa founded in Auckland to express dissatisfaction of Maori youth.
1971 Census shows 60 per cent of Maori are living in cities.
1972 Witi Ihimaera's *Pounamu, Pounamu* is the first set of short stories published by a Maori writer.
1974 Maori Affairs Amendment Act tries to pomote biculturalism.

1975 Waitangi Tribunal established by the third Labour government.
1975 September 14-October 13 Whina Cooper leads a hikoi (land march) from Te Hapua to Wellington.
1977 Ngati Whatua protest development of tribal land at Bastion Point.
1978 May 25 Massed police remove protesters from Bastion Point. Eva Rickard occupies Raglan golf course.
1979 Matiu Rata founds the Mana Motuhake (Maori sovereignty) party.
1981 November Mana Motuhake comes second to Labour in the Maori electorates.
1984 July 14 Mana Motuhake again second to Labour in the Maori electorates.
1984 Donna Awatere publishes *Maori Sovereignty*. Te Maori exhibition opens in New York.
1985 Keri Hulme wins Booker Prize for *The Bone People*.
1986 August 16 Te Maori exhibition opens in Wellington.
1986 October-December Maori Loans affair.
1987 Maori Council wins legal fight to stop disputed Crown land being transferred to State Owned Enterprises. Court of Appeal rules principles of Treaty of Waitangi override everything else in State Owned Enterprises Act.
1989 Abolition of the Department of Maori Affairs and devolution of its responsibilities to Iwi Transition Agency or Te Tira Ahu Iwi. New Ministry of Maori Affairs or Manuta Maori established in advisory role. Bastion Point returned to Ngati Whatua Maori Fisheries Act grants Maori 10 per cent quota.
1990 Criticism of the government's race relations record by both Queen Elizabeth II and Bishop Wharehuia Vercoe at Waitangi celebrations after protester throws clothing at the Queen. National Congress of Tribes established.
1991 March Winston Peters launches Ka Awatea and announces establishment of Ministry of Maori Development (Te Puni Kokiri). October Winston Peters sacked as Minister of Maori Affairs.

1992 January 1 Te Puni Kokiri commences operations and Iwi Transition Agency phased out two years early. August Sealord Fisheries deal secured under Maori Fisheries Treaty of Waitangi Act. October Peters sacked as Minister of Maori Affairs and Iwi Transition Agency abolished.
1994 Waitangi commemorations disrupted by angry protesters and Ihaka spits at the Governor-General, Dame Cath Tizard. 'Fiscal envelope' proposed by Treasury setting a one billion dollar ceiling on reparation for claims.
1995 January 1 Office of Treaty Settlements or Te Tari Whakatau Take e pa ana ki te Tiriti o Waitangi established to hasten settling of Treaty claims. February Waitangi Day cancelled and Motua Gardens in Wanganui occupied by Ken Main and followers. 'Fiscal envelope' proposal rejected even by the most conservative Maori representatives. September 107-year-old Takahue school burnt down as gesture of protest. November Waikato Raupatu Claims Settlement Act provides $187 million as reparations for Tainui.
1996 February Waitangi Day celebrations held in Wellington to avoid disruption. April Te Runanga o Ngai Tahu Act establishes this iwi as a full legal entity despite opposition of the Alliance's Sandra Lee. $170 million settlement reached with the National government before the October elections. August Taranaki settlement concedes that 'genocide' was practised against Taranaki and offers an apology and approximately $145 million dollar settlement. Local pakeha leasehold farmers placed in awkward situation by government using their 271 farms as compensation. September Whakatohea $40 million settlement secured. October New Zealand First surges to the lead in polls of Maori voters. New Zealand First takes all five Maori seats on election night.

Key Events: Political and Constitutional Developments

1837 December New Zealand Association established.
1839 February-March Colonial Office decides to intervene in New Zealand.
1839 May New Zealand Company formed. *Tory* despatched to New Zealand.
1839 August 14 Captain Hobson despatched to 'treat' with the natives.
1840 February 6 Signing of the Treaty of Waitangi.
1840 May 21 Hobson declares all New Zealand a British possession, claiming the South Island by right of Cook's discovery and the North Island by cession.
1840 September The capital is shifted from Russell to Auckland.
1840 November 16 New Zealand becomes a separate Crown colony.
1846 New Zealand Constitution Act passed through the British parliament to create the province of New Ulster in the north and New Munster in the south.
1847 The new constitution suspended by Grey for five years.
1852 A new Constitution Act establishes six provincial governments serving under the Governor and a settler assembly of an appointed upper and an elected lower house.

1853-54 Self-government and the provincial system put into operation.
1854 May 24 The first Parliament meets in Auckland.
1855 The provinces win control of their land reserves.
1856 April 18 Henry Sewell forms the first responsible ministry.
1859 Hawke's Bay and Marlborough created as separate provinces.
1861-65 A series of Goldfields Acts increases the power of central government.
1861 Southland breaks away from Otago.
1865 The capital is moved from Auckland to Wellington.
1869 Julius Vogel becomes Colonial Treasurer.
1870 June 28 Vogel introduces the idea of a large loan in his Public Works budget. Secret ballot introduced.
1875 Women ratepayers entitled to vote in local body elections.
1876 Abolition of the provincial system.
1877 Establishment of county councils. Introduction of compulsory free and secular primary education.
1877 October 9 George Grey elected as Premier.

1878 Women's Franchise Bill introduced by the Grey government.
1879 October 8 Grey defeated by the Hall ministry. Women's Franchise Bill introduced by the Hall government.
1880 The New Zealand Seamen's Union founded.
1881 December 9 Country quota introduced to protect rural electorates from urban domination.
1882 Male franchise broadened and secret ballot introduced. William Rolleston's Land Act introduces a perpetual lease with right of repurchase. Women empowered to vote for licensing committees.
1884 August 19 The Stout-Vogel ministry wins power in an endeavour to save the New Zealand Agricultural Company. Married Women's Property Act passed.
1885 Women's Christian Temperance Union founded.
1887 August 29 Women's Suffrage Bill almost passes the House.
1887 October 11 Harry Atkinson defeats the Stout-Vogel ministry. Sectional organisations – Canterbury Elector's Association and Canterbury Reform Association make their first appearance in New Zealand politics.

1888 A modest tariff is introduced.

1888 September-December The 'Sweating Scandal' breaks in Dunedin.

1889 July 11 Formation of the tailoresses' Union.

1889 September 2 Introduction of male suffrage and abolition of plural voting.

1889 October 28 Maritime Council established to unite 'new' unions of the unskilled.

1890 August-November Maritime Strike.

1890 December 5 Confused election result. Atkinson stacks the Legislative Council.

1891 Emergence of the Liberal Party. Seddon breaks the power of the Legislative Council.

1892 Ballance falls ill. Seddon takes over as 'acting leader'.

1892 October 8 John McKenzie introduces lease in perpetuity. Women's Franchise League founded.

1893 McKenzie purchases the Cheviot Estate. 30,000 signatures presented by women for the vote.

1893 May 1 Seddon becomes leader on death of John Ballance. Joe Ward secures £3 million loan.

1893 September 8 Women win the vote.

1893 November 28 Liberals win a big mandate of 51 to 20 seats.

1894 Lands for Settlements Act. Industrial Conciliation and Arbitration Act.

1896 William Pember Reeves 'promoted' to London as Agent-General.

1896 December 4 Liberals win 42 of 70 seats.

1897 Seddon attends Queen Victoria's Diamond Jubilee.

1898 Old Age Pensions Act introduced.

1898 April 15 Seddon establishes Lib-Lab Federation.

1899 September 28 New Zealand joins Boer War effort. Troops embark on 21 October.

1899 December 6 Liberals win 52 of 70 seats.

1900 September 28 New Zealand annexes Cook Islands.

1901 New Zealand rejects federation with Australia.

1902 August Formation of the New Zealand Farmers' Union and New Zealand Employers' Federation.

1902 November 25 Liberals win 52 of 80 seats.

1903 September 9 William Massey takes over as leader of the opposition.

1905 Massey establishes Reform Leagues at the local level.

1905 December 6 Liberals win 61 of 80 seats.

1906 June 10 Death of Seddon.

1906 August 6 Joseph Ward becomes Premier.

1907 September 26 New Zealand granted Dominion status. Lease in perpetuity dropped.

1908 August 4 Blackball strike results in formation of the New Zealand Federation of Miners.

1908 November 24 North Island small farmers challenge Liberal dominance but Liberals win 51 of 80 seats.

1909 February 'Reform' adopted as the name of the opposition. Creation of the Federation of Labour.

1910 Formation of the New Zealand Sheepowners' Federation. 1909 Defence Act passed into law to introduce compulsory military training.

1911 New Zealand nearly goes dry.

1911 December 7 and 14 Close election result.

1912 March 23 Ward resigns and replaced as Premier by Thomas Mackenzie.

1912 July 6 Liberals defeated and Massey takes over government after John Miller leads 4 other Liberals over to Reform.

1912 May to November Waihi strike.

1913 January 21 United Federation of Labour formed.

1913 October 22-November 28 Watersiders' strike.

1914 January 13 Miners' strike collapses.

1914 August 5 New Zealand declares war on Germany.

1914 December 10 Massey retains office by 41 seats to 39.

1915 April 25 New Zealanders take part in Gallipoli landing.

1915 August 8 New Zealanders take Chunuk Bair.

1915 August 12 Coalition government formed.

1916 New Zealand troops enter the Western Front.

1916 July 7-8 Labour Party formed.

1916 August 1 Conscription introduced.

1917 July 11 Protestant Political Association formed. Six o'clock closing introduced.

1918 March 25-30 New Zealanders help halt the German spring offensive.

1918 November 4-5 New Zealanders take Le Quesnoy in their last action of the war.

1918 November 11 Armistice Day. The influenza epidemic becomes serious.

1919 April 10 New Zealand votes to go dry. Returning soldiers reverse the result.

1919 June 28 New Zealand signs peace treaty and becomes a founder member of the League of Nations.

1919 December 17 Massey's government returned by 46 out of 80 seats. Formation of the Alliance of Labour. Women entitled to stand for Parliament.

1921 Civil Service salaries cut 7 per cent.

1922 Formation of the Country Party.

1922 December 7 Labour takes the central city seats and threatens the Liberals' place as official opposition. Reform wins 38 seats, the Liberals 22, Labour 17 and Independent 3.

1925 May 10 Death of Massey.

1925 November 4 Reform easily wins election. Coates becomes New Zealand's first locally born Prime Minister. First women's branch of the New Zealand Labour Party formed in Auckland.

1926 September 9 Family Allowance introduced.

1927 March 26-27 Labour abandons 'use-hold' policy. Coates government fails to control prices of dairy products in Britain.

1927 November Old Liberal rump and business wing of Reform form the United Party.

1928 United wins election with Labour's support.

1929 Ward tries 1890s style solutions including a land tax.

1930 May Ward resigns. George Forbes becomes Prime Minister.

1930 July Ward dies.

1931 February Hated No. 5 Scheme of Public Works introduced.

1931 March Civil servants' wages cut by 10 per cent and a further 10 per cent in June.

1931 September 18 Coalition government formed between United and Reform.

1931 December Coalition win the election by 51 seats to Labour's 25.

1932 April 8 and 11 Riots in Dunedin.

1932 April 15 and 16 Riots in Auckland.

1932 May 10 Riots in Wellington.

1933 February 8 New Zealand Legion formed.

1933 September 13 Elizabeth McCombs, MP for Lyttelton, becomes New Zealand's first woman MP.

1933 October 12 Savage becomes leader of Labour after Harry Holland dies on 8 October.

1934 Election delayed for a year.

1934 July Introduction of unemployment relief.

1934 September Right wing Democrat Party formed. The Dairy Industry Commission presents a bleak report.

1935 November 24 Coalition government jams 'Uncle Scrim's' radio broadcast.

1935 November 27 Labour wins comfortably with 53 seats plus 2 Ratana to 19 for the Coalition.

1936 'Guaranteed' price implemented for dairy products.

1936 May 13-14 National Party formed as the new look Conservative Party with Adam Hamilton as leader. Primary Products Marketing Department established. Compulsory unionism introduced.

1937 April Federation of Labour formed. John A. Lee establishes the Housing Construction Department.

1937 May Savage criticises Britain's policy towards Italy and Germany.

1938 April 2 Savage announces introduction of Social Security.

1938 May Labour refuses to recognise the Italian conquest of Abyssinia.

1938 September 13 Social Security Act passed.

1938 October 15 Labour wins hefty mandate with 53 seats and 56 per cent of the vote.

1938 December Labour introduces exchange controls and import licensing.

1939 June Nash seeks a loan in London to ease exchange crisis.

1939 September 3 New Zealand declares war on Germany.

1940 January 5 First Echelon sails.

1940 March 25 John A. Lee expelled from the Labour Party.

1940 March 27 Death of Savage. Fraser becomes Prime Minister.

1940 July 16 War Cabinet of three government and two opposition members created.

1941 March-May Defeat in Greece.

1941 May 20-27 Defence of Crete and evacuation.

1941 December 8 New Zealand declares war on Japan.

1942 June 27-28 New Zealand Division fight their way out of an Axis encirclement at Minqar Quaim.

1942 October 23-November 11 El Alamein. United States Marines arrive in New Zealand.

1943 May Afrika Korps surrenders.

1943 June War Cabinet includes 6 National MPs and they withdraw in September.

1943 September 23 Labour wins wartime election, 45 seats to National's 34 and 1 Independent.

1943 October 14 Gordon Coates resigns from the National Party.

1943 November Italian campaign begins.

1943 December Battle for Orsogna.

1944 January 21 Canberra Pact signed between New Zealand and Australia.

1944 February-March Cassino.

1944 March Withdrawal from the Pacific begins. Formation of Federated Farmers.

1945 April 9 New Zealand troops cross the Senio River, Trieste taken on 2 May. Atomic bombs end war with Japan, 4000 New Zealanders serve in 'J' Force in Japan. New Zealand plays leading part among the small nations during the establishment of the United Nations.

1946 November 27 Labour wins election by the 4 Maori seats.

1947 New Zealand loses dominion status and (reluctantly) gains full nationhood.

1949 August 3 Introduction of peacetime conscription.

1949 November 30 National wins the election by 46 seats to 34. Sidney Holland becomes Prime Minister.

1950 July 26 New Zealand enters Korean War.

1950 August 18 Legislative Council abolished.

1951 January 17 Walter Nash becomes leader of the opposition.

1951 February-July The Waterfront Strike is crushed by the Holland government.

1951 September 1 Holland and National win the snap election and the ANZUS pact is signed.

1954 Social Credit League formed.

1954 November 13 National wins the election 45 seats to 35.

1956 January 23 New Zealand forces begin operations in Malaysia.

1956 August New Zealand sides with England during the Suez Crisis.

1957 September 20 Keith Holyoake becomes Prime Minister on death of Sid Holland.

1957 November 30 Walter Nash leads Labour to victory by 1 seat.

1958 June 26 'Black Budget' introduced to stave off balance of payments crisis.

1960 November 26 Keith Holyoake wins power for National by 12 seats.

1963 April 1 Arnold Nordmeyer elected leader of the Labour Party.

1963 November 30 National wins election again by 10 seats.

1964 June New Zealand engineers arrive in Vietnam.

1965 July New Zealand Artillery arrive in Vietnam.

1965 December 16 Norman Kirk becomes leader of Labour.

1966 November 26 National wins election comfortably by 9 seats. Vernon Cracknell takes Hobson for Social Credit.

1969 November 29 National wins by 6 seats, winning back Hobson from Social Credit.

1972 February 7 Holyoake retires and John Marshall takes over as Prime Minister.

1972 November 25 Labour wins a big victory by 23 seats under Norman Kirk.

1972 December Troops brought home from Vietnam.

1973 French atmospheric nuclear testing opposed by sending a frigate to Mururoa.

1974 July 9 Robert Muldoon becomes leader of the National Party.
Accident Compensation Commission established.

1974 August 31 Death of Norman Kirk. Wallace Rowling takes over as Prime Minister.

1974 September 21 The franchise is extended to all persons 18 and over.

1975 November 29 Robert Muldoon leads National to a major electoral triumph by 55 seats to 32.

1976 July 23 National Superannuation scheme introduced at age 60.

1977 February 19 At a by-election Bruce Beetham becomes Social Credit MP for Rangitikei.

1978 November 25 National's winning margin hauled back to 11 seats.

1978 Sonja Davies becomes first woman elected to an executive position on the FOL.

1979 September 6 Gary Knapp wins East Coast Bays for Social Credit in by-election.

1980 Working Women's Charter passed by the Federation of Labour.

1981 November 28 National receives sufficient provincial seats for them to hang on by 46 seats to Labour's 44, Social Credit's 2.

1982 Sue Wood becomes first woman elected as president of a political party.

1983 February 3 David Lange replaces Bill Rowling as leader of Labour.

1984 A free-market New Zealand Party emerges led by Robert Jones.

1984 July 14 David Lane leads Labour to victory by 19 seats.
Exchange and constitutional crisis averted.
Anti-nuclear policy instituted.
Ann Hercus becomes first Minister of Women's Affairs.
Margaret Wilson becomes Labour's first woman party president.

1985 Labour moves to the right and pursues free-market policy.

1985 July 10 Bombing by French frogmen of the *Rainbow Warrior*.

1986 Roger Douglas initiates a policy of corporatisation.

1987 David Lange again leads Labour to victory by 19 seats.

1989 Jim Anderton forms New Labour Party.

1990 Limited Bill of Rights passed.
National wins landslide victory.

1991 May Employment Contracts Act passe⬛ abolishing compulsory unionism.
August Gilbert Miles and Hamish Macintyr⬛ leave National to form Liberal Party and Ne⬛ Zealand troops serve with U.S.A. in Gulf Wa⬛ against Iraq.
December New Labour, Mana Motuhake, th⬛ Greens and Democrats coalesce into th⬛ Alliance party.

1992 New Zealand wins seat on UN Securit⬛ Council.
October Winston Peters forced from Nation⬛ Caucus.

1993 April Winston Peters wins Tauranga by⬛ election against his own government.
July Winston Peters launches 'New Zealan⬛ First' party.
October National hangs onto power by sli⬛ majority once Labour's Peter Tapsell accept⬛ job of Speaker.
Electorate votes 53 to 47 per cent in favour o⬛ MMP.

1994 May New Zealand troops sent to serv⬛ as peace keepers in Bosnia.
Roger Douglas founds ACT (Association o⬛ Consumers and Taxpayers).

1995 March Prime Minister Bolger meet⬛ President Bill Clinton in the White Hous⬛ the first such meeting since 1984.
June United Party formed by seven break⬛ away MPs, 4 National and 3 Labour led b⬛ Clive Matthewson.
Christian Heritage Party launched by Graha⬛ Lee.
August Navy ship *Tui* sent to protest Frenc⬛ nuclear testing at Mururoa.
November Commonwealth heads of govern⬛ ment meet in Auckland and Nelson Mandel⬛ visits New Zealand.

1996 Various small parties emerge to contest th⬛ first MMP election.
April Richard Prebble takes over as leade⬛ of ACT.
August Bolger's visit to South Africa turn⬛ sour as demand made to pardon protester⬛ arrested in 1981. Bolger apologises bu⬛ withholds pardon.
Anti-government vote split on election nigh⬛ leaving New Zealand First as power broker⬛ New party ACT wins 8 new seats a⬛ Alliance falters and Labour recovers fro⬛ poor polling.

Key Events: Economic Developments

1769 Lieutenant Cook and Joseph Banks note the potential of timber and flax.

1792 First American sealers land at Dusky Bay.

1798-1829 Overkilling depletes the seal population.

1800-39 Main period of deep sea whaling.

1820-30 Ngapuhi agriculture stimulated by whaler's demands.

1829-44 On-shore or bay whaling flourishes with 80 stations established around the New Zealand coast.

1835-40 Traders and land speculators arrive from Sydney.

1840-45 Severe depression and lack of staple exports causes new settlements to struggle.

1842 First merino ram arrives in Nelson.

1845 Wairarapa opened up for sheep farming.

1846-51 Marlborough opened up for sheep farming.

1851 Gold discoveries in Victoria stimulate Maori farming and pastoralism.

Grey's cheap land regulations benefit the big pastoralists.
Pastoralism proves profitable in Canterbury.

1856 Otago chops the 'sufficient price' for land.

1858 New Zealand Insurance Company established.

1858-61 Depression sets in.

1861 Discovery of gold in Otago.
Bank of New Zealand established along with Wright, Robertson and Stephenson & Co. Ltd.

1863 Bank of Otago established.

1864 West Coast goldrush begins.
National Mortgage Association established.

1865 Loan and Mercantile Agency established.

1867 Thames/Coromandel goldrush begins.

1868 Depression sets in.

1869 Julius Vogel becomes Colonial Treasurer.

1870 Public Works programme introduced and £10 million loan secured.

1870-79 Artificial boom.

'Working man's paradise'.
1700 kilometres of railways built and 400⬛ kilometres of road.
6400 kilometres of telegraphs erected.
Big estates created out of runs and farms.

1871-82 Grain 'bonanza'.

1872 National Bank established.

1873 Dalgety's begins operations in New Zealand.
New Zealand Shipping Company established.
Mosgiel Woollen Mills commences operations.

1875 Union Steamship Company founded.

1877 New Zealand and Australia Land Company formed.

1878 Collapse of City of Glasgow Bank.

1879 Further loan of £10 million secured.
Collapse of British grain farming.

1879-96 The Long Depression.

1882 February 15–May 24 First successful shipment of refrigerated meat to Britain.
First co-operative dairy factories founded at Edendale and on the Otago Peninsula.

1882-89 Growth in textile factories, printing and heavy engineering in Dunedin.

1886 John Ballance begins village settlement scheme for part-time farmers.

1887 Deferred payment system introduced to encourage closer land settlement.

1890 584 individuals and companies own 56 per cent of freehold land.

1892 Department of Agriculture established.

1893 Sir Joseph Ward secures £3 million loan.

1893-95 Colonial Bank and Bank of New Zealand in trouble.

1894 Advances to Settlers' Office established.

1895 January 1 Industrial Conciliation and Arbitration Acts passed.
Liberal government rescues the Bank of New Zealand which absorbs the Colonial Bank.

1896 Prices for agricultural commodities begin to upturn.

1896-1921 Period of virtually unbroken prosperity based on the growth of small family farms.
Economic dynamic shifts from South Island to the North.

1907-09 Brief recession.

1912 Massey allows state tenants to purchase their farms at original valuation.

1915 Commandeer introduced for meat.

1916 Commandeer introduced for wool and cheese.

1917 Commandeer introduced for butter.

1921-23 Sharp recession.
Failure of returned soldier farms.

1922 Establishment of the Meat Board.

1924-26 Period of recovery with considerable public works.

1926-27 Establishment of the Dairy Board.
Foundation of Massey Agricultural College and the DSIR.
Lincoln College overhauled.

1926-29 Economic decline.
Debt and unemployment increase.
Commodity prices decline as increasing production creates oversupply.

1930-35 The Great Depression.

1933 January New Zealand pound devalued and taken off parity with sterling.
'Official' unemployment peaks at 80,000.
Reserve Bank established.

1934 Mortgage relief to farmers increased.

1935 Small economic recovery comes too late for the Coalition government.
Overseas funds reach £23 million when Labour takes office.

1935-37 Some recovery.

1936 Primary Products Marketing Department replaces old boards.
Government takes full control of the Reserve Bank.

1938 December Financial crisis reduces overseas funds to £8 million.
Introduction of exchange controls and import licensing.
New Zealand becomes a mixed economy.

1940-45 Overstrain of the war effort.

1945 November 24 Nationalisation of the Bank of New Zealand.

1946-49 Period of stabilisation and rehabilitation.

1949-57 National continues deregulation.

1950 Korean War wool boom.

1957-58 Exchange crisis.

1958-67 Last of the economic golden weather.

1967 Serious trade deficit.
Robert Muldoon becomes Minister of Finance.

1968-72 Modest recovery.

1973 The oil shock hits New Zealand hard.
Britain enters the EEC.
Overseas debt reaches $1 billion.

1973-87 Painful adjustment to a post-colonial economic world.
Diversification stepped up, especially in manufacturing, horticulture and fishing.
Frantic search for new markets and new industries.

1975-78 Muldoon increases economic controls.

1978 Unemployment increases significantly for the first time since the 1930s.

Muldoon releases the 'Think Big' strategy to promote heavy industrialisation.
CER (Closer Economic Relations) agreement with Australia.

1984 July Unemployment reaches Great Depression levels of 80,000.
Exchange crisis resolved by new Labour government devaluation of 20 per cent.

1984 July Fourth Labour government pursue a free-market policy, remove economic regulations, float the dollar in March 1985, corporatise many government departments, remove subsidies to farmers and exporters, and reduce tariffs.

1988 Unemployment passes 100,000 for the first time.
Richard Prebble closes 432 Post offices.

1989 First annual balance of payments surplus since 1973.
Reserve Bank Act passed to secure price stability through attempting to hold inflation under 2 per cent per annum.
GST raised to 12.5 per cent.
Postbank sold to the Australia New Zealand Bank.
New Zealand Steel, Coal Corp and State Insurance privatised.

1990 Telecom sold to an American-dominated overseas consortium.

1991 Unemployment passes 200,000. Inflation falls to under 2 per cent.

1993 New Zealand rail sold to Wisconsin Central Transport Company.

1994 Unemployment starts to fall.

1996 Unemployment falls officially to around 6 per cent of the workforce.
Tax cuts introduced in July budget.
First evidence of an increase in real wages since 1970s.
October Dollar soars as overseas investors speculate on post election uncertainty. Export sector complains that our currency if over valued and Peters promises easing of fiscal restraint.

Key Events: European Settlement and Social Developments

1814 First Mission Station established.

1827 Shore based whaling stations set up and traders begin operations in the Bay of Islands. The Australian connection is expanded through the 1830s.

1840 January 22 The first settlers arrive in Wellington.

1840 September Foundation of Auckland.
First settlers arrive at Wanganui.

1841 March 30 First settlers arrive at New Plymouth.

1842 February 1 First settlers arrive in Nelson.

1847 Arrival of Fencibles in Auckland.

1848 March 23 First settlers arrive in Otago.

1850 December 16 First settlers arrive in Canterbury.

1855 European population numbers outstrip the Maori.

1860-65 18,000 British troops serve in New Zealand.

1861-63 Victorian miners pour into Otago.

1864-65 Australian and Otago miners move to the West Coast.

1869 Establishment of the University of Otago.

1860-70 New Zealand's population more than doubles from 99,000 to 248,000 by the goldrushes.
Dunedin becomes New Zealand's biggest town with 14,000 people.

1870-80 A major wave of assisted (approx. 115,000) and unassisted (60,000 plus) migrants pours in under the Vogel scheme.
New Zealand's population doubles from 248,000 to 500,910.
Despite large numbers of single women the population remains young and predominantly male.
The Great Bush of southern Hawke's Bay and Taranaki is opened up.
Significant minorities of Germans and Scandinavians integrate well.

1871 Otago Girls' High School established as the first girls' secondary school.

1876 New Zealand connected to the international telegraph cable.

1877 Introduction of compulsory primary education.
Kate Edger is the first woman to graduate BA.

1880-90 Depression forces farmers to subsist and unskilled urban workers to struggle.
Growing awareness of social problems.

1884 Married Women's Property Act passed.

1885 Women's Christian Temperance movement founded.

1889 Free kindergartens established.

1890 May Royal Commission reports on sweating scandal.

1891 Factories Act passed to limit employment of women and children.
Labour Bureau established to find work for the unemployed.
Truck Act passed to ensure payment in wages.

1892 Employers' Liability Act passed to provide compensation for injury in the work place.
Labour Bureau becomes the Department of Labour.

1844 Comprehensive Factories Act passed to improve conditions.
Shop and Shop Assistants' Act passed to improve conditions and provide a half-day holiday.

1895 Grace Neill becomes first woman inspector of factories.
Daybreak, the first women's journal, begins publication.

1896 Emily Siedeberg becomes the first woman to graduate in medicine in New Zealand.

1897 Ethel Benjamin becomes the first woman lawyer in New Zealand.

1898 Old age pensions introduced.
Divorce Act makes it possible for women to divorce violent, drunken and unfaithful husbands.

1899 The Employment of Young Boys and Girls Without Protection Act passed to make it illegal to employ children without pay.

1900 Testators' Family Maintenance Act passed to force deserting husbands to pay maintenance.

1901 Registration of nurses made compulsory.

1903 Free places introduced in secondary schools.

1904 Registration of midwives made compulsory.

1905 St Helen's Hospitals established.
Triumph of the All Blacks in Britain.

1907 Plunket Society formed in Dunedin to improve the health of babies.
Dental School opened in Dunedin.

1908 Quackery Prevention Act passed to stop the sale of patent medicines.

1909 Otago School of Home Science opened.

1910 1 million population mark is passed.

1911 Census shows that the majority of New Zealanders live in towns.
Widows' pension introduced.

1912 Cost of Living Commission reveals rising expectations of the population.
District nurses appointed.

1914-18 17,000 men killed and 56,000 wounded in the First World War.
Teaching and nursing professions opened up for women.

1918 November-December Influenza epidemic claims 8000 lives.

1919 First town Planning Conference.
The Housing Act makes loans available for low cost housing.

1920-29 A decade of moral panics and technological advance.

1921 Introduction of the Dental Nurse Service.

1924 The borstal system is introduced for young offenders.

1925 Child Welfare Department and Children's Courts established.
Formation of the Country Women's Institute and the Women's Division of the Farmers' Union.
Some 9600 kilometres of electric power lines are in place by the end of the year compared with 3250 kilometres in 1919.

1926 Introduction of a small family allowance.

1927 Some 18,000 radio licences are held by the end of the year compared with 2000 in 1923.

1929 The number of cars and trucks reaches 213,000 compared with 60,000 in 1918.

1930-35 High unemployment causes mass trauma throughout New Zealand society.

1931 February 3 Hawke's Bay earthquake kills 256 people.

1935 *Working Women* begins publication.

1936 New Zealand Broadcasting Service established.

1937 *Women Today* replaces *Working Women*.

1939 April 1 Introduction of Social Security.
The *New Zealand Listener* begins publication.

1940-45 Women enter the armed forces.
Women enter the workforce.

1940 Formation of the Mobile Broadcasting Unit.
Centenary celebrations.

1942 Arrival of large numbers of American marines.
New Zealand National Film Unit established.

1944 Introduction of compulsory secondary education to age 15.

1945-47 Rehabilitation of ex-servicemen proceeds smoothly.

1947 Baby boom begins.
Landfall begins publication as New Zealand's first serious literary magazine.

1952 New Zealand's population passes the 2 million mark.

1956 New Zealand defeats the Springboks in a home series.

1957 Janet Frame's *Owls Do Cry* is published.

1960 Introduction of television.
Equal pay for women in the public sector introduced.

1964 Massey Agricultural College expanded into a full university.
Downstage Theatre opened in Wellington.

1967 Abolition of 6 o'clock closing.
Lloyd Geering faces 'heresy' charge.

1968 Waikato University opened.
Mercury Theatre opened in Auckland.

1970 *Up from Under* published as the first periodical of the 'new' feminist movement.

1971 Vietnam War protest marches reach their peak.

1972 New Zealand Film Commission established.
Court Theatre opened in Christchurch.

1972 Equal pay for women employed in the private sector is introduced.
Broadsheet begins publication.
Compulsory military training ends.

1973 Britain enters the EEC.
New Zealand Author's Fund established.
New Zealand's population passes 3 million.

1974 Second television channel set up and colour television introduced.

1975 Women's Electoral Lobby established.

1976 Unemployment appears for the first time since 1938.

1977 Contraception, Sterilisation and Abortion Act is passed.

1977-87 Women enter the medical, dental and legal professions in large numbers.

1981 Springbok Tour.

1984 Unemployment reaches significantly high levels.

1985 Sinking of the *Rainbow Warrior*.
Keri Hulme wins the Booker Prize.

1986 December Success of *KZ7* in the America's Cup.
December Homosexual Law Reform Act passed.

1987 All Blacks win inaugural World Cup and New Zealand netballers also win the World Cup.

1988 Royal Commission on Social Policy reports and sets a new model for devolution of responsibility and greater targeting of welfare assistance.
Gibb report on hospital administration recommends more business like management structures.
Picot report on education establishes 'Tomorrows' Schools' system of governance by parent dominated Boards of Trustees.

1989 Boards of Trustees meet for the first time.
Sunday trading begins.
Third television channel begins broadcasting.

1990 Successful Commonwealth Games in Auckland choreographed by Pita Sharples, but celebrations of sesquicentennial muted and unconfident.
New *Dictionary of New Zealand Biography* launched.
New National government cuts benefits in December.

1991 Welfare benefits cut further by over one billion dollars.
State housing rentals set at commercial rates.

1992 University fees raised substantially and student loans scheme introduced following Todd committee recommendation to reduce tertiary funding to 75 per cent of cost.
Regional Health Authorities and Crown Health Enterprises established to manage new health system along the lines of funder provider split.
Fran Wild elected as first woman mayor of major metropolitan centre.

1993 Privacy Act passed.
Women's suffrage celebrated and Dame Silvia Cartwright appointed as first woman High Court Judge.
The New Zealand movie *The Piano* enjoys international acclaim and wins an Oscar.

1994 November First Casino in New Zealand opened in Christchurch
Regional television revitalised.
The movie version of Alan Duff's *Once Were Warriors* wins further international acclaim.

1995 April Cave Creek viewing platform collapses killing 14 young New Zealanders. Underfunding of Department of Conservation subsequentially blamed.
May New Zealand wins America's Cup.
June All Blacks lose World Cup final to South Africa.
BCNZ commercial radio stations sold off.

1996 July Danyon Loader first New Zealander to win two gold medals in swimming at the Olympic Games.
August/September All Blacks beat South Africa in a series in South Africa for the first time.

Ministry	Prime Minister	Held Office		Governing Party/Coalition
Sewell	Henry Sewell	7 May 1856	20 May 1856	
Fox	William Fox	20 May 1856	2 Jun 1856	
Stafford	Edward William Stafford	2 Jun 1856	12 Jul 1861	
Fox	William Fox	12 Jul 1861	6 Aug 1862	
Domett	Alfred Domett	6 Aug 1862	30 Oct 1863	
Whitaker-Fox	Frederick Whitaker	30 Oct 1863	24 Nov 1864	
Weld	Frederick Aloysius Weld	24 Nov 1864	16 Oct 1865	
Stafford	Edward William Stafford	16 Oct 1865	28 Jun 1869	
Fox	William Fox	28 Jun 1869	10 Sep 1872	
Stafford	Edward William Stafford	10 Sep 1872	11 Oct 1872	
Waterhouse	George Marsden Waterhouse	11 Oct 1872	3 Mar 1873	Prior to 1887 there were no political parties as such. Shifting parliamentary factions revolved around local leaders.
Fox	William Fox	3 Mar 1873	8 Apr 1873	
Vogel	Julius Vogel	8 Apr 1873	6 Jul 1875	
Pollen	Daniel Pollen	6 Jul 1875	15 Feb 1876	
Vogel	Sir Julius Vogel	15 Feb 1876	1 Sep 1876	
Atkinson	Harry Albert Atkinson	1 Sep 1876	13 Sep 1876	
Atkinson (reconstituted)	Harry Albert Atkinson	13 Sep 1876	13 Oct 1877	
Grey	Sir George Grey	15 Oct 1877	8 Oct 1879	
Hall	John Hall	8 Oct 1879	21 Apr 1882	
Whitaker	Frederick Whitaker	21 Apr 1882	25 Sep 1883	
Atkinson	Harry Albert Atkinson	25 Sep 1883	16 Aug 1884	
Stout-Vogel	Robert Stout	16 Aug 1884	28 Aug 1884	
Atkinson	Harry Albert Atkinson	28 Aug 1884	3 Sep 1884	
Stout-Vogel	Sir Robert Stout	3 Sep 1884	8 Oct 1887	
Atkinson	Sir Harry Albert Atkinson	8 Oct 1887	24 Jan 1891	
* Ballance	John Ballance	24 Jan 1891	27 Apr 1893	Liberal
Seddon	Rt. Hon. Richard John Seddon	1 May 1893	10 Jun 1906	
Hall-Jones	William Hall-Jones	21 Jun 1906	6 Aug 1906	
Ward	Rt. Hon. Sir Joseph George Ward	6 Aug 1906	28 Mar 1912	
Mackenzie	Thomas Mackenzie	28 Mar 1912	10 Jul 1912	
Massey	Rt. Hon. William Ferguson Massey	10 Jul 1912	12 Aug 1915	Reform
Massey	Rt. Hon. William Ferguson Massey	12 Aug 1915	25 Aug 1919	National Coalition (Reform-Liberal)
* Massey	Rt. Hon. William Ferguson Massey	25 Aug 1919	10 May 1925	Reform
Bell	Hon. Sir Francis Henry Dillon Bell	14 May 1925	30 May 1925	
Coates	Rt. Hon. Joseph Gordon Coates	30 May 1925	10 Dec 1928	
Ward	Rt. Hon. Sir Joseph George Ward	10 Dec 1928	28 may 1930	United (Minority Government)
Forbes	Rt. Hon. George William Forbes	28 May 1930	22 Sep 1931	
Forbes	Rt. Hon. George William Forbes	22 Sep 1931	6 Dec 1935	National Coalition (United-Reform)
* Savage	Rt. Hon. Michael Joseph Savage	6 Dec 1935	1 Apr 1940	Labour
Fraser	Rt. Hon. Peter Fraser	1 Apr 1940	13 Dec 1949	
Holland	Rt. Hon. Sir Sidney George Holland	13 Dec 1949	20 Sep 1957	National
Holyoake	Rt. Hon. Keith Jacka Holyoake	20 Sep 1957	12 Dec 1957	
Nash	Rt. Hon. Walter Nash	12 Dec 1957	12 Dec 1960	Labour
Holyoake	Rt. Hon. Sir Keith Jacka Holyoake	12 Dec 1960	7 Feb 1972	National
Marshall	Rt. Hon. John Ross Marshall	7 Feb 1972	8 Dec 1972	
* Kirk	Rt. Hon. Norman Eric Kirk	8 Dec 1972	31 Aug 1974	Labour
Rowling	Rt. Hon. Wallace Edward Rowling	6 Sep 1974	12 Dec 1975	
Muldoon	Rt. Hon. Robert David Muldoon	12 Dec 1975	26 Jul 1984	National
Lange	Rt. Hon. David Russell Lange	26 Jul 1984	8 Aug 1989	Labour
Palmer	Rt. Hon. Geoffrey Winston Russell Palmer	8 Aug 1989	4 Sep 1990	Labour
Moore	Rt. Hon. Michael Kenneth Moore	4 Sep 1990	2 Nov 1990	Labour
Bolger	Rt. Hon. James Brendan Bolger	2 Nov 1990		National (Coalition with NZ First from late 1996)
Shipley	Rt. Hon. Jennifer Mary Shipley	8 Dec 1997		

* Died in office

Governors and Governors-General

Governors	Held office		Governors-General	Held office	
Sir George Gipps	30 Jan 1840	3 Jan 1841	Lord Liverpool	28 Jun 1917	7 July 1920
Captain William Hobson (Lieutenant-Governor)	30 Jan 1840	3 Jan 1841	Lord Jellicoe	27 Sep 1920	26 Nov 1924
* Captain William Hobson	3 Jan 1841	10 Sep 1842	Sir Charles Fergusson	13 Dec 1924	8 Feb 1930
Lieutenant Willoughby Shortland, Administrator	10 Sep 1842	26 Dec 1843	Lord Bledisloe	19 Mar 1930	15 Mar 1935
Captain Robert FitzRoy	26 Dec 1843	17 Nov 1845	Lord Galway	12 Apr 1935	3 Feb 1941
Sir George Grey	18 Nov 1845	31 Dec 1853	Sir Cyril Newall	22 Feb 1941	19 Apr 1946
Lieutenant-Colonel R.H. Wynyard, Administrator	3 Jan 1854	6 Sep 1855	Sir Bernard Freyberg	17 Jun 1946	15 Aug 1952
Colonel Thomas Gore Browne	6 Sep 1855	2 Oct 1861	Sir Willoughby Norrie	2 Dec 1952	25 Jul 1957
Sir George Grey, Administrator	3 Oct 1861	3 Dec 1861	Lord Cobham	5 Sep 1957	13 Sep 1962
Sir George Grey	4 Dec 1861	5 Feb 1868	Brigadier Sir Bernard Edward Fergusson (later Lord Ballantrae)	9 Nov 1962	20 Oct 1967
Sir George Bowen	5 Feb 1868	19 Mar 1873	Sir Arthur Espie Porritt (later Lord Porritt)	1 Dec 1967	6 Sep 1972
Sir James Fergusson	14 Jun 1873	3 Dec 1874	Sir (Edward) Denis Blundell	27 Sep 1972	5 Oct 1977
Lord Normanby, Administrator	3 Dec 1874	8 Jan 1875	Rt. Hon. Sir Keith Jacka Holyoake	26 Oct 1977	23 Oct 1980
Lord Normanby	9 Jan 1875	21 Feb 1879	The Hon. Sir David Stuart Beattie	6 Nov 1980	6 Nov 1985
Sir Hercules Robinson, Administrator	27 Mar 1879	16 Apr 1879	Sir Paul Reeves	20 Nov 1985	29 Nov 1990
Sir Hercules Robinson	17 Apr 1879	8 Sep 1880	Dame Catherine Tizard	13 Dec 1990	3 Mar 1996
Sir Arthur Gordon	29 Nov 1880	23 Jun 1882	Sir Michael Hardie Boys	2 Mar 1996	—
Sir William Jervois	20 Jan 1883	22 Mar 1889			
Lord Onslow	2 May 1889	24 Feb 1892			
Lord Glasgow	7 Jun 1892	6 Feb 1897			
Lord Ranfurly	10 Aug 1897	19 Jun 1904			
Lord Plunket	20 Jun 1904	8 Jun 1910			
Lord Islington	22 Jun 1910	2 Dec 1912			
Lord Liverpool	19 Dec 1912	27 Jun 1917			

* Died in office

General Election Results Since 1890

Year	Liberal	Conservative	Reform	Labour	United	National	Independent	Social Credit	Alliance	New Zealand First
1890	38	24[1]					12[2]			
1893	46	20					8			
1896	42	27					5			
1899	52	18					4			
1902	52	24					4			
1905	61		15				4			
1908	51		26	1			2			
1911	33		37	4			6			
1914	31		40	8			1			
1919	19		46	8			3			
1922	22		38	17			3			
1925	12		55	13						
1928			29	19	26		6[3]			
1931			22	25	29		4[4]			
1935				55		19	6			
1938				53		25	2			
1943				45		34	1			
1946				42		38				

Year	Liberal	New Labour	Reform	Labour	United	National	Independent	Social Credit	Alliance	New Zealand First
1949				34		46				
1951				30		50				
1954				35		45				
1957				41		39				
1960				34		46				
1963				35		45				
1966				35		44		1		
1969				39		45				
1972				55		32				
1975				32		55				
1978				40		41		1		
1981				43		47		2		
1984				56		37		2		
1987				58		39				
1990		1		29		67				
1993				45		50			2	2
1996				37		44			13	17

[1] Includes five Labour members
[2] Seven join the Liberals
[3] Four Independents support United
[4] Coalition government of Reform and United

Further Reading

* = easy reading

1. Vikings of the Sunrise: East Polynesian Voyagers Discover Aotearoa

*Janet Davidson, *The Prehistory of New Zealand* (Longman Paul, Auckland, 1984) for the most up-to-date archaeological account.

David R. Simmons, *The Great New Zealand Myth* (A.H. & A.W. Reed, Wellington, 1976), contains a fascinating examination of the story of the Great Fleet.

James Belich, *Making Peoples: A History of the New Zealanders From Polynesian Settlement to the End of the Nineteeenth Century* (Allen Lane the Penguin Press, Auckland, 1996), contains easily the fullest synthesis on the various theories concerning pre-European New Zealand yet published.

Margaret Orbell, *The Illustrated Encyclopedia of Maori Myth and Legend* (University of Canterbury Press, Christchurch, 1995) provides an up-to-date if somewhat universalised coverage of the world of Maori myth and story. Te Rangi Hiroa (Sir Peter Buck), *Vikings of the Sunrise* (J.B. Lippincott & Co., Philadelphia, 1938), and his *The Coming of the Maori* (Maori Purposes Fund Board, Wellington, 1949) remain the classic studies.

2. In Search of the Southern Continent: Tasman Discovers New Zealand

*J.C. Beaglehole, *The Exploration of the Pacific* (Adam and Charles Black, London, 1966) is indispensable.

Andrew Sharp, *The Voyages of Abel Janszoon Tasman* (Oxford University Clarendon Press, 1968) and Oliver E. Allan, *The Seafarers: The Pacific Navigators* (Time/Life, Alexander, Virginia, 1980) are helpful.

J.E. Herries (ed.), *Abel Janszoon Tasman's Journal* (N.A. Kovech, Los Angeles, 1965) gives something of the feel of the voyage.

3. Master Mariner: Cook Circumnavigates New Zealand

*J.C. Beaglehole, *The Life of Captain James Cook* (Stanford Univ. Press, CA, 1974) remains the authoritative biography.

J.C. Beaglehole (ed.), *The Journals of Captain James Cook On His Voyages of Discovery* (Cambridge University Press for the Hakluyt Society, 1955-69) are indispensable. Vol. I 'The Voyage of the Endeavour 1768-1771' is particularly relevant to New Zealand.

Ann Salmond, *Two Worlds: First Meetings between Maori and Europeans, 1642-1772* (Viking, Auckland, 1991) is essential reading on early culture contact, as is its sequel *Between Two Worlds*: *Early Exchanges Between Maori and Europeans 1773-1815* (Viking, Auckland, 1997).

Link: From Cook to Hongi

On sealers see A. Charles and Neil C. Begg, *The World of John Boultbee, including an account of sealing in Australia and New Zealand* (Whitcoulls, Christchurch, 1979).

On whaling see *Harry Morton, *The Whale's Wake* (University of Otago Press, Dunedin, 1982).

There are many useful articles on missionaries in the *New Zealand Journal of History* but there is no one comprehensive study. The most helpful books are Judith Binney, *The Legacy of Guilt: a Life of Thomas Kendall* (OUP for University of Auckland Press, 1968) and J.M.R. Owens, *Prophets in the Wilderness: the Wesleyan Mission to New Zealand, 1819-27* (AUP/OUP, Auckland, 1974).

Warren E. Limbrick (ed.), *Bishop Selwyn in New Zealand 1841-68* (Dunmore Press, Palmerston North, 1983) also contains some useful essays.

4. Utu: Hongi Hika Launches the Musket Wars

See Jeffrey Sissons, Wiremu Wi Hongi and Pat Hohepa, *The Puriri Trees are Laughing: A Political History of Nga Puhi in the Inland Bay of Islands* (The Polynesian Society, Auckland, 1987) and *Ormond Wilson, *From Hongi Hika to Hone Heke: A Quarter Century of Upheaval* (John McIndoe, Dunedin, 1985).

G.S. Parsonson, 'Hongi Hika', *Historical News*, October 1981 provides a lively overview. Judy Corballis, *Tapu*, is a lively novel providing fresh insights into this story.

Link: From Hongi to the Treaty

The most important books in this period are Peter Adams, *Fatal Necessity: British intervention in New Zealand 1830-1847* (AUP/ OUP, Auckland, 1977), Patricia Burns, *Te Rauparaha: A New Perspective* (A.H. & A.W. Reed, Wellington, 1980) and Alan Ward, *A Show of Justice: Racial 'Amalgamation' in Nineteenth Century New Zealand* (AUP/OUP, Auckland, 1973, 2nd ed. 1994). F.E. Maning, *Old New Zealand: A Tale of the Good Old Times* (Golden Press, Auckland, in association with Whitcombe and Tombs, 1973) remains a classic account by a contemporary. Michael King, *Moriori: A People Rediscovered* (Viking, Auckland, 1989) tells the story of a long-forgotten episode in our history – the conquest of Moriori by the northern sections of Ati Awa.

Unfortunately there is no good biography of Edward Gibbon Wakefield, nor a modern study of the New Zealand Company. We continue to rely upon *John Miller, *Early Victorian New Zealand: A Study of Racial Tension and Social Attitudes, 1839-1852* (OUP, London, 1958) and Michael Turnbull, *The New Zealand Bubble: The Wakefield Theory in Practice* (Price, Milburn, Wellington, 1959). Patricia Burns died before her *Fatal Success: A History of the New Zealand Company* (Heinemann Reed, Auckland, 1989) appeared and the book suffers as a consequence. Look out for the papers given in August 1996 to mark the bicentennial of Wakefield's birth as have been published by the Friends of the Turnbull as *Edward Gibbon Wakefield and the Colonial Dream: A Reconsideration*, 1997.

5. Scrap of Paper or Sacred Pact?: The Treaty of Waitangi

*Claudia Orange, *The Treaty of Waitangi* (Allen and Unwin/Port Nicholson Press with assistance from the Historical Publications Branch, Wellington, 1987) is indispensable. Ruth Ross, 'Te Tiriti & Waitangi: texts and translations', *New Zealand Journal of History*, Vol. 6, No. 2, October 1972, pp. 129-57; and three books: P. Adams, *Fatal Necessity*, Alan Ward, *A Show of Justice*, and Ian Wards, *The Shadow of the Land: A Study of British Policy and Racial Conflict in New Zealand, 1832-1852* (Government Printer, Wellington, 1968) are also essential reading.

T. Lindsay Buick, *The Treaty of Waitangi* (Thomas Avery & Sons, London, 1914) still contains the best account of the story of the Treaty.

D.F. McKenzie, 'Oral Culture, Literacy and Print in early New Zealand: the Treaty of Waitangi' (Victoria University Press with the Alexander Turnbull Library Trust, Wellington, 1985) is a provocative essay.

Since the first edition of this book, a 'Treaty industry' has developed. The most helpful of the new books are I.H. Kawharu (ed.), *Waitangi: Maori and Pakeha Perspectives on the Treaty of Waitangi* (OUP, Auckland, 1989) and William Renwick (ed.), *Sovereignty and Indigenous Rights: The Treaty of Waitangi in International Context* (Victoria University Press, Wellington, 1991).

Link: From Waitangi to Colonisation

See titles for previous Link.

6. Frontier Towns: Europeans Establish Settlements at Wellington and Auckland

Both cities require new and updated histories. In the meantime we are dependent upon John Miller, *Early Victorian New Zealand* and E.J. Wakefield, *Adventure in New Zealand, From 1839-1844: With Some Account of the Beginning of the British Colonization of the Islands*, 2 vols. (London, 1845) on Wellington. David Hamer and Roberta Nicholls (eds), *The Making of Wellington 1800-1914* (Victoria University Press, Wellington, 1990), contains some useful essays on the city's development.

On Auckland see Russell Stone, *Young Logan Campbell* (AUP/OUP, Auckland, 1982); and G.W.A. Bush, *Decently And In Order: The Government of the City of Auckland 1840-1971* (Collins for the Auckland City Council, Auckland, 1970) is also helpful.

7. Rebellion in the North: Hone Heke Chops Down the Kororareka Flagstaff

*James Belich, *The New Zealand Wars and the Victorian Interpretation of Racial Conflict* (Auckland University Press, 1986); and *Making Peoples*.

Alan Ward, *A Show of Justice*.

Ian Wards, *Shadow of the Land*.

Ormond Wilson, *From Hongi Hika to Hone Heke*.

Link: From Heke to Gold

On Otago see Tom Brooking, *And Captain of their Souls: An Interpretative Essay Upon the Life and Times of Captain William Cargill* (Otago Heritage Books, Dunedin, 1984), A.H. McLintock, *The History of Otago. The Origins and Growth of a Wakefield Class Settlement* (Otago Centennial Historical Publications, Dunedin, 1949) and *Erik Olssen, *A History of Otago* (John McIndoe, Dunedin, 1984).

On Canterbury see James Hight and C.R. Straubel (eds), *A History of Canterbury*, Vol. 1, to 1854 (Canterbury Centennial Association, Christchurch, 1957).

On pastoralism see *Stevan Eldred-Grigg, *A Southern Gentry: New Zealanders Who Inherited the Earth* (Reed Methuen, Wellington, 1980) and A.G. Bagnall, *Wairarapa: An Historical Excursion* (Hedley's Bookshop for the Masterton Trust Lands Trust, 1976).

On political and constitutional developments see Raewyn Dalziel, 'The Politics of Settlement' in W.H. Oliver and B.R. Williams (eds), *The Oxford History of New Zealand* (OUP, Wellington, 1981), pp. 87-111, and D.G. Herron, 'Provincialism and Centralism, 1853-1858', in R.M. Chapman and Keith Sinclair (eds), *Studies of a Small Democracy: Essays in Honour of Willis Airey* (Paul for the University of Auckland, 1963). Ned Bohan, *Edward Stafford: New Zealand's First Statesman* (Hazard Press, Christchurch, 1994) is also helpful on this period.

To understand how the South Island was alienated for so little money see Harry Evison's magisterial study, *Te Wai Pounamu The Green Stone Island: A History of the Southern Maori During the European Colonisation of New Zealand* (Aoraki Press with the Ngai Tahu Trust Board, Christchurch, 1993).

8. Eureka: Gabriel Read Finds Gold

See *Philip Ross May, *The West Coast Goldrushes* (Pegasus Press, Christchurch, 1962), Erik Olssen, *A History of Otago*, Erik Olssen and Tom Field, **Relics of the Goldfields* and J.H.M. Salmon, *A History of Goldmining in New Zealand* (Government Printer, Wellington, 1963).

Link: From Gold to Grey

See titles for Milestone 9.9.

Crushing the Kingites: Governor Grey Orders the Invasion of the Waikato

The most important recent work is *James Belich, *The New Zealand Wars and the Victorian Interpretation of Racial Conflict*.

Also see B.J. Dalton, *War and Politics in New Zealand 1855-1870* (Sydney University Press, 1967) and Alan Ward, *A Show of Justice*.

For the causes of the Taranaki wars see Keith Sinclair, *The Origins of the Maori Wars* (New Zealand University Press, Wellington, 1957).

James Cowan's two-volume *The New Zealand Wars: A History of the Maori Campaigns and the Pioneering Period* (Government Printer, Wellington, 1922-23), reissued in 1986, contains much useful information on the military side of the conflict.

James Belich, *I Shall Not Die: Titokowaru's War New Zealand, 1868-69* (Allen and Unwin/Port Nicholson Press, Wellington, 1989), provides fascinating insights into the last phases of the wars as does Maurice Shadbolt's novel, *Monday's Warriors* (Hodder and Stoughton, Auckland, 1990).

Link: From War to Refrigeration

The most important books on the 1870s are *Rollo Arnold, *The Farthest Promised Land: English Villagers, New Zealand Immigrants of the 1870s* (Victoria University Press with Price Milburn, Wellington, 1981), and Raewyn Dalziel, *Julius Vogel Business Politician* (AUP/OUP, Auckland, 1986).

On the same economic side compare J.B. Condliffe, *New Zealand in the Making: a study of economic and social development* (2nd edn. Allen & Unwin, London, 1959) and G.R. Hawke, *The Making of New Zealand: an economic history* (CUP, 1985).

Judith Binney, *Redemption Songs: Te Kooti Arikirangi te Turuki* (Auckland University Press/Bridget Williams Books, 1995) is probably the most sophisticated book yet published on New Zealand history and forces readers to rethink Maori history. Her essays in *J. Binney, J. Bassett and E. Olssen, *The People and the Land Te Tangata me Te Whenua: An Illustrated History of New Zealand 1820-1920*, Allen and Unwin/Port Nicholson Press, Wellington, 1990) are equally valuable.

Miles Fairburn, *The Ideal Society and Its Enemies: The Foundation of Modern New Zealand Society, 1850-1900* (Auckland University Press, 1989), challenges cosy notions of pioneer community in a most provacative fashion. Rollo Arnold, *New Zealand Burning: The Settlers' World in the Mid-1880s* (Victoria University Press, Wellington, 1994), trys to counter many of Fairburn' arguments but concedes that colonial New Zealand was a raw and rather dangerous place.

Geoff Park, *Nga Uru Ora (The Groves of Life): History and Ecology in a New Zealand Landscape* (Victoria University Press Wellington, 1995) provides a vivid account of the impact of bush-clearing and swamp-draining on the New Zealand environment.

10. Colonial Entrepreneurs: The First Successful Shipment of Refrigerated Meat

Martine E. Cuff, *Totara Estate: Centenary of the Frozen Meat Industry* (New Zealand Historic Places Trust, Wellington, 1982).

*Kenneth Cumberland, *Landmarks* (Readers Digest, Surrey Hills, New South Wales, 1981).

Donald Denoon, *Settler Capitalism: The Dynamics of Dependen Development in the Southern Hemisphere* (Clarendon Press, OUP 1983), for the broader perspective.

Mervyn Palmer, 'William Soltau Davidson: a pioneer of New Zealand estate management', *New Zealand Journal of History*, Vol. 7 No. 2, October 1973, pp. 148-64 is very useful on the input of big business.

Condliffe and Hawke are also helpful as is Eric Warr, *Bushburn to Butter: A Journey in Words and Pictures* (Butterworths, Wellington, 1988).

11. Sweating: Work or Slavery? Reverend Waddell Preaches on the 'Sin of Cheapness'

The most important work on this subject remains locked away in the university theses of John Angus and Robbie Robertson. Their findings are summarised in Erik Olssen, *A History of Otago*, and *Julia Millen, *Colonial Tears and Sweat* (Reed Methuen, Wellington, 1984).

*Keith Sinclair, *William Pember Reeves: New Zealand Fabian* (Claredon Press; Oxford, 1965) is also indispensable as is W.P. Reeves, *State Experiments Australia and New Zealand In Two Volumes* (Macmillan, Melbourne, 1968 – 1st pub. 1902).

Several books have also appeared on the Liberal era since 1987 which add much on the ideas, politics, land, labour and welfare reforms, and social history of the period. The most helpful are David Hamer, *The New Zealand Liberals: The Years of Power, 1891-1912* (Auckland University Press, 1989); Margaret Tennant, *Paupers and Providers: Charitable Aid in New Zealand* (Historical Branch/Port Nicholson Press, Wellington, 1989); Ross Galbreath, *The Reluctant Conservationist: Walter Buller* (Government Print, Wellington, 1989); Kerry Howe, *Singer in a Songless Land: A Life of Edward Tregear* (Auckland University Press, 1991); Michael Bassett, *Sir Joseph Ward: A Political Biography* (Auckland University Press, 1993); Miles Fairburn, *Nearly Out of Heart and Hope: The Puzzle of a Colonial Labourer's Diary* (Auckland University Press, 1995); Jean Garner, *On His Own Merits: Sir John Hall – Pioneer, Pastoralist and Premier* (Hazard Press, Christchurch, 1995); Tom Brooking, *Lands for the People? The Highland Clearances and the Colonisation of New Zealand. A Biography of John McKenzie* (University of Otago Press, Dunedin, 1996); and David Thomson, *A World Without Welfare: New Zealand's Colonial Experiment* (Auckland University Press/Bridget Williams Books, 1998).

12. New Zealand First: Women Win the Vote

The most important book remains *Patricia Grimshaw, *Woman's Suffrage in New Zealand* (AUP/OUP, Auckland, 1972). Also useful are P. Bunkle and B. Hughes (eds), *Women in New Zealand Society* (George Allen & Unwin, Auckland, 1980), Reeves, *State Experiments*, André Siegfried, *Democracy in New Zealand* (Trans. by E.V. Burns with an Introduction by William Downie Stewart and David Hamer, Victoria University Press, Wellington, 1982, 1st pub. 1904) and Betty Holt (ed.), *Women in Council: A History of the National Council of Women of New Zealand* (National Council of Women, Wellington, 1980), is helpful for later developments.

W.B. Sutch, *Women With a Cause* (University of New Zealand Press, Wellington, 1973) adds more detail. Margaret Lovell-Smith, *The Woman Question: Writings by Women Who Won the Vote* (New

Women's Press, Auckland, 1993), is a useful collection of contemporary opinion while Charlotte Macdonald (ed.), *The Vote, the Pill and the Demon Drink: A History of Feminist Writing in New Zealand, 1869-1993* (Bridget Williams Books, Wellington, 1993), and Charlotte Macdonald and Francis Porter (eds.), *My Hand Will Write What My Heart Dictates: The Unsettled Lives of Women in Nineteeth Century New Zealand* (Auckland University Press/Bridget Williams Books, 1996), constitute rich collections of women's views on a host of subjects.

Dorothy Page, *The National Council of Women: A Centennial History* (Auckland University Press with Bridget Williams' Books and the National Council of Women, Auckland, 1996), provides an up-to-date and balanced account of this important organisation, and Anne Else (ed.), *Women Together: A History of Women' Organisations in New Zealand* (Historical Branch and Daphne Brassell Associates Press, Wellington, 1993), is an indispensable source of information on women's organisations. *Sandra Coney, *Standing in the Sunshine: A History of Women in New Zealand Since They Won the Vote* (Viking, Auckland, 1993) is a lively popular history of New Zealand women since 1893.

13. Cossacks on the Streets: The Waterfront Strike

The most important work on this subject is locked away in articles and papers by Erik Olssen and an MA thesis by P.J. Gibbons. Olssen's *The Red Feds: Revolutionary Industrial Unionism and the New Zealand Federation of Labour, 1908-1913* (OUP, Auckland, 1988), made much of this material more accessible. His *Building the New World: Work, Politics, and Society in Caversham, 1880s-1920s* (Auckland University Press, 1995), is indispensable for understanding the broader context in which Labour's challenge emerged. P.J. Gibbons, 'The Climate of Opinion' in W.H. Oliver and B.R. Williams (eds), *The Oxford History of New Zealand*, pp. 302-332; Barry Gustafson, *Labour's Path to Political Independence: The Origins and Establishment of the New Zealand Labour Party, 1900-1919* (AUP/OUP, Auckland, 1980); *P.J. O'Farrell, *Harry Holland Militant Socialist* (Australian National University Press, Canberra, 1964); and Len Richardson, *The Denniston Miners' Union: A Centennial History* (Denniston Miners' Union Centennial Committee, Westport, 1984) are also useful.

The posthumous publication of Jim Holt's study of the IC&A system *Compulsory Arbitration in New Zealand: The First Forty Years* (AUP, Auckland, 1986) (edited and completed by Erik Olssen) deepens our understanding of this event. Len Richardson, *Class, Coal and Community: The United Mineworkers of New Zealand, 1880-1960* (Auckland University Press, 1995) and Richard S. Hill, *The Iron Hand in the Velvet Glove: The Modernisation of Policing in New Zealand 1886-1917* (Dunmore Press with assistance from the New Zealand Police and the Historical Branch, Palmerston North, 1995) add detail on both industrial militancy and the development of the Labour Party.

Link: From Wharves to War

See titles for Milestone 13.

14. Gallipoli: Trial by Ordeal

Much of this chapter is based on war diaries held in the war archives series at National Archives. For published material see *Ormond Burton, *The Silent Division* (Angus & Robertson, Sydney, 1935).

C.E.W. Bean, *The Official History of Australia in the War 1914-18. The Story of Anzac*, Vol. 1 and Vol. 2 (University of Queensland Press, Brisbane, 1981, 1st pub. 1921).

Kit Denton, *Australians at War: Gallipoli: One Long Grave* (Time Life, Sydney, 1986).

Bill Gammage, *The Broken Years, Australian Soldiers in the Great War* (Australian National University Press, Canberra, 1974).

*Christopher Pugsley, *Gallipoli: The New Zealand Story* (Hodder and Stoughton, Auckland, 1984).

Keith Sinclair, *A Destiny Apart, New Zealand's Search for National Identity* (Unwin Paperbacks with the Port Nicholson Press, Wellington, 1986).

15. Te Mihaia Hou (The New Messiah): Tuhoe Prophet Rua Kenana is Arrested

*Judith Binney, Gillian Chaplin and Craig Wallace, *Mihaia: The Prophet Rua Kenana and His Community at Maungapohatu* (OUP, Wellington, 1979).

Judith Binney and Gillian Chaplin, *Nga Morehu: The Survivors* (OUP, Auckland, 1986).

Peter Webster, *Rua and the Maori Millennium* (Price Milburn for Victoria University Press, Wellington, 1979).

Jeff Sissons, *Te Wai Mana: The Springs of Mana* (University of Otago Press, Dunedin, 1992) adds valuable background on Tuhoe history as does Judith Binney, *Redemption Songs*.

16. Repelling the Hun: New Zealanders Plug the Gap During the German Spring Offensive

Strangely there is as yet no major study of New Zealand's participation on the Western Front. Most of this chapter has been based on war diaries of the New Zealand First Division and the First, Second and Third Brigades held in the War Archives series at National Archives, and Colonel H. Stewart, *The Official History of New Zealand's Effort in the Great War. The New Zealand Division, Volume 2, France* (Whitcombe & Tombs, Wellington, 1921).

On the spring offensive in general see Martin Middlebrook, *The Kaiser's Battle 21 March 1918: The First Day of the German Offensive* (Penguin, London, 1983).

The four major literary accounts of the First World War also tell us much about 1918: Burton's powerful and personal account, *The Silent Division*; *John A. Lee's novel, *Civilian into Soldier* (Mayfair Books, Auckland, 1963, 1st pub. 1937); *Robyn Hyde's novel based on the story of James Douglas Stark, *Passport to Hell* (edited and introduced by D.I.B. Smith, AUP, 1986, 1st pub. 1936); and *Archibald Baxter's compelling autobiography, *We Will Not Cease* (Caxton, Christchurch, 1968, 2nd edn., 1st pub. 1938). Christopher Pugsley, *On The Fringe of Hell: New Zealanders and Military Discipline In the First World War* (Hodder and Stoughton, Auckland, 1991), adds much about the practices and problems of the New Zealand army.

17. The Black Scourge: The Great Influenza Epidemic

The major study is Geoffrey Rice, *Black November: The 1918 Influenza Epidemic in New Zealand* (Allen and Unwin/Historical Branch, Wellington, 1988). Also see his article in the *New Zealand Journal of History*, Vol. 13, No. 2, October, 1979, pp. 109-137.

R.M. Burdon, *The New Dominion: A Social and Political History of New Zealand 1918-1939* (A.H. & A.W. Reed, Wellington, 1965) contains some useful information as do two theses: Martine E. Cuff, 'The Great Scourge. Dunedin in the 1918 influenza epidemic', BA Hons, Long Essay, Otago, 1980, and Linda Bryder, 'The 1918 Influenza Epidemic in Auckland', MA, Auckland, 1981, summarised in *NZJH*, Vol. 16 No. 2 (October 1982), pp. 97-121.

Link: From War and Sickness to Depression

There is no one detailed study of the 1920s but Burdon, *The New Dominion* is a useful introduction as is R.M. Chapman and E.P. Malone, *New Zealand in the Twenties: Social Change and Material Progress* (Heinemann, Auckland, 1969).

Several political biographies contain much helpful information, especially Michael Bassett, *Coates of Kaipara* (Auckland University Press, 1995). Part III of the *Oxford History of New Zealand* is also helpful.

18. This! In God's Own Country!: Riots Break Out in Dunedin, Auckland and Wellington

See Burdon, *The New Dominion*, James Edwards, *Riot 1932* (Whitcoulls, Christchurch, 1974), Erik Olssen, *A History of Otago and John A. Lee* (University of Otago Press, Dunedin, 1974) and *Tony Simpson, *The Sugarbag Years. An Oral History of the 1930s Depression In New Zealand* (Alister Taylor, Wellington, 1974).

Robbie Robertson's 1978 Otago PhD thesis, 'The Tyranny of Circumstances: responses to unemployment in New Zealand, 1929-1935, with particular reference to Dunedin', contains much new information.

Autobiographies are especially helpful, particularly Janet Frame, *To the Island* (Hutchison, Auckland, 1982) and Ruth Park, *Fence Around the Cuckoo* (Penguin, Auckland, 1992).

19. From the Cradle to the Grave: The Passing of the Social Security Act

The main study is Elizabeth Hanson, *The Politics of Social Security: The 1938 Act and Some Later Developments* (AUP/OUP, Auckland, 1980).

See also Burdon, *The New Dominion*. *Barry Gustafson, *From the Cradle To The Grave: A Biography of Michael Joseph Savage* (Reed Methuen, Auckland, 1986); *Michael King, *Te Puea: A

Biography (Hodder & Stoughton, Auckland, 1977); *Erik Olssen, John A. Lee*; and Keith Sinclair, *Walter Nash* (AUP/OUP, Auckland, 1976). Ian Carter, *Gadfly: The Life and Times of James Shelley* (Auckland University Press in association with the Broadcasting History Trust, 1993) adds much on the cultural initiatives and experiments in broadcasting undertaken by Labour as does Rachel Barrowman, *A Popular Vision: The Arts and the Left in New Zealand, 1930-1950* (Victoria University Press, Wellington, 1991). The forthcoming joint biography of Fraser by Michael King and Michael Bassett should help us understand the complex politics of this period even better.

David Thomson, *Selfish Generations?: The Ageing of New Zealand's Welfare State* (Bridget Williams Books, Wellington, 1991), argues somewhat controversially that the welfare state created by the generation covered in this chapter became a nightmare for subsequent generations.

Margaret McClure, *A Civilised Community: A History of Social Security in New Zealand 1898-1998* (Auckland University Press in association with the Historical Branch, Department of Internal Affairs, Auckland, 1998) and Bronwyn Dalley, *Family Matters: Child Welfare in Twentieth Century New Zealand* (Auckland University Press, 1998) both examine the innovations of the 1930s within a longer timeframe.

Link: From Social Security to War

See titles for Milestone 19.

20. Learning the Hard Way: The Italian Campaign

On the campaign see the Official War History volumes by N.C. Phillips, *Italy, Volume 1, The Sangro to Cassino* (Government Printer, Wellington, 1957) and Robin Kay, *Italy Volume II, From Casino to Trieste* (Government Printer, Wellington, 1967). Also see John Ellis, *The Hollow Victory, The Battle for Rome, January-June 1944* (Sphere Books, Sydney, 1984). *John McLeod, *Myth and Reality. The New Zealand Soldier in World War II* (Reed Methuen, Auckland, 1986) and *Dan Davin, *The Salamander and the Fire: Collected War Stories* (OUP, Auckland, 1986).

On the home front see Lauris Edmond (ed.), *Women in Wartime: New Zealand Women Tell Their Story* (Government Printer, Wellington, 1986), and Nancy M. Taylor, *The Home Front, New Zealand in the Second World War 1939-45*, 2 vols (Government Printer, Wellington, 1986). David Grant, *Out in the Cold: Pacifists and Conscientious Objectors in New Zealand During World War Two* (Reed Methuen, Auckland, 1986), tells the story of opponents of the war effort. Gaylene Preston's wonderful film *War Stories* evokes the Second World War story as well as anything else, but the Communicado series *New Zealanders at War* is very uneven and frequently inaccurate.

21. Labour Self-Destructs: The 151-Day Waterfront Strike

The major study is Michael Bassett, *Confrontation 51: The 1951 Waterfront Dispute* (A.H. & A.W. Reed, Wellington, 1972).

See also Erik Olssen, *John A. Lee* and Keith Sinclair, *Walter Nash*.

C.K. Stead's novel *All Visitors Ashore* (Collins, Auckland, 1984) catches the feel of the time, while Claire Matthewson's 1986 Otago PhD, 'From Subject to Device: History as Myth in Action. The evolution of an event from mythic processes as revealed in Waterfront Dispute fiction', provides a completely new look at the event.

Link: From Holland to Te Maori

On post-war New Zealand in general see Part IV of W.H. Oliver and B.R. Williams (eds), *The Oxford History of New Zealand* and G.Rice (ed.), 2nd edn.

On the economy see J.D. Gould, *The Rake's Progress? The New Zealand Economy since 1945* (Hodder & Stoughton, Auckland, 1982) and *The Muldoon Years: An Essay on New Zealand's Recent Economic Growth* (Hodder & Stoughton, Auckland, 1985).

On social change David Bedggood, *Rich and Poor in New Zealand* (Allen & Unwin, Auckland, 1980), Brian Easton, *Income Distribution in New Zealand* (New Zealand Institute of Economic Research, Wellington, 1983), and Brian Easton, *Wages and the Poor* (Allen & Unwin/Port Nicholson Press, Wellington, 1986). Micheal King's superb biography of Frank Sargeson,*Sargeson: A Life* (Penguin, Auckland, 1995), makes clear the enormous difficulties overcome by our writers.

22. The Rogeronmics Revolution

*Colin James, *The Quiet Revolution: Turbulence and Transition in Contemporary New Zealand* (Allen & Unwin/Port Nicholson Press, Wellington, 1986) is sympathetic towards these big shifts. Bruce Jesson, *Behind the Mirror Glass: The Growth of Wealth and Power in New Zealand in the Eighties* (Penguin, Auckland, 1987) presents a much more critical view. Brian Easton, *In Stormy Seas: The Post War New Zealand Economy* (University of Otago Press, Dunedin, 1997) provides an up-to-date coverage of the radical reforms of the late 1980s and early 1990s. Jane Kelsey questions their worth in *The New Zealand Experiment: A World Model for Structural Adjustment?* (Auckland University Press/Bridget Williams Books, 1995). A fascinating inside justification is provided by Richard Prebble in *I've Been Thinking* (self-published, Auckland, 1996). Anne Else, *False Economy* (Tandem Press, Auckland, 1996) provides a feminist critique of new right policies and argues that there is no economy without community. Bruce Jesson (1999), *Only Their Purpose is Mad: The Moneymakers Take Over New Zealand*, Palmerston North, Dunmore Press, updates his critique of 'New Right' policies and their impact.

23. Te Hokinga Mai (The Return Home): Te Maori and the Cultural Renaissance to the Rejection of the Fiscal Envelope

George Asher and David Naulls, *Maori Land* (New Zealand Planning Council, 1987).

Donna Awatere, *Maori Sovereignty* (Broadsheet, Auckland, 1984) remains a provocative classic statement of radical Maori opinion.

Witi Ihimaera and D.S. Long (eds), *Into the World of Light: An Anthology of Maori Writing* (Heinemann, Auckland, 1982) is still the best introduction to Maori writing.

*Michael King, *Maori: A Photographic and Social History* (Heinemann, Auckland, 1983, to be reissued 1997), was controversial when published but still contains striking images of Maori history.

*Sidney Moko Mead (ed.), *Te Maori: Maori Art from New Zealand Collections* (Heinemann with The American Federation of Arts, Auckland, 1984) catches the look and feel of the exhibition.

Erik Schwimmer (ed.), *The Maori People in the Nineteen-Sixties* (Paul, Auckland, 1968) is a useful collection for learning about the aspirations of that time.

Hiwi Tauroa, *Race Against Time* (Human Rights Commission, Wellington, 1982), stresses the urgency of the many race relations problems confronting New Zealand.

Ranganui Walker, *The Years of Anger* (Penguin, 1987) and *Ka Whaiwhai Tonu Matou: The Struggle is Without End* (Penguin, Auckland, 1990) assert the Maori point of view.

Andrew Sharp, *Justice and the Maori. Maori Claims in New Zealand Political Arguments in the 1980s* (OUP, Auckland, 1990) is very helpful on the setting up and early work of the Waitangi Tribunal. So too is W.H. Oliver, *Claims to the Waitangi Tribunal* (Waitangi Tribunal Division, Department of Justice, Wellington, 1991). William Renwick (ed.), *Sovereignty and Indigenous Rights: The Treaty of Waitangi in International Context* (Victoria University Press, Wellington, 1991), places the New Zealand story in a broader global context.

To understand how the failure to provide adequate reserves forced marginalisation upon the southern section of Ngai Tahu, see Bill Dacker, *Te Maemae me te Aroha: the Pain and the Love: A History of Kai Tahu Whanui in Otago* (University of Otago Press with the Dunedin City Council, Dunedin, 1994). Similarly, the re-issue of Pei Te Hurunui Jones, *Nga Iwi o Tainui: The Traditional History of the Tainui People*, edited and annotated by Bruce Biggs (Auckland University Press with assistance from the Tainui Trust Board, 1995) provides vital background material on the Tainui claim and explains the bitterness felt over confiscated land, or raupatu. Real enthusiasts will find the various reports on the claims, especially those relating to Ngai Tahu, Tainui and Taranaki, extremely rich sources of information.

Two matching books provide an interesting survey of both Pakeha and Maori views on Maori sovereignty and reveal a surprising degree of tolerance on both sides. See Hineari Melbourne, *Maori Sovereignty: The Maori Perspective*; and Carol Archie, *Maori Sovereignty: The Pakeha Perspective* (both Hodder Moa Beckett, Auckland, 1995). This hopeful tone is off set by Stuart C.Scott, *The Traversty of Waitangi* (Campbell Press, Dunedin, 1995). This is the most carelessly researched book to be published in New Zealand for a very long time, but reveals much about the pathology and fears of late twentieth century Pakeha. Its success (it sold over 12,000 copies) suggests that much fear and ignorance has to be overcome before the process of reconciliation and reparation is complete.

For useful updates on recent happenings in Maoridom, especially in relation to Treaty matters, see Mason Durie, *Te Mana, Te Kawanatanga: The Politics of Maori Self-Determination*, OUP, Auckland, 1998; and Alan Ward, *An Unsettled History: Treaty Claims in New Zealand Today* (Bridget Williams Books, Wellington, 1999).

General

For information on **people** see the four volumes of the *Dictionary of New Zealand Biography*, volume one W.H.Oliver (ed.) and the rest edited by Claudia Orange, Bridget Williams Books/Department of Internal Affairs, Wellington, 1990, 1993, 1996 and 1998.

On New Zealand **literature** see Terry Sturm (ed.) *The Oxford History of New Zealand Literature in English* (OUP, Auckland 1991) and 2nd edn. 1998; and Nelson Wattie and Roger Robinson (eds), *The Oxford Companion to New Zealand Literature*, Auckland, 1998.

The excellent new *Historical Atlas of New Zealand*, Malcolm McKinnon (ed.), David Bateman, Historical Branch of the Department of Internal Affairs, Auckland, 1997, contains many striking **maps and visual representations of historical change** and is the most useful aid produced for both history teachers and students in many years.

217

Index

Page numbers in italics refer to illustrations.